PHILOSOPHICAL EXPLORATIONS

A Series Edited by George Kimball Plochmann

Creative
Ventures

Paul Weiss

Foreword by
George Kimball Plochmann

Southern Illinois University Press
Carbondale and Edwardsville

Copyright © 1992 by the Board of Trustees,
Southern Illinois University
Printed in the United States of America
Edited by Dan Gunter
Designed by Edward King
Production supervised by Hillside Studio
95   94   93   92   4   3   2   1

"Anecdote of the Jar" and "Theory" by Wallace Stevens. Copyright 1923 &
renewed 1951 by Wallace Stevens. Reprinted from *The Collected Poems of
Wallace Stevens,* by permission of Alfred A. Knopf, Inc. Reprinted by
permission of Faber and Faber Ltd. from *The Collected Poems
of Wallace Stevens.*

Reprinted by permission of Farrar, Straus and Giroux, Inc.: Excerpt from
"Epilogue" from *Day by Day* by Robert Lowell. Copyright © 1977 by Robert
Lowell. Excerpt from "Sextet" from *To Urania* by Joseph Brodsky.
Copyright © 1988 by Joseph Brodsky.

The appendix essay, "The Dunamis," originally appeared in a slightly different
form in the *Review of Metaphysics* 40 (June 1987): 657–74. Reprinted
by permission.

Library of Congress Cataloging-in-Publication Data

Weiss, Paul, 1901–
Creative ventures / Paul Weiss   :   foreword by George Kimball Plochmann.
p. cm. — (Philosophical explorations)
Includes index.
1. Creation (Literary, artistic, etc.) 2. Philosophy. I. Title. II. Series.
B945.W396C74 1992
128—dc20   91-7731
CIP
ISBN 0-8093-1729-X

The paper used in this publication meets the minimum requirements
of American National Standard for Information Sciences
—Permanence of Paper for Printed Library Materials,
ANSI Z39.48-1984. ♾

For Kim and Carol Plochmann
Friends of the Excellent

Contents

Foreword

IF PHILOSOPHIZING in its most proper sense is the steady determination to make clear what underlies the essential and even the accidental characters of things natural, conventional, and artificial, of ideas by which these things are known or constituted, and of the symbols whereby these otherwise fugitive ideas are edged, communicated, and recorded, then Paul Weiss is one who has spent all the adult years of his long life ardently philosophizing. His first large project, when he served as co-editor (with Charles Hartshorne) for the first six volumes of the monumental *Collected Papers of Charles Sanders Peirce,* published in the late 1930s, was followed by a stream of works long and short, dealing with topics central to logic and mathematics, and to the problems arising in the defining of the self and its relations to God, nature, space and time, organic bodies, other selves, and the arts (among them cinema), all showing the deep imprint of the metaphysical premises from which his thinking starts and to which it has always returned. These premises account for the existence of theoretic and actual realities that can be combined many times over, reseparated, and again organized in fresh ways. Their author has kept them under constant scrutiny and revision.

Creative Ventures conceives creativity very strictly and thus accords success to a relatively few possible creators, no matter in what manner of enterprise. This book is a serious general discussion that includes neither the individuals and their sleeves-rolled-up procedures nor references to interrupted laudanum binges or the famous boarding steps on a French trolley said to have occasioned great insights. Rather, it is written under the conviction that the results of its inquiry can be communicated philosophically when its concepts have been cleansed of their immediate and particular references.

The evident phase of the method espoused in this book is the one that ever since his *Modes of Being* (1958) and even earlier the author has used with much skill. He begins here with what he calls ultimates, and these are of two kinds, the first of them dividing into five conditions. At the outset, each is conceived as operative primarily on one of five kinds of creative ventures. The way these conditions—in company with the second kind of ultimate, which Professor Weiss calls the Dunamis, a raw power, a force, a potency (not unlike Schopenhauer's Will)—produce meaning and life in creations is the chief subject of the book. For all six ultimates, the language used to name them and track their interminglings is perforce abstract, but despite what at first blush seems a remoteness from daily living, the six are so bound up with life itself that without them the whole of experience would collapse and nothing of ourselves and our lives would remain, not even the "extensionless point" that Ludwig Wittgenstein once thought constituted the ego. By interweaving these ultimates with each other and with the stuff of art, mathematics, moral agents, a people, or rulers and ruled, they become known, felt, enjoyed, lived, as the author says, with and through. As a result, creative works can be examined not only in painting, music, and literature but also in mathematics and the sciences, in moral self-development, in social movements requiring impressive leadership, and in just government. In all five ventures, however, significant distinctions and instructive likenesses are found, so that there is no blanket assertion of a featureless cloud to descend upon these types.

One must disentangle the ultimates from the tangibles and visibles that both manifest and conceal what underlie their true natures, so that the natures and their recombinations can be understood. The important Appendix to this book, on the Dunamis, is thus a much-needed propaedeutic, or at least a clarifying parallel, to the entire account, explaining as it does the ways that the powerful workings are brought to fruition. Correlatives to this power are more nearly self-explanatory, for they are closer to and in one instance identical with the rational. The principal interrelations of all these can be glimpsed in the "map" that precedes chapter 1. In this very capacious matrix, the basic structure allows for analogies at every point between the columns denoting sorts of ventures, but the progress from unformed materials to concluded achievements runs through stages peculiar to each of the kinds. In neither case, however, are the terms allowed to run away from the tight meanings originally allotted; this is no Hegelian dialectic in which categories merge into their opposites and again into more wide-embracing concepts all under the sway, and forming portions, of the Idea that is identical with all reality. It may be useful to point out that these five conditions represent painstaking reworkings of the four modes of being that the author described thirty-odd years earlier.

Much less explicit in this book is the way he has come to his grasp of the ultimates, for otherwise the charting of their combinations would seem to certain readers an exercise without solid foundation. I have known Professor Weiss for many decades, during which time I have felt a mounting admiration for the unquenchable enthusiasm that he shows for the varied facets of creative human life. As a philosopher he can talk to artists on a familiar level of their profession; as a philosopher he talks to mathematicians about countless issues in their spheres of interest; and again as a philosopher he confronts the most exasperating and recurrent moral problems besetting human beings everywhere. He has provided himself with a rich armament of facts about and exercise in the arts—this one must gather from personal acquaintance, not from this book—that lends a strength to his reasoning in what otherwise would be abstractions regarding music, poetry, sculpture, architecture, and the rest. His discussions of these and the other disciplines are buttressed in his mind (though not in this writing) by music studied, easel paintings executed, theater engaged in, and much more; he has made corresponding efforts in the other four fields so carefully examined in this volume. The emphasis throughout is on what is worked with and what is made under the guidance of the ultimates, and so the reader is not invited to follow intricate psychological analyses, such as one meets with in writers as different as Coleridge and Freud, or to follow reactions of audiences more proper to rhetorical studies but found also in elementary shape in Horace's *Ars Poetica* and in Tolstoy with his theory of the moral enhancement of the populace through the best art. *Creative Ventures* traces instead the route traversed by materials that are combined and again combined until at last a purpose is fulfilled and a form conferred on the work that was to be made. In mathematics, the creations of one epoch become the materials for another, so that the integers of the early Greeks are taken up as materials for the creation of natural numbers, which are in turn used as material for the rationals, and then the irrationals, the imaginaries, and so on.

Though not often stated, one controlling distinction in this theory is that between active and passive. The painter is active, his paints and brushes are passive to his thoughtful touch; they are partly resistant, partly pliant, for matter is always both, though never to the same degree. The leader of a social movement is active; his people (an entire population) as such is passive. In a larger sense the great conditions are by reason of their purity the active agents that invariably make their way into the unique creations occasionally appearing in a world cluttered with misalliances, failures, forgeries, and that in relation to the conditions are also clay. More vital still than the five conditions is the Dunamis, the power, and this is doubtless the first and last activity against which all else must be partly resistant and partly pliable.

Gustav Mahler once said of the stupendous opening bars of his Symphony no. 8, with its huge chorus backing and backed by a much-expanded orchestra, "The universe begins to vibrate." If this *Symphony of a Thousand,* as the work soon came to be called, has expressed such a force, has not Paul Weiss sought to catch some of this rending vibration, to put it into language?

The style of this book, with its deliberateness and sobriety, even so betokens an innate exuberance, an impulse untamed by any ordinary standards of writing that would cabin, crib, and confine usage, word order, or effects of sound. It is an exuberance that manifests itself as well in the unusual variety of subject matters which the author has sought to master, analyze, and at length codify, during all stages of his career and now in this volume. His massive *Philosophy in Process,* a kind of journal of philosophic communings and sketches, some of them quite long and all of them substantial in content, is not a finished work in the customary sense but is rather like what Berkeleyan scholars used to call the Commonplace Book; it is a record of ideas, far from being a treatise or series of treatises, though one finds virtually no references in it to the author's daily life—few accounts of lectures given, friends visited or received, letters written, or concerts enjoyed. *Creative Ventures* stands, so its author has said, about midway between a treatise and some of the entries in *Philosophy in Process.*

As with so many philosophers, the vocabulary is the author's. *Privacy* is a word that behaves as a concrete noun denoting a kind of transcendental self. An *excellence* is the name not of a quality but of the *prospective outcome* of a creative act. The *conditions* are not meant to be states or causes of the usual sort but are instead the bases, the universal grounds, for any thing being what it is. They do not include any mechanical connection or sequence; they most resemble formal causes of the classical and medieval traditions. *Voluminosities* is a concept replacing older notions of what is spatial or is at the root of particular temporal and causal occurrences. The *Dunamis* (with the Greek upsilon thus transliterated) is the source of the reality present in every thing. If a painter were to present this Dunamis symbolically, it might well be with a sunburst of red and gold against a blander, finely drawn filigree. If a composer were to put it forth in sound, he could use a staunch bass tuba grounding a surge of authoritative trombones and frantic trumpets, all set against another modest filigree, this in strings and the woodwinds in their treble registers.

This is not a book on which to exercise much editorial control, for the author has already chosen his language with care and has employed it independently in what stands somewhere between the spontaneous and the formal; it is written partly for the author himself and partly for a wider public. He uses metaphysical and other premises in an almost Euclidean profusion of reassertions. Much of the inspired roughness of the Gargantuan *Philosophy in Process* (twelve thick volumes have been published, and more are on the way) can be found here, but now tempered by a march of propositions showing the author's close attention to what Aristotle called *taxis,* the arrangement of parts. Stylistic adroitness, phrasing for the sake of phrasing, have not been summoned to disguise the seriousness and inevitability of the progression in this unique interpretation of the primary creative ventures in superior walks of life.

George Kimball Plochmann

Preface

CREATIONS are more than the outcome of the masterly use of techniques and cultural influences. They are also quite different from the creation that some attribute to God, who supposedly produced a universe in place of, or as it is sometimes oddly said, out of, nothing. They will be dealt with here as outcomes of activities in which only a human being can engage and which can be brought to a successful close only if he is persistently occupied with producing an excellent work in one of a number of equally basic ventures.

One of the great gains that such a study yields is an understanding of the ways irreducible ultimate factors can be used in maximal, mutually enhancing ways. It also should make clear how all else uses those very factors in lesser and more limited forms. Knowledge of those factors is not readily had. In any event, over a series of faltering, unsteady steps and missteps I have now come to see them with only a flickering clarity. They have nevertheless enabled me to make some headway in understanding the nature of creative work in process and in outcome. A knowledge of them and their functionings makes it easier, too, to see how all else uses them in less controlled, less basic ways. As I now understand them, they have a being and a power not exhaustively expressed in any outcome and can therefore be expressed again and again, sometimes in and by means of what they have already constituted. As standing apart from one another and so far as together in another way, they are the proper topic of a metaphysical and, more particularly, an ontological inquiry. If successful, this inquiry should make evident the underpinnings of all studies, including this one.

Created works readily lend themselves to classifications of various kinds. Some are usefully grouped as having been produced in a particular historical epoch or culture. A number of them can be dealt with as exhibiting a common style, as expressing a common outlook, as using distinctive material, or as employing special instruments. Such classifications presuppose the existence of excellent works; they cannot account for them. An examination of creativity will also be unduly limited if it is restricted to a consideration of what artists do, and surely if it is focused

xiii

mainly on what a special group of them—composers, painters, or poets—usually produce. Not only are there artists engaged in other kinds of activities, such as the writing of novels, dancing, and acting, but there are creative mathematicians, others who actively forge great characters for themselves, creative leaders, and those who occupy themselves with creating a state. The understanding of each of them requires references to five different, irreducible, ultimate conditions. An emphasis on any one requires use of all the others as well as of a primary vitality, an ideal, a privacy, and obdurate material.

The present method is reconstructive: it follows a dissolution of the daily known into constituents, with an attempt to trace these back to their sources and to understand how those sources act, come together, and can be deliberately united. Every item provides evidences of all of them. In this book, the reconstruction is restricted primarily to showing how the ultimates make possible the process and outcome of creativity. A chart at the beginning of the work indicates how the emphases and uses of the various creative ventures differ and are related.

I owe much to Dr. Richard Beals, Dr. J. Gastwirth, Dr. Florence Hetzler, Dr. L. Somer, Dr. Nils Tongrin, Jonathan Weiss, and my graduate students for their detailed and careful criticisms. I am also indebted to George Kimball Plochmann for editorial work on this book and for his Foreword.

1 May 1990
Washington, D.C.

Creative
Ventures

Creative Ventures

Primary Factor	Art	Mathematics	Character	Society	State
Creator	Imaginative	Penetrative	Dedicated	Inspired	Supplementary
Condition	Voluminosities	The Rational	Stratifier	Affiliator	Coordinator
Dunamis	Vibrancy	Synthesis	Insistence	Fraternity	Flexibility
Ideal	Beauty	Truth	The Good	Glory	Justice
Material	Texturizers	Variables/Values	Habits	People	Role Bearers

1

Created Works

A Survey

CREATIVE WORK turns a prospective excellence into a single unification of a plurality of separately produced parts. Initially indeterminate, the prospect is made more and more determinate until at the end it is no longer distinguishable. It is then present as an effective bond, enhancing what has been produced over the course of the activity realizing it. In art, the excellence to be achieved is beauty; in politics, justice; in other ventures it has other forms. In all of them, work, hard work, is done. Success demands that habitual ways and irrelevant tendencies be countered and that effective use be made of resistant material. If the creative venture is successful, the different parts will be transformed from demarcated items, bounded and aggregational, into a singular, interlocked multiplicity of functions. Often the work will exhibit the outcome of ingenuity, innovation, spontaneity, and invention, but these marks will be incidental, produced along the way, spicing and qualifying a more basic, overriding activity. Creativity differs from all other kinds of ventures in intent, course, content, and outcome.

One is tempted to look to creators for information and clues regarding the nature of their activity. Only they have mastered the creative process. They alone have given themselves fully and effectively to a task that ends in what has no duplicates. Creators, though, are so thoroughly engaged in producing their works that they have little time and often little desire to give a good account of what they have utilized, or how. Few are equipped to report what they did or are able to express it in precise, well-controlled ways; few have the ability to provide good analyses; few are masters of self-reflection. Even those adroit in the use of words, the best of poets, storytellers, and playwrights, do not usually know how to use language in the way it must be used in order to state exactly what they have done creatively, even with words. Some make a great effort to remember, to reflect, and to speak precisely about what they have used and how they have used it. What is then said, though, is often overrun with analogy and is so charged with hardly noticed expressions of pride and hope, unexamined suppositions, and tags taken from critics, historians, teachers, and philosophers that they tend to obscure more than they clarify. Creators sometimes protest that accounts of their activities go counter to what they know of themselves or to what they did. Unfortunately, that does not mean that they, better than others, are able to understand or communicate what they do.

Creativity is carried on outside the sphere of daily activities. Some think that it requires references to the unconscious, infantile traumas, the muses, or unsuccessful love affairs. We know that some creators have been quite ill in mind and body and have shown remarkably poor judgment in politics and elementary economic matters. Some have treated friends abominably. To be sure, others exhibit similar deficiencies but show little indication that they have creative abilities. Everyone has hidden impulses; most men have undergone some traumatic experiences; each does some things that are regrettable and fails to be all a human might conceivably be. The limits and vices of everyone play significant roles in their acts, as surely as do their powers and virtues, but none explains what creativity is, requires, and achieves. Past good and bad experiences contribute to the determination of the course and outcome of poor as well as of great works, in what is carried out with little effort or concern, as well as in what is achieved only through hard work of a distinctive kind. Creativity requires a study of its own in which its indispensable components are exposed and its distinctive nature, course, and outcome are dissected and clarified.

If a creator were able to make use of powers unavailable to the rest of men, or were he so privileged that what he used was available to him alone, he would be a special kind of human being, if only for the short period when he was being creative. He would also baffle the rest of us, even those who attend to what he says, what he has to do, and what he in fact does.

The powers, dedication, efforts, and opportunities of which a creator makes such splendid use are available to others but are not used in the same ways, to the same degree, and with the same effectiveness. The most routine of men makes an unduplicable use of his privacy. He has ends in view and brings about what is new in fact. This activity is not often of much interest; the results are usually quite commonplace and are rarely worth comparing with what is achieved creatively, even by one who is somewhat careless and not among the very great. The difference between the two, though, does not suffice to show that they make use of different factors or that the one or the other's activities are not intelligible.

No matter how great he may be, a creator remains a human being among others, making use of powers latent in all. In his weaknesses and in his strengths he is one of us, and no matter how distinctive his activities and accomplishments, he continues to be so. His course and activity require neither supernatural help nor the use of mysterious gifts, for he differs from the rest of us not in nature but in what he seeks and tries to achieve, and succeeds in doing.

A study of creativity, an acknowledgment of its components, procedure, and products, begins where all inquiry does—with whatever is at hand. That is where the needed evidences are. Were one to focus on nothing but signal occurrences there, more likely than not only those components and problems would be dealt with which were common to or emphasized in them. It is better to look for the components that are present in any and everything and trace these back to their sources, for if successful, one will then be in a position to understand creative works in terms appropriate to all other occurrences and will therefore be able to see how both good and bad works can be produced and how the useful and the useless, the satisfying and the regrettable, can be in the same world.

Since adventitious traits could be present anywhere, one is forced to check and recheck what is initially surmised to isolate what must be present in every one of them. The sciences carry out a related venture but restrict themselves to seeing what observation and experiment, backed by theory, will allow them to say about the nature of bodies and their interplay. Since the sciences are not in a position to tell us about the nature of privacies, individuals, values, or transcendents, or about beauty, truth, and other excellences, recourse must be had to a different method if we are to say anything about them that does not set them entirely apart in a separate, detached realm. One must dissect whatever one happens to focus on and see if the outcomes are obtainable everywhere. If they are not, one must press further, until one finds the constituents of every item as there specialized and evidencing their sources.

Since one can never be sure that every type of object has been found and that what has there been focused on is present in all in some form and degree, it is never possible to do more than offer a better, more satisfactory account than is presently available. A good check, though, can be provided by facing oneself with hard cases. Created works provide such a challenge, one that has not been met even by the towering figures in the history of thought. None of them has made evident just what creators presuppose and utilize, how they proceed, or the nature of that with which they end, in good part because their examinations were not preceded by a successful attempt to know what all the ultimate factors are and how they are and could be joined.

Particular occurrences of different kinds have to be analyzed and the results checked against what can be analyzed out of what else is encountered, produced, or imagined. The result will not have the color, vigor, specifications, or connections that any actuality—adventitious, natural, or created—exhibits. That is one reason why it is not possible to become a creator by learning what a creator aims at, confronts, uses, does, has experienced, or believes. It does, however, make it possible for others to know what creators do and achieve.

All actualities provide evidences of the same ultimates. These ultimates are specialized and intertwined in each and can be distinguished when attention is paid to their distinctive natures, interrelations, and activities. The observation is not especially new. The Aristotelian dissection of daily occurrences into matter and form, the Thomistic analysis into essence and existence, and the Hegelian isolation of thesis and antithesis with their negative thrusts, offer conspicuous, impressive illustrations of the ways actualities can be analyzed and more primary realities made evident. None of them, however, acknowledges all the factors present in whatever there is. These three views in particular have difficulty in dealing with the temporal side of things. They also overstress what is intelligible or categorized and fail to show how the noted factors might be more effectively joined or brought together in better ways. To know the essential constituents of every item, whether it be humdrum, technically exact, unexpected, undesired, or created, and to do so with minimal distortion, we must deal with whatever we daily confront in a spirit at once more innocent and more resolute than that required elsewhere. Dealt with as being pertinent only to the tasks of logic, science, cosmology, theology, or some other special enterprise, the nature and scope of the essential elements would be unduly limited or distorted.

Great masters produce works spoiled by what we now see to be distortions, omissions, embellishments, and confusions. The more daring the venture, the more likely it is that it has these and other flaws. This risk every creator runs; it will be run, too, by anyone seeking to know what creativity is and does, especially by one who tries to attend to its essential components, who seeks to understand how these have to be used and what is finally achieved.

It would take a long, quite different treatise from this to do justice to the problem of knowing the natures of all the factors which, in limited forms, constitute any and every particular. To carry out that project, one would have to make evident how, starting with specializations of the factors which constitute every item, one can come to know what those factors are and how they are and can be joined. Without some knowledge of the nature of these "ultimates" or "finalities" (as they deserve to be termed) and the ways they are and can be brought together, it could not proceed far in the understanding of anything, and surely not of creativity and its outcome.

Ultimate factors are of two basic kinds—a number of *conditions* ("modes of being" I once termed them) and a primary pulsating ground, or *Dunamis*.[1] These

1. The Dunamis, which has close connections with various basic powers acknowledged over the course of history, East and West, was freshly examined by me in a recent article, reprinted as the Appendix to this volume.

factors come together in uncontrolled ways to constitute limited, distinct, existent actualities as well as future, indeterminate prospects. Some of the actualities are complex. Humans form one class. Each member of it is an individual, expressing himself through, and both possessing and maintaining himself in opposition to, a body and a privacy. The study of privacy has been rather neglected today, except by some therapists and existentialists and those few philosophers, ethicists, and theologians who concern themselves with the nature of responsibility and virtue and their possible outcomes and just rewards. In a study of creativity, account must be taken of both the privacies and bodies even when the study is occupied with understanding performances or the formation of a noble character.

In the West there is a strong tendency to consider only pervasive factors, formally expressible, flat, steady, and answering to clear concepts. Individuals, ideals, ongoings, contingencies, and pulsations are then usually bypassed or are dealt with as instantiating some endlessly applicable condition. Becoming, time, emotions, intentions, fear, hope, and action are found to raise intractable problems. Much time is spent by some in trying to show that these are illusory occurrences or could somehow be reduced to variants of what is fixed and forever. In the East, and occasionally and most recently in the West as well, this view and its procedures have been criticized for ending with what is unacceptably thin and abstract. It would be an error, though, to suppose that the acknowledged factors were not present in every item or that they did not have an irreducible reality.

Conceptualization, categorization, and formalization are not to be rejected; what is needed is an understanding of their proper objects and use. Indeed, the conditions on which the Western tradition has focused are unduly limited in number and are then treated as though only one way of reaching and expressing them was possible or permissible. Most Western studies focus on the purely rational; some attend to a primal being, still others to the formal structure of time or, more recently, to a space-time. All of these conditions can be conceptualized and then presented in formal terms. There are, in fact, at least five primary conditions, reachable through distinct, intensive moves. These moves end in more than mere forms that are somehow hooked to irrelevant agents enabling those forms to acquire a local role.

One ultimate condition is *the voluminous,* a condition most pertinent to the arts. There it is dealt with as being primarily spatial, temporal, or transformative. A second condition is *the rational,* sheer intelligibility or form. This condition is most signally and effectively utilized by creative mathematicians. A third condition, *the stratifier,* an assessing, ordering power, is utilized in the forging of a noble character. A fourth condition, *the affiliator,* enables items to be interinvolved with one another as more or less compatible and supportive. Its use is prominent in acts of creative leadership. Finally, the creation of a state requires that primary emphasis be put on a coordinating condition, or *the coordinator*. All of these conditions are operative in every occurrence, created or not, good or bad, with different types of creative work fastening primarily on one, specializing it, and joining the result to other factors, again and again, under the aegis of a distinctive, progressively realized prospective excellence.

Ultimate conditions are sources of fixities. Even temporality and causality, as versions of the voluminous, provide stable structures. None enables one to see why or how anything comes to be or passes away, or why anything pulsates. To account for these occurrences, reference must be made to what is at once potential, powerful, and dynamic. I refer to it as *the Dunamis* in order to point up the double fact that is has been historically used in all three ways and that it contrasts with all five conditions. Creative ventures move beyond the usually manifested layers of the Dunamis to become involved with it on a deeper layer preliminary to its interplay with some emphasized condition. Were it alone dealt with, one would be caught up in a sheer flow, a single ongoing in which nuances could be distinguished without being set apart from one another.

Like the conditions, the Dunamis is never fully probed. Like the conditions, too, it can be reached only by going through an intensive move, involving one with what is more and more remote, insistent, and self-maintained. Some Eastern thinkers carry out a long-established practice of deconstruction, freeing what they encounter and know from whatever can be distinguished; they do not, as some of the later Western practitioners do, try to peel away layer after layer, apparently without end. Most of them believe the Dunamis can be reached most readily by retreating into oneself until one arrives at a position where the Dunamis is able to engulf everything without remainder. Although it does not, I think, act in this fashion, and although it can never be fully probed, it can be reached and utilized as readily and as directly as any of the other ultimate factors can.

Because each actual entity is constituted by all the ultimates, each will provide evidences of them in the guise of limited specialized versions. Each is extended; each is intelligible; each is more or less valuable in relation to others; each is more or less relevant, germane, congenial to others; each is as real as any other. All pulsate. One arrives at the ultimates by freeing what is initially acknowledged from the limitations that their specialization and meeting introduced. The process may be carried out over a series of steps, as both Plato and Hegel held, or it can be reached in a single move as creators do, and speculative thinkers sometimes do as well. The latter, though, try to understand what it arrives at; creators begin at once to specialize and to use all of them.

As singulars, conditions and the Dunamis meet without guidance or control. The meeting occurs in two ways. One yields units in a universe. The other constitutes a prospective future, specialized in ideal excellences and possibilities.

Each actuality, paltry or important, natural or worked on, is unique. So is each created work. The one holds a plurality of parts together from a depth they only partly reveal. The other has its units interlocked by an ideal realized over the course of a creative venture. There is nothing mysterious in the existence of the one, though it is not reducible to either a particular or a universal; there is nothing hidden in the other, though what is there may be hard to discern or decipher.

Not an individual, a creation nevertheless has powerful affects as well as an identity that may be maintained over a period of time. Internally limited, it has externally imposed boundaries determining its position in relation to what is other than it. Endlessly nuanced, rich beyond anyone's capacity to exhaust, a creation is the outcome of an individual's specialized use of conditions and the Dunamis, as joined again and again under the guidance and control of an ideal that a creator has committed himself to realize. The result is sustained and grained through the use of recalcitrant material. This material does not jeopardize the continued independent operation of the conditions, the Dunamis, the individual, or the ideal. Even the parts, which are finally unified and which are therefore interinvolved with one another, continue to have their own separate natures, each bounded off from the rest.

A created work utilizes and overrides what is used to produce it, but it annihilates nothing. Conditions and the Dunamis are joined in its units; a privacy enables its excellence to be focused on and realized. The material used gives it a grain and stability, as well as a purchase on the world beyond. None of these constituents is at a spatial or temporal distance from the creator, the work, or its parts. Such a distancing would require them to be in a common space or time. Since space and time also realize the ultimates, they, too, would somehow have to find a position in some other space and time, and so on without end.

No distance needs to be traversed in order for a creator to make use of ultimate factors. They are present in all actualities. One of them will be dominant in all actualities of a particular kind. A speculative thinker comes to know them in their unspecialized forms. The constituents of any and every entity, they are reached by carrying out intensive moves. A creator reaches those same factors by beginning in his privacy and from there specializing and using them while facing an ideal prospect that he has committed himself to realize. If the factors are to be properly specialized and used to produce an excellent work, he must be free enough to commit himself to realize the sought excellence as he carries out the acts needed to turn it into an actual unification of produced parts. To the degree he accomplishes this unification, to that degree the parts become functions interinvolved with one another.

If anyone could unite the various ultimates as they are in their full, independent majesty, he could produce a universe. Our finitude denies us that privilege. Instead, the most we can do is join specializations of the conditions and the Dunamis in part after part under the guiding, increasing control of a gradually realized excellence. In the absence of this excellence, we can produce only pluralities of units, each constituted by a distinctive joining of the conditions and the Dunamis.

Were a prospective excellence alone to dictate what parts are produced, the Dunamis, conditions, and creators would all be its instruments. No one would act, no one would create, and the ultimates would not be independent sources of the constituents of the parts. Not only do creations require work, they also require their creators to subject themselves to a sought excellence. Only then will they join the very same factors that all particulars do, but they will do so as a consequence of acts carried out in order to realize beauty, truth, or some other ideal.

At the beginning of a creative venture, a sought excellence is indeterminate, faint, weak. Over the course of a creative act it becomes more and more determinate in the form of connections among and stresses on the parts produced until it is finally realized as the unification of them all as so many different operative units. Not until a creator has joined specialized forms of a condition and the Dunamis many times is he finally freed from his involvement with his work. At that time the prospective excellence will have vanished as a distinguishable item. Its complete determination is one with its transformation into a single operation. The result is not an organism, for an organism is alive.

Had an organic being no bounded parts and could it realize a particular type of excellence, it would still differ from a created work in not being dependent for its existence on somebody's acting to realize what is initially a radically indeterminate, prospective excellence. Were it produced in a laboratory, through a joining of various items, it would still differ from a created work, being independent of the need to realize an ideal prospect. Without this prospect, there would be nothing created. Were an experimenter to produce various parts and enable them to flourish together, he still would not be creative since he would not have adequately expressed his own privacy, nor would he have made proper specialized use of ultimate factors, committed himself, or grained and sustained his production by embedding it in appropriate, recalcitrant material. After a while, the organism he produced would act apart from him and, in effect, itself complete what he had begun. A creator is not granted that privilege. He must produce a work fully completed, needing nothing to nourish it.

Creativity presupposes a privately exercised ability to act in considerable independence of vagrant tendencies and established habits, even those built up over the course of a successful, productive career. Although the habits and tendencies may promote a good and needed use of techniques, these techniques must, in a created work, be kept subject to the demands of the gradually realized excellence.

Never entirely freed from his past, always more than spontaneity incarnate, a creator carries on his work between the extremes of established fixities and a prospect that is being made more and more determinate. The former provides the factors to be united; the latter helps determine if, when, and how what is available is utilized. Accounts of creativity which are primarily biographical, historical, or cultural, so far as they treat the achievements as primarily the outcome of uncontrolled forces, repeat in a different way the error attributed to their romantic opponents, who take a human creator to be a medium through which some alien creative power surges.

Medieval thinkers knew that "truth," "goodness," and "beauty" were not predicates like "human" or "fat" and that they referred to what was eminently desirable. What they did not see was that their realization of those ideals required them to be changed from guiding, indeterminate prospects into agencies by which separately produced units became actively interinvolved with one another.

When a work is said to be beautiful, good, and so forth, reference is made not to some feature characterizing the whole but to the need to read it as an irreplaceable singular with mutually enhancing, diverse functions. Words, shapes, numbers, colors, and other units are there turned into stresses, separations, connections, climaxes, and backgrounds without thereby destroying their different natures as so many distinct units, with their own modes of action and effects. Often enough, various aids, in the form of titles, settings, familiar or arresting components, or knowledge of what was intended, might be used to help others locate foci, crucial turns, rhythms, contrasts, supports, and spacings.

An excellence plays a different role in each created work, even in those of the same genre, for its realization is one with its operation as a unification of particular parts. Were it readily discernible, it would not always be as difficult as it now is to distinguish a copy from an original. The fact that the most minute examination of each item and its position in a work may well leave its originality in doubt does not jeopardize the radical difference of the one from the other. No matter what men know or say, a creation remains a creation, and a copy a copy. Both may please to the same degree. A copy may even be preferred to the original by someone forced to choose between the two. When a supposed original is discovered to be just a copy, its market value will change, and there will be a decrease in public interest in it; yet nothing will have been altered in the work itself. Instead, one will have become alerted to the fact that the various parts are externally joined and bounded in a copy, and that an original has them internally connected. We may not always become aware that some purported creation is in fact a copy until we discover that the material used by it had to have been produced at a time and place when it could not be, were it an original work. If this alone were what was amiss, there would be no reason why the copy should not be cherished and perhaps even preferred, even when we learn that it is only a copy.

A good copy may be all that one can obtain. It may provide a deep satisfaction, its parts being so well joined that an encounter with it would be virtually indistinguishable from an encounter with its original. It would still have been put together by adding part to part under the guidance not of a realizable excellence but of a realized one; it would therefore never get beyond the point where a unification was suggested but was not in fact present.

Conceivably, a copy might be unified by one who appreciated it, but a creation is unified even when not appreciated. Both are unities, distinct, bounded. The two may bring equal rewards and give equal pleasure. An original may even have more flaws than a copy has, in which case the copy will be superior to the defective original and yet continue to have a radically distinct, deficient nature. If it is too different, it will cease being just a copy and become at best a forgery with an evident affinity to some created work.

If part of an original work has a boundary separating it from other parts, it will so far not be part of a created work. A copyist, even before he begins to copy, will at least tacitly take the original to be dissectable into an aggregate of such parts. Even if he has a sound appreciation of a great work, he abstracts an aggregate from it. He may thereby do a service, acquainting many with a work to which they may have no access. Beginning his own work, as he does, with an abstraction from the original, he could not, strictly speaking, reproduce the original itself.

We are readily deceived by copies because we readily allow our appreciations to dictate what our readings are to get out of them, without also using them to enable us to get back to the original. There a good reading would end with an affect no copy can bring about. A good reading of an original ends with one's being pulled beyond the point at which the reading of a copy necessarily stops. Originals make it possible for a reader to confront a primary condition in depth; a copy can do no more than help one go part of the way.

The problem of distinguishing originals from copies does not arise in mathematics very often; the physical sciences offer more instances. There are, too, some individuals who only seem to be noble, and some groups which only seem to form a well-led people. There are also states which appear to be but are not just. In all, unities are mistaken for unifications, aggregations for interlocked functions, imitations for originals. The differences may have little significance for one who is content to enjoy what he confronts. It has great importance for one who seeks to learn what only an original created work can make evident—how ideals are realized and what is beyond whatever one daily knows, could encounter, or could use. We can know ultimate conditions, for we can find evidences of them and follow those evidences back to their sources; but we need a good reading of a created work to put us face to face with a condition in-depth, powerful, all-encompassing, at once terrifying and satisfying.

A creator begins by detaching himself as well as he can to be free enough to attach himself to a prospective excellence. He then specializes and uses conditions and the Dunamis to produce what is required by this prospective excellence, by what he has already brought about, and by what is then required. Rarely will he stop to contemplate, know, or enjoy what he uses; instead, he will specialize and join ultimate factors again and again and thereby make the sought excellence more and more attractive, more and more determinate, and more and more in control.

Creators are producers, not critics or conceptualizers. They respond and do not merely attend to the factors they use. Their responses to the condition of which they make primary use are as unlike their confrontations with that very same condition at the end of a good reading of a created work as their experience of being in the present or at a place is from their experience of being in time or in space.

The accepted task of a creator is to produce units supplementing one another inside an internally bounded, unsurpassable, singular outcome. Conceivably, mutually enhancing parts could be provided without showing any interest in the realization of an excellent prospect. Parts might be produced which do not affect one another maximally but still carry out interlocked functions. What is not subject to guidance and control by a prospect does not have a creator, condition, and Dunamis intimately together. If it has well-joined parts, these parts will not supplement one another to the degree they do when an ideal outcome is realized.

In a creation, a sought excellence becomes progressively more and more effective in determining the roles of what is produced. A pause, an accent, a connection introduced into an early or late phase of a creative activity will be affected by and also affect what is produced later or earlier. Ideally, each will make a difference to the others. There is no rule or formula which a creator might follow to enable him to maximize the contributions made by each factor. That loss may be more than balanced if the creator is prompted to concentrate on doing what an ideal prospect, and both produced and needed parts, demand.

Sometimes creators thematize themselves, the factors they use, the course of their venture, some area, or the outcome, and then use these to make evident something encountered, remembered, or imagined. Some appear to be occupied with making evident the nature of love, hate, death, or some other crucial occurrence, to make pure essences visible, to capture the glory of God, to express the power or grandeur of nature, or to elicit hidden forces. Reduced to categories, claims, labels, or even made the object of concern, what is then focused on will at best enable one to note pivotal positions in excellent works. A creator overrides all such positions, making what is there serve as co-contributors to a singular outcome.

If we improved our instruments or narrowed our interests, a created work could conceivably be dissected into smaller units, each of which could perhaps be subdivided further. Creators sometimes carry out such dissections, but mainly to help them obtain a better mastery of the structure of their compositions. A created work interrelates functioning units, each with its own components. Some of these components are essential to the units' existence, others not. Creativity makes primary use of the units an excellence requires, with other items being treated primarily as props, guides, aids, or supplements, affecting and being affected by what is more central and deserving of greater emphasis.

For his last eighteen years Rimbaud apparently wrote no poems and spent his time in travel and engaged in business; nevertheless, we are forced to conclude that unless he was able to split himself in two, the particular foci, emphases, uses, and concerns which once occupied him played some part in what he subsequently did. The conclusion could be avoided if creative work could be carried out without the need to bring otherwise unused dimensions of ultimates to the fore or if once used they would leave behind no indication of their use in whatever else was done.

As collectors sense, creators leave traces everywhere of their attitudes, power, and usages. Rarely do collectors think that the incidental products of mathematicians are to be treated with the same reverence, mainly because they do not think that the achievements of the mathematicians have the kinds of repercussions that the works of artists have. This notion is most likely due to the fact that the works of mathematicians are not readily understandable by the collectors, even when they are expressed in long-established notations. The mathematicians, moreover, are usually thought to express so little of their privacies as to make it not worth attending to what else they might do.

Mathematicians do not usually express much emotion. They rarely provide evidence of inward travail, struggle, or doubt. We know too little of what they privately are and do to make them of much interest. At the height of their powers they may be marked out from all others as abstracted, disengaged, disoriented; later, when they are no longer creative, they may be taken to be just like other men. Yet unless the past could be wholly lost, or individuals could be split up into pluralities of well-bounded parts, mathematicians, like other creators, must leave some mark of themselves in whatever else they do.

It is possible to discover unsuspected aspects in creative works by noting what is stressed at other times—and conversely. Knowing George Bernard Shaw's admiration of dictators, one is encouraged to look not necessarily for clear signs of this admiration in his work but for its effect on the impulses, values, and judgments he expressed in the course of his productions, where they may have unduly skewed some items.

An individual is undivided; so are the privacy and body he sustains. His unitary nature is not without some effect on the particular things he does. Artists, though, stress sensibility, whereas mathematicians stress thinking. Whereas the noble emphasize the will, leaders express a desire to realize an incomparable glory, and those involved in the production of an excellent state take account of common, pressing needs. All depend for their satisfaction on privately initiated actions.

What a creator alone is able to produce might be approximated by his assistants and deputies. If these follow his instructions, they will act as extensions of his privacy and body. Architects depend on builders, sculptors rely on foundries, an arthritic Matisse gives instructions to assistants on where and how to place the pieces of his cutouts.

The noble, the leaders, the rulers and ruled—all use auxiliaries and agents. The creators' achievements are not compromised so long as it is they who decide where to act and how, where to begin and where to stop. Since no humans are simply puppets, all will leave their mark, but created works are still to be credited only to those who dictate what parts are to be produced and how.

The acting of a play, the performance of a concert, the production of a film involve activities other than and in addition to those required for a creation by just one individual. All are to be guided and controlled by the same prospective excellence. All the preformers will, so far, be cocreators. This cooperation will not preclude one or a few from having dominant roles at various places.

Sometimes the needs, problems, or achievements in one work will prompt creative activity elsewhere. Property rights in land prompted measurement, and this achievement in turn promoted reflections on the nature of areas, shapes, lines, and their conceivable divisions and transformations. A geometer, though building on them, may not know of these origins. Probability theory long ago left behind the problems that gamblers presented and that gave the theory its impetus, but it did not lose its bearing on the crude results that had been obtained. Although one has no opportunity to confront all the units in them together, a script, as well as the memories of performers and the spectators, can keep a work in being by providing a hold both on what was done and on the prospective excellence that was operative from beginning to end.

Unlike one who seeks only to know, a creator opens himself to the ultimate factors as they exist apart from him, preliminary to producing a limited, controlled combination of all of them. At the end he arrives not just at a closure but at the completion of a process in which the prospective excellence was made determinate in the form of an actual unification of what was produced to realize it. He will then be in a position to confront the primary condition he had specialized and used. One who reads the work well arrives at that very same position. This reading will not require him to follow the creator's steps. Even when he attends to a performance and is most ready and willing to allow it to dictate to him, he will stress, qualify, and join units in a distinctive way, never coinciding exactly with what the performers did. Many are able to share in final realized excellence and are able to confront what it signifies, but they will do so from different positions, carrying out differently toned actions.

Created works are both internally constituted and locatable; they may have quite familiar roles in economics and in daily life. We move to the right because a sculpture blocks our way; we walk up the stairs an architect designed; we journey the globe in accord with long-established mathematical rules extracted from mathematical creations. We can see that a hero's living and breathing, eating and walking, are similar to those carried out by others. We can note the responses of a people to its leader and can make detached observations of ways in which rulers and ruled interplay. Were only this much known, created works would have to be viewed as though they were ordinary things with heightened features, raising no special problems. Conceivably, they could then be produced by accident, by machines, by animals, or through a good use of technical skills. Not only do creators unite ultimate factors in tighter and mutually enhancing ways; they also enable an ideal excellence to exist throughout. Were the excellence attributed to the parts, or were these imaginatively abstracted from it, the work would still have them interrelated in a way not possible in other kinds of productions.

Appreciation of works already completed must start with outcomes. These outcomes are accepted as presumably excellent, worth exploring. Appreciations of ongoing performances must instead be content to accept a prospective excellence and to carry out a reading that keeps pace with what is being gradually revealed. At their best, appreciations at both times are backed by an alertness to the fact that what has been achieved is singularly unified, with the items in it having reverberations throughout. The "syntheses" that Kant thought were involved in all countings, and that Hegel thought characterized everything intelligible, have their counterparts in works of art, mathematical creations, noble characters, a glorified people, and a just state. They occur not because someone acted over a stretch of time or used concepts and categories but because some unifying prospect was operative throughout in each.

Usually, one or more items will be considered to be pivotal, serving primarily to determine where attention should be centered and how other items should thereupon be approached and dealt with. Established critics often stop at such pivotal items. Teachers, by contrast, are inclined to focus on techniques and the way one could adroitly move from one position to some others. Rarely does either follow the path actually traversed by a creator. What he does is not fully known, even by the creator himself. Scholars and skilled interpreters usually have a surer knowledge of what was intended and done than others do, but they often lack the kind of sensibility or openness that a proper appreciation requires.

Rarely does a proper assessment of a creation await a reading of it along the lines its creator would endorse. Rarely can a creator do more than provide others with hints and clues on how to read it. Composers and mathematicians are content to use an accepted notation to be read in well-established ways, but these notations provide at most only hints and clues. What is produced is novel, with nuances, relations, tensions, and an import the creator neither planned nor anticipated in its full concreteness and splendor. Still, creators, like lovers, the religious, and prisoners, are often quick to note when others fail to grasp the import of what is for them a crucial move or part.

Creators are not particularly interested in appreciating or enjoying their creations. Their lives and energy, what they cherish, and their ability to be free enough to specialize and to combine ultimates over the course of a distinctive venture— these take up most of their time and effort. They may end exhausted, with little interest in what has required much painful labor and concentration, while others who seek only to appreciate may come to the creations innocently and relaxed and then carry out a careful reading, ending with an insight into what is at the root of the familiar. Most appreciators have to content themselves with reading what is made available to them by noncreators and which, therefore, are at best creations that have been given a new status and perhaps thereby radically altered.

Recognizing that a musical composition was completed long ago, one might suppose that even excellent performances of it could have no other status than that of agencies, making it possible for those who come later to become acquainted with otherwise inaccessible works. This supposition is countered by another which denies that any work is ever completed until it receives a public status and perhaps a public endorsement. Rightly rejecting these views, a few take improvisational works or great technological achievements to be genuine creations—perhaps even the only ones. In opposition to these widely held opinions, it will be here maintained that there are two kinds of creations, each with its own special excellence.

A great musical composition may be splendidly as well as poorly played; great actors may provide great performances despite the fact that the text used has little merit. Just as a musical composition is to be distinguished from its performance, so the work of creative mathematicians is to be distinguished from the scientific works which make creative use of the result, the noble from the virtuous, a glorified people from one producing a new era, and an internally produced state from one just maintained alongside others.

Creativity is not compromised because use is made of someone else's creation. If it were, Joyce would be disqualified because he made use of Homer and Vico, Picasso because he studied Goya, Descartes because he knew his Euclid, and Gaudi because he studied the Gothic masterpieces from whose grip he tried to escape. Creations can serve as stimuli, material, provocations, and challenges for others without compromising what those others then do.

Every creation has a past and a future. It partly incorporates them, while they continue to remain outside it. Inevitably, the result will fit into a context of similar works, and this context will fit into others. Paintings belong together with paintings, sculptures with sculptures, algebras with algebras, the noble with the noble, leaders with leaders, and states with states. The contexts, with their members, fit into larger contexts and so on until we come to a single civilization, the locus of the best that men achieve. That civilization in turn fits within a history embracing the minor and the trivial, the accidental and the intended, failures as well as successes, individuals and groups, together with what they do and produce. All can be set in still larger settings. Any can be subdivided. Whatever course is followed, the creations in it will still be unduplicable.

Some take creation to refer primarily to a supposed divine, free production of the universe. To adopt that approach one must know that there is such a producer and that his creation is what humans can at best faintly imitate and, to that extent only, be creative. Unfortunately, a study of human creativity, difficult though it be to understand, can gain little from even a strong confidence that one understands God's ways. Presumably limited by nothing, he could produce excellences without end, not having to grope, backtrack, change, correct, or submit to the demands of a gradually realized excellence. A human creator, by contrast, makes free use of an ideal and freely reaches to and uses factors already present.

It makes more sense to try to understand a possible divine creation after one has mastered the nature of human ones, rather than the converse, for only the human can be known in process and in outcome. The variants, limitations, failures, and benefits of human creations are open to a checking against what is produced elsewhere. A supposed different kind of creation, guided by no separate prospect, not needing to specialize ultimate factors, apparently not even able to fail or to produce what is flawed, can provide little help in understanding what a human could do. Human creators are all fallible beings who have managed to use available factors in ways other humans conceivably could but do not, and who must make an unusual effort to produce their splendid works. Those works are inevitably limited and flawed, though subject to the controlling presence of a realized excellence. A god who was like them would really have had to rest on the seventh day of creation in order to recover his energies and to rethink his options, perhaps to try to improve on what he had already achieved.

No human creation is entirely explicable in terms taking no account of what men privately do; but also, none is entirely explicable in terms taking no account of ultimate factors and materials. Because the ultimates are always available, there can be any number of creative ventures, each specializing and using them in distinctive ways; because each uses material, each is also publicly datable and locatable and sometimes able to be confronted again and again.

Without losing our place in the daily world, we must, to appreciate any created work, ignore its daily status and try to read it as having its own constituents, rhythms, subdivisions, and irreplaceable excellence. Because what is created and what is not are the outcomes of a joining of all of these, one can understand and locate a created work in the daily world and yet be able to deal with it in a distinctive way. Creations—and appreciations of them—differ from all else not because they use otherwise unavailable powers and realities but because they use them in radically individual manners to obtain radically distinctive results.

Attempts to understand creations by attending only to what can be learned from language use, community attitudes, psychology, sociology, logical analysis, the history of art, political history, or some other specialized enterprise will inescapably turn matters upside down since unduly limited forms of the ultimates will then be considered, followed by examinations of a number of limited ways they could be joined. Creations are surely beyond the reach of any who confine themselves to a study or use of agencies in a guise unsuited to creative work. The factors utilized by both are dealt with at greater depths and with greater boldness by the creators to bring about incomparable results.

The greater is not always a variant form of the lesser; often the lesser is the greater in a more muted, poorly ordered, more dispersed form. If we free the lesser from its limitations, we will still not know what other limits are to be overcome. No one produces a great work simply by rejecting the limitations characteristic of a poor one; the needed factors must be dealt with. Because they are always available, one can always try to bring them together so that the outcome promotes the realization of what would otherwise remain just prospective. Although ultimate factors need no help to fit together, they do need to be deliberately joined under the guiding control of an ideal if a created work is to be produced.

The best and the worst, the better and the poorer, are not inverses of one another. Newton is not a schoolboy doing his sums, magnified, speeded up, using notations suitable for dealing with incredibly large numbers and difficult cosmological issues. A schoolboy is not even a Newton in miniature, stumbling, not yet in full control. The boy is in fact unaware of the constituents of what he is producing. Just as theoretical physics cannot be learned by studying engineering and then freeing the results from their involvement with machines and daily affairs, and just as metaphysics cannot be carried out by exaggerating aspects of what science, religion, or experience find, so creations cannot be understood by studying lesser works and re-presenting their procedures in heightened forms. It takes a signal act to reach the ultimates; another to specialize them; a third to use them together with others; and still another to have the result produced within the limits of a gradually realized beauty, truth, good, glory, or justice.

Poor works are produced as freely as great ones. The first are to be measured in terms of the second since the latter deal more adequately with what the others use and do so often enough to serve purposes independently determined and operative. We should study creativity to learn what other kinds of production are possible.

Creative and Created Work

Creativity requires distinctive kinds of work and ends with a work of a distinctive kind. The fact requires one to discriminate among a number of ways in which the term *work* is pertinent to what is done and achieved through creative activity.

There are at least fourteen different senses of *work* bearing on what creators do:

1. Without thought, over the course of life, bodily habits are gradually built up, enabling one thereafter to act promptly and with considerable surety. Work in accord with those habits promises efficiency and success with the routine, with the established, and with what has been successfully mastered in the past.

Every creator puts up some resistance to the unreflective and often unsuspected ways in which he is accustomed to act in daily life. Some of the arresting quality of his achievement is due to his successful defiance of what served him so well in everyday affairs. He must work in a new way to counter what makes other kinds of work successful. He may even deliberately reject what has been most successfully used in previous creations. In both cases the work will allow for accommodations and modifications. Both creators and noncreators usually act in well-established manners, modified to suit new circumstances, all the while that they are engaged in making new efforts which challenge well-established patterns.

2. There are not only bodily habits; there are bodily tendencies as well. Some are common and daily, others novel and singular, to be counted on to promote a ready satisfaction of appetites, needs, and desires. Creators must, to carry out their distinctive tasks, subject them to new aims.

The most abstracted of humans, the most austere and self-denying of them, tends, as others do, toward what quiets hunger and thirst and helps him to avoid injury. Those who abstain from food or drink or who deny themselves ease, as well as those who create, make evident not that they have different tendencies but that they intend to prevent, and to some degree succeed in preventing, those tendencies from being carried out.

Creators, however conscientious and concentrated, have the same kinds of appetites, needs, bodily tendencies, and some of the habits that others do. For a while, they do and should qualify, limit, and defy those bodily inclinations which require them to turn away from their occupation with what they seek to produce. Like others, they must hold their bodies in check, but in different ways and on different occasions, for the sake of bringing about different outcomes. At the end of their creative ventures they may allow a greater play to the tendencies that they have limited, deflected, or qualified. After a created work is completed, other tendencies, which have been ignored or suppressed, may be manifested in a way and with a strength they otherwise would not show.

It requires effort to hold one's body in check, whether that be momentarily, persistently, loosely, or tightly. Since a creator is primarily occupied not with qualifying, withstanding, or even using bodily tendencies—though this is what he must do—but with his creation, he will work against those tendencies only incidentally, while stressing other ways of using his body in the course of his creative activity. Much as a preoccupation with a conquest of evil provides no assurance that good will thereafter be done rather than what is indifferent, routine, or merely acceptable, so a preoccupation with the overcoming of wayward or irrelevant bodily tendencies may not promote a creative venture. One must work against those tendencies, but incidentally, and then primarily to get on with the creative work.

3. There are nonbodily inclinations, quite different from bodily tendencies in nature, course, and outcome. Privately begun and sustained, desires and needs come to the fore and recede and are often enough expressed in unexpected ways, leading one to turn suddenly in this direction rather than that, and then perhaps suddenly following this alteration with a new turn. Some of the desires and needs may be long entrenched, the products of unnoticed fears or of insistent causes originating in early experiences. Much is made of these experiences in familiar accounts of great creators, leading to a search for indications of the presence of disorders in daily living or of self-hidden responses to parents, siblings, lovers, and strangers.

It is often supposed that the contributions of creators can be explained as representations of what was long hidden but is now revealed in ways calculated to mislead. The supposition has the merit of alerting one to the creators' use of their privacies at depths not particularly pertinent to daily affairs. It may also lead one to overlook the fact that those tendencies may have been resisted or been allowed only a minor role because the creative work was accepted as the most attractive option.

No one is a mere locus of suppressed forces. Few can be said to do no more than just exteriorize these. The determination, persistence, devotion, the hard work that creations require, makes most implausible the idea that creators are puppets pulled by invisible strings, manipulated by hidden powers.

4. Having partly freed themselves from habits operative in satisfactory daily living, creators must still take account of the habits acquired in the course of mastering what they have used in previous creative ventures. In contrast with the ways they defy their private and bodily inclinations, they must both yield to and qualify the very habits and practices that enabled them to be skilled. Advantage must be taken of those habits in order to carry out needed technical work with ease. To escape being just dexterous or glib, it will also be necessary to avoid merely slipping into those habits. One must remain constantly alert to the danger that technical

proficiency may lead one to become no more than skilled, perhaps dazzling, endorsed, and honored, but still not a creator. Technique is needed, but it contributes most to achieving excellent work only if controlled.

Creativity requires that some items be given the role of intermediaries, with others having pivotal or climactic roles. A mastered technique makes it possible to provide these stresses when, where, and how needed, but if excellence is to be achieved, the technique must be kept subject to what the work itself requires. Creativity serves ends that techniques alone cannot promote. Creators must work against a tendency to display their skills.

Lacking an interest in producing what is excellent, and therefore in having what is done be affected by its prospect, one may still be able to produce an aggregate of parts, perhaps tightly and well joined, beyond anyone's capacity to improve upon. A creator, instead, will from the first turn parts into interlocked units through a persistent use of a sought excellence. To realize that excellence, he must convert his skills into subservient aids, not allowing them to dictate what he does. Some of the items he produces will be given major, others supportive roles; some will be focused on, and others will remain in the background. He and technicians both work, but at the service of different objectives and outcomes.

A technician is alert to the fact that his work is to be well made; a creator is occupied as well with the production of a self-maintained, internally constituted singular. He may be as skilled as any technician; he may successfully control what he does as well as any virtuoso does, but he also labors to satisfy an effort to have his work be permeated by a feeling that reflects the enhancing presence of a gradually realized excellence. (Josef Albers kept feeling out of his paintings and consequently exhibited great skill but no creativity. His works can be admired, but not enjoyed.)

The techniques that musicians display are not those that were used in the course of the creations they utilize. Those creations required distinctive skills, enabling their creators to use established agencies in ways that might be matched by noncreators. Even apart from accepted notations, a musical composition demands a mastery of considerable technical skills and an effort to prevent technique from slipping out of its subordinate, contributive role.

5. The five ultimate conditions and the Dunamis have ranges and a purity beyond the reach of anyone not privately and bodily freed from control by external determinations. By making free use of his privacy, a creator can specialize the ultimate factors in distinctive ways.

The privacy and body are opposed, interrelated, and possessed by an irreducible individual. At different times, if he is a creator, he will make each play a different role in relation to the other and to interplay in different ways and degrees with the ultimate factors. Before he can make use of a condition and the Dunamis, he has to carry out hard work to make possible a primarily private occupation with what is to be achieved.

To the degree that a creator sets his privacy in contrast with his body, to that degree will it be possible for him to be so positioned that he can begin a private act. What is finally realized will of course require him to make use of his body as well. This use will not only help fix and grain what the privacy does in interplay with a condition and the Dunamis but will also make possible the use of various materials providing other, public, and brute fixatings and sustainings. The free, fluid movement of creativity is stabilized by the body and what it is able to use—and that requires work of a distinctive kind.

6. No one ever becomes entirely free from what he has achieved or has learned. If he is to engage in a creative venture, he must so utilize what is privately and publicly available and pertinent that the work is supported and lodged in what allows the work to exist, sometimes for a considerable period after the creative act is over. Each effort begins a new adventure, demanding its own kind of venture.

Even when prompted and guided by what has been achieved in the past by himself and others, a creator begins afresh, as free as possible from the grip of what he has already done well or poorly as well as from extraneous influences and settled habits. There is no way in which he can rid himself completely from all of them; he cannot transform himself into a pure, untrammeled spirit.

The style that a creator achieves and usually freezes in his creative works could be turned into a factualized, abstractable component that he should be neither interested in nor concerned with. It should not be allowed to guide him, for his is individual work, then and there produced. His style is a steady precondition which can too readily interfere with the distinctive work that has to be done at a particular time. To produce an excellent work, he must therefore strive against the inclination to allow his achieved style to rule him, at the same time that he seeks to utilize it in a new way.

7. Although it is both yielded to and utilized, a prospective excellence imposes limits on what is acting to realize it. If no effort were made to realize it, a creator would have no way of determining how needed factors are to be joined in act after act. Work must be done to keep the prospect in focus; effort and attention must be directed at making it determinate. Were it not kept in focus, were it not brought to bear and yielded to, there would be no way of knowing what should follow on what has already been achieved in order that an excellent outcome be promoted.

An ideal prospect is too indeterminate to allow one to read from it just what is to be done next. A creator responds to it from a private position and is thereupon able to see that what was achieved needs supplementation and support from other items. These, together with what has been produced, make the prospect more and more determinate. Unlike a possibility (i.e., what can be instantiated but not gradually converted into a unifying operation), an ideal prospect requires actions serving to make it more and more determinate. Unlike a possibility, too, the prospect contributes to its own realization by guiding and controlling what is done. The actions of men here and now qualify the excellence being realized. As the creation progresses, the excellence becomes a greater and greater agglutinative force. Creativity is autotelic, with a limit in the form of a splendid prospect made more and more determinate as the work progresses.

What is produced through a joining of the conditions and the Dunamis makes a privacy and a prospective excellence increasingly interinvolved, the one thereby becoming better focused and the other more determinate. Subsequent joinings of the ultimate factors continue the process. At the end, the sought excellence will be present as a power enabling the different items that the creator produced to make a significant difference to one another's import.

The more determinate that a work, the roles of the produced units, and the excellence become, the more thoroughly will the parts be turned into interplaying functions. Finally, the sought excellence will be present only as an effective internal connection, exhaustively expressed in the unification achieved. The excellence cannot then be abstracted from the completed work, for it is there only as a determinate interinvolvement of what was initially produced as distinct units. Both the excellence and the units will still be available for other creations, the one as a prospect, the other as distinct parts.

The conversion by an excellent prospect of separately produced parts into interinvolved units overrides the boundaries of those parts without annihilating them. The words of a poem do not cease to be words of a common language when they reverberate throughout the poem; their common meanings serve to anchor them outside the poem, while they are given new meanings within it. What metaphors do so conspicuously—yoke different words and meanings together so that they emphatically affect one another—an excellent poem does to the words it encompasses. It is therefore as legitimate to take it, or any other creation, to be a grandiose metaphor as it is to take it to be a new necessity linking otherwise contingently joined items or to be a complex in which distinguishable units are intimately interrelated.

8. Created works are made available to others through the material in which they are embedded. In musical and mathematical creations, the material may be no more than an established notation and the grammar implicit in the notation's proper use. The common use of the term *work* refers to what must be done to make such material fixate, support, and strengthen what is otherwise achieved. Even language, though it can be manipulated in an apparently endless number of ways without great effort, can be creatively used to yield new units and connections only in the teeth of established usages.

A poet, more evidently than most other creators, keeps conventional connections and usages at bay in the course of an effort to join what otherwise would be disconnected and apparently discrepant items. He does not, could not, and will not want to eradicate all the meanings and connections that his words have in daily discourse. Still, with other creators, he will accept no antecedently defined restrictions on what is to be done; yet he will inevitably find the work to be subject to qualifications by what is not within his full control.

Language in its daily use clings to the poet's variants and modifications. Like other creators, the poet accepts no antecedently defined restrictions on what he is to write about or how he is to write it. He can, and often does, listen to criticism by other poets. It would be unwise for him to listen to anyone else, though it may be good policy to heed his patrons, his rulers, or his publishers. The words he uses are parts of a common language that his own usages may override but cannot extinguish. Whatever he does makes a difference to his work in ways not entirely within his power to overcome.

Improvisational musicians and dancers evidently, but no less surely painters, the noble, leaders, and political beings, try to master recalcitrant materials. The improvisionalists differ from other creators primarily in making more conspicuous and sometimes more radical use of their materials than the others do, though they, too, must work if they are to take advantage of their materials. Creators, when carrying out their different enterprise, become as fatigued as others do.

Created works may but need not have economic importance. They may neither be wanted nor cherished by others. Supply and demand, suppression and exploitation may dictate where and how physical energies are to be employed. Were the economic sense of work alone considered, poets and composers would often have little or no role to play. Yet they work against obstacles as obdurate as others face; in their own ways they work as hard as do those who are engaged in producing other excellences. Goods that no one wants or needs have little economic import, but creations lose nothing of their excellence even if neither wanted nor needed.

9. Insight, inspiration, impulse, and determinations do not last long. Every creator tires. Effort must be made not only to work but to keep at work, to resist fatigue, to remain involved, to bring a work to its proper close. Reserves must be called on if one is to continue. A creator must make himself work even when he willingly engages in an act of creation, for new efforts must be made again and again. He has to work in order to work.

Caught up in his project, elated, absorbed, lost in his venture, hardly aware of himself or of what he is making use, a creator often finds himself unable to go on, not because he is unable to see what he has to do next—though this surely does happen—but because he cannot make satisfactory use of needed private and bodily powers. It is possible, at times, for him to force himself to continue and to do so with some success. Eventually, though, he must rest, eat, and sleep. The work that he must do in order to keep on working he can command for only short periods and in limited quantities.

One not guided and controlled by an ideal prospect will produce only externally related parts. These parts could, and sometimes do, add up to a work well done, but even then reserves will have had to be called on. All tasks impose their own demands, sometimes getting in the way of those made on a creator's energy, time, and interests.

Were a creator to depend mainly on outbursts of energy, exuberance, spontaneity, sudden insights, and the like, he would work only occasionally, and then usually for short periods. Whatever plans he had could then be readily overwhelmed, made subject to uncontrolled impulses; they would, more likely than not, lack direction and not be prepared for use. The additional vitality he introduces makes a difference; it thrusts him forward, allows him to look back, enables him to move in ways he otherwise would not. Work must still be done to keep his efforts confined to the piece at hand. There are lucky strikes, sudden hits, but if anything is to be created, these fortunate occurrences must be harnessed, limited, made to act on behalf of what is sought. Occasionally they may open up a course and invigorate activity in desirable ways. To benefit from them, work of another kind is required, one that channels, orders, directs, and constrains what they make available.

10. It may be of no great importance to say that everyone has creative moments or to take *creative* to characterize only the work done to produce excellent works— provided only that the great differences separating creators and noncreators are not overlooked and that mankind is not divided into two classes, with the creators in one and the rest in the other. Geniuses are human; so are clods. No matter what they do, they all express a common human nature, marking them off from other kinds of beings. Each is a distinct, unduplicable individual, able to carry out private and public acts different in kind from those carried out by what is not human. Each, unless radically distorted or immature, can assume accountability, be responsible, imagine, be self-critical, will, and believe. The difference that separates creators from other men is one of degree within a common nature—a degree, though, that enables them to achieve what is different in kind from what the others do.

A tendency to read back into creators the presence of incomparable gifts, as though the creators did nothing but make evident what was latent, awaiting only an opportunity to become active, overlooks the humdrum character of the lives of many creators, while the supposition that those who fail lack some special abilities unilluminatingly attributes actual failures to supposed incapacities. Some men have better ears and eyes, defter fingers, a better grasp of spatial relations than do others. Some have perfect pitch, others perfect vision, still others fine physical control. The fact that they can do what many cannot is insufficient to show that they are or will be creators. Not only may they not use these agencies, but those less favored may be able to create by carrying out other kinds of work, as Matisse so brilliantly demonstrated.

Creators differentiate themselves from others as they work, bringing into play powers others do not use as persistently or as well. They begin, act, and maintain themselves at deep private positions which others only occasionally reach and rarely utilize. They keep focused on a prospective excellence that others may glimpse but which they do not commit themselves to realize or do so less effectively. Creators persist where others act for only a passing moment or so or yield to the temptation to settle for easier work or quicker satisfactions.

Mastery of techniques, training, acquaintance with great achievements, quick success, and rewards sometimes help some to continue beyond the point where noncreators stop, either because they have been overwhelmed by forces beyond their control or because they have been lured in another direction. Prodigies make evident that some individuals can master techniques quickly and exceptionally well; they do not show that they have a creative power denied to others. Conceivably, a physiological or psychological quirk might enable some to find some prospective excellence more attractive than a more immediately realizable prospect attracting most others. Whether this be the reason or not, creators sooner or later reveal themselves as persistent and able to back with well-honed techniques their occupation with some ideal prospect.

Not all who dedicate themselves to a creative life are creators, while some who have spent their time at other work may suddenly decide to, and may in fact, create. Novelists and playwrights sometimes begin to flourish long after the age when mathematicians come to the end of their creative careers. There seems to be no distinguishable trait or occasion prompting some persons to create, no distinguishable trait or occasion keeping them fully occupied with creative work while others engage in it for only short periods. When the difference is credited to special endowments and gifts, the difference is displaced, not explained.

Everyone is faced with short- and long-range goals and can see that the latter sometimes promise more, but also that they demand a neglecting of what is more easily realized. A few settle for a life devoted to an end to be reached after that life is over; others settle for what will now please or appease a hunger. Early training and institutions encourage the one; familial and social training discourage the other. Most find a position in between. Creators are among them. Without necessarily losing interest in immortality or in a limited end promising immediate satisfactions, they focus on the kind of excellence many others could also achieve were they willing to work to realize it. It seems to be as difficult and as easy to account for the failure of these others to engage in creative work, or even to overcome what stands in the way, as it is to account for a preference to swim, run, sing, or dance.

Bodily constitution, opportunity, and guidance surely play a role. Attitude, early success, training, and encouragement help account for many, but not for everyone willing to go through a period of difficult apprenticeship and self-criticism.

Although we can never be sure exactly what has made someone give himself to a creative life, we can find a good explanation in his decision to try to realize excellence rather than work to bring about another kind of prospect. Once this explanation is accepted, we will be able to distinguish those who rightly persist from those who do not, and the successful from those who fail. One thing is certain: the work creators carry out make the work they produce worth the effort.

11. Explosive expressions of energy make a difference to what is encountered and done. The outcome is not properly termed *work* unless the word is permitted to characterize any kind of activity. Spontaneity is too irregular in its appearance, course, and emphasis to be useful; control must be exercised. At a minimum, work is needed to regulate the use of one's energies.

The fact that creators are caught up in the work they are producing often suffices to determine the work they are called on to do in order to make themselves function in needed, steady ways. They must take advantage of sudden spurts of energy, opportunities that happen to arise, and be ready to press advantages suddenly glimpsed. Not to work to control and use is to allow opportunities to appear and disappear. Creators are usually signally alert to what could contribute to the success of their ventures.

12. The decision to stop at some particular point or with some particular work is not hard to make, though it is often quite difficult to carry out and hard to see why it was made. Some stop too soon, give up too easily. That surely happens more often than its opposite, the failure to avoid adding irrelevancies. Hopes, conceit, and desire all play a role in prompting some creators to pass beyond the point where they are being effectively creative. Work is therefore needed not just to make a decision to stop—although this decision may sometimes have to be made in the face of enticements attracting one in some other direction—but to make the decision play an effective role in what one is about to do.

No one knows himself so well that he surely knows when he has reached the limits of his creative powers. Each must make a decision to stop at some point in his work, marking that point as the furthest he is then able to get without blurring and blundering. He must decide for himself that what he once could and did do, or what he is now at last able to do, is not now to be done. He must make his determination to stop be effective, as surely as he must work to carry out a determination to continue.

It is tempting to refine, embellish, add, or subtract this or that detail. No work is perfect; yet no one knows when he, at least, can do nothing more to improve it. Sometimes a creator stops because he does not see how to go on. Rarely does this cessation occur at the very place he should have stopped. Since the recognition of his ability to go on does not coincide, except accidentally, with what is required if there is to be progress toward the achievement of an excellent outcome, he must use what he has achieved and what he discerns of the excellence being realized to tell him that he must do nothing more. What has been produced might well need additions, improvements, alterations, but this work may be beyond his capacity to produce without spoiling what has already been achieved or precluding what is yet to be done. Work must be done if a creator is to keep himself in check, if only to avoid doing harm.

A piece of work, having been begun and carried out in a particular way, is to be brought to a close. Independently of the question whether or not a creator could continue with it, he must decide whether or not the work needs further work. To stop with what is not unified is to stop with what is truncated, partial, unfinished, flawed, but if a more or less completed work is not left alone, what has been achieved may well be spoiled. Able to continue, one should have refused to do so. Unfortunately, creators are not always the best judges of what they have achieved or of what they could achieve. Sometimes they focus on what should have had only a minor role within an excellent whole. Though they may then improve what they attend to, they may also get in the way of achieving what they had dedicated themselves to produce.

A work might not be as good as it could be but still may not be open to improvement, precisely because, with all its defects, it could not be improved, given such and such abilities, circumstances, materials, or interest. The best work has blemishes; none is perfect, but the needed improvements might not be achievable. Sometimes great scores, stories, plays, proofs, and courses of action are well emended by others who have markedly less ability. These others change the role of some of the items on behalf of a work that otherwise would have avoidable defects, accomplishing this improvement in ways and with a success its creator apparently could not.

Fortunately for some writers, there are editors whose main task is to restrain and direct those in their charge. The editors of mathematical journals do not work that hard at helping mathematicians perfect their work. The noble have usually had teachers early in life. Leaders are too dominant to be in a position to benefit much from criticism, while rulers and ruled are too much involved in daily tasks to listen carefully even to wise statesmen. All could benefit from help from those who are not creative, but to whom flaws are patent and who can suggest remedies not beyond the creators' abilities to provide.

13. The outcome of creative activity is properly called a *work,* for that term sums up the efforts made to realize it. Some of that work is not exhibited in what is produced, having been spent in correcting, adding to, and supplementing or in

modifying or suppressing tendencies to add or subtract. Throughout, in one way or another, energy must be spent to control, act, organize, resist, and transform as preconditions for the realization of a prospective excellence.

It is to the outcome of a creative activity that others initially turn to enjoy and perhaps to read a realized excellence on the way to making contact with a primal condition at an otherwise undiscerned depth, there exercising an otherwise unsuspected power. These appreciators also work, though their work is quite different in kind from that carried out by creators. Sometimes they will get more from a creation, and often what is quite different from what their creators do. What the appreciators discern may even be unknown to the creators, since the latter may not have rested sufficiently long with their works to grasp their full import. Critics are sometimes alert to the fact. To make it their own, though, they, too, must become appreciative, perhaps alerted and guided by others.

It is one thing to know what work was done and another to know what work was produced. The one knowledge falls short of the other because the completion of a created work is one with the vanishing of the excellence as something distinctive, not yet realized. One looks in vain for a well-demarcated beauty, truth, goodness, glory, or justice in a completed work. At the beginning of creative ventures these prospects are too indeterminate to be more than hardly noticeable beacons, while throughout the course of the creation attention has to be directed at what has to be done, what is being done, and what is next to be done. Work is needed to get one to attend to what a creation makes it possible to discern, just as surely as work must be done to keep one from using the work as just a means enabling one to attend to something else.

At the end, a created work must be held in equilibrium between an appreciation of it as self-contained and a use of it as a sign enabling one to confront an effective, all-encompassing condition. A creator must work to keep his work from having too large or too small a role. If he fails, he will not maintain a needed distance from the work throughout and at the end. It takes work to keep him steadily positioned toward his creation, so that it is neither just enjoyed nor just employed, but both, with now the one and then the other to the fore.

Two poets among many others make evident how concerned an artist may be both with a work and with what it signifies. Since the first piece is given only in part, it is not offered for appreciation but as an aid to understanding; the second escapes that limitation. The first is from "Epilogue" by Robert Lowell:

> Those blessèd structures, plot and rhyme—
> why are they no help to me now
> I want to make
> something imagined, not recalled?

The second is from Joseph Brodsky's "Sextet":

> Petulant is the soul begging mercy from
> an invisible or dilated frame.
> Still, if it comes to the point where the blue acrylic
> dappled with cirrus suggests the Lord,
> say, "Give me strength to sustain the hurt,"
> and learn it by heart like a decent lyric.

14. The hardest part of creative work, and the hardest to understand, is the actual process a creator goes through, making use of all the ultimate factors, step after step and concomitantly, to turn a prospective excellence into a determinate unification of all the parts. The difficulty is in some degree owing to the creators being caught up in their work. When they reflect on their activity, they must rely on much that has been only incidentally noted. Creators, moreover, are not usually acute self-observers, masters of analysis, or sufficiently attentive to what they have made it possible for others to discern. When they move back into their privacies, however, and focus on a prospect worthy of being realized, they are positioned not only to make use of ultimate factors but to utilize an ultimate condition in a way others do not. Different types of ventures emphasize different conditions; different subdivisions of those ventures use the same conditions to carry out more limited functions. The ways in which each kind of venture embraces, modifies, relates, and empowers what occurs is made evident in the special ways in which beauty, truth, the good, glory, and justice are realized.

Seldom are creators interested in the nature of what they use or in the ways they use it. Usually they content themselves with trying to do what is required if an excellent work is to be produced and initially discerned depths made more evident. Working characterizes their entire venture within the compass of a faintly discernible prospect and as subject to the commitments their acceptances and accomplishments entrain. Insufficiently prepared to report what they had initially acknowledged and too caught up in what has its own rhythms, requirements, and outcome, creators are unable to help others learn much from what they report about their beginnings, activities, or achievements.

Work, whether elicited, carried out privately, or exhibited over the course of a venture in producing an excellent, revelatory product, is to be dealt with by engaging in such an account as this one, devoted to understanding. The task is in principle no more difficult than that of grasping the way an arm is successfully lifted or the heart is made to beat more quickly even when one makes no move. Physiology may lay bare the muscles and other necessary parts; observation may allow one to remark on the beginning and the end of an act, or any point between, without actually subdividing, hindering, or quickening it. Although the primary concern of a creator is not to understand what he uses or how, or even what he discerns of the depths of things, of a prospective excellence, of himself, or indeed of anything else, he, too, could benefit by working to understand what he confronted or accomplished—if only to reassure himself in moments of doubt or to forestall an apparent failure.

These fourteen instances of types of work make evident that a creator must work against habits, bodily tendencies, private inclinations, and constraints produced over the course of his activity, to use ultimates, to free himself from limitations induced by his previous activity, to make what is indeterminate determinate, to use materials, to keep on working, to bring neglected powers to bear, to regulate the use of his energies, to make himself stop, to enable the creation to act as a sign, and to yield in understanding of what is done. He must not only make an effort to become as free as possible but must insist on, direct, restrain, and utilize his powers, both those that are well entrenched and those that come to the fore to a degree not antecedently determinable. These are just a selection from a multitude of challenges he faces, none easily distinguished.

A creator does not have access to the items he uses to a degree or in a way necessarily beyond the reach of noncreators. He cannot discern otherwise unfathomable depths in ultimates; if he could, he would be a distinctive kind of being, if only for the short period when he was creative. He would also baffle us, we who seek not to imitate him but to understand him and what he does. References to problems requiring solution, to combinations and separations of items in new ways, to inventions, to sudden changes in direction, fall short of telling us about the nature of the work that must be done if an excellent work is to be produced, while references to inspiration or to different parts of the brain, like references to genius and the muses, presuppose that the answer is to be found in unprobed or unknown regions.

A creator does nothing that is not in principle possible for anyone to do. Nor does he make use of what is not available to others. He differs from them mainly in taking account of factors in a form purer than others use and then specializing them in distinctive ways, while progressively realizing a prospective excellence that the others do not work hard enough or well enough to make fully determinate. What he initially discerns, they can, too. They do not, mainly because they are occupied with other matters. That, of course, does not mean that a change in interest or effort will turn them into creators. They will still differ in their commitments and how they satisfy them.

Ultimate factors—conditions and the Dunamis—are evidenced in everything and can be reached by moving intensively from the places where they are together in limited, specialized forms to where they are apart from one another, dense, self-maintained, able to come together in multiple ways. A philosophy that concerns itself with stating what these ways are makes it possible to know what a creation requires. The knowledge will not enable anyone to create. Still, it may help a creator learn where and how to work more effectively and—more evidently—to see how his achievement is related to the achievements of others who use the same factors in other ways to bring about different, excellent works.

Creators, again and again, deliberately join limited forms of the ultimate factors. To justify that claim, it is necessary to see how this joining must be done if excellences are to be produced. The needed study will be abstract and general, in contrast with anything done creatively. It would be even more, indeed overly, abstract and general were it to deal indiscriminately with all types of creativity. Major types of creative work need to be distinguished if the quite different uses of the factors all creators use are not to be overlooked. The present examination of five quite diverse, readily recognizable ventures in creativity is carried out in the hope of making the work of each more evident and the distinctive nature of creativity and created work better understood.

Topics, Themes, Emotions, and Feelings

Most discussions about creativity center about works of art. As a consequence, what concerns artists and leads them to create becomes most prominent. There are good reasons for this approach. The achievements of artists are usually more accessible and more quickly appreciated than other creations are. At least they seem to be more easily read and often have a wider appeal over longer periods than do other types of created work. What is created in other areas, though different from what is achieved in art, is still cognate with what occurs there. Those others should not be neglected even by one concerned primarily with understanding works of art, for they make it possible to detect aspects in art—and in one another—that would otherwise be overlooked.

Creative works in art, in mathematics, in the achievement of a noble character, in social life, or in politics emphasize different things. Each endeavor focuses on what the others neglect or minimize. Studies in creativity are unduly hobbled unless they attend to what can be learned from all the major ways in which creativity is carried out.

Occasionally, the arts are approached from the position of mathematics—or conversely. The word *art* is also used sometimes to characterize whatever exhibits some spontaneity, freshness, or inventiveness. Sometimes, some such enterprise as psychiatry is used as a guide to or source of the categories to be employed in an analysis of the arts or other creative work. No help is to be despised, but none should be allowed to take one away from the creative activity and its outcomes or to stop one from considering what it is necessary to use and do in distinctive ways in different creative ventures.

Creative activity begins with an attempt to produce an excellent work. This attempt may be elicited by what is beneath the surface of things; that is often what prompts artists to create. It may be provoked by glimpses of a prospect worthy of being realized. That is how some individuals apparently become committed to realize an ideal good in themselves. The creative effort may also be elicited in response to what has been achieved in the past; mathematicians and scientists are often led to venture into new areas because of limitations found in the already accepted. Leaders act to transform a people, taking themselves to be the agencies through which the people's common glorification will be achieved. States are created when rulers and ruled, with the help of statesmen, reach the position where they act together and thereby realize an ideal justice. These different creations are backed by the different creators' expressions of emotions and are quickened by the presence of distinctive feelings.

Like everyone else, creators are affected by their individual involvements in limited situations, remembered, expected, confronted, or imagined. When the results are kept in focus, these situations may be treated as topics, that is, as subject matters or as themes, in other words, as ideas. Painters and writers usually, and composers, sculptors, architects, and choreographers occasionally, do this. Sometimes topics and themes are discernible in the works of those mathematicians who are attentive to the needs of theoretical science. The formation of character may exhibit them when it is approached by following precepts and revered masters. Leaders present topics and themes in the form of myths, while historians sometimes remark on them in the recalled highlights of extinct states. Despite the conspicuousness of topics and themes in these instances, they are the most dangerous of reefs, quickly bringing accounts of creative work to disastrous conclusions.

Anything can be used as a topic—a death, a wall, a sunset, a sound in the night, something remembered, an experiment, a task, an injunction. An old woman paring her toenails is as good a topic as the Crucifixion; a dead flower is not inferior to one in full bloom; a shriek makes as good a topic as a smile, an ocean, or the earth. The topic may be noted by means of a name or a title, may be underscored, emphasized, pushed to the fore, or made focal and bounded off in some other way. Novices and dictators, some religious leaders and educators, most critics, censors, and guides attend to topics primarily, sometimes exclusively, supposing that they are what interested the creator and are or should be attended to by all others. Soon it is held that there are suitable and unsuitable topics. Yet topics are at best aids, helping one to get a purchase on a creation. Sometimes they make one miss what was in fact accomplished. Othello's killing of Desdemona is as good a focal point as any other in the play. It is more correct and often more helpful to take it—or any other topic there—to be nothing more than an important stress within a single, unified whole. Multiplying the number of topics still leaves one with a plurality of bounded units and, therefore, with an aggregation. Such an aggregation is considerably short of what a created work embraces.

In the ordinary course of life we make do with proper names to take us toward individuals as existing apart from all else. Those individuals are mediated by what appears. Were creators engaged in doing just this, they would have to be said to be engaged in a kind of "rectification of names" in order to obtain those which were in accord with what is discerned of realities, behind their ostensible appearances.

Matisse said that every object has its own sign; I think he meant that every object can be grasped in depth by a singular, created referent to it and that artists produce such signs. He seems to offer a splendid reason why one should focus on topics. Yet, if a creation were nothing more than the presentation of a topic as a sign, no particular attention might have to be paid to the entire work or to its production. Even topics arousing a creator's joy, fear, or anger, which excite him, jog his memory, reveal his desires, or are expressly named by him, are to be submerged in the making an excellent, single, undivided work. That is one reason why some artists designate their works simply by numbers.

Mathematicians, the noble, leaders, and political beings make less evident use of topics than artists do. With artists, however, these other creators make distinctions between major and auxiliary items, decisions, incidents, moves, and acts. For all of them, topics enable one to read their supposedly excellent works. Since they may make evident a creator's root concerns, biographers attend to them. In a created work topics are chiefly a means enabling one to attend to major foci and crucial turns, thereby helping one to read it well.

A good reader will finally confront the condition that was primarily used, but at a depth and as having range and import otherwise not discernible. Once it is recognized that a good reading of a created work ends with it functioning as a single sign, different stresses within it can be attended to as so many subordinated Matisseans.

It seems not difficult to understand the way painters, sculptors, architects, composers, poets, novelists, playwrights, and choreographers—and sometimes mathematicians and leaders—enable one to confront a final, insistent, conditioning power at the root of all particulars. It is more difficult to deal in this way with the noble or with a created state, owing in part to our being unaccustomed to so reading them that they make evident a condition as it lies behind and affects whatever occurs.

When a created work is used as a sign, a topic may enable one to focus on a distinctive qualification of the ultimate condition there emphasized. This condition will then be faced as insistent, independent, somewhat mysterious, and having a great depth. Topics may also enable a reader to concentrate on a qualification to which other ultimates subject the condition that the created work signifies. They may also promote the distinguishing of different genres in a particular type of creative venture.

Religious art exhibits ways in which voluminosity is subject to a primal assessment. Realistic art attends to a primary affiliative condition. Collages make evident how a primal voluminosity is qualified by a coordinative condition. Abstract art shows a primary rational condition providing such a qualification. In each, different degrees and modes of qualifications of a primal voluminosity occur, with the results able to be combined in multiple ways.

What holds of art holds differently in other kinds of creative venture. There is a warrant, therefore, for dividing mathematics into branches, one emphasizing space, another transformations, a third affiliations, and so on. A created character signifies a primal ordering that may be affected by rationality, equality, solidarity, history, and combinations of these. Societies and states not only signify affiliative and coordinate conditions but are strongly qualified by space and time. In each a created work signifies the primary condition that is so used that it pervades the whole.

A theme, unlike a topic, interrelates a plurality of parts so as to explicate what none of the parts can. Since in order to present a topic one must produce and order parts, a topic can be treated as a limited theme, or in turn, a theme can be identified as a topic presented through an ordered set of parts. If beauty, truth, or some other ideal excellence is taken to be a theme, the distinctive functions that are unified in a work will be minimized or neglected, and what is indistinguishable in the final outcome—the excellence—will be credited with a role it does not have.

Topics are in a work. A theme is explicated. Excellence is creatively produced and exhausted in the act of unifying the produced parts. No creator takes beauty, truth, goodness, glory, or justice as his theme; these ideals are all to be realized by carrying out the work of creation. Each of these excellences interrelates the same items that a theme or thesis does, but where these use them for an articulation, the excellences join the items intimately.

A well-read, finished work acts as a sign of a final condition giving a distinctive import to any and every object. A well-read painting opens one up to a space as able to enclose, pull, divide, absorb, relate, or sustain what occurs. Making use of a brutal act of war as a theme, Picasso's *Guernica* enables one to sense the power of space as able to separate what belongs together. The named theme serves mainly to sharpen our apprehension of but one expression of that power. Whether or not Picasso was concerned with having it do so, the painting acts as a sign for a good reader because it is an excellent painting.

When a created work is used as a sign, it continues to be excellent. Were it viewed as though it were a sign and nothing more, it would not be attended to but would instead be reduced to an object used. It is to be lived in, lived with, and lived through. Only then will it mediate an appreciator—who may, of course, be the creator—and what is omnipresent and effective, able to make a difference in the course, nature, power, and role of whatever occurs. We learn from a created work not primarily about some focused object, but what is revealed about an effective, ultimate condition existing apart from it.

A topic is at best a region focused on, never properly separated from the work. As caught up in a work, it is changed in import, with the role of an emphasis. It may there be subordinated to other emphases as surely as they may be to it. Since anything that might antecedently limit a creation could compromise it, instead of allowing any chosen topic to constrain him, a creator uses it mainly as a suggestion or as a pivot.

Not itself a topic or a theme, a created work is a self-effacing means for confronting a permanent, operative condition. Read again and again in diverse ways, the final outcome of the reading of a work could reach the condition on a very deep level. Since, however, the various levels of a condition are not neatly divided from one another, it is difficult for anyone to be sure that it was encountered at a depth not reached before.

A boy at a piano, a singing cigarette girl's violent independence, or a flying buttress cannot be isolated without seriously compromising the work in which they occur, precluding good readings of them. Each offers a highlight, a pivot, a focus not fully operative until its ostensible nature is used within a larger whole. It is the singular unified work that primarily functions as a sign. Each of the stressed items reverberates over a larger area; what else is there affects it and alters its import and role. A thousand painters could depict a pair of peasant shoes more precisely and more illuminatingly than Van Gogh did or could. Not trying to acquaint anyone with the nature of shoes, peasants, or even of the nature of a conditioning, voluminous space, he occupied himself with the creation of a painting, with shoes as but one, though perhaps the main, focal point.

When topics alone are noted, a work is treated as little more than a message. When the message is taken to be important because of its endorsement or its defiance of prevailing values, the topics are made unduly prominent. In a painting of a hero, a poem about peace, a story emphasizing the punishment of a criminal, just as surely as when a national flag is submerged in urine, a king portrayed without his pants, or a leader shown in an embarrassing posture, attention is pulled away from the work as a whole and concentrated on some demarcated part of it. Whether a topic is acceptable or unacceptable, pleasing or disturbing, it is wrongly focused on if it is considered only so far as it stands in the way of the creation or appreciation of a single, interconnected excellent work.

The error in supposing that a created work is necessarily or primarily occupied with a presentation of topics or themes becomes glaring when some subject matter is introduced from the outside and then focused on inside the creation, with all else ignored or made subservient. This error is committed when *Hamlet* is read or performed from Hamlet's point of view, with Polonius treated as an old fool or Gertrude taken to be the object of Hamlet's Oedipus complex.

If *Guernica* were given another title, or none at all, it might not be so easy to read, but nothing in it would be changed. The title helps us to sharpen our attention and to place emphasis at particular places. Picasso himself may have sought to do so; quite evidently he wanted viewers to be reminded of Fascist brutality, especially in war. We do not really know his intent; if we did, it would make little difference, for the work is to be read and judged as a painting.

Topics are not swallowed up in a work; they must not be separated from the rest of it. To do so would be to give them boundaries, set them apart, deny them their interplay with other, more or less distinguishable items in the work. These items function as contrasts and supplements and might themselves be taken as topics by those interested in the effects other artists had on the creator, the symbols characteristic of a culture or a time, inadvertent expressions of mood or experience, and the like. Surely there is nothing amiss in saying that all works are *about* something, particularly when the works point up where turns, similarities, and contrasts are to be noted and where emphases are to be placed. Still, in and of itself a created work is single, undivided, with each part qualified by the presence of the others and is therefore effectively present throughout.

No created work is perfect, but neither is it successfully completed if it contains bounded items to be aggregated with others. Even the distinguishable items in a splendid collage or montage have repercussions throughout the work and, in turn, have their natures enriched by what else is there. A work may have to wait an indefinite time before there is someone who knows how to read it well and, at the end, becomes aware of a signified condition, indefinite in range, sinuous, powerful, giving a new import to whatever it affects.

There do not seem to be any creations through which we come to know either a creator or the Dunamis in its effective depths. We are forced to learn about the one primarily by attending to topics and themes, and about the other primarily by attending to the ways techniques and materials overcome obstacles. The first may be known well before the work is completed, and even without attending to it; the second may require an occupation with the entire work as though it contained only separately produced parts and was not single, unified, completed, lived in and through. A portrayed jealousy, used to frame and provide connections for this or that assumed beginning of a work or to point up some crucial part, will be pulled toward and pull on what else is produced there. It, too, will be subject to a progressively realized, unifying ideal. If excellent, the work will have a beginning and a discriminable end; what lies between will be so interinvolved that a bounding of any part will compromise the excellence. If what is separated is itself well unified, it will constitute a single work in which distinguished items in it have some roles different from those they had in the original.

Much creative work is carried out cold-bloodedly. Some of it is overrun with corrections and refinements. It may surprise or dismay, awakening emotions in others that crowd out any the creator may have had or sought to elicit. The dynamism of the whole, the ways in which each functioning unit affects the others, takes over, with the consequence that all are qualified.

Every part of a work is produced against resistances that topics tend to emphasize or conceal. At their best, topics provide occasions for attending to the objects of proper names, calling attention to places where crucial emphases or turns occur. They are to be utilized, not made the primary objects of a reading. Each is like a part of an organism that cannot be separated from the rest without destroying the whole; it is not to be considered primary, with all else incidental. Despite their complexity, created works are more like single-celled organisms than like those more developed, since their unifications play so great a part in determining what they are.

When privately grounded efforts are expressed through the body, they are resisted and thereby qualified. The private expressions, as a consequence, acquire new tonalities; the reverse activity, with the body acting on and being resisted by the privacy, yields other kinds of qualifications. The former are usually more conspicuous, for the body clearly limits and sometimes gets in the way of privately grounded expressions of the understanding, responsibility, desire, and other epitomizations of the privacy. Again and again the smooth course of bodily activities is disrupted by nameless fears, changes in interest, and expectations. As a consequence, the constant, normal joining of privacy and body in consciousness is qualified, turbulently filled out, not readily controlled by the individual who possesses both.

Noble spirits, particularly those who emphasize the importance of knowledge and self-control, join those who cherish clear minds or well-functioning bodies in treating emotions as kinds of topics, but regrettable. What is required is only that the privacy remain relatively dominant at various times. It is not emotionality that needs to be rejected or suppressed, but those particular emotions that are in the way of the desirable functioning of an undivided privacy or body.

There are many who want the privacy to be guided by the body's needs and dispositions. Others want the body to be limited to minimize pains and frustrations. It is not to all the emotions that either group should object but to particular ones, those so primarily and improperly biased as to preclude the proper expressions of either the privacy or the body. They would be right to object to such emotions, though their theories mistake the what and why of the occurrences. Emotions color consciousness; one could be free of them only if one could keep apart and in a permanent equilibrium the contributions which privacy and body are able to make to one another. The freeing is neither desirable nor possible, for sometimes the body's requirements and sometimes the privacy's deserve to dominate and make possible a readier satisfaction of both.

The privacy and body are alike possessed by the individual. The point at which they meet and are in equilibrium is consciousness. The emotions reflect the imbalances produced by emphases introduced by the one or the other into that common point. Inheritances from the past fill out the consciousness with the outcome of competitions carried out among different epitomizations of the privacy, the jockeying for positions that different bodily tendencies express, and the resultant meeting of private and bodily emphases. Some of the emotions will be the result of, and thereupon will accompany, whatever work is done, since this work is always carried out against resistances; other emotions will reflect the ways in which private plans, expectations, and desires are qualified by the body through which they are expressed. It is impossible to free oneself completely from every emotion; even if one could live mainly as a private or bodily being, the other will always have some effect. Even a blissful calm is an emotion with minor perturbations.

Every act consciously expressed, privately or bodily, has its emotional tone, for it is set in place of what has been, makes use of what might be, and is carried out against influences and resistances by the other. The fact that emotions sometimes flood what one does privately or bodily shows that sometimes great intrusions from one side or the other are consciously experienced. Just as one cannot free oneself from all emotions, even when acting as a merely private being, so one cannot do so in a life devoted to bodily action. At both times it is necessary to struggle against overemphases by the one or the other.

Emotions are neither just private confusions nor bodily disturbances. They depend on the existence of a consciousness, and therefore on an individual joining his privacy and body. His actions, no less than his reflections, are emotionally toned. If he were unaffected by his privacy, his would be a life indistinguishable from one of mere bodily movements and rests. Many of his bodily acts, as long as he is conscious, are affected by what he does privately. The resulting emotions, like others, are not to be isolated as though they were separable from the privacy, the body, or their common possessor.

The so-called mind-body problem was already solved in principle by those who presented it. Only because a mind and body had already been acknowledged, each with a distinctive nature but joined in a consciousness and there affecting one another, was it possible to know them and then imagine them set apart from one another as separate realities. The consideration of them together enables one to identify each as qualified by the other.

Neither the mind nor any other epitomization of the privacy is a clear pool into which items can be dropped without a ripple. To have an absolutely clear mind would require a freeing of oneself from all entanglements with the body—an impossibility. Conversely, although the body is not just at the service of the privacy, its actions are affected by what is privately thought, decided, and projected. Since a creative venture makes distinctive use of both privacy and body, the emotions a creator or an appreciator undergoes will have a nature distinct from those lived through when they ruminate or are confronted by bodily challenges.

Emotions are vibrant, sometimes upsetting, sometimes violent, and may so overwhelm that one loses one's way. As long as an individual is conscious, he will undergo some emotion, reflecting the dominance of his privacy or body in the consciousness he jointly conditions. Some of these emotions will be faint, some strong, some momentary, some persistent.

The term *emotions* can also be justifiably used to refer to what is undergone in confronting ultimates. We rightly speak of emotions of wonder, awe, or reverence which mark the outcome of a meeting of consciousness with the ultimates, with a primary stress being laid on privacy. The Romantics so reveled in some of these emotions that they sometimes forgot that there was work to do.

Emotions of joy and relief, the awareness of being successful, of an acceptance of others, or of the coming to an end of an arduous task—all seem to belie this account, for they seem to involve no imbalances in a consciousness where the privacy and body are joined. Furthermore, such emotions as wonder, awe, and reverence seem to be determined by what accepts and lifts up and not to depend on the way privacy and body are possessed. Still, it is an individual who wonders, is in awe, or is reverential. If he did not remain distinct over against what makes these and other emotions both overwhelming and desirable, there would be no one who could be said to be subject to them.

The arts are sometimes denigrated for being produced with the help of the emotions. Balancing the assumption that emotions are unintelligible, confusing, or to be enjoyed as one might a meal or a swim, not having any significant merit in themselves, there is the supposition that some activities are or should be carried out freed from all indications that an individual is conscious and that the possessed privacy or body has a dominant influence. The arts are then held to be work to be left for leisure hours, not to be taken seriously, not supposed to be illuminating, but at best to be sources of private pleasures or bodily determined outcomes, and at worst to express disturbances and confusions.

Both creators and appreciators of works of art, occupied with attributing to each part its full import in the course of grasping the nature of the whole, make use of their emotions. A mathematician, too, is emotionally involved in his creative work. He is not the calm, separated, private mind that the reports of his results are sometimes taken to imply. Even those who seek to be noble or to be just are emotionally involved, though neither is upset or whirled about.

Those who follow Aristotle take participation in art to be purgative, allowing one to live through emotions with salutary effects. They offer a plausible and even an illuminating way to take account of the effect produced by a number of great Greek tragedies. Limitations of this view become evident when one considers comedies, architecture, the dance, or other types of creative work.

Although he said that he heard "the scream of nature," no one knows just what Edvard Munch privately underwent when he produced *The Shriek*. Conceivably, he was emotionally aroused. He surely did not experience at the time what he would have had he met the woman on the bridge. He may possibly never have known such a woman. He may have met one younger or older, fatter or thinner, on the riverbank or in her home, or he might have observed her quite calmly. He surely made her a main topic, but we do not know whether she occupied him as much as did the rest of the scene. Fortunately, it makes little difference to the merit of his work or to our appreciation of it to know exactly what he was living through before, after, or in the course of his creation. It would, however, make a great difference if we took the screaming woman to be the only or primary focal point and treated the rest of the work as though it were no more than background, enabling one to concentrate on the woman.

Although *The Shriek* is not a great work, it offers a good illustration of how a topic might tempt one to take a work to convey a message. If Munch had tried to produce an excellent work, he would have envisaged the screaming woman as little more than an important pivotal figure. Even if we knew what Munch underwent before, while, or after he was working, it would still be a good policy to try to read the result as having no isolable parts, topics, or themes. Even if we knew that he did want us to concentrate on the woman, to be emotionally aroused by her shriek, we would, to appreciate it as a created work, have to use her only as a clue and otherwise ignore her, for it is the entire work that is to be appreciated. Such an appreciation requires us to respond not to some focal figure or features but to the work as an undivided singular.

Feelings are to be sharply distinguished from the emotions—particularly when reference is made to what is present in a created work. There is nothing emotional in it. The work is nevertheless affected by a prospective excellence interconnecting the various parts. The result is a pervading feeling. This feeling is most evident in the rhythms, stresses, tensions, oppositions, supplementations, and thrusts which crisscross the work. Whether or not it contains strong feelings, a work may arouse a spectator's emotions. The anxiety felt as one reads a well-told tale of a planned murder has a different cut, length, force, and effect from the emotions undergone when one is actually confronted by an assassin.

Were it possible to follow the way in which a prospective excellence became more and more determinate, one would be in a position to see how feeling is introduced into a work. That feeling has no necessary relation to the emotions the creator may have undergone in the past or even in the present. We come to know that a work is infused with feeling when we read it, aware that what is focused on here or there is part of a single, final excellence. For a work to be appreciated, the feeling in it must guide and enrich the reading.

To say that a work was produced with feeling, is deeply felt, or is pervaded with feeling is not to impute a consciousness or sensitivity to it. Instead, one underscores the fact that the clusters, combinations, separations, and distancings in the work are due to the presence of beauty or some other excellence realized over the course of a creative activity. Conceivably, the feeling could be present in the work even if neither the creator nor the appreciator were subject to any distinctive emotions. It is this sense of the term of which one usually takes account when a work is criticized as being dead, impersonal, or clever. Such characterizations remark on the failure of the producer to make the pertinent excellence present throughout. Were he a creator, he not only would have made the work be permeated with feeling but would have made this feeling intrusive, evidencing the ways in which stresses, separations, and combinations were intimately interlocked. A great technician, a superb virtuoso, a splendid craftsman is too much occupied with the production of his work to allow himself or others fully to share in it as a single, felt, unified whole.

A focus in art on topics and themes or on occasions for emotional arousal has its counterparts in a concentration on the parts of mathematics which are appropriate to some other enterprise; on those parts of science which are of interest to technology; on nobility as confined to some incident or individual; on leadership as pivoting about some current issue; and on politics as centered on legislation. Each of these ventures, in turn, exhibits counterparts of the feelings present in works of art. In mathematics, the feelings are exhibited in the affect the latest creation has on earlier ones; in science, they are manifested in the ways claims are framed and experiment required; in nobility, feelings are evident where efforts and actions exhibit an ideal good; in leadership, they are discernible in the effect a promised glory has on a people; in politics, they are discernible in the influence exhibited by an ideal justice. When feelings are not discernible in these different areas, we tend to speak of what is done as being lax, dogmatic, indifferent, unresponsive, or routinized. A double loss is then at least tacitly recognized: the appropriate ideal is not lived with as it guides and governs, and one is unable to reach the point where the created work opens one up to a confrontation with a primal, insistent, powerful condition. One might undergo a pleasant experience and even have it come to a satisfying close, enjoy it as "consummatory" (as Dewey took it to be), but nothing excellent would so far be encountered, and nothing basic discerned. The truth that there was an excellent work confronted, lived in and with, self-sufficient as an achievement and yet self-effacing as a sign, would be overlooked.

We are now in a position to deal more confidently with a primary set of creative ventures. There are five of these, each making use mainly of one condition and occupied with realizing just one kind of excellence. Each has subtypes and distinctive problems. All deserve careful examination, with their pivotal problems and resolutions kept in focus. Unfortunately, little more than essential distinctions, inescapable problems, and plausible solutions can be provided, even in a work as long as this one.

2

The Arts

Feeling and Emotion

ALMOST ALL, perhaps even everyone—creators, critics, those who are appreciative, and others who have little interest in the arts—find one and sometimes a few arts to be interesting, attractive, or rewarding. Among those who favor but one art, a few seem to doubt that there are others no less important. Most people seem to grant that painting, sculpture, music, fiction, and poetry require creative work and that they are severally faced with distinctive problems, follow distinctive procedures, end with unduplicable outcomes, elicit different appreciations, and provide some insight into the creators, their times, and a reality otherwise only faintly discerned.

There are many reasons why one of these arts, or architecture, theater, or dance, might be set above all the others. It would be an error, though, to dismiss those others or to deal with them in terms not singularly appropriate to what they achieve or reveal. There are many sincere and sensitive persons who find incomparable excellences realized in them; these, too, may be genuine products of creative activity. No art is a limited form or a variant of some other.

There is perhaps no way to persuade those who are indifferent to or who reject what is produced in some particular art or in some other field that excellent works can be found in them. Still, they should in principle be able to be persuaded, could one make evident that the works they dismiss or denigrate make use of similar factors to produce what is genuinely appreciated by perceptive readers with results comparable to those achieved in their preferred field. One way to persuade them is to make evident how different types of creative ventures are caught up in cognate tasks, each distinguished from the others primarily in its concern with a particular kind of excellence, other ways of employing ultimate factors, the production of other kinds of units, and a successful, technical mastery of special materials.

Bach is incomparable. So are Dante, Molière, Balzac, Martha Graham. These are just a few of a large number, though this number is quite small when measured against the total population. Each of these creators produced excellent works, self-limited, singularly illuminating and satisfying. Each ended with an effective unification of what was produced step after step. The beauty they finally realized, like the truth, good, glory, and justice others turn into effective unifications, was a prospective excellence that was suffused with feeling on being made fully determinate.

Like other ideals, beauty is initially faced as an indeterminate prospect. It guides and lures, gradually becoming more and more determinate as it more and more achieves control. Were a work perfect, every distinguishable item in it would have endless repercussions throughout, evidenced by a pervasive feeling tone. It is doubtful that there are any such works, and there surely are not many that fully measure up to so severe a standard. But quite a number come close enough to allow them to stand out against all the rest. Some items in them will stubbornly continue to be mainly bounded-off parts, unable to have an appreciable effect on more than an occasional neighbor, while some will affect a few others at a distance but have no appreciable effect elsewhere.

There are no known ways by which we can measure precisely the difference between the perfect, the almost perfect, and what is just less than this. We are rarely sure that failure to find a work well unified may be due to its being poorly read. We must be content to go over an initially appreciated work again and again, starting at different points and following different routes, to see if it is still unified, with each part having an affect on the others.

A reader who has initially identified a work as excellent should follow the lead of the feeling in it and thereupon be able to read it as an internally constituted, vitalized, unified whole. There, every item is to be dealt with as an operation having some bearing on every other. If a person is not sure but still thinks that a work is excellent, he must try to read it in this way. If he fails, little confidence can be placed in his judgment until he carries out several such efforts, beginning at different points and moving in different directions. Only then can one have some confidence that the failures are in the work and are not due to him.

Overwhelmed by a first encounter with a Raphael, a Rodin, or a Gaudi, one has good reason to suspect insensitivity if various readings do not successfully follow the course of a feeling connecting the beginning, ending, and points between. If the work is splendid, each reading will end with the reader being opened up to depths intrusive on what is daily confronted. A good reading of it should be a fresh reading, carried out by one alert to the ways in which different parts bear on one another and, so far, exhibit a prospective excellence successfully realized as a feeling pervading a unified whole. Subsequent readings may then not be needed except to uncover subtleties or to enable one to penetrate a little more deeply into a primal reality already made evident.

Sonnets are different from epics, and algebras are different from geometries. Painters and poets know that they are not producing mathematical truths; mathematicians know that they are not writing poetry. If either follows the route provided by a pervasive feeling, he will be alert to the differences that focal points make to one another. The observation will be readily accepted by those interested in painting and poetry, but the formulae in which mathematical creations are presented will make most overlook the way a mathematical creation is read by mathematicians.

As not yet realized, beauty is an ideal, prospective and indeterminate. It can be realized by creators who proceed along different routes, make use of different kinds of material, and apply their privacies in different ways. Like all other excellences, the beauty depends on creators who specialize the ultimate factors as these exist apart from one another and who so unite them again and again that the sought excellence finally becomes an operative unification of the parts produced along the way.

A creator begins by so withdrawing into his privacy that he is maximally free of his habits and other established limitations to fresh moves. The withdrawal is accompanied by a focus on the ideal prospect to be realized and is followed by a move toward the ultimates. A specialized use is then made of the ultimates under the guidance and control of the prospect. To do this, the creator uses distinctive epitomizations of his privacy, in particular his sensitivity and sensibility. What he confronts as a prospective excellence can then be realized in ways he could never have fully anticipated.

When artists couch their reports in technical language, they tend to emphasize their skills. Since they are also men among others, they usually emphasize familiar, commonsense distinctions. The gain in communicability that they thereby achieve is offset by a failure to make evident what in fact was done and how the result is best read. Teaching helps; exposure to great works is desirable; the judgments of others and self-criticism will reduce the number of possible blunders a reader might make. Often these aids will prove of more value than the obiter dicta of even the most self-conscious and articulate of creators.

What no one is sure of is just how some particular great work was produced or what it finally achieves. The most careful watching of a creator at work falls far short of discovering the way he used his private powers or the nature and strength of his commitment to the ideal, to what he had already produced, and to what is yet to be done. Neither creators nor appreciators are sufficiently detached from their works to carry through reliable acts of introspection, recollection, or observation. There is, to be sure, no unbreakable barrier behind which they live. Again and again they discern what others miss or slight. Still, what they say will often be so charged with both subtleties and irrelevancies that they will offer only uncertain help and dubious guides. Nor will a sound knowledge of what creators can and in fact do be established by attending to what their critics say. Their comments are best used when treated only as suggestions, guides, and warnings.

It helps to tell someone to free himself from established bonds and thereupon to be free enough to create, to appreciate, or to read a work properly. The advice needs to be followed by the performance of different and difficult acts by which one frees oneself from hardly sensed and rarely understood constraints. Because it is not possible to enter into someone's privacy as lived through from within, it is not possible for anyone to be sure just where another's creative endeavors begin, how the prospective excellence has been envisaged, or what was intended. One is not even sure how particular acts were carried out or how far the creator retreated within himself when he began to create.

Literature clearly reveals that what goes on in the minds and bodies of creators is not clearly or fully known. It cannot be discovered by interrogating the creators or by studying what they say they have done. Despite the tinge of arrogance and the willfulness that seems to accompany the observation, there is little hope of understanding what is involved in creative activity except by turning away from it for a time to attend instead to the factors that are used there, and then trying to understand how they are best utilized again and again until an excellent work is produced.

Some great achievements can be returned to and dissected at leisure. They may then yield clues about the functioning of particular units and may make possible a better grasp of what is finally achieved. What was in fact done will, though, be difficult for the creator to recall, since he was caught up in the task of producing something rather than in contemplating or dissecting it, or in understanding the nature of what he was using or doing. It is therefore better to look for guidance to those who are concerned with knowing what he accomplished and who may not be especially interested in creating something themselves. When a creator studies the biography and practices of another, he does so, not mainly to know about him but to benefit from possible hints pertinent to what is to be independently produced.

Although no creator ever frees himself from all constraints or is in full control of every move, he still is in charge, doing more than mechanists allow and more than sheer spontaneity could sustain. It is not possible to say in advance or even to be precise about the private position at which he begins his creative venture. Wherever it may be, this position and the end at which he is directed are opposites in a single stretch, with the privacy aroused and insistent and the prospect alluring and confining.

A creator needs multiple skills; he must be able to distinguish the unpromising from the promising, failure from success, insight from vain imaginings. He may carry out mental rehearsals and test imagined outcomes against likely consequences. None of these preliminaries will contribute much to his creative effort if he does not first reach a position in himself from which he can freely act to consider and do what the realization of a prospective excellence requires. There are no rules, no guides, no teachings which will assure success, though they often can provide useful indications of the places where failure is likely to take hold.

A creator moves back into himself to consider what is to be achieved. That backward movement might be initiated to get a faintly glimpsed prospective excellence into better focus, to enable him to make readier use of ultimates in as pure a state as possible, or to help him escape from the limits within which he usually acts. Whatever the prompting or the reasons, he must retreat in order better to advance. He here does, acutely and forcefully, what everyone else usually does loosely, with less concentration and effort, when getting ready to make a concerted effort to carry out a more limited project.

Moving into one's privacy allows for a movement into a deep level of a condition and a deep layer of the Dunamis. Sometimes in the course of daily living, beset by a nameless terror, these ultimates are reached without one's having engaged in a preliminary move back into one's privacy. Instead, the privacy is quickly affected by what is encountered. Sometimes it is overwhelmed. A creative activity is carried out more deliberately, even when charged with spontaneity. While continuing to be directed at a prospective excellence, a creative act reaches toward the depths of ultimates and makes immediate specialized use of them. At both times a creator escapes for a while from the effective operation of indurate habits, at considerable risk to his control, so as to be able to reach and use what is needed.

Creativity depends on one first getting to the point where he is as free as possible from external determinations; he will then be in a position to act in fresh ways to realize what is initially indeterminate and vaguely appealing. If he is an artist, he will favor an ideal beauty rather than some other ideal, in part as a consequence of the route his retreat into his privacy took and where it ended. There he begins a thrust toward the ideal as a prospect he is to realize. Committing himself to realize it, he allows it to guide him while enabling it to be joined with and made determinate by what he produces.

No one ever wholly frees himself from the limitations that daily practice and circumstances impose. When materials are used, special skills and techniques have to be employed to overcome encountered resistances and intrusive irrelevancies. Sculptors, occupied with creating within the compass of some such condition as a voluminous space, sooner or later will so accommodate and manipulate their stones, metals, woods, or other materials that they support and qualify what is otherwise produced. An architect will take account of what environs his structure, adapting the structure to make it a work in a setting. Wallace Stevens, in "Anecdote of the Jar," made evident how the environment makes a difference to everyday things:

I placed a jar in Tennessee,
And round it was, upon a hill.
It made the slovenly wilderness
Surround that hill.

The wilderness rose up to it,
And sprawled around, no longer wild.
The jar was round upon the ground
And tall and of a port in air.

It took dominion everywhere.
The jar was gray and bare.
It did not give of bird or bush,
Like nothing else in Tennessee.

Again, in "Theory":

I am what is around me.

Women understand this.
One is not duchess
A hundred yards from a carriage.

These, then are portraits:
A black vestibule;
A high bed sheltered by curtains.

These are merely instances.

A philosopher is somewhat like the jar, a technician like the duchess. An architect joins the two. All make their works pull in their environs in a way jars can, but to a degree and with an effect these cannot produce. Since paintings, sculptures, poems, compositions, and stories have no fixed environments, they have to be dealt with primarily as self-enclosed. That approach will still allow them to have repercussions on those who make or appreciate them.

Training, experience, and familiarity with great achievements in a chosen field usually make it easier to engage in effective acts and therefore make it more likely that an excellent work will be produced. They may also set unnoticed blocks in the way, making one too much a creature of the past to be able to do something great thereafter. Understanding the role that the past now plays helps to put a stop to the demand that one refer to unknown powers in or outside a creator, supposedly limiting him at some times and exciting him at others. Unfortunately, it may also prompt one to try to rest with historic, physiologic, and similar accounts of created works. These accounts do explain some things. Usually, though, they lead to over-contextualizations and unduly confine what is produced.

Like everything else, a created work is both affected and enriched by the past, the future, the conditions, the Dunamis, the privacy, an ideal, and materials. The past and future, to which the work is subject, relate it to a remoter past and future; the conditions pull it toward themselves on deeper levels; the Dunamis subjects it to influences from deeper layers; the privacy enables it to be subject to free acts; and the materials both stabilize and enable it to be located in a public world. As a consequence, the work will be both privatized and enabled to find a place in a number of complexes. Most of its roles and effects will be of interest mainly to those who deal with it as an object in history, society, or the economy. Since these factors contribute something, a created work, in its full concreteness, cannot be well understood without taking all of them into account. Still, one interested in the work itself will find most to be of little additional interest, perhaps contributing a grace note here and there to what is accepted as a single realized excellence.

Since no one knows how to dissect even a familiar burst of anger exhibited by someone well known, we cannot expect to achieve full understanding of the nature, thrust, and outcome of more subtle, more recessive, personal efforts, particularly when they are confined in and qualified by the larger enterprise of creating something through the help of other, more basic factors. It is unnecessary, however, to suppose that one is ever faced with unknowables. If we could know any, we would deny them that status. We have no warrant for claiming that anything is wholly hidden, but only that we now have nothing but a thin, faint knowledge of it, itself passing imperceptibly into what is thicker, awaiting further dissection.

We can, in principle, know privacies, conditions, the Dunamis, materials, the ideal, the course of creativity, and final outcomes. There is no reason why we may not to come to know any of them as well as we can a stone or a sneeze. Yet while we are content to stop with quite general knowledge about stones and sneezes, we would like to know the others in their full complexity and irreducibility. We can— if by *knowing* we mean philosophic comprehension and what is achieved when a work is read well. The reading will not exhaust the work, triangulate it in concepts, not because the work has an unintelligible core but because it is unfathomably rich, allowing for distinctions, stresses, and connections without end. That richness does not preclude a reading of it that not only is better than those that had been achieved before but is alert to the bearing multiple distinguishable parts have on one another. What satisfied an initial appreciation makes possible a final satisfying confrontation with an operative condition, to a degree and in a way nothing else can.

An actuality is able to stand apart from the ultimates constituting it because it continues into a field in which the conditions dominate over the Dunamis, and into a region where the Dunamis dominates over the conditions. To the degree that the actuality is able to be in the field and region, it has a public body and an involved privacy. If it is a human or some other higher living being, it joins the body and the privacy to constitute a consciousness. That consciousness will be overlaid with emotions so far as the insistence of the privacy or the body is dominant over the other. Emotions are consciously lived through outcomes of a private intrusion on a body, or conversely, of a bodily intrusion on a privacy.

The emotions germane to creative work are of three kinds.

1. The most common emotions result from a meeting of an individually grounded, private thrust into what is external to, but countered by, the body. We are frustrated, upset, annoyed, disturbed by what terminates private expressions in and through our bodies. The more successful the encounter, the more readily will we become relaxed and adjusted, with our emotions losing their negative import.

2. A second type of emotion, the object of most studies, reflects the oppositional natures and mutual qualifications of an individual's privacy and body. Unavoidable, being integral to all activities in which privacies and bodies effectively interplay, they are conspicuous usually only when either the privacy or body is prominent. The supposition that what is eminently desirable is a clear mind that knows truly and leads one to behave splendidly takes emotions to be mainly of this second type. They are then denigrated, overcome, or avoided as distorting and distracting.

3. Most pertinent to the understanding of creativity is the third type of emotion. This is aroused when we encounter what seems to be beyond complete conceptualization and therefore has to be treated as brute and resistant, frustrating the attempt to understand it. Since it blocks the way to a steady use of what is needed for a creative work to be carried out successfully, it (and the other two types of emotions as well) makes a difference not only to the nature and course of creative acts but to the final outcome, particularly as satisfying an individual's insistence on what he wants to have realized.

All three kinds of emotion occur daily and are elicited by what is encountered as having an insistence or a resistance not easy to master. A creation depends on the creator achieving some control over them to make possible his successful withdrawal and insistence, to free him from an absorption in technical activities, and to enable him to keep focused on his task. Creativity is inescapably qualified by them, though one can often reduce their effects.

Whether strong or weak, a creator's emotions are rarely recollections of daily ones. Such recollections would yield what was quite feeble and in any case would be too firmly bound to daily encounters and what may have been disturbing events to allow him to be occupied with or to try to reproduce or imitate them. Although striking encounters may resonate in his memory for a considerable time, often coloring much of what is done thereafter, they are sometimes corrosive, making an undesirable difference to his outlook and activities.

Illness and sad experiences may provide occasions for someone to want to create or to express himself forcefully. They are, though, no more indispensable than the emotions that may accompany them. A creator is rarely excited when engaged in creating, being absorbed in the tasks set by what he has already accomplished, by what his accomplishment seems to require, and by the excellence he seeks to realize. In any case, the emotions he once underwent, and whatever emotions he may undergo while creating, are not matters of great importance to him. Usually he spends those emotions while actually undergoing them. Not transferrable, they cannot be introduced into his work. Evidently, they should not be identified with the feelings encountered there.

A painting, poem, story, or building is incapable of feeling anything; the feelings that pervade them reflect ways in which their parts are interinvolved because of the effective presence of an ideal beauty. Whereas a technical expert occupies himself with fitting items together splendidly, a creator is concerned with having them make a difference to the import of others within the compass of his gradually produced ideal. Careful examinations of his body or reconstructions of what he may have undergone or intended need have little or nothing to do with the feeling present in his work.

Emotions reside in individuals, feelings in what is produced. When performers are told to carry out their work with feeling, they are being asked to take account of the excellence that is already operative in a composition and, in addition, to act so that the sought excellence will be operative in their performance. Simple faithfulness to what was produced by some other creator would require the performers to avoid introducing feeling into what they did. A justification for taking performances to be arts to the same degree that compositions are—or more generally, for taking all the arts, indeed all creations, to be set alongside one another and not ordered as superior or inferior, apart from special uses and interests—is that from different positions and in different ways they not only realize coordinate excellences but also allow for the produced parts to be intimately joined with feeling to the same degree.

When read as having its parts interrelated with feeling, and therefore able to constitute a sign of what is more insistent, permanent, purer, more inward than any condition could be as it is operative in what is otherwise encountered, a created work will not enable one to discern a feeling in what is then signified. Instead, the emotions of an appreciator will be invoked, the feeling in the work being left behind with the use of the work as a sign.

It is one thing to share in the feeling that permeates a work. It is another to be emotionally affected by the work. Different individuals undergo emotions of different kinds even when attentive to the same feeling. The emotions aroused by what is confronted when a created work functions as a sign are different from those undergone when it is being read, for what then affects one is not something created and appreciated but an irreducible condition, with an unprobed depth, insistent and all-encompassing.

A great painting allows us to move to a space as primarily voluminous; sculptures open up a space that can be occupied and possessed; architecture reveals it to be multidimensional. All enable us to confront space as encompassing, accommodative, absorptive, relational, dispersive, and insistent, in any one of an indeterminate number of ways. A deep emotion, reflecting the way the privacy was brought into prominence, may then be aroused.

The *ananké*, "necessity," of which Aristotle spoke as being able to arouse and purge one of pity and terror, refers to a primal causal power. It is but one among several. A Platonist takes himself to be well purged of confusion by the rational; a Franciscan of a conceit by what enables all actualities to be equally real; a Schillerian of an indifference by what makes evident the kinship of all that occurs; and a Plotinian of insensitivity by what orders all items as better and worse.

"Emotion" and "feeling" have so many overtones, and prompt so many to expect excitements, disturbances, the unintelligible, the radically personal, the compelling and the absorptive, that the use of such cognates as "sensibility," "interest," "qualification," or "cause" will sometimes better serve the purposes of communication than "emotion" or "feeling" do. Whatever the terms, most noteworthy is the fact that a creator must strive to free himself from both private and public constraints, act within the compass of a gradually realized excellence, and take each part to be at the beginning and end of a plurality of a possibly endless number of vectors. He may or may not have a good idea of what the final outcome will be like. He may accept an assignment, plan with considerable care, produce sketches and diagrams, set himself to make some item vivid and unforgettable, and even have a message he would like to convey. His primary task will remain unchanged: the production of an excellent work.

Commitment

Like other creators, an artist begins his venture from a position where he is relatively free from habits, both those characteristic of him as an individual and those which reflect the practices of a particular discipline. He need not close his eyes, turn away from what he might perceive; but if he is to attend properly, he must tear what he observes away from its neighbors. Only then will he be able to reach its irreducible constituents and immediately specialize them on the way to joining them in his own way.

Like everyone else, a creator is affected by his past. Like everyone else, he is also a creature of habit. Some of his habits may reflect a previous occupation with creating, but most will be like those that others have. He, too, will remember and expect. When he strives to do what others never do, he will not cease to be a human alongside them. What he lived with and through over the years he will, like them, retain more or less, and for an indefinite time. It will probably affect what he does, sometimes indelibly.

Throughout a creator's effort to realize a prospective excellence to which he has committed himself, he is committed as well to doing this or that because of what he has already done. The one commitment is global, the other local. If he tries to satisfy the first without satisfying the other, he will not use it as an effective guide. If instead he tries to meet the second in the absence of the first, he will not act to realize an excellence and will not know when his work is completed. A creator must pass from the satisfaction of the second commitment to the task of enabling the outcomes to act as supplements and enhancements.

Asked what he is about to do, an artist will doubtless say that he is going to write a sonnet or a lyric, a short story about a homeless man, build a fire station, and the like. He will not usually say that he wants to produce a beautiful work. Such a remark would be treated by him as abstract, academic, and perhaps as expressing conceit and pride, referring to what he could neither define nor describe. His prospective excellence is indeterminate, difficult to focus on. Yet so far as he knows that he commits himself to realize it, he knows that he cannot be occupied just with writing down something, putting paint on canvas, and the like. He knows that he must instead make a concentrated, singular effort to produce a self-contained work. He did not have to take on that task. He may have done so to satisfy some social or other obligation. Once, however, he decides to act as an artist, these obligations have to be subordinated to the effort to produce what is beautiful. If he is a poet laureate, required to write a poem on his monarch's birthday, he will usually produce something for the occasion, but he will function as a true poet only if he gives himself to the writing of a splendid poem.

As an artist progresses in his work, his ideal prospect becomes more and more determinate. Consequently, he and what he has accomplished become more and more subject to that prospect. At the same time, both what seems required by what he has done and what he is about to do will be checked against one another and against what the prospect requires. No one of these will be clearly focused on; none is resolutely carried through without regard for the others. At the beginning he is beckoned by the prospect; throughout he faces now this demand, and now that.

Some artists say that they had envisaged an entire work before they produced it. If they did, every conceivable part would have had its full import already realized, and all that needed to be done would be to make the result available to others.

The only work that the artists would have had to do would be to fixate what they had already made present. Since each act of fixation detaches an item and gives it distinctive borders, a work going beyond a private envisagement would then add nothing but irrelevancies.

No merely envisaged space, time, or causation is actually operative. No imagined vitalization vitalizes. Therefore, when artists say that they had an entire work in mind before they did anything, they must mean that they knew its highlights, the main pivots, the cut of the whole, not the actual work itself. There is a big difference between such an envisaged work and an actual one; only in the latter can items be lived with and through, satisfying commitments and grounding others.

A good deal can be anticipated—but only in outline. Use always makes a difference. The reverberations of actual occurrences have an import known only when they are worked through, with each item, act, commitment, and accomplishment requiring a distinctive effort. Were these efforts carried out in a privacy, they would still have to be continued with the help of the body, if only to take advantage of or to overcome tendencies and intrusions from the world about.

Aristotle held that ethics and politics were not proper subjects for a young man, "for he is inexperienced in the actions that occur in life. The end aimed at is not knowledge but action." The young, of course, can understand theoretical accounts; they also have enough experience to make sound, practically pertinent distinctions between right and wrong, the reasonable and the unreasonable. Even more evidently, their inexperience does not preclude them from carrying out creative work, and doing so with great success. References to the youthfulness of a creator should serve only to accentuate the fact that action and often considerable time are needed before techniques are well mastered and before one knows how to ignore some alluring leads. These considerations do not constitute a denial that the young can both devote themselves to the production of great works and bring their ventures to successful closures.

No creation is possible just by taking thought. Even mathematicians, occupied with what does not appear resistant, have resistances to struggle against. Some of these are present in what has been previously achieved and must be overcome in order to produce something else. Tendencies to engage in other activities must be countered in order to carry a work to a successful close. All creators commit themselves in the large and in the small to work in distinctive ways to produce distinctive outcomes. Their thinking involves struggles, stresses, retreats, as well as advances, hesitations, leaps, and absorption in the work of creation, all the while that they continue to live, with bodies carrying out distinctive functions and interplaying with what was privately done.

Although a creator brings together many loose ends, concentrates energy and interest in a particular kind of activity, and inevitably makes it personal, his life is too multidimensional and variegated, too much involved with a plurality of limited activities and emotional occupations in adventitious occurrences, for him to provide a good counterpart of it in what he creatively achieves. If we know what he privately brought into play in his work, we will be helped only incidentally in our effort to understand what he did, for his private acts are but one of many factors transformed in the venture. Disentanglement of a contribution will not disclose what it is as interplaying with others. If we are to know the interplay, we must find a way to reach the contributors as operative on one another. Only then will we know their effective strengths and import.

A commitment is realized by doing what it requires. It is to be understood not by carrying out an act of abstraction but by seeing how what was accepted, projected, and achieved requires that something else be done to provide supplements and supports. Since a creator has a nature and life making demands that he must meet more or less well, he must make a special effort to satisfy his commitments if an excellent work is to be produced. Others may be able to learn what he used and achieved, but his creative act, in its full concreteness, can be only surmised by them, and then only by their reflecting on what a good reading made evident. References to organization, perspective, foreground and background, abstract from the actual involvement of a creator in his work.

Like other transformative forces, commitments can be dissected and their natures understood, but their actual operations must be lived with and through. This does not mean that they are undesignatable, mysterious, or unintelligible. We can name them, can gropingly reach them, and can study them. We can keep ourselves attentive to them and note their direction, insistence, and force. Sometimes we can anticipate what they direct us toward, but this end, when arrived at, will be as different from what was anticipated as the particular is from the general, performance from promise, encounter from expectation, present from future. It will have its own identity, with a nature maintained apart from the process by which it was reached. Even a formally defined conclusion must be detached from its premiss, thereby enabling it to stand apart as a distinct outcome. This outcome can provide a premiss that is able to entail another conclusion, requiring still another act by means of which one can in fact arrive at that conclusion. Creative activities are like inferences, not like formal entailments, for what they achieve is partly owing to the manner in which one moves from an accepted position to an acceptable terminus.

Creators begin their ventures as private individuals involved in persistent efforts to specialize and use a plurality of irreducibles to produce a plurality of interinvolved units. Initially confronted as quite indeterminate, lacking definiteness, the work requires needed parts and a prospective ideal to be intimately joined. Their joining alters their import. Since the unification is expressed in feeling, an alert reader can become aware of the excellence the creator committed himself to realize.

A common restrictive use of language allows one to refer to feeling only as something personally undergone, thereby denying its actual presence in a created work. Because artists and those who appreciate their works are more concerned with what they are involved with, turning away from what seems to be abstract or conceptual, or just emotionally undergone, they refuse to be so restricted. Artists remain alert to the presence of a prospective beauty so far as it has been realized in the work, while continuing to be committed to realize it more fully. For them, as it should be for the rest of us, a created work is the outcome of limited commitments well met, pervaded by a feeling that is due to the effective satisfying of a commitment to a prospective beauty.

Artists do not usually acknowledge their commitments to a prospective beauty. Most of them would say that they were not interested in and know nothing of beauty, that they are never aware of it, and that they are not sure just what they would have to do to realize it. They do not, of course, attend to it as something cognized; instead, they yield to it, allowing it to dictate where they should attend and what they are to do. The dictation is not specific; the ideal is too indeterminate, the next steps not well enough demarcated, and what has already been done too limited and apparently too well bounded from all else to make their demands evident and imperative. The commitments are accepted and met as enticements or requirements to act in this or that way, not as forces or causes. Creators are never certain that their acts will be fully in accord with what a prospective excellence requires, with what has already been produced, and with what seems to be called for by what is next to be done.

So far as it is realized, a prospective beauty, even when it is hard to discern, describe, or locate, is no longer distinguishable, being exhausted in its unifying of what otherwise would be just bounded units. Such an excellence is most clearly discerned when one comes toward the end of a creative venture, for it is then quite determinate and still distinguishable from what is being produced. When the end of the venture is reached, the excellence is indistinguishable from an actual unification of a plurality of interlocked functions.

No realized excellence is an adjective, predicate, or feature. It is an operation, exhausted in its act of interinvolving an indefinite number of operative units. It is not, therefore, identifiable with radiance, symmetry, purity, clarity, or harmony— the features which have been favored by philosophers and critics over the centuries. None of these features may be present in a created work; many may be present in poor ones—even in some not created, characterizing only aspects, effects, or externally produced results.

Objective idealists, conventionalists, and other community-oriented thinkers make claims about their chosen works somewhat similar to those pertinent to art and other creations. Explicitly or sub rosa they take all items to be "internally" related to one another and to be sunk within an all-encompassing absolute, language, community, state, or history. Usually they try to avoid references to commitments, taking them to be at best incomplete ways of referring to complex occurrences in which individuals, objects, language, practices, habit, or customs are intertwined. None grants effective roles to a prospective excellence or to produced or needed parts. Since only contexts and/or demarcations in complex wholes are acknowledged, no place is made for creators—or even for the theorists themselves as so many undivided singulars. Contextualism has no room for individuals who are able to present that view. In addition, since contextualism has no room for works of art and other creations, since these both stand away from all else and are internally constituted, it must finally rest with references to common influences to which the creators and their works have been subjected and to their relations and effects on what else is in the supposed all-encompassing context.

One may be obligated by an all-encompassing whole, but it is impossible to be committed to realize it, since it is already in existence, evidently omnivorous, letting nothing escape its clutches. Nor could anyone be committed to realizing anything within it, for whatever is there is exactly what the whole requires in that place and time. Everyone, of course, is influenced and restrained by some of the complexes in which he is a part. These complexes, though, are dealt with by them as individuals, and on the individuals' terms. If those individuals are creators, they will produce new complexes, having their own integrity, self-enclosed, and providing a loci for fulfilled commitments.

There are encompassing wholes, dictating to whatever they include—but not without meeting resistance. Some of those wholes may have been creatively produced with the help of a creative leader or by a statesman. No matter how effectively the result encroaches on individuals, some of them may still be able to act as creators who, by meeting their commitments, produce excellent works.

There is no question but that the works we seek to interpret are overlaid with irrelevancies, reflecting the intrusive presence of what obscures and distorts. A deconstructive elimination of these and their effects would not expose the original created work, unless it presented this work as having been able to give the rejected items distinctive roles. Bracketing off all the additions would leave only an abstract, impoverished object. One avoids overlays by reading within the confines of a realized excellence. The opposite stress on just the context precludes references to ultimates, individuals, privacies, prospects, and commitments. Yet without these factors, there would be no creations.

The beauty that is faced at the beginning of a creative, artistic effort is faintly attractive, almost completely indeterminate and powerless. At the end it is exhausted in the ways in which different parts are interinvolved with one another. Some of those parts were separately produced. Because of the creator's involvement in the production, a well-executed work will also exhibit his meeting the outcome of his commitments to those parts. Some of these commitments will have been evoked by what was and by what is still to be done; still others will depend on the prospective beauty, itself an object of a distinct commitment.

Works of art are not agencies enabling one to make contact with their creators. They do not send messages from them to others. Like other creators, an artist frees himself from an occupation with daily issues for a while and, so far, takes himself away from the arena where messages are produced, conveyed, and received. He has his appetites, desires, and personal interests, but they, without being altogether denied an influence, will more likely than not limit his creative activities, spoil his aim, and preclude the production of a successful work, unless subordinated to and qualified by the creative effort.

Having detached himself so that he might focus on a prospective excellence, an artist tries to make effective use of all the ultimate factors, again and again, so as to produce what promotes the realization of the prospect. As not yet creative, he could be committed only to joining ultimate factors again and again. When creative, he does more, trying to satisfy his commitment to an inviting excellence as well as his commitment to do something next because of what he has already done.

If only possible outcomes were to guide one, they would, unlike a prospective excellence, be simply accepted. If accepted as obligating, they would still differ from a prospective excellence, for this excellence awaits, not someone who will be subject to it, but someone who will try to realize it. One is obligated by what makes demands; commitments instead accept demands. One may therefore be obligated but not committed—as are those who forget their debts—just as one may be committed and not obligated—as are those who create.

Sometimes successful withdrawals into one's privacy are achieved by following various routines designed to enable one to be relatively unaffected by habits, tendencies, attitudes, or emotions, or by what is bodily or at a distance. It is not necessary to know of these routines in order to be able to withdraw so that an unusual private use can be made of the ideal prospect and other factors. What is needed is only a concentrated effort to get the committing, prospective objective into better focus.

Creative work cannot begin without one having escaped for a while from daily matters, practical problems, appetites, and desires. Inevitably prompted by something encountered or surmised, committed to excellence and to providing what various parts require, satisfied with a work only if it is well done, an artist finally confronts a primal operative condition with a directness and at a depth he could not otherwise achieve. Picasso's *Guernica* presents space as it can be occupied by what is radically sundered; Renoir's *Boat Ride* offers a primal set of resting places; Gaudi's *Park* is a sign of space as sinuously traversable in multiple directions; Bizet's *Carmen* makes one aware of a distinctive, compelling beat to time, with its performance making evident that what occurs in such a time has acquired a radical transformative power. These signs, emphasizing different aspects of dominating types of extension, are matched in other kinds of art. They also have counterparts in the signs produced in other creative ventures, where other conditions are signified, faintly at the beginning, strongly at the end.

This account of the signification of an appreciated work seems to be biased, in a distinctively Western way, toward persistent conditions. A more balanced approach, it would seem, would make evident how readings of created works also signify the Dunamis, the privacy, and perhaps an ideal. There is no question but that one can signify these factors, particularly when account is taken of materials, topics and themes, and the feeling in a work. A good reading allows for such factors, but, occupied as it is primarily with a particular kind of work—spatial, temporal, causal, rational, hierarchical, affiliated, or coordinate—it attends to the ways in which distinguishable parts in these works exercise interinvolved functions and the whole signifies a primal condition.

If one sought to reach time as a powerful extension, one would have to write or read a great story, play, or poem. Cognate acts are carried out when one dreams, thinks about an eventual sanctification, or exercises control over what is brute, and thereby makes evident a privacy, the future, or the Dunamis operative in ways not otherwise noted. Works of art signify these primarily when an occupation with the works as singulars is replaced by a stress on those contributing factors. A condition, unlike these other contributors, is signified by the entire creation. A good reading of the creation provides an acquaintance with the condition, more than matching the acquaintance provided when one attends to aspects of the work or to the intrusive presence of some other factor.

Creators are not metaphysicians in disguise or by indirection any more than dreamers are. Their main concern, first and last, is with the production of excellent works. Yet if that were all that they did, they would spend their lives producing nothing else, never admiring what they had achieved or learning from it. They, like one who reads their works well, also finally confront the condition that they have unreflectingly specialized and used, since their making is also a kind of reading, but at a pace and in a way different from that carried out by one who appreciates what is produced.

Freudians and other psychiatrists are receptive to accounts of creativity which put great emphasis on the individual and what he has suppressed and may betray. Artists interest them in a way other creators do not, in part because there are so many, their works so widespread, their influence considerable, their activity so impractical, and their frustrations so often and poignantly expressed. The topics in the creators' works provide the psychiatrists with unusual clues to personal experiences and presumably help clarify what was done and why. Yet what is then made evident about the artist may have little to do with what he created. One who wanted to learn about him and the powers he has but does not use, what he underwent when young, and the like would have to read back into him supposed origins of what he did. He differs from other artists in the different ways he responds to the same prospective excellence, the same ultimates, and even the same achieved and prospective parts. A knowledge of his use of unsuspected powers, the experiences he underwent when quite young, or his use of symbols which others in different cultures and epochs might also have used—these may help us learn something about him. Such studies will not usually provide any insight into the work produced. More likely than not, they will get in the way. Themes and topics in his work often contain clues enabling one to discover what affected him deeply as an individual. Although there is nothing amiss in looking for such experiences as perhaps providing a clue to what he intended, it does require that one, so far, ignore the work as a singular, unified excellence.

Deeply devoted to the task of producing what is excellent, and not something else, an artist charges his efforts with emotion, enables his work to be suffused with feeling, purges himself, and meets his commitments. Occupied with bringing about what otherwise would not be, he ends with himself exposed to what his creation signifies.

At the end of a successful venture an artist may feel purged, at peace, having learned something about himself and other things. His creation may provide a kind of therapy or serve as an agency for his self-discovery. It will best serve these other purposes though, if he gives himself to the task of producing an excellent work, since this task exposes him more, demanding as it does his full attention and effort. All humans are devious, but there is no reason to suppose that artists are more devious than anyone else. If they sought to purge themselves of regrettable experiences, motives, and promptings, they could do so in better ways than by carrying out creative work.

Nothing is gained and much is lost if one turns from a probing of individual creators to take account of an assumed cosmic set of forces or of a supposed distinctive type of judgment. The first will keep one focused on topics or themes, but not in their ostensible forms; the second requires that excellent works be judged in ways other occurrences are not, without thereby making evident how the judged works were produced, how they were constituted, and how they are to be read. After the nature of creativity has been understood, these and related approaches to excellent works will be able to add desirable footnotes and may sometimes provide good clues on how to read them well. In the end, though, all have to be blamed for ignoring the work as a single unification of a plurality of functions having a nature and a status apart from the creator.

Beautiful works are often created only after much work has been done. Those who create, and those who appreciate what creators do, are primarily concerned with the works and not with the creative activity. The condition, which the work finally discloses and a good reading makes evident, was not hidden. It did not need the artist or his work in order to be operative. Always present, it becomes evident, as it were, as a kind of reward for his having brought a creative venture to a success-ful close. The condition is then exposed at some depth, making one aware of what was always insistent. The work, though, is not primarily a device by means of which one effectively signifies an effective condition. If it were, one would be faced with the question why this difficult means rather than an easier might not have served, why an artist is not usually enlightened or purged at the end, and why he sometimes works over and over what he has done rather than just trying to get to the condition in some other, easier way. What a creative artist seeks is usually nothing less and nothing more than to make an excellence be realized, thereby gain-ing an eminently desirable, often unexpected insight into a permanent, effective condition.

The excellent attracts. It does so the more surely a creator moves back into him-self until he arrives at the position where he is singularly free to do what promises to end with what is worth the effort. Not engaged in forging a symbol of himself or of anything else, he does not create to reveal powers in anything. His final acquain-tance with what would otherwise not be grasped about the ground of passing things is an unexpected gratuity. For him, as it is for the rest of us, his work, if excellent, needs neither apology nor defense. Indeed, its revelation of a primal condition is obtained only if it is not sought, particularly since a seeking would take him to it as manifested, not to it in its depths, insistent and omnipresent.

A number of those who choose the life of an artist are willing to make great sacrifices if only they could thereupon produce something great. They prepare themselves carefully, work hard, reject temptations to settle for easily produced or quickly satisfying results. Often aware of the defects in what they produce, they listen to criticism; yet try as they might, they fail to achieve anything of conse-quence. Like successful artists they may have dedicated themselves; they may have had similar experiences, traumas, and made as great an effort. Yet even when they have some of the same skills and the delicacy of touch that the others have, what they accomplish is different in kind from what the artists produce precisely because they do not carry out a creative venture in which a prospective excellence is made fully determinate.

A poor poem may contain a brilliant line or two; a poor play may have some great scenes; a weak novel may have a strong passage here or there. We may isolate these achievements and treat them as unduplicable perfections. Although they may then be able to be put alongside what is achieved in other works, they will still fall short because the wholes in which they occur do not provide a prospective beauty with the scope it needs in order to become fully realized. The fragments had in fact committed their creators to doing what continued the work of realizing that ideal. Their failure (to meet commitments to do needed particular things with the fragments) made it impossible for them to realize beauty in a single work in which those fragments function as interlocked components.

The fact that a fragment is memorable, worth cherishing, and perhaps not even recognized as a fragment may make its identification difficult or even impossible. It could conceivably be accepted as excellent by taking it to be a single work, not a part torn away from a defective whole. Instead of being a poetic part of a play, it could be treated as a poem found within a play; instead of being part of a poem, it could be treated as a stanza misplaced. It would be right to take this approach so far as it reveals depths of the very condition used in the production of the work.

It is possible to continue working on what has already been completed. Although one might become aware that commitments to what has been done and to a prospective excellence have been met, an effort might still be made to produce unnecessary and even undesirable additions. The fact that depths of an effective condition have been discerned may not suffice to bring one to a stop, primarily because the condition is not focused on and has no well-defined boundaries. Evidently, there comes a point where a creator must stand back and allow the work itself to tell him that he has not yet or has already completed it.

Creators have periods when they seem unable to create. Some of those who never create commit themselves to working on important projects. The one passes into the other too often to permit the placing of them in clearly distinguished classes. Yet they do have and meet different commitments. Unfortunately, the difference is not always discernible except to those who are aware that they are engaged in different types of work.

It is possible to have such a strong sense of self that one resists being subject to needed guidance and control by what initially seems remote, indeterminate, of little value, and apparently impossible to realize. Others, willing to devote themselves to the task of creating an excellent work, do not keep themselves well focused on their task—or do not carry out their commitments fully. We may attempt to account for the differences between them and those who are successful as being just a matter of genes, circumstances, gifts, or some incomparable, inexplicable powers present in the creators and not in others; such explanations, however, make too sharp a distinction between creators and noncreators, or between a creator when successful and when baffled, perplexed, or blundering. A good ear, a good eye, training, a sense of rhythm, an alertness to feeling, the need to have beauty permeate a work—these qualities make success in some places easier for some than it is for others, but none will produce excellent work if commitments are not well met.

Toward the end of a long life, when energies fail and the difficulties of daily living increase, when it is hard to free oneself from the encrustations that experience, habits, tradition, custom, and unexamined presuppositions introduce, it becomes harder and harder to create. An occasional Sophocles shows that creativity need not end at an advanced age. Others despite incredible achievements when quite young, soon give up all attempts to create and unaccountably spend their lives occupied with minor matters. Many things demand attention; it is hard to keep oneself at a high pitch; success at some minor task is often pleasant, while a failure, even for one who has exhibited remarkable abilities and unusual persistence or who has completed great works with considerable ease, appears to be likely and so disagreeable that it seems better to turn in other directions. Some who have been successful creators at an early age and who have produced great works with apparent ease might stop creating because they can no longer bring new projects to a successful close. Only a few Van Goghs keep on creating in the face of almost total neglect. No one knows whether or not others might have done as well as he did in similar circumstances.

An artist might sell his work, give it away, forget about it. Completed, it may no longer interest him, in part because the beauty he there realized is limited in range, and in part because he has lived through its production and perhaps has already fully appreciated it on coming to the end of his work. Good, patient readers of it may discern what he never knew was there, particularly since he was immersed in fulfilling his commitments to what he had done and was about to do, and especially to the excellence he faced throughout his entire venture. His, of course, is not the only worthy undertaking. If it were, there would be something condemnable in the lives of other creators and surely of historians, engineers, craftsmen, or philosophers, for these are not concerned with creating anything.

Voluminous Regions

Some artists achieve success in a number of arts. Da Vinci, Michelangelo, and Picasso come readily to mind. No one, though, is known to have been creative in all the arts, and surely not in all other fields, partly because each type of excellence requires that primary use be made of a distinctive condition. Beauty must be displayed over an extensive stretch; truth is realized in the rational; nobility depends on the use of the stratifier; glory requires the affiliator to have a primary role; a realized justice depends on the successful use of the coordinator. Each of these ultimate conditions must be joined with the Dunamis if one is to produce what the different ideal prospects require in order to be realized.

The conditioning, voluminous regions, with which artists are primarily concerned, are conveniently distinguished as the temporal, the spatial, and the transformative. Further specializations of these regions allow for distinguishing architects from sculptors and painters and for setting all three over against composers, novelists, playwrights, and poets, and the members of all these groups against performers. The various subdivisions can be combined in multiple ways to yield such compound arts as opera and film. Some arts, like the dance, can be treated as being both single and compound. In different ways they are all concerned with making specialized use of a primary conditioning voluminosity, unitary and undivided, without separate parts, governing no traversable distance, occupied by nothing. Each of these conditions can be specialized to yield a sequential, concurrent, or transformative set of units in a temporal, spatial, or causal art.

Voluminosity was taken by Saint Augustine to be essentially a temporalized "distension of the soul." His reference to the soul unduly confined the voluminosity, while his emphasis on time unduly identified voluminosity with just one of its primary modes. It was he, though, who first clearly acknowledged it. Other thinkers, in speaking of "an eon," "the whole of time," "the whole of space," "a realm of causality," "extended fields," or a "continuum" credit those voluminosities with a more depersonalized status. They are right to do so for their purposes, though it is not altogether clear just what kind of being the voluminosities then have, nor is it evident just what role they will play in the constitution of the occupied regions with which we are familiar or in those regions so clearly displayed in the different arts.

Once it is recognized that voluminosities are preconditions for existent, limited regions of occupied space, time, and causality and that they are intensive and undivided, occupiable and conditioning, and neither remote nor alien, they will be more readily seen to provide essential, though not the only, factors constituting every item, created or not. Creations make free use of them and other ultimate factors; daily occurrences exhibit them as joined in looser ways. An occupation of extended regions, by either the one or the other, does not break up the voluminosities; instead, the voluminosities continue to provide conditions for what occupies them.

Kant is one of the few masters of thought aware of the voluminosity of both time and space and their availability for use by a private individual. It was his view, also, that causality was not as basic as these. Sometimes, too, he spoke as though both time and space were themselves produced piece by piece. Still, again and again, he spoke of "the whole of time" and the "whole of space" as somehow available. He also treated them as if they were primarily at the service of knowledge, particularly of the knowledge of primary mathematical and scientific truths. That move was neither necessary nor desirable. Still, he recognized that each was undivided, that both were presupposed by whatever occupied them, that they had a status apart from all knowers or users, and that they joined other factors to constitute daily objects. He did not go on to say, as he might have, that creators make distinctive uses of them.

A primal voluminosity is specialized as a space, time, or causality at the same time that these are specialized as delimited regions, preliminary to their being joined with other factors, so as to constitute a limited, occupied space, time, or causation. When items are identified as here, now, and involved in this or that activity, all three types are acknowledged. Apart from those voluminosities, the items might conceivably be extended, but they would not then be related over distances, just as, apart from all occupants, the nuances in the different voluminosities could not be well joined to one another.

Voluminosities are not abstract entities somehow fixated. Nor are they the outcome of human acts that cut them away from all content and divisions. Everything whatsoever, apart from any human interest or activity, makes specialized use of and fits into one or more of them. It is within the compass of a voluminosity that something is produced.

Distinct actualities, despite their independent natures and activities, are all able to be distanced, to enter the next moment together, and to affect one another because they are inseparable from a voluminosity as not yet specialized as a space, time, or causality. In the absence of that voluminosity there would be only unit, unextended bodies, unable to be spatially, temporally, or causally connected. The actual occupation of extended regions is bypassed when voluminosities are treated as though they were imaginary or in the mind.

As dominant over the Dunamis, voluminosities determine the nature of extended relations occurring in the cosmos; as subordinated to the Dunamis, they define humanized relations. The relations joining the units existing in the universe have the two in balance. A creative act recaptures the balance, but as qualified by the different relations, since it depends on individuals using their privacies and embedding a work in graining material.

Like other conditions, voluminosities allow for multiple levels to be distinguished within them, each with a distinctive insistence. Intensively rich, insistent, self-maintained, always available, able to be joined to the Dunamis, itself also effective, intensively rich, insistent, self-maintained, and available, they constitute distinct units and their connections. The voluminosities and the Dunamis come together adventitiously; creative artists join them deliberately. At both times the outcomes are unduplicable.

Were the total scheme of things excellent, one would have some warrant for referring to a creator of it. Unlike a human, that creator would not have had to contend with an unconquerable resistance in each factor. Since each factor maintains itself in depth, only a nonhuman could make all factors so interplay everywhere that a single excellence was produced. The existence of evils, ugliness, chaos, irregularities, and contingencies makes evident that this interplay did not occur. Conceivably, the regrettable parts of what exists might be no more than isolated intervals and contrasts, but we have no way of reading them as having only those roles.

In saying that there is a creator of all else, *creator* is evidently being used in a way we cannot rightly compare with the way it is used when referring to human beings. Sometimes we can see the excellences that humans produce. If all the entities in the universe together were excellent, only a creator of it would be in a position to know that it was so. Unlike the excellences men bring about, this universal excellence would, moreover, acquaint such a creator with nothing it might not already know. What such a creator might have done, but apparently did not do, human creators in fact do, though on a small scale and through the use of quite limited specializations of ultimate factors. Only humans make what is excellent by overcoming part of the resistances and making do with what is then available to produce the needed parts. Since men always create under confining limits, we can hope to learn little about human creativity by imagining how or what some other type of being might create—nor can we learn what its creation might be like by building on what we know of human creations.

Because they are objectively real, conditioning voluminosities can be used in the creation of works of art; what is produced is thereupon able to be spatially, temporally, and causally related to whatever else there is. The created outcomes will be misconstrued if not taken to be self-contained, set apart from all else, and yet related to whatever may be exterior to them in space and time. Each creation can be both self-contained and bounded because the very factors that constitute it also act in other ways.

A distinction made, say, among the arts of painting, poetry, and dance makes necessary the acknowledgment of different types of voluminosity. If the three were taken together, they would contrast with other kinds of creations—mathematical, ethical, social, and political—primarily because these creations make use of conditions other than voluminosities and are the outcome of a successful realization of ideals other than beauty. These others also make use of distinctive materials in distinctive ways and are related spatially, temporally, and causally to what is exterior to them. Whatever voluminosities nonartistic creations specialize and use are subordinated to other conditions having a primary role.

Because voluminosities have beings of their own, they can affect, limit, and add to that which they join. To neglect them is to fail to take account of essential components of any and everything. Yet Aristotle dealt with space, time, and causation as though they were not ultimates and usually envisaged the Dunamis as being no more than a passive carrier of particular, intelligible structures. As a consequence, he had little recourse but to take space to be a region presupposing and occurring within the confines of some body, time to be identifiable with a sequence of numbers (that is, distinguishable positions in a process of change, coming to be, and passing away), and causality to be a necessitating rational, analytic component of what in fact occurs. His view reverberates throughout the history of thought, affecting the views even of those who take themselves to be anti-Aristotelians.

A walk is as good an illustration as any other occurrence of the role voluminosities play in ordinary life. Taking place over a terrain and involving a multiplicity of causal acts, it is a single event embracing a plurality of steps. Its extended thrust is a distinguishable, bounded form of nuances in undivided voluminosities of space, time, and causality joined to nuances in the Dunamis. From the position of an actual walk, the steps, and also some such enterprise as paying a visit to a friend down the street, are dissectable, abstractable aspects. The walk itself depends on actions spread over a limited, distinctive, temporal, spatial, and causal region. As a delimited part of a visit, as well as of a region within which steps occur, the walk has an integrity of its own, able to interplay with the visit as well as with the steps. It is a walk-for-a-visit, encompassing steps, without compromise to its status as a single activity. So far, it is like a part of a created work, differing from this part primarily in the way its prospect operates and the voluminosity and Dunamis are used.

By introducing imagined distinctions into a voluminosity, it is sometimes possible to anticipate some of the moves one must carry out in the course of a creation. One will not then have a faint version of what will or should be subsequently produced, for in an actual production units are actually joined. Anticipation does not make them be affected by commitments actually accepted and carried out.

Were one engaged in the creation of a musical composition, a prospect would effectively control what was being produced, and a temporal voluminosity would be used to help constitute units for that prospect to unify. Were one instead engaged in creating a musical performance, the same prospective excellence would exercise an effective control, but the voluminosity used would be primarily causal, not temporal. A composer, even one occupied with producing a work for a performance, deals with a privately confronted, temporal voluminosity in which the divisions, lengths, and combinations needed to produce a fine performance can be only indicated, suggested, not fixated or exhibited. His imagined divisions of the voluminosity may be vivid and may be repeated in a performance. Even when there is an attempt to make the performance be most faithful to the composition, it will qualify what it uses with the beauty it realizes, unifying quite different kinds of entities from those a composer does. Actual sounds differ from imagined ones, no matter how vividly lived through, for they fill out an actual space and come toward and move away from the listener from different places and with different emphases.

A composer's imagination of how a piece will sound will contain units and intervals different from those an actual performance provides. His anticipations cannot, therefore, be equated with a performer's acts or even with a performer's anticipations. Their anticipations are directed toward units and combinations of different types, carrying out different roles. Their units and acts have distinctive locations, divisions, lengths, and affiliations, revealing them to be in different kinds of artistic creation.

A composer can indicate, suggest, but he cannot fixate or exhibit what the performer will do. When a performer uses a composer's notations, he inescapably qualifies them. Different instruments will help him qualify them in different ways. When a number of instruments are used consonantly, they do more than provide different media through which the composition is conveyed. The reverse holds in fact: a composition provides a common, constant occasion, enabling different performers to make creative use of ultimate factors on their own, limited and mediated by a conductor or other agency enabling them to keep in accord.

When the use of a voluminosity is of primary interest, as it is in the arts, it is tempting to treat a creator as one mainly occupied with filling out the voluminosity with other factors. The temptation must be resisted, for the voluminosity plays as active a role as other conditions do in other types of created work. While a voluminosity provides an opportunity for parts to be related over a distance, it is itself not subdivided; subdivisions exhibit it in specialized forms. Once this fact is recognized, there would be little harm in following the usual practice of supposing that an imagined composition is set inside an extended region, could one but make sense of the idea that anything unextended was able to find a place in what is extended.

A musical composition makes use of a voluminous temporality, bringing it to bear in a series of distinguishable efforts to produce a sequence of interlinked parts. The efforts require a concurrent use of the Dunamis, the privacy, and the excellence to be realized. The rhythms, phrases, combinations, and separations which the composition then exhibits were neither discovered nor invented, the one because there are no such separations and relations in the voluminous time that was used, the other because what a composer produces is no mere outcome of a search for novelty or a solution to a problem. One does most justice to a composition not by giving it an occasion to be displayed in another medium but by playing it creatively, thus making independent use of a different voluminosity and other factors. A musical composition has an integrity of its own, with its own distinctive units. So does a performance. The excellence of neither is jeopardized by the other. Both, too, are loci of distinctive feelings, because the same prospective beauty acts on and is qualified by different kinds of units.

A performance cannot be properly said to be at the service of a composition. It has its own requirements, with distinctive separations and connections. These are not sunderable from the obdurate natures and capacities the performance produces through the use of distinctive acts employing distinctive agencies and materials. If creative, the performance uses different material while bringing ultimates together again and again in a distinctive way under the controlling guidance of a gradually realized excellence. Making independent use of all the ultimates, a creative performance is no more a composition made public than a created composition is a pale version of a performance.

By making a composition part of a new creative venture, a creative performance gives it a new role, producing a distinctive set of units and interlocking them in a distinctive way. Where the composition is primarily occupied with filling out a voluminous time, the performance also makes use of a voluminous space and causality. The relation of composer and performer is thus somewhat like that of a mathematician to a theoretically guided, creative experimenter.

A poet uses ordinary language and grammar but transforms them in the course of his creative venture. An architect uses and transforms established spatial affinities. A sculptor interrelates filled and empty spaces. A novelist interinvolves different episodes in a story. A choreographer sets out different positions of the body and their place on the stage. All act somewhat in the way a composer would were he to use an established notation and have the result embedded in freely produced sounds, occupying a region encompassing the performer and his audience.

The pace at which a composer goes through his work, despite all markings showing where one must play slowly or quickly, emphasize or deemphasize, combine, rest, and the like, is different from the pace exhibited by a performer. The one may take years to complete his work; the other is finished in an hour or so. The one may make sketches, diagrams, go through a multitude of preliminaries, but will engage in the process of creation for only a short period, helped perhaps by the use of an instrument or two, imagination, memory, and a sense of the bearing that different sounds have on one another. A performer rehearses and practices, sometimes for long periods, helped by the use of imagination, memory, and a sense of the effects different sounds have on one another. He may use a great composition as a guide or inspiration and take whatever sounds he produces to commit him to others, even though this approach may make him deviate from explicit formulations in the composition. When we try to identify the work of a composer and a performer, we must ignore the latter's rehearsals on the supposition that they are intended solely to get the performance to provide a good representation of the composition. Its primary purpose, though, is not this. A rehearsal enables a prospective performance to be corrected to promote the production of a new, excellent work.

Skilled musicians read the notes of a composer the way sensitive readers read the words of a poem. Both might like to do no more than share in the original work and its feeling, but both inevitably introduce new stresses into what is being appreciated. A good reading and a consequent performance, if they begin with appreciations of an excellent, completed work, will try to share in the feeling that the work contains, but only a reader who allows the work to dictate the pace and connection, only one who introduces no acceptances or anticipations, only one who does not himself try to realize a prospective excellence, could achieve such a reading.

A production makes a difference to the ways in which a voluminosity, perhaps already functioning, will be utilized or is improvisationally filled out with actual sounds affecting one another. Composers and performers, this performer and that, will also provide for the presence of different kinds of feeling in their works, whether or not they undergo similar emotions. Each will lead a reader to keep himself subject to what a work contains. A reader will not escape making some modifications, unless it were possible for a reading to be wholly passive. The most that a conscientious reader could do is to keep the emotions that his reading arouses subordinate to the feeling the work contains. Such a reading will lack the kind of vigor and freshness that a splendid performer introduces into his renditions of a great work, since the reading is occupied with the task of trying to share in a feeling already present.

An appreciation of a completed created work begins with an excellence already realized and tries to keep in accord with its rhythm and pace. Inevitably, it will be affected by that excellence. Were the reading a creative act, it would make a distinctive use of the excellence as well as of the ultimate factors. If it did, it would carry out a distinct creation, even though it used the other as material.

A familiar illustration may make this much-disputed distinction between a composition and a performance even more evident. One can rehearse a speech, noting where one will accent and hesitate and taking careful account of the time in which the whole will be recited. When the speech is actually delivered, it will not only be in a different setting, and thereupon be affected by the need to speak with a fresh emphasis, expressiveness, and pacing, but will also involve the use of the voice, hands, eyes, and the rest of the body in ways that cannot be completely anticipated. The relation of a delivered to a rehearsed speech is like that of the latter to something initially written, perhaps by someone else.

When he bounds off a nuance in a voluminosity, a creative performer does not affect the voluminosity's indivisible, unbounded singularity. His creative act utilizes limited parts of joined voluminosities without jeopardizing the status of the components of those parts as so many distinguishable nuances in the various irreducible, undivided ultimates. The short interval of time, the small distance in space, and the limited productive power of causality of which the performer makes use are bounded-off areas united with delimited, specialized versions of other factors. In the absence of an undivided voluminosity the different parts would be interinvolved only so far as they were encompassed by some other ultimate or by a prospective excellence. The use of the voluminosity assures that they will be joined extensionally at various distances, but no sooner is the bounding produced than it has to be overcome with the help of the prospect to be realized.

Although a builder may use an architect's achievements in somewhat the way a creative performer uses a composer's, a playwright's, or a choreographer's, it would not be correct to pair them. A performer treats a creator's work as a distinctive voluminosity for which he will provide units to be turned into interlocked functions in a single, excellent work. A builder, by contrast, is primarily occupied with embedding what an architect created; he is not himself a creator. A builder may actually have no interest in the initial creation and may do nothing more than produce item after item as required; a creative performer will instead use the original creation as a single voluminosity, in which positions and relations are indicated, as a component in a new creation. Like a performer of a created work who treats the functioning units in it as so many distinctions which he will convert into new functioning units over the course of his performance, a builder brings his materials into play with what an architect produced. The materials will then serve primarily to provide an embedment, able to give the architect's achievement a new grain and a public location.

The freedom that an artist achieves by retreating within himself must be used in part to specialize and join a voluminosity to the Dunamis under the aegis of a more and more determinate outcome. The work to be produced requires him to free himself from subjection to the voluminosity to be able to use it in the light of what is required by the sought excellence. Although not free from ambition, pride, and the other traits which characterize all, he will try to forget himself in order to produce what is excellent. This prospect is able to exist apart from him and thereupon is able to be used. Had he not used other factors in addition to the voluminosity, his work would have been without tensions, pulsations, or feeling.

Creations in mathematics or in some other enterprise take account of specialized, filled-out regions of a voluminosity while making primary use of other conditions and other factors. They are not thereby turned into works of art, or made subordinate to these. Similarly, a work of art makes use of an affiliator and other conditions without turning into an instance of some other creative venture. All creations occur in time, involve transformations, and are embedded in what occupies a space.

The Dunamis and Materials

The Dunamis is as basic as any condition, making a needed contribution to each part of a creation and to the work as a whole. Because of it, parts pulsate, and the whole work has a vibrancy the creator did nothing to produce, though it is due to him that the Dunamis is present there. That vibrancy is distinct from the feeling in the work. The same feeling could be evident when the vibrancy was hardly detectable; a great vibrancy could be exhibited where there was little feeling. Feeling, while varying in density from place to place, forms a continuum; vibrancy, while occurring throughout, affects each unit by itself as well as the relations it has to others. Feeling is global, though recognized here and there; vibrancy is particulate though everywhere.

Beyond all particulars, too fluid to be a condition, pulsating throughout, nuanced but not subdivided, possessing an endless number of layers, with an unprobed, intensive depth, the Dunamis is a constituent in every actuality and is used in every act of creation. An awareness of its presence is evident in the writings of most of the great philosophers; it is emphasized, indeed, overemphasized by Schopenhauer, Nietzsche, and Bergson. Its irreducibility has long been insisted on by Asiatic thinkers. Designating it as the *Dunamis* underscores its long-acknowledged presence and the fact that it is at once potential, powerful, and dynamic, present to some degree not only in every natural and created object but in every condition as well. The conditions in turn affect it as it is apart from them. Only as wholly in themselves are conditions and the Dunamis free of all qualifications by one another.

The neglect of the Dunamis in most studies is due in good part to an overemphasis on the need to use categories, to attend to rules, to be efficient by making use of technical aids. All these elements, though, are also affected by the Dunamis, as an occasional, inexplicable aberration in the course of what seems stable and regular makes evident. Like the conditions, of which voluminosity is but one, the Dunamis has its own contribution to make to whatever it affects. Because of it, each condition is able to have its nuances bear on one another, just as it is due to the conditions that the Dunamis can be categorized. Contrasted with conditions, the Dunamis is identifiable as "becoming," "process," "transition." Without it, space would be a single undifferentiated stretch; time would not pass, and causation would be just a gigantic if-then. But if it alone were real, all occurrences would be unintelligible.

The presence and effects of the Dunamis are most noticeable in the performing arts, but they are inescapable and detectable even in such apparently static works of art as buildings and sculptures. Those works do not have units merely set alongside one another, exhibiting the conditioning presence of a spatial voluminosity. They, too, vibrate. Were there no feeling in a work, or were it minimal, as it is in mathematical creations, the Dunamis there would not be compromised.

A created work sets a limit to the use of the Dunamis without interfering with its continued presence, undivided and undeniable. That is one reason we must take account of the boundaries of created works before we attend to their self-limiting unifications of what is present. That taking account may be so sudden that one passes without delay into the work as a self-contained singular. In galleries, museums, and other established settings one must usually make an effort to get into a work because one comes to it as a unit alongside others, already characterized perhaps as belonging to or standing in contrast with them. Similar problems arise in connection with books of poetry and fiction and with buildings, sculptures, and other locatable creations. Indeed, since one lives for the most part in a world of objects externally bounded off from one another, an extra effort must be made to attend to anything that is also self-limited.

Individuals are self-limiting from intensive depths; creations are self-limited as fully present. The distinguishable parts of both have intensive depths of their own. All are unduplicable, all have structures, all pulsate. Creations, though, are without power to act. We speak metaphorically when we say that we are disturbed or pleased *by* a play or story, for all that could have happened was that we were affected by what these works enabled us to discern. This affect is primarily a distinctive condition, with the Dunamis incidentally revealed as qualifying it. The neglect of the condition, partly corrected by his Platonism, led Schopenhauer to minimize the common, constant nature of musical works and other creations as well. Insistent, with endless levels, a transformative voluminous power is too readily categorizable to be identifiable with the ever-restless Dunamis.

Even when presented in writing and prevented from decaying or fading, a work of art is subject to change. It is at best a slow-moving instance of a process of transformation. All the while it remains completed, fixated, within whose limits distinctive, limited transformations occur. As the material of the work changes, so does the work. Its excellence may still continue to be present for an indefinite time, and then some other condition, not controlled in a creative act, might take over. If it does, it will do so adventitiously, without being well joined to the Dunamis in part after part.

If something is fixated by a notation or other material, and if its parts are set alongside one another with the work held away from every external influence, it will nevertheless inevitably crumble, because the Dunamis continues to affect it. We may want to explain that crumbling as owing to specific causes, but as fractals, quanta, and contingent occurrences make evident, we cannot always do so. The crumbling exhibits the effects of the Dunamis as never wholly constrained by any formal necessity.

The Dunamis is confined and limited in every occurrence; it is not then cut off from itself as having a greater depth. As a factor distinguishable in every item, created or uncreated, momentary or persistent, steady or turbulent, present everywhere, it is still not as all-engulfing as Bergson's *élan vital* or as illusory as formalists take all passage to be. If it were the one, nothing would be structured or individualized; if it were the other, nothing would really exist through time, pulsate while in space, or be transformed even in the absence of exteriorly imposed forces.

It is partly owing to the Dunamis that indeterminate prospects can be converted into present unifications. Although it takes a creator to produce the conversion, the outcome is not the creator himself exteriorized. The not fully determinate ideal as then and there available, and whatever material is needed to fixate what is privately produced, will also make a difference to the product. The singularity and vibrancy of the Dunamis, in addition, limits the ways conditions are utilized and the prospective ideal is realized. Since a creator's efforts must be supplemented by the persistent presence of the conditions and the Dunamis, what is created is the creator's own work in but a limited sense. While it is he who is committed and who uses and delimits the Dunamis and the conditions, it is they that provide the work with content. It makes as much sense to say that they are a creator's agents as to say that he produces such a commitment to a prospect that they are enabled to produce needed parts.

Creators, the conditions, the Dunamis, the ideal, and materials all make needed contributions to the existence of a created work. Each has its own role; each is indispensable. At one moment one is emphasized, at another moment some other, but all are operative all the time.

The conditions and the Dunamis are not passive, to be molded as one sees fit. Each has its own nature and an insistence of which a creator must take account. There is no creation out of nothing; each created work is the outcome of a utilization of available factors again and again in the effort to make an ideal excellence become a determinate unification.

Dedication, responsibility, and commitment are to be attributed to a creator since it is he who brings the conditions and the Dunamis together in a distinctive way under the aegis of a prospective excellence. Parts are joined in consonance with his commitment to an ideal prospect and to what has been and is yet to be produced. His creative activity seems to begin and end at particular, determinate moments. Treated as coming to an end with each part, his creativity would be reduced to a series of stops and starts.

Although a creator may rest in the course of his creative activity, his work is not thereby turned into a set of detached items. It is singular mainly because of the persistent presence of the prospective excellence but also because both the conditions and the Dunamis are there in undivided forms. Because creativity is oriented toward the achievement of a final excellence, and because a creator accepts commitments to realize that excellence and to provide what particular results along the way require in order to be supplemented and enriched, it is possible for him to carry out and complete his venture.

Throughout, a created work will exhibit a vibrancy due to the Dunamis. Also, a prospect is able to affect the creator, turn him toward itself because the Dunamis connects them. When he withdraws into himself, preliminary to focusing on the prospect, the Dunamis will keep him connected to it. With its assistance, he is able to help the prospect intrude on what he does.

Although it is possible to reach the Dunamis as it is apart from its interplay with ultimate conditions, it is not possible to probe it altogether, get to it as separate from all else, any more than it is possible to get to a privacy or to ultimate conditions as these are completely in themselves. Able to be realized in an endless number of particularized forms, always present as an ongoing vibrancy in and connecting what it impinges on, having no separate parts, the Dunamis pulsates throughout its length and depth. Occasionally one can distinguish passing nuances in it, but a concentration on them in particular places or times will unduly specialize them and wrongly bound them off from one another. Its pulsational, uncharted exhibition is present in even the most impersonal and trivial occurrences. A dead leaf, wind, dust, mud, and rust are not the outcomes of interpretations somehow imposed on qualityless, monotonously acting, law-abiding objects, denied all tonality and transitions; if they were, they would at best reflect the ways in which humans adjust themselves to the presence of what is alien and perhaps would be so apart from and indifferent to human interests and needs that their presence would not be suspected. We have no warrant for supposing that there are any such unknowns or unknowables.

The Dunamis makes all entities able not only to be together but to be related to one another in root without denying them their irreducible, separate realities and activities. It is unbounded, with transitory nuances, varying in emphasis. Those nuances that are most prominent are most likely to join insistent stresses in conditions and thereby, with these stresses, constitute actual entities. The joining is one with the distinguishing of nuances in both the Dunamis and the conditions, without denying those nuances their interinvolvements with one another in their respective ultimates.

Commitments take advantage of the presence of the Dunamis to obtain effective thrusts toward areas where they can be satisfied. In its absence the commitments would at best be obligations privately accepted. Because of the Dunamis, also, the commitments imposed by actual and prospective acts have a different force from that which a prospective ideal has. It is because of the Dunamis, too, that a commitment to others, characteristic of the wise and the heroic, is able to reach them and become both operative and directive.

The Dunamis, like the conditions and the privacy, has depth. Layer on layer, one more intensive and inward than its predecessor, can be successively distinguished within it while still continuing to be unseparated dimensions in a single, pulsating, undivided intensity. At once absorptive and intrusive, it qualifies whatever it enters into and whatever may penetrate it, insistently affecting the rhythms and activity of the intruded and the intruding. No thinking could possibly extinguish it; none ever wholly bypasses it. The more it is participated in, the deeper the layer where it is penetrated. On all the layers it is undivided, with passing emphases at different positions, none of which is separated from the rest. As brought into play in a creation, the Dunamis is already partly affected by other factors. Always available, qualified by and qualifying both privacies and ultimate conditions, converging with conditions at a common point and there constituting an ideal, the Dunamis must be used in a distinctive way if an excellent work is to be produced.

The Dunamis is no less an ingredient in the conditions of which mathematics and other enterprises make use than it is in the voluminosities that interest an artist. It is also present in a privacy and helps constitute its acts. As a consequence, conditions and privacies, as well as the creations they help to constitute, reverberate throughout, both when apart from and when joined to one another. In the absence of the Dunamis, creations would quickly fall apart.

A realized excellence unifies all the parts of a creation; feeling pervades the whole; the Dunamis vitalizes both the parts and the feeling. Already qualified by the privacy and a voluminous condition, the Dunamis continues to exist apart from these. It can therefore enable an artist to produce new vitalized parts. Were it absent, these parts would not be subject to a common dynamic interconnection.

Nothing is so available as the Dunamis is, yet nothing is so difficult to isolate or talk about. Nothing is so insistently present in other factors and in the outcome of their joinings, yet nothing is so obscured. Nothing is so often neglected in philosophical accounts, yet it plays a distinctive role in whatever is, acts, or is created.

Both the Dunamis and the conditions are distinguishable in actual occurrences and can be used to begin moves into them. One reaches into the Dunamis itself by taking advantage of its presence in whatever one confronts. Even moves into the conditions need its help, evidencing its distinctive and intensive thrust. Without the Dunamis, there would be nothing to enable one to pass from what is evidenced toward the evidenced as it exists apart from all else.

Artists differ conspicuously from other creators in the way they open themselves to the presence of the Dunamis and thereby allow themselves to be pulled into a layer of it not otherwise reachable. That layer is specialized and used in the course of the creative activity. Rarely does much deliberateness, specific planning, or programming precede or govern the efforts. Devices designed to get some to a position where they will be able to create are primarily ways for getting them to free themselves from constraints. To be creative, they must, of course, not just be freed, but must themselves freely make use of both the Dunamis and conditions to produce units enabling a prospective excellence to be realized. If it is, it will enable those units to make a radical difference to one another's import.

A creator is usually alert to sharp focal points. Often he is aware of the degree of success being achieved over the course of his venture so that he ends with a sense of having more or less achieved what he set himself to do. Not precluded from appreciating what he achieved, he is usually so preoccupied with making what is worthy of appreciation and deserving of a careful reading that he may not be as appreciative of his own work as others are. Sometimes he is glad to rest, feeling released and perhaps relieved.

A creator's appreciation, like the appreciation of others, requires him to attend to pivotal, functioning items as limiting and enhancing one another. Some of these items will serve mainly to pace, others to join, and still others to contrast and supplement. References to fate, a primal will, a splendor at the root of things, an ultimate being, or a collective unconscious are all unnecessary. They are also regrettable, tempting one to deal with creators as though they were passive beings, manipulated by impersonal powers.

A painting hangs unseen on a wall, a building stands empty at night on a deserted street, a poem is printed on a then-unopened page. All seem to exist as aggregates of particulars in an indifferent world and, so far, not to be works of art at all. If so, the qualitative and the quantitative, the personalized and the impersonal, structure and passage, would be separated from one another. Because conditions, the Dunamis, and the ideal are interinvolved in a creative work, it is able to continue, and can continue to be excellent.

Because conditions and individuals have their own irreducible integrities and insistencies, the Dunamis cannot absorb them without a trace. Still, since it is always present and operative, they are caught up in a pulsating process having an indefinite range and an unprobed depth. Without the Dunamis there would at best be only particulars in an indifferent, structured time; and without the conditions there would just be an uninterrupted flux.

Artists may not attend to the Dunamis to a degree greater than they exhibit toward conditions. Still, while making use of all, they are not primarily concerned with trying to understand or enjoy them; their focus, instead, is on what they are to make and achieve. They can be aware of the different factors and may even dwell on one or the other for a time, but since they are primarily interested with creating, they will attend mainly to the dunamically quickened work in process and not to what is being used. Like a seasoned driver who is aware of the road, his hands on the wheel, his speed, and the pedestrian about to cross the street, a creator focuses on this factor or that so far as he must in order to make the best use he can of all.

Chinese calligraphers and painters—or, as was often the case, Chinese calligrapher-painters—traditionally began their works by first trying to reach a position where they were at their most serene, freed from all involvements. Some artists in the West try to achieve a similar position before they begin. The Chinese, though, sought to become one with the Dunamis at a depth below that at which it is normally operative, experienced, or acknowledged, while artists elsewhere, lacking a tradition in which the importance of the Dunamis is constantly insisted on, usually have to discover for themselves that they make use of it. All creators, East and West, though, use it at depths below those utilized by others, no matter what the prevailing outlook, but none probes it entirely, nor, apparently, do many see that still deeper layers could be brought into play.

A rejection of formalism as too rigid and conceptual is sometimes expressed by Chinese artists, thereby balancing the professed avoidance by many Westerners of the Dunamis as too inchoate or fluid to be well understood or able to be used. Yet each side takes some account of what the other insists on. Even Western studies of creativity, despite an overemphasis on symbols, traditions, topics, themes, and techniques, remark on the transitory nature of things and the vibrancy that great works insistently exhibit. The attitudes and practices of the two do not differ in kind but in degree, though the degree may be so great at times that they can be taken to be engaged in different kinds of creative work. Not only are the arts of neither culture tightly sealed off, but a concentration on either or even on both will fail to do justice to the arts produced in what is quaintly called "the Third World."

The arts, though surely culturally qualified, can be appreciated by those who know nothing of the culture of their creators. Sometimes the works in one culture are carried over into another. Sir Henry Moore's sculptures continue a primitive South American tradition; Lafcadio Hearn was aware of the nature of the work carried out in a number of different cultures; some Japanese musicians exhibit a profound appreciation of the works of Mozart and Beethoven. Although artists benefit from what is familiar and established and are readied to work within the compass of established norms, these influences evidently have no designatable minimum, maximum, or predesignatable role.

When Easterners remark on the importance of the Dunamis, they usually also recommend that one relax, stop conceptualizing, planning, or thinking about oneself. It is good advice, but it is not properly used if it requires the rejection of everything one knows or might imagine. One should reach a private position where one will be maximally free from determinations by what is external and thereupon be able to make adequate provision to use not only of the Dunamis but also of conditions and a sought excellence as well.

Creators face a common dilemma: the purer the factors used, the greater the possible achievement, but also the more difficult it is to join them. In the course of an actual creative venture it is usually necessary to move back and forth, sometimes stressing one, sometimes another factor in the attempt to find a position where the factors constitute what is required if an ideal prospect is to be realized. Conceivably, an artist might privately imagine distinctions in a specialized voluminosity and emotionally so qualify the result that it would acquire an enhancing vibrancy in an extended unified region. If that were all he did, he would have to be satisfied with the hope that the outcome would turn out to be satisfactory. Even then, to produce such an outcome he would have to contribute to it by joining the Dunamis and a condition again and again. If creative, he would, in addition, act under the guidance and control of a gradually realized excellence to which he had committed himself. If he had to overcome strong inhibitions and bad habits, it would also be necessary for him to be more attentive to some one or more factors than he otherwise would.

Exaggerations are sometimes useful in getting timid students, or those who are so occupied with some one factor that they are unable to achieve anything worthwhile, to move toward the position where they might be able to create. This is particularly difficult to do in mathematics, ethics, social life, and politics. It may sometimes prove too dangerous to insist on. Still, both timidity and fear of failure have to be overcome if great work is to be achieved. Conceivably, one might produce distinctions in a specialized voluminosity and so qualify the result that it acquired an enhancing, dunamic pulsation. In that way a charged region might be produced. If one went no further, one could only hope that something excellent might eventuate.

To produce an excellent work, it is necessary for a creator to contribute to it. Not only must he use the ultimates and focus on the objective to be realized; he must also act so that he satisfies his commitments to the prospect, to the particulars already produced, and to what seems then to be required. If he meets those commitments, he will have so used the Dunamis that it modifies and is modified by a voluminous condition again and again, in part after part, in the course of a production both personally and impersonally determined.

Occupied with writing a poem about a sad moment in childhood or the flight of birds, with trying to write a musical composition that captures the quality and lilt of a battle or a circus, or with designing a building for a bank or a church, an artist produces distinctive unions of conditions and the Dunamis. He has no need to remember some previous occurrence or achievement. Nor need he relive the emotions he once underwent. If he did relive them, it would be in reverie. If he dwelt in some remembered experience, it might upset him. Rarely does he want to live through it again, even in tranquility. He does not often take his work to be a device for freeing him from the sufferings which experience or memory produced. He is not primarily a self-healer, using creative activity to bring him surcease from regrettable intrusions from the past. Nor is he a cheery archivist, preserving pleasant experiences in a more available form. He does not try to reinstate the past in the present, though his past will surely have repercussions in what he subsequently does. He seeks to purge neither himself nor others of stresses, emotions, experiences, or memories, using his art to bring these into the open. Such purgation, though, might be incidental. His is primarily a new, freely entered but still limited venture in the making of an excellent work, not an attempt to cure himself or to please.

One sometimes lives through an enacted tragedy, vicariously going through stresses, tensions, relaxings, tightenings, and a final satisfying resolution, to end with a sense that a deep question has been answered. Not all tragedies, though, have such consequences. *Othello* and *Hamlet* leave one vaguely dissatisfied, not so much with the plays as with one's grasp of what they signify. It is also quite hard to apply purgational theories to architecture, sculpture, painting, music, poetry, and dance. In any case, purgations or other benefits could be achieved without requiring one to attend to imagined dangers and dramatic resolutions. The kind of peace finally arrived at, moreover, could conceivably be attained more readily by becoming noble or wise, with art serving as a possible but not an essential agent. Were such benefits made the object of one's work, they would rarely be obtained. Art benefits most when its benefits are not sought.

We do not ask a mathematician to justify himself by demonstrating that his work will somehow benefit himself or others. We should also accept other kinds of creation as needing no further justification. All have consequences. Some of these are eminently desirable, warranting an interest in those ventures. The merits of the creative work will not thereby be enhanced or compromised.

Creators do not often take themselves to be more than creators. They may be stimulated to deal with particular problems, to respond to certain demands, to respond to the needs of other disciplines or kinds of activity. Their desires might influence their choice of topics and themes. Once they take up the task of creativity, different problems, commitments, and solutions will become their main concern.

There are branches of mathematics that have no known use. Virtue is said to be its own reward. A successfully led people is content to be glorified. Most citizens would be happy to be active contributors to the existence of a just, well-run state. Almost everyone can derive some pleasure or insight from some works of art, but none of these, or the others, depends for its merit on an ability to provide such benefits. Excellence needs no justification, though if realized in works well read it will yield a satisfaction of a distinctive kind and may help illuminate what otherwise had not and would not have been discerned.

Some readings will be better than others, making a reader more easily and readily aware of the excellence of the whole and what it signifies. A spirited reading of an indifferent work will be open to the charge of being histrionic, bringing to bear too much of the Dunamis, and sometimes too much of oneself, and not enough of whatever excellence may in fact be operative in the work. Such readings introduce new paces and divisions, usually telling us more about the reader than what is actually read and what the work reveals.

Like an actuality, a creation has its own being and nature. Like an aggregation of items, it has no privacy. Unlike the one, its singularity depends on the gradual realization of a prospect in the form of interinvolvements among distinguishable subdivisions. Unlike the other, it is unified, singular, with functioning units qualifying one another and, so far, denied the status of separate parts. The Dunamis is present throughout, limited by the condition with which it is joined and helping to keep creator and prospect effectively together.

A privacy could of itself be committed to the realization of a prospect. The prospect on its own could attract and guide. Neither separately nor together would they then provide all that is needed to assure the realization of the prospect. This requires the creator to tap forces other than his own. The Dunamis will be needed to take him from one item to another, some near, others somewhat distant. In an aggregation it will do so incidentally, connecting bounded items; in an actuality it will do so as a component in a single unity, where it may have a dominant role at one time and recessive ones at others. Only in a creation will it be so utilized that it gives a creator's commitments effective roles as so many incipient connections between what has been done, what is to be done, and what is to be achieved, at the same time that it provides the work with a distinctive vibrancy.

If the vibrancy were like a feeling, it would vary in its intensity in different parts of the work; if a feeling were like a vibrancy, it would not be an integral part of a unification, be dependent on a prospective, and be sustained by a realized excellence. A vibrancy, with its varying stresses, contrasts with a feeling in a created work. The feeling, though not divisible, has to be lived through in every part.

As merely envisaged, not yet expressed, a poem, a musical composition, or a novel will at most utilize a specialized form of a temporal voluminosity, subdivided into a plurality of interlocked, limited stretches and united with nuances in a specialized version of a layer of the Dunamis, below those usually evident or utilized. Were no notations or linguistic accompaniments provided, the result would offer no more than an instance of the way in which the voluminosity was privately utilized, the Dunamis confined, and the sought excellence realized. It also would not yet be available for appreciation by others. Were the works to have such accompaniments but did not also incorporate a distinctive layer of the Dunamis, one would not be able to move toward the voluminosity as a primary condition encompassing and affecting all occurrences in basic ways.

The writing of a poem, composition, or story does not merely add a public creation to one privately completed. If it did, the writing would not be part of the act of creating and would do little more than allow for an exhibition of writing skills. As a consequence, the work would not be enriched by the sounds and grammatical connections the words have in daily language. Daily use and associations make a difference to the contribution language makes in a work and help dictate how the work is to be read. Other materials play similar roles. Whenever use is made of material, a privately produced outcome is able to be fixated and joined to what is external to it.

If there were no dunamic passage to what is beyond a created work, a reader would be unable to discern an operative condition; he would in fact be so immersed in the work that he would be completely closed off from all else. A great achievement not only pulls one into it, overcoming whatever may have bounded it off from all else; it also leads an appreciator to attend to an insistent condition and thereby overcome his tendency to be satisfied with just having read the work well.

The notes set down by a composer are not just reminders; they also enable those who appreciate his work to become acquainted with something other than it, just so far as they live through it as a single, vibrant, unified excellence. The work allows them to discern the way a voluminosity affects anything and everything in multiple ways. Creations in other fields open readers to conditions other than a voluminosity, but these conditions, too, operate on and affect whatever exists.

One is able to reach what is made available by a completed, created work because the Dunamis carries one toward it. Without the Dunamis, the work would at best be a sign awaiting use. Because of it, the work can act as a sign for anyone reading it well, thereby enabling him to encounter a condition giving a distinctive import to whatever it affects. The Dunamis enables him not only to name or to refer but also to reach toward what operates everywhere. Because it allows created works to be articulated without being fragmented, vitalized without being reduced to turbulences, it can also take one behind what is daily evident.

In all works of art the Dunamis is already present in the voluminosity, in the produced parts, and in whatever connections these have to one another. Used by an artist on a layer deeper than those usually utilized, it is also present where its user is. Present in him and in everything else as a constituent, it is available for probing and use on deeper layers.

It is as right to say that the Dunamis acts without regard for what men do as it is to say that they use it. The one truth expresses the role that the Dunamis plays in all activity; the other emphasizes the individual, particularly when he creates. Yet some of those seeking to be creative are not sufficiently aware of their need for the Dunamis or of its availability. Could they be awakened to its importance, they might enable it to have a greater play. That would still not suffice to turn them into creators, for at the very least they would then have to join a voluminosity or some other condition many times over the course of a production under the guiding control of an ideal prospect.

A technician may be alert to the presence of the Dunamis. He may even be aware of the feeling present in a work and may want to be opened up to the presence of an operative condition. Since he does not allow the Dunamis to make its needed contribution to the work, he will be inclined to suppose that if he could master his materials more, he would be able both to create and thereby reach what creations make available. If he followed that inclination he would then not just spin his wheels but would let them whirl on their own, arriving nowhere.

A neglect of the roles of conditions in constituting the parts of a created work leads to the supposition that those parts have no intelligible structures. Bergson's fear that conditions alone would be considered in accounts of what exists in nature or in what is created is amply justified, as the history of thought shows. Still, confinements of the Dunamis, to which he so strongly objected, are not only inevitable but desirable, reflecting the presence of conditions which enable a work to have a nature.

A voluminous space, time, or causality has no distances within it, no positions marked out, no bounded parts. When any one of the voluminosities is joined to the Dunamis, the result acquires a single vibrancy and structure. Their juncture could be imaginatively subdivided, but that division will not affect either of them. Distinct units are produced only when conditions and Dunamis are joined, with nuances in the one fitting together with nuances in the other.

There is no arriving at ultimates simply by removing the accretions of history, politics, language, or theory. The removals are themselves never free from extraneous accretions from the past; still others are introduced in the act of removal. The ultimates can, though, be reached directly in one move by attending to their attenuated presence in any item and then intensively passing toward their origins. Everyone carries out such a move when remarking that there is a space in which some item exists, for its spatial extent is space itself in a delimited form, interlocked with other conditions. Those other conditions can be reached just as readily. Like a voluminosity, they are omnipresent. Each is undivided, terminating single, intensive moves, passing from limited uses of it to it as not yet joined to other factors.

No work will be successful if a condition and the Dunamis are not well united in what is done in the course of its production. Were the activity not subject to a gradually realized excellence, the condition and the Dunamis would connect the parts of the work adventitiously, somewhat in the way they connect those parts with what is outside the work. If the Dunamis or the conditions did not play any role, the sought excellence would not be a realizable prospect, effectively controlling and guiding what is produced; there would not even be contingent occurrences, since these, too, are the products of the meeting of specialized forms of ultimate conditions and the Dunamis.

What artists and other creators inherit they use, subjugate, transform, and make important by turning them into constituents of excellent works. These works make use of much that was previously achieved. Their topics and themes often bear the marks of customs and outlooks long passed away. Not just private productions, then and there produced in the imagination, the creations are also not mere functions of what once was earlier achieved, itself presumably traceable back to antecedents, and so without end.

The singular, essentially unified being of a creation stands in the way of an adequate dissection of it into a purely private, personalized product and a publicly available form of it. It has a public role because its materials are two-faced, both integral to it and part of a public world. The material makes a difference to the texture of the work and enables it to be stabilized and preserved, at once grained and fixated with a public location. To appreciate it, its publicly available material should be used to enable one to enter into it. The material will then act in ways similar to those followed when one hears a cry as the cry of one in pain. To respond to such a cry is to pass from an aspect of it as heard to its aspect as lived through. The two are not separated from one another any more than material used when producing a work is separated from itself as a constituent of the work.

No matter how deep the sympathy, no one reaches another's pain as it is suffered. One is affected by the cry and then paced by the way the other lives through it. At both times something of one's own will be added without necessarily obscuring what is there. Just as a cry of pain reports a pain having distinctive emphases and effects, so a private creation, through the material used in it, may introduce one to it as that which was being privately produced and textured.

Public language is a context able to be qualified by what is privately expressed. Though no one has a sure knowledge of what is so expressed, and though the making available of what is private adds modifications to it, nothing need be wholly hidden, altered, or annihilated by it. Often, others are able to correct misapprehensions of what is being undergone. There is a rough-hewn agreement among men regarding the way expressions requiring quick action of a particular sort are to be understood, even when the common situation is assessed in different ways. Just as public attributions of accountability are met by private acceptances, so an established language, or any other context, is met by other private acceptances. Just as privately grounded demands and intentions are interpreted in different ways in different places and times, so private meanings are changed when expressed in different contexts.

A public language is a publicly available context containing materials individuals use in diverse ways. The individuals are not solely language consumers interplaying with language producers; what is publicly produced is privately used by each. Nor are they just individuals thrown into a completely alien world; they act there with some regard for what they will encounter. Material is needed to complete what is privately done, and this in turn gives the material a new status and role. An essential part of every completed creation, whether as intangible as a language or as dense as a stone, the material textures a work at the same time that it enables it to be distinct from the material and in the same world with other objects. The divisions characteristic of the material may be overridden in the work at the same time that the material qualifies what is there achieved. The material also subjects the work to irrelevant contingencies. The paintings by Mark Rothko which changed color radically over recent decades are not now the works he created. They formerly had material different from what they now contain; yet all the while that his works were subject to what occurs in an indifferent world, they continued to have integrities of their own, remaining self-limited, cut off from all else as so many different unifications of interlocked functions. Sometimes, though, changes in materials make a great difference to the nature of the whole—apparently, in Rothko's paintings, enough to change the nature of some of his creations.

Conceivably, an altered work might be superior to the original, making its restoration a dubious enterprise. Sometimes the alteration will yield an entirely different beauty. Great ruins do. Not themselves creations overlaid with random intrusions, ruins have distinctive natures midway between created and natural wonders. They point up the fact that there is no predetermined point at which material is no longer able to be an integral part of a work. Within the work, the material is a component in each part; outside, it is obdurate, with its own career.

The performance of a composition has a distinctive grain, place, and relation to what else exists. Without obliterating the texture that it has owing to its notation, a performance adds another of its own, making the whole a distinctive creation in which every part will, at its best, affect every other in a new way.

The notes that were written down are never the notes played, though the former surely have a role in the latter. Yet it is sometimes said that a composer already hears the music as it will be played in a performance that is fully faithful to the composition. In a written interchange with Louis Schlosser (in *Composers on Music*, edited by Sam Morgenstern), Beethoven is recorded as saying, "I turn my ideas into tones which resound, roar, and rage until at last they stand before me in the form of notes." In the same volume, Mozart is reported as having said that he heard an entire piece before he wrote it down. He also remarked, "Nor do I hear in my imagination the parts successively, but I hear them, as it were, all at once . . . producing takes place in a pleasing, lively dream. Still the actual hearing of the *tout ensemble* is after all the best. What has thus been produced I do not easily forget." He has also been reported as saying, "Everything is already finished and it rarely differs on paper from what it was in my imagination." What he set down on paper, though, grained, sustained, and textured his work in ways he did not and could not imagine.

It is wrong to say that Beethoven or Mozart actually heard anything in his privacy. Hearing requires ears. What is heard by means of the ears fills out a volume of space and exists over a period of time. When made available to others, it unfolds at a rate different from that at which a composer wrote what he said he heard. Just as one can imaginatively distinguish the voice of one's mother from one's father or shudder at the imagined screech of chalk on a blackboard, so a composer can imaginatively distinguish sounds without in fact hearing any of them. What a composer "hears" does not fill out a room; it is not loud or brassy, coming to him from all sides; it was not sent out; it does not reach him from a distance. If, when he composes, he imagines what might be heard, each stage in his production will be imagined without his living through the full length of it or the feeling it has when it is well played. He will not actually go through all the pauses and rests he distinguishes in it, nor will he experience the reverberations characteristic of sounds actually heard.

A performance, because it is embedded in its own material, gives a composition a new pacing and fits it into a new setting. Inevitably, it distinguishes what is used from what is produced. It does not make someone's privately heard music available to others, using a composer's notes to recapture the tones he supposedly heard. How could it? Not only does no one know what was privately heard by another, but a performer is occupied with the use of an instrument having a unique timbre, yielding distinctive items to be intimately joined. We require of a faithful performer no more and no less than that he join the units of a composition in such a way that an excellent, temporalized, vitalized unification, with a distinctive feeling tone, is produced.

Performers can be creative; they are not all reducible to technicians or communicators. The greatest of pianists and violinists do more than publicize the privately produced, notated work of a composer. They are not related to the compositions they perform as contractors are to architectural plans, welders to sculptural designs, framers to paintings, or printers to poems. They are more than technicians making a difference to the way material is used so as to enable the works to serve some external end.

There are some who create works improvisationally, without attending to any compositions, their own or another's. Producing distinctive pacings, insistencies, tonalities, nuances, and unifications, they make what is performed be different in kind from what could have been used to guide them. If creative, they produce excellent works, suffused with feelings, with singular textures, able to be appreciated by those sensitive to the difference between high and low sounds, short and long separations, the sharp, the brittle, the coarse, the soft, and the hard.

Beethoven's resounding, roaring, raging, privately "heard" tones and Mozart's "hearing in [his] imagination" make evident the effective private presence of a voluminous time joined in masterly fashion to the Dunamis. Both composers articulated and qualified their private compositions by making use of notations. When their works are played, the compositions acquire other sustainings and grainings and, so far, are differently textured and thus effectively altered. Recorded performances are qualified in still other ways. The high note that is transmitted through some device and shatters a glass with a dramatic crash is a different note from one not so transmitted.

Works that are privately composed are not identifiable with what is notated, performed, or recorded, primarily because they incorporate different materials. Indeed, since each performance makes a different use of the same instruments, each is turned into a distinctive work. Even so, while materials make a real difference to the nature of a created work, the result is usually one in which the original creation makes the greatest contribution. Consequently, when a composition is identified in various performances and recordings, its dominant role, in contrast to the materials in which it is embedded, is rightly remarked.

A discrimination among imagined sounds, and particularly their placement relative to one another, may occur well before a temporal voluminosity and the Dunamis are united or are fixated through an established method of recording the result. Related anticipations of publicly recorded works occur in other arts. A painter may imagine possible positions for his colors; a novelist can think of his character in many different situations. If they did nothing more, their works would pass with the moment into the recesses of their privacies, to which only their memories could ever penetrate.

What was privately undergone is inescapably qualified both by what is made into an ingredient of it and by what is done to push something away. Yet those who stand out above all others in character and virtue are often spoken of as though they were pure spirits or souls, though they, no less than others, breathe and hunger, need food and drink, and live in distinguishable environments. At best they could exist apart from all else only by holding it at bay. In that very act they would give a role to what they face, as that which has to be overcome in order to carry out a private activity.

Just as it has been claimed that a composer "hears" his entire creation before providing notations and before it is performed by an orchestra, so it could be claimed that architects and others envision fully completed works before they are embedded in their appropriate, obdurate, publicly available materials. They, as well as painters, poets, choreographers, novelists, and playwrights, supposedly produce completed works in their privacies and attach them to privately imagined materials that adequately punctuate, connect, and even alter what is attached to them. The idea is no more legitimate here than it is when it is brought to bear on musical compositions.

The material aspect of formal expressions is neither as common nor as commanding as pragmatism affirms; it can be dealt with well apart from the demands of experience. Nor are those demands as irrelevant or avoidable as formalism takes them to be. Pure forms are nowhere to be found. Even the rational is insistent, intensive, and possessive; it is not a passive, contemplated object. What is there known, and surely what is there created, has its own material and texture. Materials, there as elsewhere, affect and are affected by what they stabilize. Those who use mathematics, or any other created work, do not compromise the privately qualified achievement.

No improviser merely accepts the materials he uses. He acts on and with it, to give it more than an adventitious, casual role in what is being produced. Aware of the difference that diverse materials make, he must work on them to produce his creation. When he envisages what the material can do to what it grains, he emphasizes salient features and the major differences that the material makes. No matter how vivid the anticipation or the private activity, the material, obdurate and insistent, will inevitably make a difference to the outcome.

What is used to fixate the private work of a composer, poet, writer, architect, sculptor, painter, or other artist is not an idle accompaniment, simply attached to what has already been freely achieved. If it were, it would add irrelevant or regrettable qualifications to what was excellent without it. Sometimes performances provide means whereby others become acquainted with a privately produced work, and they may be admired for that reason. What was used as material will then be treated as a means for acquainting others with whatever a creator had not made widely available. That creator would be set apart as one who awaits help from intermediaries. The best performers on such a view would be self-effacing, and what they did would allow their listeners to face what alone was created. Virtuosos would then be ideal performers, since they more evidently than others do not create and therefore do not get in the way of an encounter with a creator's work. Yet virtuosos are criticized precisely because they are unable to give their works the feelings they deserve.

To do justice to a great composition, play, or dance, a performed work must be permeated by feeling. Since a virtuoso's performance is excessively subject to the desire to exhibit technique, he stresses texture unduly, with the consequence that what he does is too dependent on the material he uses dazzlingly. One must reverse the virtuoso's emphases and thereby risk making poorer use of the same materials. An innovator, in contrast, often produces a texture not altogether appropriate to the work he is performing.

A musical composition is properly called a "work" since it results from something worked over, usually carrying a strong charge of feeling. A different feeling will be exhibited when the piece is creatively performed. Since the works are different, the feelings in them will have distinctive qualities and ranges. Conceivably, the different ventures could have the same emotional impact.

Great performers of great works provide textures appropriate to their playing, phrasing the compositions afresh, creatively combining needed factors and new materials. The results are more than reinstatements of the original compositions. Similar differences are evident in other arts and, indeed, in all other creative enterprises. All shape their works in their own ways, demanding that the materials used promote the production of an excellent work.

A great composition deserves more than a great performance. Performers should freshly combine it with the material provided by their instruments. The result should be a new creation, with its own texture, feeling, and beauty. Although great compositions—and great plays and other works—may be backed by instructions as to just how they are to be carried out in another medium, a creative performer will not allow himself to be confined by them. Bernard Shaw gave detailed instructions for performances of his plays, but these instructions are rightly ignored by the best directors, who give a new import to the plays. A playwright is not an authority on how this new import is best achieved. Similar observations make it desirable to distinguish pure mathematics—even when expressed in established notation and ready to be applied—from theoretical science and other enterprises in which mathematical achievements obtain new embodiments. These embodiments turn the mathematics into a modified part of a different enterprise. Imagining the texture that might result cannot possibly provide the graining that eventually will be produced.

A causal movement plays a dominant role in musical, theatrical, and choreographic performances. These performances take an audience from place to place so that what occurrs earlier is affected by what is later produced. The change is prefigured in a commitment aroused by what has been done. The various parts, despite the different times of their production, interplay with one another as functioning units in a single unification.

Different types of performance vary primarily in what they stress, a musical performance emphasizing a process, a theatrical performance filling one out, a dance identifying itself with it. Other works of art place diverse emphases on temporal or spatial units and their relations. Those stressing the role of a conditioning space yield what allows for ready movements backwards and forwards, up and down. Other types of creation rely on other materials to provide them with related opportunities.

The second act of a performed play, like the second act in a written one, affects the meaning of what occurred in the first act, and conversely. So far as the actions required both by what was achieved in the first act and by the prospect are produced, occurrences there will acquire the additional roles of occasions, premonitions, purposes, or causes. So far as the reverse occurs, and what the earlier prefigures is carried out, the later will have the role of continuations, progressions, justifications, or explanations. A performance moves forward as a result of productions required by an effort to supplement and enrich what has already been produced at the same time that the realization of an accepted excellence is promoted.

In those musical performances where there is no plot or character development, the acts of the performers often seem to be the primary determinants of what occurs. There will, of course, be no performance without them, but the performers' actions need not be part of the causality that is in fact generating the performance. That causality is distinctive, since it allows for subsequent occurrences to turn antecedents into preliminaries. It makes no difference whether or not those antecedents are initially produced primarily as consequences of what was done before or are items then and there required; what is done later changes their import.

Spatial or temporal arts are not necessarily superior to the transformative, or conversely. Even when one depends on the others for control, inspiration, or guidance, it will have its own components, course, and outcome. Each art specializes a single voluminosity and joins it with a specialized layer of the Dunamis to realize a prospective excellence, textured by the material used. Since certain parts must be produced or placed in some particular order, the material will have to provide more than a texture and fixation for the whole. It does so on being used over the course of the production. The most vividly imagined piece is integrated with material step after step, each changing the pace and bearing of what was and still is to be done. One must, therefore, not only master the best ways to retreat within oneself, to focus on a prospect, to combine ultimates, and to make use of material but must also know how to control the ways each is joined to the others.

The achievements of great composers and mathematicians are so astounding that one is inclined to overlook the roles that their notations and an established grammar play. One is then likely to take what they have created to be distorted on being expressed in notations or performances. Consequently, the excellence promoted by private achievements will be treated as though it were sullied by uses elsewhere, precisely because the new material alters what has already been achieved. One would then be justified in holding that performances spoil what it would be better to leave alone, except insofar as one wanted to carry out a separate, uncreative act of practice, communication, or preservation. Yet just as the material used by the original creator was made integral to his work, so is the material that enables the result of the original creation to become part of another.

Action painting and chance-governed productions seem to be like performances. They apparently make use of material not only to sustain and grain but to determine what is to be done next, and then adventitiously, in ways not controlled by the creator or his material. Although a good deal is left to chance, the nature of what has been produced and embedded will still be dominant. Related observations are pertinent to sculptured mobiles. A mobile caught up in a gale is just a work tossed about; it is a mobile only so far as the movements caused by changes in air currents are identifiable as its movements. Created as an intricate number of joined pieces in a pleasing pattern, it is not yet completed. Without subordinated currents of air functioning as part of its material, it is an incomplete mobile.

Not all the readings of a created work are equally good. The best will allow a place for the others as forms of itself, subjected to special qualifications and limitations. So far as a work does not allow for such readings, it is not excellent. If it is excellent, it allows for an endless number of movements from part to part, each adding new meaning to the others. The same words used by a poet and by a novelist, because utilized in different ways, can so far be said to be different. Where a poet will give each word a distinctive role, a novelist will subordinate a number of them to the needs of an incident. Climaxes obtrusively, but asides, connectives, and repetitions also, reverberate throughout a work; all are pulled into and pull on the rest, affecting the import.

It would take unusual insight and control, and a kind of double vision, for creators to know all that they will do and what else occurs in creating a work. Neither automata nor passive instruments, they can complete their works only if they use material to texture them. Topics and themes may help them determine just what material is to be used and how. This material may then be worked over and radically altered. No matter what is done, the material will still have made its own contribution, for though it is possible to accommodate and modify what is obdurate, it cannot be deprived of all its insistent resistance and therefore of its ability to make a difference to what accommodates or even subjugates it.

It makes no difference whether one counts fingers or toes; one ends with ten. If that sum is not at all affected by the nature of the counted units, it is conceivable that some things and perhaps works of art might also not be affected by the material used. Still, if the ten of the fingers and the ten of the toes were affected differently, *ten* could be considered apart from both without apparent loss and perhaps with some gain in range. We might therefore feel warranted in trying to understand created works apart from their materials. Putting aside the fact that counted items have a different relation to numerals from what the materials have to a work of art—

the items offer locations and opportunities to count, whereas the material gives creations their distinctive textures—the numerals not only enable one to obtain sums but can be used again and again.

It is we who correlate numerals and objects. The latter neither accept nor are affected by the former. Although we would be disturbed if we found that the numeral we reached, on counting our toes, fell short of the usual ten, our dismay would not be because the numeral could no longer find lodging there. We could also arrive at a final ten with a shout of surprise or joy, but this would not show that the numeral qualified or was qualified by a toe.

Counting involves a correlation; whatever is accepted as a locus, whether it be a unit or a group, could be correlated with any numeral. Similar correlations could be made when dealing with a work of art. The number of colors or shapes in a painting might be counted by the very numerals used to count toes. The correlations would set the numerals over against the objects counted, thereby giving the objects the status of countable units; but as part of the work, the colors and shapes are not bounded off from one another and thus cannot be counted. We can distinguish them as so many units only because we ignore their interlocked functionings in an unduplicable singularity.

Weights and magnitudes are major concerns of both architects and sculptors. The quality of the paint and the resonances of actual colors give a new import to whatever painters may have in mind. Novelists work within the realm of accepted, plausible connections between grounds and consequences. Poets write against the dead weight of a common language with its familiar associations and meanings. Choreographers are confined by what human bodies can do. Novelists, playwrights, and directors are all subject to the limitations under which communication operates. Each is free to create by bringing a privacy into play with a conditioning voluminosity and the Dunamis, under the controlling guidance of a cherished beauty, at the same time that the result is limited by whatever is used to grain, stabilize, and communicate what has been achieved. Each work is textured by what continues to remain outside it. A reading of it will often benefit from the identification of a familiar object, from a title, or from some other device enabling one to imagine something familiar and thereby be in a position to attend to focal points in what may have been confronted by the creator or may have interested him.

A materialistic interpretation of art adds a needed corrective to a romanticism that takes what is created to exist in some ethereal realm, neither using nor interacting with what is brute, despite conspicuous evidence of decay and the effects of the elements and history. Neither view, apart from its function as a corrective, is tenable. The private and the public are intimately joined in a creation, while continuing to exist and function independently of it and of one another.

No one fully controls the material part of a work. Recalcitrant, it allows for modifications but not for a complete subjugation of what is otherwise done. Rarely does it play as important a role in a creation as other factors do. What it helps constitute may have ultimate factors already joined. If one produced a work without being guided by a prospective excellence, use could be made of the primal factors, but one would not yet be able to produce a completed, internally constituted singular. Although the outcome of a creative work may contain much that was unplanned and will yield surprises, it must have been produced over the course of a persistent venture where it is made more and more determinate. There will always be something in a created work beyond what the outcome of chance combinations of parts could possibly match, unless a plurality of externally related items could be identical with a unification of internally related ones.

Beauty

The special excellence of a work of art is commonly designated as *beauty,* which is usually set alongside *truth* and *goodness*. There are sound reasons for adding *glory* and *justice* to that list. None of them, as radically indeterminate prospects, usually holds the attention of creators. They are more interested in producing an excellent work.

A creator must free himself both from established constraints and from tendencies pointing him toward his daily needs, confrontations, and actions. As he progresses in his venture, the excellence which he is committed to realize will become more determinate and more effective. Whether noticed or not, from beginning to end it will guide his activity. His work will, so far, be distinguishable from all others. Even if it has serious defects, a distinctive prospect will have been faced and realized, to some extent, throughout. Because of the presence of the prospective excellence to which he is committed and whose realization he acts to promote, even what is flawed in his work will be different in nature from what is produced in other ways and for other reasons and which may at times even be more interesting, pleasurable, appreciated, or profitable.

Thousands of sonnets have been produced by following established rules. Few are creations, even flawed ones. Although many exhibit masterly workmanship, they give evidence of no unifying excellence. Since the excellence is initially indeterminate and is to be finally converted into a unification of what is produced over the course of a creation, it can be identified only so long as it is not fully realized and the work not yet completed. When the excellence is realized, the work will exhibit a feeling connecting pivots, climaxes, thrusts, and rests.

One may commit oneself to realizing a prospective excellence. No one commits himself to providing an occasion for a possibility to receive a filling; at best it is focused on, perhaps because one is obligated to carry out some task. A prospective excellence is a constant indeterminate, filled out by but unchanged when content is just added to it.

A commitment to an ideal prospect enables it to acquire greater and greater control; an obligation can do no more than relate a possibility to an area where specific acts should be performed. The one is made more and more determinate; the other remains unaffected even when made to encompass a plurality of particular determinations. Possibilities acquire new locations as a consequence of occasions provided for them; prospects cannot be abstracted from completed works, though these works will allow for the abstraction of an indefinite number of possibilities. Guided by a prospect, a creator realizes it through a production of parts connected in mutually enhancing ways. There is no way of his knowing in advance exactly what contribution a sought excellence or produced parts will make to a final outcome, for their actual contributions are affected by their interplay.

Human beings alone have individualized privacies affected by and able to be partly expressed in and by means of their bodies. What they then produce may have little or no bodily value. Their distinctive privacies provide one reason why their works are superior to those produced by other living beings, even those whose desires, fears, and expectations dictate what they do. Those humans who are corrupt, mutilated, sick, or seriously defective in mind, body, morals, or ways of acting are superior even to the greatest of created works, for humans have at least a latent ability to assume accountability for public acts and to become responsible for privately initiated ones. Only they are free to act and are therefore able to create. If denied the opportunity to develop or to realize their potentialities, they will still differ radically from all other kinds of beings and occurrences precisely because they alone are persons, beings who alone have those potentialities. Although creations have an incomparable nature and may be more attractive and pleasing than those humans who are radically incapacitated, they are inherently inferior, for they do not have privacies and, despite their singularity, lack individuality. Humans are individuals continuing into, possessing, and able to use their privacies and bodies and to make specialized use of all the ultimates.

The beauty of a created work makes singular demands on one's attention through its appeal, not through the exertion of force or by limiting one's actions. The work is self-limited, but unable to hold itself off from all else, it cannot impose boundaries on anything. Not a predicate or a category, beauty lacks individuality, substantiality, and productive power. Not itself unified, it cannot itself be excellent. Like all other excellences, it presupposes realities existing apart from it, enabling it to be realized.

Natural beauties are excellences which are realized without any effort being made. Occurring in nature, they are of two types. One exhibits beauty in unbounded splendors—a sunset, a mountain, a forest, a waterfall. The other exhibits it in well-bounded complexes—a web, a hive, a snail, a rose, the lithe movements and springs of a panther, the running of a colt, an athlete's body at rest and in motion, a young woman at once innocent and attractive, the serene look and posture of one both old and at peace. These are all well marked off from what is alongside them. Both the bounded and the unbounded beauties are constituted by the same ultimates, but the bounded have the junctures of ultimates mediated and thereby limited by singular beings.

Whereas humans create beauties by joining ultimates again and again under the guiding control of an ideal beauty, nature produces beauties without being occupied with the realization of such a prospect. Whereas nature happens to have conditions and the Dunamis joined as undivided ultimates with the result exhibited here and there through the agency of distinct actualities, creators use their individualized privacies to unite specialized forms of the ultimates under the guiding control of a gradually realized excellence.

Uncreated beauties require no reference to a purpose in nature any more than created beauties do. They are also as objective as any other feature of actual entities or any other product of human activity, existing apart from judgments or appreciations of them. Like other natural occurrences, they are grounded in actualities. The actualities, though, may be so affected by what nature expresses through them that they are readily credited with the beauty that is due to nature's adventitious union of conditions and the Dunamis.

Natural beauties may evoke emotions, but they contain no feelings. Feelings pervade creations, but they may be encountered without evoking much emotion. Both created and natural beauties unite ultimates in a singular way, but whereas creators act deliberately to realize an excellence, nature has ultimates joined as a matter of course to achieve what otherwise would not be realized. Nature acts without deliberation, uses ultimates globally, and exhibits the fact in limited places and times; men compensate for their partial uses of the ultimates by subjecting them to the control of a sought excellence.

Natural objects and occurrences all have appearances enabling one to grasp what they are, if their appearances are used as beginnings of intensive moves into their possessors. The appearances are all "appearances of" and cannot be neatly sheared away without being radically changed. A created work has no appearances. Endlessly rich, its content awaits an attentive reader. Whereas the appearances of things lead one into them, creations enable one instead to confront a condition as a primary, insistent power.

Not dependent on a privacy attending to a prospect and carrying out a plurality of acts, a natural beauty is the product of unguided combinations of ultimates. It does not provide a sign of the natural world, nor does it help one to reach that world. More like a created work suddenly come upon and not yet read, a natural beauty is neither articulated nor able to signify anything. No foreshadowed specialized excellence is realized in it. If one reads it as one reads a created work, its beauty would be misconstrued since it is natural in origin and exhibited only here or there. Whereas the reading of a created work introduces one to a beauty in its full concreteness, a natural beauty has to be yielded to.

If on first entering a great cathedral we are awed, we have taken the first step toward achieving an adequate appreciation of it. A natural beauty, in contrast, must be accepted as it appears; a reading of it, carried out by attending to part after part, would be one with its dissolution. When we call a natural beauty "sublime" or "awesome," we are asking that it be accepted as it presents itself. A work of art, instead, is to be lived in and lived with, and thereby enabled to function as a sign of an insistent, ever-present condition.

The different parts of an excellent creation may have either a condition or the Dunamis in a dominant position, but the final outcome will have them supplementing one another over the entire work. That result is one with the realization of the excellence, itself constituted by the convergence of all the ultimates. The beauties of nature do not have the different factors so well balanced. Here the Dunamis may be in ascendancy, there a voluminosity, the rational, the affiliator, the stratifier, or the coordinator.

No one knows the whole of nature. We cannot say it has all the ultimates in balance. When we speak of some part of it as beautiful, we take some particular expression of it, here or there, to contrast with or balance some disequilibrium elsewhere. The glorious starry heavens are beautiful against a dismal darkness. When we speak of running wild horses as beautiful, we speak elliptically of them as seen against an indifferent or uninteresting background.

Although natural occurrences do not function as signs of conditions, they can alert us to localized occurrences as compensating for what occurs elsewhere. If they do, it will be nature that will be beautiful, though the beauty will be discerned only here and there and in a limited form. An isolated natural beauty is like a grand climax compensating for what seemed to be a tepid prelude, or like an oasis that turns a desert into a needed background.

The difference between creations and anything else can be best seen if they are set over against machines, rather than over against natural events, for the bounded character of the different parts of the machine and what the machines produce are far more evident. The excellence of a created work is an undivided ingredient; a machine and its products need someone to give them the status of single units.

A created work and an organism are both unified, the one by a realized excellence, the other by its possession of its appearances. Aggregates, whether natural or produced by men, have only externally produced, bounded parts. When taken as single entities, the aggregates may, like a copy of an original creation, be mistakenly held to be unified and thereupon be identified with an actual creation.

Montages, collages, and assemblages may seem to be no more than parts added to parts, unified perhaps through the act of a spectator and, so far, not actually unified; if created, they will not differ in principle from other kinds of paintings or sculptures. Their parts function more readily as focal points, transitions, pauses, climactic turns, and intermediaries than the units in other works do; but if the works are created, the parts will be unified by a realized excellence, and a feeling will be present throughout, thin though it may be.

Although a complete understanding of what has been created includes a reference to other works and whatever else has an effect on it—perhaps even a reference to what might have been produced later—and although the work's very existence depends on the use of ultimates having their own integrity and power, the focus of the understanding must be on the created work as a unique singular, already unified. One cannot always differentiate between such a work and a copy of it or always distinguish an act of appreciation from an act of interpretation. A copy never allows for an appreciation, though an interpretation of it may yield as much satisfaction and may even alert one to the presence of an insistent condition.

A distinguishing of an original and a copy may prove exceedingly difficult, mainly because we do not know how to read very well. While the difference between them may remain undetected indefinitely, that does not mean that it is absent. Usually we need some clue, perhaps even a confession or a betraying, improper use of paper, canvas, notation, language, paint, or the like, before the distinction is suspected. Judgments and appreciations are not without their prejudgments and dangers. Whatever excellence a copy is taken to have, like the supposedly excellent product of a machine, is a consequence of a mistaken tacit supposition that it is unified. The discovery that it is only a copy or the work of a machine makes manifest that a unification has been wrongly attributed to it.

Forgeries differ from copies. They are original works, requiring some creativity and offered as belonging together with other acknowledged originals. Since they are intended to fit into an established canon of some creator or period, their outcomes are antecedently limited. Whatever unification a forgery might produce could never be more than partial since it will have been limited by the need for the work to be compatible with some already accepted, complete creation.

A unification, though due to a creator, is inherent in the created work. Its prospect guides and controls. Forgeries depend on the existence of other works, on prevailing notions of what some figure or period accomplished, or on an ignorance by many of the way works of a certain kind were produced. Usually forgeries use partial unifications to lull the viewer into accepting the whole as fully unified.

Where creators allow their works to be bounded, forgers produce boundaries designed to mislead one into taking their works to be self-contained. Original work is carried out by a forger, not to produce something excellent but to fit in with what has already been accepted as being excellent. Sometimes forged works closely approximate created ones, exhibiting a common style and stressing various obtrusive functioning items. Nevertheless, created works contrast radically with forged ones, since the former are not limited by the demand that they fit in with other creations of a particular individual or time.

If the excellence of a work were thought to be due to someone appreciating it, that work would be treated as if it could have been produced noncreatively. When it is supposed that a copy, a forgery, or the product of a machine could be excellent, it will be mistakenly supposed that it is unified. There will have been reductionist mistaking of a unity for a unification or, at best, a subjectivistic misconstrual of a unification as being due to a reader of it.

Machine products, copies, and forgeries, in order to be thought beautiful, have to be misinterpreted, for excellences are realized only by those committed to them and to what is required to produce them. Since we may not be sure whether some particular work is a creation, a copy, an aggregate, or something wrongly identified as one of these, in the end there can be only one recourse—seeing if the work can be read as an interlocked set of functions, imbued with feeling and signifying a primal condition.

Experiments trying to show that there is no sure way of determining whether something was produced by a machine or a human being presume that the machine is a single entity apart from its place in a humanized world and that a string of marks is in principle indistinguishable from an actual message. Were there no human beings, there would not be anyone able to decide that there was no actual or determinable difference between what was and was not machine-made. Questions of the differences between machines and humans are addressed to the latter and are answered by them, and then only because the machines have already been viewed as being more than an aggregate of bounded units.

The cosmos and the universe are indifferent to human existence. They, too, depend on the operation of ultimates. An isolation of an item in these areas dislocates it. We produce such a dislocation when we refer to some plurality of units as a machine, a message, a copy, a forgery, or a creation, for we then set them in a humanized world, where human values and organizations give them new roles.

Some painters—montagists, those using found objects, collagists—seem not to produce interlocked, functioning units within the compass of a gradually realized beauty. Many of their works are apparently begun without preliminaries; some apparently end with new ways of exhibiting separate items in relation to one another. "What you see," some minimalists maintain, "is what you get." Supposedly, there is no feeling present in any of these works, no excellence affecting either the production or its outcome. If so, these works are not genuine creations.

Traditionalists dismiss minimalism as debased, perverse, anarchistic. That, of course, is the reaction we expect from those who reject deviations from accepted standards, procedures, or conventional topics. Such rejections should be avoided as at least begging the question; new genres deserve the same consideration that more traditional genres receive, particularly if an initial appreciation of them is supported when they are read with care. Still, if the new lacks the essential characters of a creation, it is not to be placed alongside those works that have them.

Radically new creative achievements may not be properly approached or characterized even by those who favor them. It is difficult to deal with them since their materials, techniques, topics, and themes are so novel. We should not be surprised, then, to find that the terms and categories for explaining or justifying them are principally negatives of those that have long been used.

Innovators demand that traditional techniques, established canons of good taste, and traditional themes and topics not be treated as sacrosanct. Those innovators are right: nothing should be allowed to keep creators from utilizing new units, new combinations, new materials. The new, of course, does not deserve acclaim simply because it is new. One does a work justice only by taking time to learn how to read it, even if the reading ends in rejecting it as not well enough unified to merit acceptance as excellent. Fortunately, a new work is seldom so radically different from the old as a program claims it to be, in good part because its novelty and the ingenuity of its makers are not essential parts of it. The innovators, of course, may be creative. By freeing themselves from unnecessary restraints or ways of realizing beauty, new ways to read old works may then also be promoted. What was once taken to be auxiliary, mediocre, or incidental may then also be revealed as crucial and illuminating.

Since we can envisage a work by merely imagining the divisions on which a diagram or other device might fix, we should distinguish between those who deliberately set about to realize an ideal prospect and those who occupy themselves with working over material until a prospect is discernible. It is well to do both, since an exclusive occupation with satisfying an ideal may lead one to overlook the demands each achieved part makes on others, while an exclusive occupation with these parts or with material may lead to a neglect of the demands made by a prospective excellence.

Beauty is an ideal and, like others, specializes a more general excellence. In different fields of art, creations are occupied with distinctive versions of it, to be realized by carrying out distinctive acts. In the absence of a common, more indeterminate beauty that diverse arts focus on and attempt to realize, they would produce what could be called "beauty" only by analogy. It is only a matter of ingenuity, however, to find analogies between any items. There are analogies, for example, between a brook and a computer: a brook runs on without supervision, a computer has a location in a public world; a brook is the outcome of physical acts, a computer receives and changes what is put into it, sometimes into what is better. Similar analogies hold between any other arbitrarily selected objects, for all are constituted of the same ultimates playing comparable roles in diverse settings.

Beauty, like other excellent prospects, functions as a guiding ideal because it has a status all its own, though this status is not always acknowledged until a work is completed. This lack of acknowledgment does not mean that beauty does not guide and control what is done. Nor will a failure to acknowledge it affect either a creator's commitment to realizing it or his ability to produce the parts that promote the realization of a final unification. Like other prospective excellences, it can guide and control. In its absence there would be only stimuli, provocations, arousals, terminating in a miscellany of items getting in one another's way, unable to sustain, modify, or enhance one another.

Within the externally determined boundaries that creations acquire by being placed in a public world, creations closely interrelate what is within them. Just as more loosely joined objects carry out functions even when observers are absent, the roof stopping the rain, the floor holding up the table, roots feeding a tree, so the functions acquired in a creation continue to be exercised within the unification that a creator achieves.

Anthropologists have long struggled with odd marks, trying to determine whether they were caused by weather or were deliberately set down. A kind of Turing experiment, which asks one to determine whether or not some presented set of items forms a message sent out by a person, could have been formulated by anthropologists well before the age of the computer, for one cannot always be sure that something is a message any more than that it is a copy. Just what kind of functions distinguishable items actually exercise are sometimes very hard to discern. Poor readers of great works miss many of them. If the question of whether something is unified cannot be definitely settled, one still has no right to conclude that there is no difference between created and noncreated works or that we cannot know what the difference is. Failure to determine what is well unified in this or that case does not preclude its being present, nor does it show what will be known if other attitudes are assumed and other clues followed. Had we additional data, the issue could presumably be resolved.

If we cannot determine whether a work is well unified, we cannot know whether or not it is beautiful. Sometimes we can see that it is beautiful; at those times there can be no question but that the work is unified. To be sure, one might wrongly suppose that a unification was operative. To test that supposition one would have to begin a reading at other places and then follow other routes. We know we are reading a splendid poem when we see how words and meanings reverberate throughout, making a great difference to some, little difference to others, and hardly detectable differences to the rest. In the end we must be content to settle for a recognition of interplays greater than those to be found in most other poems, with the entire poem acting as a sign of a primal, effective condition.

Each work of art has its own "language." That language does not mediate the work and a reader. It is part of the work, to be lived in and through. That, it might be contended, is why there could never be an agreement on whether something is beautiful. There are, though, other ways in which persons agree besides employing some common language, mediating a human being and what he confronts—as rowers and relay runners show. If everything but language were dismissed or subjectified, we would, at the end, be left with no one to speak to, nothing but language to speak about, and no one able to understand what we said. A history would never be lived, a society would contain no one, or both would come about when men begin to speak. If instead all else but history, society, economics, or some other context were alone objective, the users of a language would exist only when and where those contexts enabled them to be.

People make a difference to what they confront and use; they utilize what has a status of its own, joining it in new ways in distinctive, separately existing singularities. Even with the vanishing of the last human being, there will continue to be beautiful, created objects and other results of human interest and effort. Were this not so, paintings would even now turn into congeries of physical units during the night, and a poem would vanish with a closing of a book.

A work of art is externally related to all else, but it still can be made part of some other. It can have many different influences at different times and on different objects. It does not thereupon lose the excellence it possesses. Its economic and political dimensions, like its weight, will not necessarily affect it, since it is internally constituted, self-limited, stopping at its boundaries.

Creators control their works. This control is best achieved if they first retreat deep into themselves before they begin the hard task of creating. William Butler Yeats's "Circus Animals' Desertion," like other great poems, speaks both opaquely and clearly, thematically and unthematically, illuminatingly and darkly, about this, while making one aware of the insistent nature of a conditioning time—here the locus of origins—and making evident a basic problem that every poet must solve:

> Now that my ladder's gone,
> I must lie down where all the ladders start,
> In the foul rag-and-bone shop of the heart.

A creator is also appreciative. An appreciator, from beginning to end of his reading of a created work, is pulled into it and then directed beyond it. The entire enterprise is accompanied by multiple tensions and various degrees of relief, absorptions, and satisfactions. At the end the work remains between what it signifies and what is privately undergone, enabling each to affect the other. The condition signified will not only be privately reached but will have an effect on the reader. The work will enable him, as it does the creator, to face the condition directly. At the same time, as bounded off, the work will be subject to and instantiate all the ultimates, together with other occurrences, created or not.

The mastery of one kind of art makes evident what in other kinds might be overlooked. Nothing less than a detailed study of all will expose every aspect that an adequate account of any should consider. It is equally important to realize that other creative ventures emphasize what none of the arts do. They, too, are occupied with realizing excellences. Each makes use of individualized privacies and uses a distinctive ultimate condition; each joins nuances of this condition to nuances in the Dunamis again and again in distinctive kinds of acts; each texturizes and stabilizes the result by using distinctive kinds of materials and realizes a distinctive kind of unification. The result should make one alert to otherwise slighted aspects in the other kinds of created work. These aspects, in turn, make more evident what is present in every art, though there slighted and sometimes misconstrued. By contrast, but also by bringing new issues to the fore, other kinds of creation should be able to illuminate what has now been said about art—and conversely.

3

Mathematics and Science

The Nature of Mathematics

AT LEAST seven views of mathematics have found advocates among distinguished mathematicians and philosophers. Each has singular merits, rarely acknowledged by the defenders of the other approaches. Each has its defects as well, precluding it from being accepted, whether by mathematicians or by those who try to express what mathematicians do and affirm. An understanding of their strengths and weaknesses will help make the nature of mathematics more evident.

1. *Platonism* maintains that there is a realm outside the transitory, contingent world. There, fixed and fully intelligible items supposedly exist, presumably to be known by pure intellects. Some forms of Platonism are content to claim that the realm contains only the natural numbers and that mathematicians must make use of these numbers if they are to know other truths not discernible there. The radical Platonic view takes all mathematical truths to await discovery in an eternal realm open only to pure spirits. The difficulties besetting it have qualified forms in the other, more limited Platonisms.

If all mathematical truths were already present in some eternal realm, one would have to accept what appears to be the outcome of great creative mathematical work to be the result of fortunate accidents or of a dialectical progress up a fixed hierarchy of truths. If the realm were occupied by one part of mathematics alone—the natural numbers, for example—the rest of mathematics would have to be created or deduced, or variations would need to be played on the occupying part. One would then be faced with the difficulty of knowing how it was possible to reach what is outside the finite, transitory world in which the adventure presumably begins and is carried out.

Discoveries presuppose something to be discovered. To account for the presumed discovery of some or all of mathematics, what has been discovered must have a nature of its own. Platonism tries to meet that requirement by remarking on the fixity, universality, and intrinsic rationality of mathematical truths, differentiating them from whatever else is producible and from what was part of an apparently transient, not altogether intelligible world. Because the supposed discoverer is in and is affected by that world, it must also be held that mathematical truths must be envisaged by a supposed eternal side of man. Plato accepted that consequence but was thereupon left with the problem of understanding how that side was related to what was transitory. That problem he never did solve.

In the end, Platonism cannot avoid dichotomizing both men and what they know, for it sets a knowable realm of eternal truths against transient human beings existing in a contingent world. Left unanswered are the questions How can one apply the discoveries of the eternal to temporal events? How can what was discovered at one time help one make discoveries at others? A Platonist has too little respect for what he and everyone else daily encounters to be able to get to the eternal except by turning in an entirely new direction and losing himself in what he claims to encounter there. How could he ever come back to where he started and where, in fact, we mortals find him?

There are fixities that everyone can reach, but evidently no one of them can be marked off from all else. They are impervious to change because, like time itself, they do not exist in time. As related to other eternal entities, they are limited as surely as transitory things are.

A pure Platonist must either point insistently to where some other being is insisting on itself or must deny that he is more than a faint version of what he arrives at, since this alone is supposed to be real. The latter idea was affirmed by later Platonists, with the consequence that the more surely they reached what was real, the more surely they themselves had to vanish. As long as a pure Platonist supposes he is other than what he takes to be eternal, he will not arrive at what he affirms.

2. *Formalism* treats variables as terms, concepts, meanings, or symbols that take what is distinct from but pertinent to them to be their values. It could function on behalf of a Platonism, expressing in formulae what are supposedly eternal mathematical truths. More modest formalists would instead hold that their formulae recapture or give the only appropriate, usable meanings to those truths. They are deontologized Platonists, saying nothing about the reality of their subject matter while claiming to present in precise form what mathematicians are presumably able to know when they confront what awaits the confrontation.

The masters of precise formalizations are symbolic logicians, whose classic is Whitehead and Russell's *Principia Mathematica*. Beginning with a few assumptions, logically expressed and precisely defined, that work attempts to derive the basic truths of mathematics in the shape of well-demonstrated consequences. Their approach is now recognized to lead to apparently irresolvable paradoxes and to be faced with Kurt Gödel's proof that it allows for the formulation and assertion of a theorem whose truth or falsehood cannot be demonstrated.

Formalism appears only after creative mathematics has provided it with something to dissect, reorganize, and restate. No one occupied solely with it ever produced, or could be expected to produce, an important mathematical theorem, for that production requires one to carry out acts of inference.

Implications connect antecedent and consequences in a single fixed structure. Inferences begin with premisses, then leave these premisses behind to end with conclusions able to be affirmed as distinct truths separated from the premisses. Implications hold onto their premisses; inferences do not. An implication is a complex, to be characterized as valid or invalid; an inference is a production ending in an outcome having a feature that owes its presence to the fact that one started with that premiss and then arrived at what can be formally accepted as a necessitated conclusion. Because inference is a process, and because a formal expression presents only a static implication, the latter can never fully accommodate or explicate the former. It could only rigidify it, thereby denying to the inference its characteristic movement and productivity.

Extant modal logics are occupied chiefly with possibilities and necessities, yet they do not differ essentially from the familiar two-valued, extensional logic, for their possibilities and necessities are made subject to the same kind of implications and inferences accepted by this logic. One can obtain a logic distinct from either only by formally relating premiss and conclusion in a new way or by carrying out inferences that the others do not warrant. Since an intensional logic does the latter, it needs its own set of expressions. Attempts to provide these expressions have so far succumbed to the temptation to produce formalizations which imitate those characteristic of extensional logic.

The truths of mathematics are not jeopardized by the provision of logically exact, symbolic formulations of what mathematicians have created and affirmed, but if such formulations were taken to capture the whole meaning of mathematical truth, mathematicians could supply no more than anticipations of the logical tautologies to which extensional logicians reduce valid implications. All of mathematics could then, in principle, be produced by purely mechanical means. As a consequence, mathematicians would have to be said to reach their results swiftly, perhaps anticipating or inventing neat expressions and ingenious proofs, but they could not be properly credited with the ability to create. Galois, Gauss, and Bolyai would all be logicians in a hurry.

Creative mathematicians may express their results formally, though these results are obtained by carrying out inferences. What they achieve deserves and profits from formalization, somewhat as a musical composition deserves and benefits from a good musical notation. What would otherwise slip away is thereby fixed. But pins should not be confused with butterflies. Formalists are ready with the one; they need creative mathematicians to provide them with the other.

3. *Axiomatics* is concerned with the provision of precise expressions of axioms or principles from which all mathematical truths are rigorously derived. The pivotal figure of this approach is Hilbert. He made no attempt to ground his formulations in a more general logic. As a consequence, he avoided the familiar logical paradoxes and tautological formulae to which traditional formalism reduces necessary truth. He, too, though, depended on the completion of creative work by those taking no account of his axioms or his procedure. Definiteness, care, and proof should not be permitted to obscure the fact that creative mathematicians open up new areas. Systematization, like Formalism, belatedly reexpresses what creators independently produce. Both can provide good checks on the correctness of what the creators affirm. The checks, like a speedometer, do not duplicate what they confirm.

4. *Constructionism* assumes that the natural numbers are marked out in a kind of Kantian pure time. It then proceeds to use some of those numbers to obtain others by following careful, step-by-step procedures. Taking what is only possible to be indeterminate, it properly denies that the law of excluded middle applies to it. Recognizing that this law holds only of what is well distinguished, Brouwer refused to affirm that everything that is the outcome of a merely possible procedure has a mathematically acceptable form and may be characterized as either true or false. A mathematical truth will be, and will be known, he claimed, only if it is in fact arrived at through well-demarcated stages as a distinct, well-bounded outcome, cohering with what is already known. Some later Constructionists allow for well-defined infinite processes, but it is not clear precisely where they stand between Brouwer and the Cantorians whose multiple infinitudes they take not to be constructible and whose novel language and methods they treat as questionable.

So far as Constructionism treats some of the natural numbers as distinct units, it takes them to be subject to the law of excluded middle. It is unclear whether its defenders take that law to apply to all the natural numbers or to all the real as well, even those never counted. Apparently they do not allow for those that cannot be reached by proceeding step by step. Transfinite numbers, in any case, are to be ignored or at best to be taken as indeterminate, allowing for neither affirmations nor denials.

It is not quite clear whether Constructionism allows that what is once distinguished remains so, is fixed in notations, or has to be recovered again and again. Presumably the first is intended. If so, some of the natural numbers will today have to be treated as "given," thereby leaving open the question of how they were initially obtained and how they are kept from vanishing. While avoiding purely imaginative leaps into realms which cannot be otherwise reached or utilized, Constructionism joins Intuitionism in radically limiting the scope of mathematics at the same time that what is being presupposed is left unexamined.

Since the rule that one should proceed from one position to another in a well-specified manner is stated in general terms, it, too, should be unacceptable to the Constructionists. There is, moreover, no way that they can show that they embrace the entire range of constructional entities or even the entire range of those that are desirable or useful. To do so, they would have to put aside their intuitions and the work of construction and attend to what these presuppose.

Constructionism would be unduly restricted if it did not accept all the natural numbers, even those not counted or deduced. Furthermore, if it is to avoid the kind of criticism that it levels at others, its own general claims must be shown to differ in kind from theirs. Even if one were to grant the Constructionist view a dispensation that it denies to its opponents, one would still be left with a program to be carried out, but neither defended nor justified. Constructionism provides a cautionary note. What is not clear is what it precludes, and therefore what its program allows.

The thesis that only what can be constructed is acceptable tells us nothing about the possible legitimacy of operations on the natural numbers that have not yet been performed. Also, not only is it unclear what status the view accords the finite numbers which no one has yet arrived at or formulated, but it is apparently also being assumed, in a quasi-Platonic spirit, that there are numbers having definite, fixed properties, whether or not the numbers or those properties are known.

Constructionism will not be well grounded until it can show why one must construct, why what is constructed is a proper part of mathematics, and why types of construction other than those now certified are either undesirable or impossible. It does, though, offer a good, albeit partial account of what is done in mathematical creations, since these creations determine what would otherwise remain indeterminate or be without existence proofs. The proofs need not be expressed in diagrams or by moving from one definite position to another. Certain operations cannot be carried out on transfinites, but this fact does not entail that there are no legitimate operations pertinent to these numbers. Thus, Constructionism, evidently, burdens us with an unduly limited view of what needed determinations are like and how they are to be produced.

By taking a firm stand with the natural numbers, it is possible to create other kinds of numbers and other mathematical units. Those results could be called "constructions" provided that they were recognized as the outcome of creative acts and did not have to be attained only after one had actually stopped at every designatable position between an accepted beginning and a justified end. Most creative mathematicians do not accept the Constructionistic restrictions of mathematics to the natural numbers. Instead, they move into higher levels of the rational to give new roles and a new import to what was previously achieved at a lower level.

5. *Operationalism* is the view maintained by Benjamin Peirce, his son Charles

S. Peirce, and Alfred North Whitehead. Mathematics, for them, has neither a distinctive set of premises nor a distinctive subject matter. They say instead that mathematics vigorously and surely carries out inferences from highly general principles. The view has evident affiliations with Constructionism since it assumes that the conclusions of some inferences are more limited forms or continuations of the premises. Constructions, though, are used primarily to make evident what is achieved in other ways. With Axiomatics, Operationalism is also too much occupied with proof, the nature of which it does not stop to examine.

Charles S. Peirce observed that practicing mathematicians are occupied with drawing conclusions, while logicians are interested in breaking down the movement into as many well-defined, intelligible steps as they can. He assumed not only that logicians deal with the very inferences that are carried out by mathematicians but also that the logicians do justice to the nature of those inferences.

Every inference could be credited with a modicum of creativity since it freely moves to a terminus whose nature is determined in part by the way in which it is reached. Yet were it held that everyone is creative whenever he thinks, provision would still have to be made for the distinctive kind of inference that creative mathematicians carry out. The conclusions at which they end are used sooner or later as occasions for lifting the premises to the level of those conclusions. The two are joined there in a new truth with those premises and conclusions having the status of two intertwined components. New creations in mathematics, unlike those elsewhere, can be used to make an advance on the old, for they can be—and often are—joined to what was created before.

Inferences can be part of creativity, but no matter how free and bold, their use does not suffice to turn a person into a creator. Although they can reach what no one has even surmised and can end with conclusions having a determinateness lacking to a prospective outcome, they usually leave their premises behind. Creative mathematicians can and do use what they arrive at to affect what they began with. Unlike other creators, who enable previous achievements to benefit from what is subsequently done, mathematicians creatively produce new truths by bringing the old alongside the new.

Truth is not merely attached to what is mathematically created. It is integral to it. An otherwise distinct, bounded, accepted beginning is therewith given the status of a functioning part of an outcome of which the ending is another part. The truth of a mathematical creation is thus no more like the truth of some statement about a matter of fact than the beauty of a painting is like the beauty sometimes credited to a copy. After a mathematical creation is completed, it will, as other creations do, have all its units coordinated. Achieved in its own way, the outcome of the creative venture will be a single truth realized as an interplay of multiple working units, some of them having more important roles than others. Some roles will be achieved only after one has passed beyond the reach of any commitment, grounded in what has been produced before.

Because what is already achieved makes possible an entry into a higher level of the rational, creative work in mathematics may invite more daring moves than are carried out elsewhere. Whatever use other creations make of what has already been done may be simply repeated along the lines of a commitment grounded in what has been accomplished earlier; creative mathematicians thrust beyond all such commitments.

Mathematicians are masters of inference. The truths that interest them have a great range and hold forever, whether or not they have application in science and daily life—though such application surely is desirable. Unlike the inferences envisaged by the Operationalist view, mathematical inferences are not at the service of deductions; instead, they may penetrate into new levels of a condition already utilized in other mathematical creative acts.

Mathematicians infer, but not by conforming to the structures of known, valid inferences. Those acknowledged and approved structures rarely help one even to understand what mathematicians do, not only because these infer in single, bold steps and do not attend to the stops and connections that logicians distinguish, but also because their inferences end with what gives their premises new roles.

Inference is an act. Properly carried out, it ends with what can be shown to be necessitated by what was accepted at the beginning. If a conclusion is necessary, it can be formally defended. After being detached, it will possess the same kind of truth that the premisses had. It can rarely be anticipated, despite a subsequent proof that it is warranted.

One can take many routes and reach a conclusion identical with what is formally required without thereby being rightly accused of committing a logical blunder. Creators follow such independent courses; inventors do so as well, their discoveries also being made by following no previously known route. After conclusions have been arrived at by either, they can usually be exhibited as necessary.

Given "Horses fly" and "If horses fly, snow falls in the tropics," it is right to conclude that snow falls in the tropics—if one accepts that premiss and that implication. Nor need one get to the conclusion straightaway. It makes no difference how the act of inference twists and turns so long as it arrives at a conclusion endorsed by a logically certifiable rule.

There are formally certified inferences ending in what is more general than their premisses. Those conclusions share the same kind of truth with the premiss, having in fact inherited it. Despite their greater generality and their being on a higher level, able to encompass the initial premiss and other items, and despite the fact that they possess the same kind of truth, the conclusions are not identifiable with the kind of results achieved by creative mathematicians. Not only do the mathematical outcomes not need to have a greater generality than their premisses, their conclusions both allow the premisses to remain as and where they were and may also give them positions alongside the conclusions.

Creative mathematical inferences, though they proceed hierarchically, end with premiss and conclusions coordinated. Zero is a number alongside the very numbers that served as the beginning of the act of creating it, giving them a new status. *Number* is a general term having a constantly increasing richness.

The Operationalist view offers a good account of what mathematicians do when not creative, allowing as it does for proofs whose results could be produced by machines. It also accords well with the fact that most mathematicians unreflecting-ly and with surety arrive at sound conclusions. It should be noted, however, that creative mathematicians also carry out inferences different in kind from those used by other mathematicians, or by anyone else, and do so in areas distinguishable from those which concern the others.

6. As Ludwig Wittgenstein forcefully stated, a relativistic *Conventionalism* de-nies that mathematical claims have an intrinsic truth, supposing instead that they reflect what a number of people, or a society of them, agree is a sound outcome. The view explicitly allows for any number of opposing claims to express what is acceptable, one being no more justified than any other. Explicitly opposed to For-malism, such a Conventionalism limits itself to what happens to be endorsed and not to what is certified by some formal rule expressed in a canonical form. Some possible group, it is held, could claim that the number of counted items was prop-erly designated as "six" where we would say "five." To any protest that we might make, those in the other group could respond that we had unwarrantedly omitted something, while we would reply that they had unwarrantedly added another nu-meral when acknowledging or reporting the result of their counting. This counting, and presumably all other mathematically grounded operations, would, on this view, follow a course and end with whatever some community settled on.

Putting aside the fact that Conventionalism itself tacitly assumes a supposedly nonconventional position neutral to both sides, so as to be able to credit them with equal validity, and putting aside the fact that it pays no attention to creative mathe-matics, it has nothing to say about the truth that the same mathematical results have been accepted by members of diverse groups and that the results have been effective and illuminatingly incorporated into scientific accounts confirmed in many different places and times.

Different communities carry out different practices. A process of counting (or measuring) is inescapably tied to activities that could be subject to multiple irrele-vant, nonmathematical requirements. Other groups may not impose the same ones that ours do, but that variance need not affect what is being subjected to the different practical qualifications. Nor is mathematics a "language"; it is a congeries of truths, some of which are created.

Mathematicians form a limited community in which they create what is always true and for everyone. That theirs or any other practice is endorsed by a community does not and could not justify it. If it did, one would be able, in similar ways, to justify the cannibalism of a group of warriors living in an approving tribe. Practices are not justified merely because they are accepted. Only if an agreement on the way one counts sufficed to legitimize the practice, could the practices of one group be taken to be as good as any other's. We rightly criticize deviations as mistaken because we can justify the way we count.

A relativistic Conventionalist view of mathematics does not allow for universal necessities, prescriptions, proofs, or truths. Still, better than the preceding views, it can allow a place for creative activity and its results. These results, though, will be accorded no other dignity than that which a community ascribes. Implicit in this view is the idea that mathematics is necessarily applied and that any mode of application is satisfactory so long as a number agree to engage in it and accept the outcome. The necessity, prescriptiveness, and creativity of mathematics is thereby bypassed for what has no warrant in fact.

Relativistic Conventionalism makes several assumptions that it neither notices nor questions. It takes some others, identified as human beings like us, to be members of a group in the same sense that we are members of our own group, and not aberrant individuals who happen for the moment to be in some accord. The fact that other groups—astrologers, cabalists, and numerologists—use numerals in other ways is not considered. It also assumes that the members of an acknowledged group do not try to mislead; that they are in fact counting and not playing a game or carrying out a ritual; that the numerals used in their presumed counting are allied to numbers used in mathematics; that the acts then carried out are similar to those carried out everywhere; and that no one errs. It is difficult to see how these conceivable occurrences could be known *not* to occur if all one could know is what happened to be agreed on. Could all of them be known or even assumed, so could the correctness or incorrectness of some way of expressing the outcome of any counting.

If these issues were dealt with satisfactorily, one would still be left with the prospect that counting by the members of one group might come to results different from those reached by ours and that their practice might be as legitimate as our own. That would still allow for some in either group to create what is true everywhere and always, whether or not it was acknowledged or misconstrued by others. Practice enjoys no absolute role, beyond all questioning; it can be assessed and ordered in terms of its difficulty and congeniality and the provision of reliable means for comparing aggregates.

If all agreements, whatever the time and whatever the group, however reached, and for whatever purpose, are equally valid, the claim that this is so must be set alongside no others; otherwise, the most it could properly maintain is that it is no worse than some other claim, including its own denial. Conventionalism is an absolutism placed beyond all justification.

Aristotle found no need for zero or one in his arithmetic. We do, for we have a warrant for acknowledging numbers not reachable by counting. Aristotle was mistaken; since he was no Conventionalist, he would presumably have admitted his error on becoming acquainted with the range of natural numbers.

7. An *empirical approach* to mathematics was defended by John Stuart Mill with a vigor and disregard of consequences few others rival. He held that mathematical truths are derived from experiences with numbers in actual countings and measurings. Contrary to relativistic Conventionalists, he also supposed that counting and measuring were carried out by all people in the same way. Why, he did not say. Nor did he account for creations which had no evident application or for those not derivable from the practices of either ordinary or scientific men.

Creative work in mathematics does not happen at random. Previous achievements set the stage for work in particular areas and the use of particular methods and procedures. Today, mathematicians often respond to the pressures or needs of scientific theory and practice, technology, and practical life. They need not so respond, and sometimes do not. Conceivably, they might not have even thought of any measuring or counting.

Initially, as the term itself makes evident, geometry was limited to measurements of land. Elementary arithmetic arose even earlier, apparently to record the outcome of a counting of weapons, cattle, children, and other familiar items of daily life. Fingers and toes provide a constant base for comparing various pluralities. Being always available, the fingers and toes are evidently able to be brought into play on many occasions and can therefore offer eminently desirable, constant units in terms of which one can readily characterize and compare different aggregates.

Numerals are not numbers but standard designators in terms of which the magnitudes of various pluralities are conventionally expressed. Unlike numerals, numbers have no necessary reference to any plurality. There is only a single number seven, or twelve, or eighty-six. When it is said that seven is two more than five, the "two" uses a numeral to mark the number of steps needed to go from five to seven in the natural number series. When the numbers are counted, numerals are used in the way they are when cats, pauses, clouds, or commas are counted. When, then, it is said that "one" is added to "one," or "seven" to "eighty-six," the most that could be legitimately claimed is that it is necessary to make a specific number of moves to get from the one to the other.

The acknowledgment of numbers as distinct from numerals is endorsed by Platonism. It is also acceptable to the next two, and perhaps the fourth and fifth, of the examined views. There is no necessity, though, even in pure mathematics, to take only numbers to be unduplicable and forever the same; there are also known, nonnumerical mathematical units worthy of whatever status numbers may have.

Well before a plurality of numbers was explicitly produced as a consequence of the use of Giuseppe Peano's postulates, grounding a derivation of the natural numbers, some numbers were widely known. The Pythagoreans divided them into even and odd and described them as having essentially light and dark sides. For them, numbers were neither closed off in some ethereal realm nor identified with numerals. It is often said that the Pythagoreans discovered that the diagonal of a unit square could not be expressed as a the ratio of two whole numbers, as though all they needed was a change in their established procedures to be able to discern what was already present. If so, they, and presumably all other mathematicians, would not be creators.

Empiricism supposes no mathematical truths to have been created. With Platonism, it supposes all to have been discovered, with a multitude of others perhaps waiting for later discoverers. Great discoveries are not to be denigrated, but they are also to be sharply distinguished from creations. Pythagoreans created irrationals in their effort to solve an otherwise intractable problem. Those numbers did not exist before the Pythagoreans created them. Their creations were as daring and startling as those produced later; they required the same abilities that great mathematicians have always exhibited. Even such currently familiar numbers as zero and one were once the product of creative acts that subsequent mathematicians took into consideration when they went on to produce still other creations.

Empirical approaches to mathematics make provision for the fact that mathematics does begin by taking account of various practical needs, but they then suppose that it is forever occupied with that task. Yet irrationals, non-Euclidean and other geometries, the calculus, topology, and transfinite numbers are informative and precisely formulable. They do not need to be shown to be of use in empirical, scientific, or other practices before they can function as parts of mathematics.

Not all of mathematics today has an application. What does not have an application does not lose its truth if one is found. Applications of mathematics presuppose that what is already at hand is respectable. This is together with what is not or never was used or usable.

Although it was once the startling creation of a great mathematician, the Pythagorean theorem is now part of elementary geometry, intelligible to a bright child. Today we readily speak of mathematical points, lines, planes, square roots, and imaginaries, no one of which is the object of everyday information or experience. Many youngsters manipulate them easily. Some outcomes of mathematical creativity—Fermat's Last Theorem and Goldbach's Conjecture—are not now known to be true or false, but one thing about them is certain: they were not reached by drawing diagrams, relating quantities, formulating tautologies, or deriving theorems from postulates or axioms.

Composers sometimes create in response to the limitations discerned in performances, using those flaws to provide a base which their creations are to transcend and transform. In a similar way, mathematicians create by using previous achievements as occasions or provocations. Previously reached results are joined to what is newly created, within the compass of a single, unifying truth. This truth is forged in an ultimate, rational condition. That condition is not frozen, filled with units. It is an endlessly leveled irreducible; it can be instantiated in actual occurrences, reached through the use of its instantiations as evidences, and subdivided in creative acts.

Most accounts of mathematics ignore the entry of creative mathematicians into the conditioning rational, while a formalism that acknowledges that condition supposes it to be already subdivided into a plurality of distinct units. Not remote, the rational condition is not arrived at by going through a series of steps until the daily world is left behind. Nor are any distinct items in it known by a pure intellect. Nor is it where actual objects exist, confined within boundaries separating them from one another.

Irreducible and insistent, like other ultimates, the rational can be specialized. Joined to specializations of the Dunamis, it constitutes fields, regions, relations, and units. Operating under the aegis of an ideal truth, it helps constitute the units that mathematicians create.

Like other creators, mathematicians avoid a preoccupation with daily affairs and their constraints. As other creators do, they retreat within themselves to be free of established habits so that they can attend to and make use of what is available. There, they may mark off units and examine some of them, all the while that these units continue to be together in a single, unifying truth, as realized thus far.

Mathematical truth is an excellence which, like beauty, nobility, glory, and justice, must be achieved by introducing determinations in an ideal prospect, thereby converting this into a realized excellence embracing otherwise distinct parts. The final truth with which mathematicians are concerned, though aimed at all along, is an ideal rarely kept in clear focus. Like other ideals, it is gradually transformed from an indeterminate, privately faced prospect into a unification of what was once achieved and what is newly distinguished. The truth that is achieved in mathematics at any given stage is different in nature and scope from what it has been and will be in the history of mathematical creation. Over the course of its realization it will take on different forms at different times. As an ideal, to be made fully determinate over all that is produced, the truth that creative mathematicians seek to realize will allow for the acknowledgment of the whole of mathematics as a single work. Mathematics must therefore be recognized as having a threefold truth: a first, characterizing its distinct achievements; a second, the whole of mathematics so far produced; and a third, the whole of mathematics as not yet completed.

Much as it takes time to free the mind, will, desire, and other epitomizations of privacy from the other powers with which they so often unreflectingly merge and by which they are modified, so it requires time for a creative mathematician to use and unite the primary, irreducible factors so that they supplement one another. If a mathematician were to remain at his center, he could perhaps be at peace, but more likely than not he would be empty of thought, perhaps without desire, selfless, ready to be flooded by the Dunamis, but not yet ready to create a truth. Those who claim that one must not only attain to but remain at some such state if one is to create, or even to shoot an arrow properly, need to show why anyone who succeeded in reaching that state would make the effort to create anything, or to shoot an arrow. Presumably, he would have already arrived at a position where nothing else would have any appeal.

The privacy of a human being is not a closed-off nucleus. A person is able not only to affect its different epitomizations but can also open himself to the other needed factors and to join himself to specialized uses of them. No matter now self-controlled a man might be, he is inescapably affected by his past; thus, he will at first place more emphasis on one factor than on others. There is therefore some validity in the claim that his experiences and envisioned prospects determine what and how he will create, and then in one field rather than another. However, there is a considerable difference between the claim that one does not know everything about the production of a created work and the claim that it is altogether unfathomable or irrational. Once it is known what the different conditions are like, that they have an indefinite number of distinguishable levels, that an apparently endless number of layers and distinguishable in the Dunamis, that privacies and individuals are never fully penetrable, and that excellence permits of an endless number of determinations, one can readily see that there can be no end to the creations possible in mathematics—or in art.

A creative mathematician arrives at his starting point from an individual way of living in the daily world. As other creators do, he specializes and uses the ultimate factors available; unlike those others, he is concerned with working within the confines of the rational, no matter where he lives or when. The outcome, if excellent, will have no geographic taint, though it may be expressed in a distinctive notation and conceivably be translatable into some limited, commonly used, daily language.

It is surely desirable to achieve serenity before being caught up in any venture. One can even imagine a kind of primal serenity at which every creator should arrive before engaging in a creative act. There is, however, no need for this serenity; creators, when they penetrate deep into themselves and then act with maximum freedom, immediately commit themselves to realize a distinctive excellence. The relaxation precedes the creative act; like the hesitation of a pole-vaulter or a high-diver, it is part of a moment of concentration preliminary to a daring move.

Mathematical creations, like those of artists and others, make use of ultimates having a reality apart from their users. Those ultimates, in specialized forms, are constituents of whatever occurs or is made. The Dunamis is also a real and effective ultimate, not a mere receptacle or irrational surge; specializations of both it and the conditions are produced by all creators. Without the Dunamis there would be no distances between mathematical units, no interweaving of beginnings and endings of its theorems. The informative, "synthetic" nature of mathematical expressions is due mainly to it.

Mathematics is not an art; beauty is not its objective. It makes no demands on sensibility and does not concern itself with making use of a primal voluminosity, even when concerned with creating new geometric truths. Because of its acceptance of previous achievements, its history, though dotted with extraordinary creations, is more unified than other histories are. Creative mathematicians are not only chiefly directed toward a primal rational condition; they use it to adopt and redefine what has been previously created.

Mathematics never loses contact with its first creations. Those creations may continue to be used apart from what is done later. The rational numbers can be redefined or reexpressed as ordered pairs of natural numbers, the real numbers as ordered pairs of rationals (backed by Dedekindian cuts), and so on. Allowance may also be made for the production of new theorems and proofs on the old level, ignoring the fact that the old has been joined to the new.

When mathematicians arrive at results seemingly opposed to what was achieved previously, they in effect point up the limits within which earlier results were obtained. Non-Euclidean geometry does not show that Euclidean geometry is in error but only that it is one of a number of ways in which a primal, voluminous spatiality can be articulated. Any one of the geometries, or a number of them together, might serve as an occasion to formulate another geometry, with the earlier ones treated as specializations of, variations on, or additions to it.

Each generation of mathematicians speaks as though it has finally probed the depths of the rational and implicitly supposes that its successors will be able to go no further. It often seems incredible that one might use their achievements as an occasion for producing fresh creations, giving a new import to the old. This reaction is understandable, for not only is it impossible to envisage what subsequent creators might produce, but it is also reasonable for a creator to suppose that, for the first time, he has opened up an area in which all other creations would be placed alongside his. The old and new can be found alongside one another. The old, without losing its established position, has been brought to a new level to become part of a single mathematical truth beyond which others can be created on other, more remote levels of the rational.

A number of creative, baroque musicians together made baroque a well-defined musical style. So, it might be said, creative algebraists contribute to a single algebra having a number of subfields. Nothing is amiss in taking this stance. It also accords with the way algebraists and historians of the subject speak of the field. The attempt, though, should not be permitted to obscure the significant difference that separates creations on one level of the rational from those beginning where these end and going on to something else. While it is possible to understand the creations of a great modern artist without having a knowledge of the past, one cannot understand the creations of a great modern mathematician without recognizing that he accepts previous creations as determining what he will use and that he will eventually treat them as coordinate with what he creates.

Later mathematicians create with the help of the rational as it has been reached on a lower level. Past achievements are then brought up to the level newly conquered and are thereby able to benefit from a realization of a truth pertinent to all of the mathematics produced so far. A formalism or Platonism that tried to accommodate that result would have to allow for an apparently endless number of distinct levels in its eternity, the mastery of any one of which would make possible the discernment of still others, with a consequent enrichment of the old by its being set alongside them. A formal hierarchy and a Platonic ladder would then not only have distinct steps, but each of the later ones would somehow pull a preceding one up to where it is.

Both artists and mathematicians are able to produce combinations of ultimates which, while having little value by themselves, may enhance one another inside the creations. The artists may make use of some combinations of little or no importance to produce excellent works in which some items function primarily as contrastive units. Mathematicians begin and end with units having the same status; that a circle cannot be squared is for them not a nobler, surer, different kind of truth from that expressed by $1 + 1 = 2$ or from one expressed in the statement that the sum of the angles of a triangle in some non-Euclidean geometry is less or more than that of a Euclidean triangle.

Because mathematicians begin with what their forerunners have established, they can be part of a single community of thinkers, stretching over a long time and passing beyond all political or social boundaries. Artists do not belong to anything similar, although limited numbers of them do form schools or develop characteristic ways of working, using particular themes or adopting a common program. We can set all their works within a single domain, or in an epoch of which they may know little or nothing. Mathematicians, in contrast, know and accept what has been previously achieved.

"Zero is a number" has a meaning today that it did not have when first created. "Number" here, instead of being an idle universal under which particular numbers fall, provides a way of presenting the meaning of a single mathematical truth as unifying and being exhausted in a plurality of more particular truths. Since at each stage of mathematics "number" refers to a new unification, the expression "Zero is a number" must be understood as shorthand for "Zero is a number which others join on a common level of the rational."

Each number has a fixed nature, as does any variable having a well-defined range. It can thus be a value for a higher-order variable. This variable is a surrogate for "number" itself, and like it ranges over a plurality of unspecified numbers. This sort of plurality is suggested when, for example, one states some such arithmetic law as that of distribution. At all times, what is affirmed in mathematics are truths at once universal, formally expressible, and able to have either variables or constants as values.

What is true of the numbers that interest mathematicians is true also of the figures, structures, operations, relations, descriptions, and other matters that concern them. Whether or not all of these can be restated in terms of some use of numbers, they are reached and studied as having their own natures. Like the numbers, they can be concluded to on distinctive levels of the rational and serve to bring to the newly entered level what has been accepted previously. Since mathematics pulls its history into every advance, what is now accepted serves to enrich what has been achieved in previous creative acts.

Once zero was created, it gave the known numbers a new, coordinate status, to be taken as numbers in another, richer sense. Only after zero, which was perhaps initially conceived as the result of moving back a designated number of steps from some actual number, was identified as being a number were the already accepted numbers able to achieve the new status of being numbers coordinate with it. Numbers, nevertheless, can still be understood today as they were before zero was created, for their entry into a higher level does not deny that they are also on a lower.

The Hierarchy of Creations

The creative activity of mathematicians today does not differ in principle from that of their predecessors. Like them, they, too, know that there is only one number twelve and only one mathematical straight line, for they enter a realm where the number and line have been created and still remain. The numbers one, two . . . twelve, like a line without breadth, are all singulars, demarcated and located in the rational, where they were initially created.

The rational is a condition. Like other conditions, it is a distinguishable aspect of what occurs. Because it is not confined to these, no one can control it. Like all other conditions it is irreducible but can be utilized in limited forms. Without parts, independent in being and operation, the rational condition can be entered into by a creative mathematician in a distinctive way on a level not previously reached.

Counting and picturing are practical acts. Creative work in mathematics neither pictures nor does anything practical in a similar sense. When the results of mathematical creativity are said to do so, perhaps when applied or used, they are confused with substitutes, which alone can be connected with what is external to mathematics. No number plays a part in any practical act, though the study of some numbers may help us find our way about in physics or in daily life, where they mark out consequences, properties, and relations that might otherwise be missed or misconstrued.

The first mathematical creator obviously used numerals in a form available in daily life; perhaps he deliberately produced them to facilitate easy communication. Initially related to actual items, they enabled him, in any case, to remain oriented toward the familiar. In his first creative act, these numerals were presumably used to establish positions from which he could enter into a low level of the rational and there, aided by the Dunamis, create a mathematical truth. A notation was then needed to help him fix his results and to enable others to know of his achievement.

Only the first entrance into mathematics leaves its beginning entirely behind. What is left behind might be used as numerals, at once affecting what was created and enabling a mathematical creation to be related to what is outside mathematics. Whether so used or not, numerals are at best materials, not intelligibles produced by entering a level of the rational in a creative act.

If there is an earlier creation, now on a lower level, it will be joined to the new creation on a higher level to become a part of a single body of truth. Once zero, the square root of minus one, or the like is created, a mathematician may leave to others the task of showing that it could be necessarily derived from established mathematical truths. Or he might, as Pierre Fermat did, claim that he had reached a new truth without showing that he had done so.

Whatever he does, as long as a mathematician is occupied with creating, he will end with truths carved out of a distinctive level of the rational. The more detached he is from bodily involvements and particular tendencies of his privacy, the more he will be able to confront, specialize, and explore the rational and be ready to create on a new level of it.

What mathematicians are able to do today would not have been possible without the work of their predecessors; in turn, they make it possible for their successors to create on higher levels of the same condition. Since what the later creators produce lifts up the previous achievements to that level, at any given time all mathematical achievements will be together as so many coordinated truths while still able to function as they had on their original levels. The reverse is also possible. By being freed from confinement to rough-hewn practices and to well-stated laws of nature, theoretical results are able to be brought to bear on technology. Theoretical science, by boldly utilizing mathematics in formulating theorems pertinent to experiments, carries out the process more widely and in ways having both theoretical and practical justification.

Scientific and practical applications of mathematics are special cases of the applicability of mathematical creations to the levels where they began and obtained needed fixities. The integrity of the creations is not thereby compromised. A further step is taken when mathematical expressions are freed from a concern with what science suggests or needs and the result is fixed in an established notation precisely used, making possible a better formulation of what was done earlier.

Just as speech can have its words freshly disjoined and joined by one who reads them, so mathematical creations can be dissected and codified by those who seek to reexpress them in logically endorsed forms. None of the formal devices or externally imposed methods enters into the regions where the creations are produced. Formalized proofs and codifications await the creative activity of mathematicians and, at some remove, offer frozen reconstructions of the process. Mathematical logicians presuppose the achievements of mathematics, tailoring their formulations to express what has already been created. Usually the logicians hold that their affirmations fully capture what was achieved and that they present the achievements in more general, precise, and communicable forms. Rarely do they refer to them as having been created; rarely do they speak of anything other than numbers and combinations of them. When they restate what has been done, they make no provision for future creations. What they present lacks the vitality of creative mathematics, the series of radical entrances that are made into level after level of the rational, and the initial as well as the continued rootage of the mathematical creations in daily experience. Logical formulations either keep too close to what is daily said and done or move too far away from it to be able to recapture the freshness of creations or the historicity of mathematical work. Mathematicians usually ignore them.

The numbers which mathematicians acknowledge are all on the same level of the rational, with segments of them also present on previously entered levels, where they are able to fixate what is subsequently achieved. All the natural numbers are unified on one level of the conditioning rational; with each new mathematical creation they become part of a new unification while still able to be distinct units as well as components in former unifications. Every number acquires additional meanings on being joined with what is created on new levels of the rational. The number is thereupon able to be part of a new base from which a mathematician may move to a still deeper level of the rational in a new creative act. On each level of the rational, all natural numbers will be present, unified with other items there, but they will also remain on previous levels and there provide sustainers for whatever is thereupon created.

We speak of subtracting numbers from one another, and even of subtracting a number from itself, but that surely is impossible. There is only one number six, with levels on levels of meaning. At its thinnest, six is directly attached to an accepted numeral; at its most ample, it is unified with what is on the most advanced position mathematicians have been able to reach.

Geometers have long maintained that their points, lines, planes, triangles, and circles are "ideal" entities, perhaps existing in a pure space. It is unclear, though, whether it is being supposed that the crude observations of daily life are thereupon refined or whether all that is done is to distinguish the members of some supposed abstract realm from one another. Both views have been held. They should be— separately and together. Like numbers, lines and the other geometric entities are created products. Like numbers, they, too, are fixed, sometimes by notations, sometimes in diagrams. Denied these fixations, they would have to be recreated again and again. Denied the status of a creation, they would have to be tied to particular locations and usages, making impossible any study of a geometry in which a point has no particular magnitude, a line no particular width, and a triangle no particular size.

When numbers are dealt with from the position of new creations, the stages traversed before arriving at the newly attained position are easily overlooked. The fresh creations give the old ones features and roles they did not have before. Still, no matter what functions numbers take on, they also continue to be what they were. Somewhat like a piece of land that also has the status of property, an initial meaning is marked off from, at the same time that is encompassed in, another.

Creations in mathematics, like those elsewhere, require one to retreat far enough into one's privacy to make it possible to avoid habitual paths and conventional routes and to be able to focus on an ideal. Previous achievements must be bracketed to make possible a direct occupation with what is reached at another level. Since the rational, like other ultimate conditions, has a reality of its own, it will never be completely probed. Mathematical creativity, as a consequence, need never come to an end. Axiom systems and formal accounts of mathematics close their books too soon.

All types of creative ventures have futures, contradicting the claim that there is nothing more to be created. That does not stop a few in every epoch from declaring that some venture has come to an end. Everyone, in effect, is then asked to avoid entering into new levels, though these levels are no less available than the one now occupied was to those who had been on a lower.

Reports of creations yield what cannot be identified with them; they are desirable so far as they serve to communicate what has been creatively produced. Not substitutes for creations, they still have value. If one takes them to be adequate representations, a discovery of their inadequacies could lead to a nihilism in which they were both rightly criticized and wrongly identified with what deserves to be cherished.

Formalists not only neglect the role that the Dunamis plays in a creation but also overlook its presence in their own procedures. Where mathematicians move away from their premisses to arrive at conclusions held apart from them, Formalists keep antecedent and consequent joined and, so far, are unable to arrive at anything.

Inferences would be indistinguishable from surmises and conjectures were they not formally justifiable. Anyone who provided such a justification for what is done in mathematics would do something similar to what is done in the arts by critics, historians, analysts, and copyists. The fact is obscured because so many can make a successful use of notated mathematical results in daily practice. Something similar would occur in music if most of us could readily read the notations of a composer and, with teachers of composition, use them as counters in our conversations and practice.

"If John loves Mary but Mary hates John" can be formally stated as "If John loves Mary and Mary non-loves John." The bitter meaning of the "but" is here abstracted from, and hate is denied its characteristic bite. At the very least, one should read the statement by passing, without regard for rules, from one to the other expression, perhaps within the compass of some such supposition as that John and Mary are mismatched. John may love Mary because she hates him, because he thinks he ought to do so despite her hatred, or because he takes her hatred to be an attractive quirk, and so on, without apparent end. Where an inference comes to a conclusion, the described situation is properly read backward and forward, with different components treated as coloring one another.

One interested in formulating rules and operating in accord with them will properly understand most and perhaps all expressions as having a plurality of meanings, each of which could be given a formal expression, marking out the limits and path through which one might move from one end to the other. Socrates dies not because all men are mortal and because he is a man, but because he is a mortal who drinks the hemlock. The formalization of this occurrence as death, instancing a mortality to which all are subject, abstracts from the actual interinvolvement of the components.

No less than painting, mathematics must be lived in if its achievements are not to be rigidified or trivialized, with abstractions replacing internally constituted unifications of what has been achieved. Yet in effect, such abstractions are what is dealt with when numbers or other mathematical entities are used as though they were all present on only one, presumably readily reached level of the rational. Inferences are not creative acts. They surely could not be if all they did was to replace a premiss with a conclusion. "Inference" would then be what Gilbert Ryle calls an "achievement word." It refers, as he did not seem to allow, to an activity having a necessitated conclusion.

It is not implausible to say that there are four numbers between two and seven and that one can progress from the two to the seven by going through five separate steps. Those steps are taken on a level of the rational where the initial two and the terminal seven are already specified. The two and the seven, and any of the numbers in between, are not tied to the world. They cannot be duplicated. When these or any other numbers are counted, they are treated as correlatives of whatever numerals one is using. The best numerals are those used to count what is on any level of the rational, thereby permitting a stable distinguishing of items on any level that one's creativity might utilize.

Were numerals numbers, they would have to be credited with new meanings and roles as one progressed creatively in the use of the rational. Once the nature and role of numbers are recognized, the mathematical hierarchy of creative achievements can be dealt with by making use of the same set of numerals. One will then act far more boldly than is done when one uses some system of notation to record the greatest of musical compositions or to mark out positions and intervals in paintings or words in poems.

So far as anything is used as a numeral, it is treated as a mere particular. Although each numeral is distinct from what it is related to, it does not, as material used in the arts does, make a difference to what it enables one to distinguish. Since it provides no apparent graining, it makes little difference whether it is supposed to occupy the lowest level of the mathematical hierarchy or to exist outside it altogether. If the first, a numeral will be treated as though it were outside; if the second, it will add an inert part to the numbers it enables one to count.

Since what is achieved on one level of the rational is retained, mathematics, it has already been suggested, could be said to be the most historical of subjects, never letting go of what has been mastered in the past while remaining occupied with the mastery of what has not been acknowledged before. It is not a history, of course. A history attends only to what has occurred. Since nothing in mathematics need be taken to produce something existent, mathematics can also be said to be the most nonhistorical of enterprises, despite the fact that, more than most, it deliberately builds on what has been previously achieved.

What holds of mathematics here holds also of theoretical science, though in a more limited degree. Achievements of the past in mechanics, optics, and other disciplines both continue to be accepted and are given additional meanings over the course of time. The sciences also formulate some theories in the light of what mathematicians have made available. Again and again they deal with occurrences not envisaged earlier. So far as the outlook of the scientific community changes in the light of great scientific achievements, its history will, of course, be exhibited mainly in a series of cataclysmic, revolutionary changes, each beginning a new period of comparative calm. There, as Thomas S. Kuhn observes, many will be content to work within the limits set by a great creator. Since no scientific epoch can be understood if its use of established techniques, effective instruments, and accepted ways of measuring and recording are ignored, the sciences must be said to be historically minded in still another sense.

Unlike what is done in mathematics, what the sciences affirm is fixed by scientific claims made in some epoch. While mathematical truths are dateless, though created at particular times and dependent on what was created before, scientific claims are dated, though presented as permanent truths about an abiding cosmos.

The introduction of arabic numerals and zero marked sharp advances in mathematics. On the whole, though, mathematics has made only a limited number of signal moves, and then sometimes only after long intervals. The changes in religions, societies, states, language, and cosmology are at times more radical and sometimes more sudden. None encompasses, any more than mathematics does, all that there is; none has come to the end of its possible achievements. Unless we arbitrarily suppose that we have arrived at the end of all mathematical creative work, the present stage of mathematics should be expected to give way to another, using the results of the most advanced achievements today to provide the appropriate starting points.

What is used to fix or frame anything has a being and course of its own. Effective use of it requires that it serve the purposes of what differs from it. If it did not also continue to function in its own way, it would cease to be of much value; at best it would be usable again and again, neither affected by nor affecting what it serves. Viewed historically—as it can be, as surely as it can be studied sociologically or linguistically—mathematics brings earlier achievements alongside later ones. Yet, since mathematics embraces a series of mathematical creations in a single whole of coordinated truths, it is to be viewed and used at any given time as though it embraced just a single unification of coordinated truths.

Great creators in mathematics are often quite young: Evariste Galois, after a brilliant five-year career, was dead at twenty-one! Many are singularly inexperienced, quite innocent of what occurs or is required in the daily world, or are much involved in established customs and language. More readily than other creators, young mathematicians confront primary factors with directness and innocence. Some great composers, such as Mozart, and some great poets, such as Keats, seem to approximate them, but these other creators are apparently never as free as the mathematicians are from the strong emotions that frequently accompany other types of creative activity.

No one seems to remain so deep within his privacy and for as long a time as mathematicians do. Even great chess players, many of whom have dispositions somewhat akin to mathematicians and who may flourish when quite young—at fourteen Bobby Fischer was the United States chess champion and an international grandmaster—do not appear able to get to the positions from which mathematicians begin their creative ventures. This failure is due in good part to the fact that the task to which they devote themselves is too often confined by well-established rules, a bounded field of operations, and the contests in which they engage. If chess players began their work by first moving back deep within their privacies, they would still not act with the freedom that creative mathematicians express—nor need they, since they deal only with particular problems and devise only particular solutions. Mathematicians open new fields of investigation, and the solutions they provide, even when answering particular questions, transform the entire enterprise.

Variables, Sets, and Classes

Some current students of the foundations of mathematics treat mathematics as a single, unified, already completed field, best expressed as a plurality of interlocked sets. Their next great advance, most likely, will use set theory in the way that it used numbers, number theory had used arithmetic and geometry, arithmetic and geometry had used controlled practice, and practice had used the roughshod occurrences of daily life. These sets are composed of variables ranging over values instancing those variables. Since the variables can apply to all, some, one, or no items, an understanding of sets presupposes an understanding of the nature of variables, values, their relation to one another, and the kinds of restrictions that "all," "some," "one," and "no" introduce. A technical treatise of some length would be needed to do justice to all the issues. Fortunately for present purposes, it will be enough to examine what helps clarify the nature of mathematical creations. This task will require focusing on a number of questions having counterparts in other creative ventures, though not always of major importance in these.

Were there a final level of a condition, and were this level ever to be reached, the mathematical variable used in expressing the fact would range over everything previously produced on all other levels of the rational. If there were not some variable having that range, no variable could encompass all of mathematics. Paradoxically, also, were it not possible for a variable to range over all others, we could not say that there could be no variable having such a range.

A variable is a one for a many, of limited scope and different from its values. Were those values other variables, they would still be distinct from the variable that ranges over them. If it were held that there was a variable for all variables which did not have themselves as values, one would be caught in the paradox Bertrand Russell made famous: that variable neither could nor could not have itself as value. If it did, it would violate the condition that the values are variables which do not have themselves as values. If it did not, it would conform to the demand that it not have itself as value and would then be a value of itself. No such difficulty would arise if a variable existed only for variables which have themselves as values, though that variable would still have to be distinguished from itself in the role of a value.

There can be no warranted bracketing off of a one from every many whatsoever, since there would then be a one that could not be reached and no many to which a single reference could be made. Unless a one and a many are recognized to be contrastive, each presupposing the other, there will be irresolvable paradoxes. The one and the many presuppose one another; the fundamental fact is the two yoked together, as correlative limits of a one/many. The one and many, as distinct from one another, are mutually referential limits of that one/many.

Creations are always ones, though complex. They can be manys only so far as their units are bounded off from one another. It is as having units so bounded that mathematical achievements provide occasions and bases for subsequent creations. Those creations are radically singular but need the help of what was left behind in order to be both articulated and established. Consequently, when we deal with sets in terms of which the numbers may be expressed, ones, not manys, will have to be used. Those ones cannot be completely freed from a relation to the many units over which they range.

For some set theorists, mathematics has reached the limit of its movement into the rational. What is there, they suppose, is expressible in terms of a one for a many of any kind. Five difficulties block the way to that claim. All have to be overcome if the nature of a set is to be fully understood.

(1) There might be only one item able to provide a value for a variable, thereby denying the variable its "many"; (2) there might be only propositional functions, and thus no items which, in fact or in principle, could be pertinent to the one; (3) what was subject to the "one for . . ." might be unintelligible; (4) the "one for . . ." might be so indeterminate that it was prevented from uniting with a many, thereby apparently requiring a reference to another "one for," and so on without end; (5) the Russell paradox would be reinstated if a set were referred to as being a member of itself and could encompass what could not be a member of itself.

1. There might be only a single unit value. If so, there would then be no many for a one unless that unit could be referred to again and again. If each reference

marked off a distinct item, the single unit would so far be dealt with not only as apart from the one but as a many for that one, contrary to the hypothesis. The one would be a one for a many while continuing to be a one without a many.

Were a supposed single unit value a number, it would be the correlate of the variable "number." In that guise, it could be referred to again and again as "a number," for it would be a unit with other units, all of them set over against the one "number." The one "number" that had it as a referent would apply to it as "*a* number" and thus as a unit among many others.

"A number" and "this number" refer to units. Those units are in a set only if they are already ones in a plurality of possible numbers. Were it just a unit, a number would still be a member of a possible plurality of numbers, its status as a correlative of a one having been assured by its already having been characterized as "a number." Because it is designative as a unit for the variable "number" and therefore able to be referred to as a unit in multiple ways from other positions, it can provide a many for a one. Even if there were only a single unit, therefore, a set can have the status of one for many unit values.

2. When preceded by "some," "all," or "no," the *x* in "*x* is a number" is credited with an independent status as a value. It is, so far, a many, able to be distinguished without being subdivided. Symbolic logicians today use "all" to refer to such an undivided many and therefore do not allow for the derivation of "some" from it. This approach requires them to deny that "Some hippogriffs are fat" follows from "All hippogriffs are fat." If the denial is to be avoided, some such quantifier as "every" should be used to make evident that it is legitimate to deduce "some" from "all," not only (as Aristotle saw) when one is referring to classes of real objects but also when referring to classes of imaginary ones.

A propositional function or incomplete expression such as "*x* is a number," instead of being presupposed, is a derivate from a complete expression, such as "2 is a number." Although the propositional function is still to be completed, some other completion precedes it; otherwise, there would be nothing to be referred to as an appropriate filling. The point is obscured if it is supposed that an incomplete expression has a blank in it. The supposed blank provides a place for a distinctive kind of filling. In effect, it presents a completion in a highly general form. The fact that one cannot know, by attending to the blank of a propositional function, just what is to complete it does not show that it allows anything at all to fill it.

We can know that an expression is incomplete because we know what a complete expression is. If this were simply general knowledge, telling us that a blank is to be filled out somehow, the blank would not be a blank-in-that-expression. It is, nevertheless, not a singular blank, for that does not need any filling any more than a pause does. It allows only certain kinds of fillings, limited by what the rest of the expression already contains.

Every assertion is partly completed before being finally completed. It would seem, then, that one might stop before the completion and thereupon produce an incomplete expression that might never be filled out. The remaining place, though, is pertinent to the rest of the assertion. So-called free or incomplete expressions, no matter how exhibited, are all complete expressions presented in general terms, one of which is represented by a blank or by a variable of an unspecified range. Understood to refer to "a certain kind of entity," the blank or variable will help constitute some such complete expression as "a certain kind of entity is a number." Propositional functions have subjects which are types, not particulars or groups of them.

3. Zero is a number. It cannot be properly defined by means of a set having what is self-contradictory as a member, for there is nothing that is self-contradictory. Zero can, however, be taken to be the terminus of an ancestral relation that begins with some already acknowledged number. If it were not also possible to create it in the same way other numbers could be created, or if it could not be expressed through the use of variables and values in the way other numbers are, it would be anomalous. In one sense it is, for the numeral representing it cannot be used in multiplication and division in the ways others can. That, however, does not affect its status as a number, any more than being a prime affects the status of the number eleven.

"There are zero dinosaurs today" is not equivalent with "there are no dinosaurs today." The first assigns a number to the dinosaurs; the other refers to their absence. The distinction is obscured when we say that there are three cats in the room, for then we use "three" as though it refers both to what is a number and to what is present. Recognizing that zero is a number just like any other should make it easier to see that the "three" in "There are three cats" and the "no" in "There are no dinosaurs today" make use of numerals.

When at the outcome of a creative act some mathematician concluded that "zero is a number," he freed mathematics from a limitation characteristic of both the Hebraic and Aristotelian views, which had no place for zero. Yet zero is relatable to other numbers as these are to one another, all the while that it differs from these in somewhat the way in which a point differs from a line. As a number, zero need not be defined in terms of variables and values. A definition of it requires, as Zermelo observed, no more than the affirmation that it is a number.

4. Plotinus, Spinoza, and Leibniz all took an absolute One to be at the beginning of their "chains of being." Could that absolute One be distinguished, it would, together with that from which it was distinguished, be subject to still another one, and so on without end. There is, though, no need to take a one to be apart from everything else. Indeed, we cannot do so without losing the position from which

the one is acknowledged. Whatever one may be realized, whether it be in the form of a unity or a single many, it is always distinct from a supposed, final, absolute One. Mathematicians face an unlimited future in part because there is no such final One for them. They are forever able to use ones having greater and greater ranges. A final, indeterminate one would be outside their reach—as it is outside their concerns.

Anything that can be isolated is subject to a one for it. "One for" characterizes, from a position on a higher level, what is on some lower level of the rational. A known One is always a One of or a One for, and consequently not identifiable with an absolute One. An absolute One could be on no distinguishable level of the rational, for it can never be derived from or subordinated to anything.

5. Russell's attempt to give mathematics the widest possible range ended with a paradox. A variant of it remarks that if the "one for" embraces whatever there is, it would encompass itself, since it, too, is something; if it does not encompass itself, it would, together with other items, be subject to still another one. Either there exists an endless number of ones, none of which could apply to what was on the same or on a higher level, or there is a final One that could not be acknowledged. These alternatives face the same fact. A knowable one is both involved with a many below it and is part of a many above it.

One and many are correlates. Only by being abstracted from their correlative roles can they be set alongside each other. Since there are no correlatives unless there are items to be correlated, the correlatives must be separately maintained. By itself, a one has its own distinctive nature and reality, but from the standpoint of that with which it is joined, it is a correlative, able to be maintained in contradistinction to this other. From a position neutral to them, both the one and the many have the status of limits.

If we begin with the many, it will be with what has a status of its own. Whatever it terminates with will, so far, be "of" it. If what is terminated with also has a status of its own, it will be more than what is being terminated with, more than just an "of." It will, therefore, itself be able to terminate with what is "of" it. A many and a one are correlatives, each "for" and "of" the other.

When it is supposed that a many is a value for a variable one, the one is not yet credited with the status of what could be "for" that many. For the one to have the many as a value, the one must not only have a status of its own but must also be "for" that many. Whatever values there are "for" a variable will make that variable be "of" those values; whatever variable there is "for" some value makes the value be "of" that variable. Variables and values are correlatives, each an "of" and "for" the other.

A variable, and therefore the One, may be "for" different manys, but that will not compromise its status as a correlative for whatever many is accepted as a value. If the One be final and the many encompass all else, they will always be "of" and "for" each other.

This or any other solution to the problem raised by set theory does not interest creative mathematicians. What they want to do is to create new truths. Although a creative mathematician today, unlike creators in other areas, works from a base that his predecessors mastered, he also acts as freely as they did and other creators do. He may also benefit from what his predecessors achieved, beginning from positions and using factors that they did not. All can contribute to the same enterprise and produce what is to be joined to what is subsequently created. There is a sense, then, in which creative mathematicians today are greater than creative mathematicians yesterday, and a sense in which they are not. Starting deep within their privacies and reaching deeper into the rational than their predecessors did, they carve out new limited forms in the rational condition and join these to nuances distinguished in the Dunamis. Their creations build on what their predecessors did; in repayment, as it were, for the bounty, they enhance what they have benefited from by coordinating it with the newly created.

Both previous and present creators produce truths at once intelligible and informative, necessary yet "synthetic." Kant knew that the truths of mathematics are all synthetic, which is to say that they are the outcome of activities joining disparate entities to produce necessarily true, informative singulars. The informativeness, he thought, was owing to their presence in a pure time or space, but something more is needed to enable any one truth, and surely all the truths of mathematics, to be unified. Like the phrases in a musical composition, or the colors in a painting, the units in mathematics are both vibrant and vibrantly together.

Kant unduly limited his examination of mathematics to acts of adding and diagramming, neglecting to observe that the one is occupied with numerals and the other with particular figures. He also failed to note that his $7 + 5 = 12$ required not just one but five distinct syntheses. To reach twelve, we do not, as Kant supposed, add seven points to five others and only then engage in a synthesis to equate the result with twelve. We must first synthesize seven distinct, counted units, then five other units, then the synthesized seven with the synthesized five, and finally that result with the acknowledged twelve points which, presumably, had been separately synthesized. Many other mathematical truths can be obtained apart from such syntheses and addings. Only a few of them will be occupied with units distinguished in a pure space or time. All have to take account of what is on some level of the rational.

The angles of a triangle, like numbers, are manipulated in synthesizing acts, operating on what had first to be synthesized in order to gain the status of single units. Any extension in which the results are to be embedded, whether pure or empirically lived in, awaits what is done in the rational. The time then employed encompasses not what is focused on but the act of focusing on it.

Georg Cantor was a creative mathematician who stated new truths about the nature and relationships of previously unknown numbers, the transcendentals. There was no way of knowing the bearing of his work in advance, for what he achieved was synthesized, that is, unified, by his going through creative acts. If we blame him for the way he entered into a new level of the rational, we should also blame those of his predecessors who left behind the natural numbers in order to create other kinds, presumably unacceptable to any constructionist living at the time.

Cantor was also the first to present a usable and intelligible set theory. Like many other creative mathematicians, he was not interested in understanding the nature of the rational but only with making use of it on a level not previously reached. Like other creative mathematicians, he approached it by starting with what had been achieved on a more accessible level. The fact that what he and others created can be expressed by means of Φ's and Ψ's, and x's and y's—that is, by variables and values having no specific designations—makes possible the use of other, more limited variables and values having a plurality of instances. When these are used, what had been expressed through the more general Φ's and Ψ's, and x's and y's, will be specified.

It is sometimes unclear precisely where a creative mathematician began and how he proceeded. It may then not be possible to determine just where he ends. Fermat is an instance. He said that he could prove his last theorem. We have no reason to doubt him, even though no one since his time has been able to produce the proof. Nevertheless, we cannot say flatly whether he did or did not prove it. Not knowing where he began and what he did then, we are left today with his unrefuted affirmation of a supposed creation whose existence is not evident to us.

It is not difficult to see how the creations of a painter are grained and fixed by the paints and canvas he uses. It is a little more difficult to see how a musical composition is grained by its notation. It is most difficult to see how the creations of mathematicians, particularly when they are occupied with what is to be presented by means of variables and values, could be affected by what is used to fixate them. A grain, though, need not compromise the nature of what is achieved apart from it. Numerals can be changed in many ways without having any effect on what is known of numbers.

All of us, mathematicians and others, insist on the integrity of the number system, even when confronted with Wittgenstein's imaginary—and as we saw, not well conceived—group that always counts the aggregates we do by means of a sequence of numerals that could not be simply interchanged with ours. Granted our known system of numbers, the numerals used by his imagined group evidently refer to the same numbers that ours do, though in a different way—unless what they do is not related to numbers at all. Yet, though numbers have natures apart from any use, they can, through the help of numerals, become involved in situations in which they would not otherwise participate. This involvement would be impossible were their distinguishable units and combinations not fixed and thereby kept from disappearing. One might remember the result, but unless what was then remembered was available to others, it would vanish with the forgetting.

Numbers are grained just so far as they are connected with numerals. Numbers can also be understood and manipulated without regard for the numerals and their graining. The grain will be present even when the levels where creations occur are numerous, making possible a movement from numbers to numerals. Only if it were possible to get to the last rung of a Platonic hierarchy, and there free oneself from all connection with previous achievements, would it be possible to arrive at a mathematical truth lacking all graining. There would then be no way to return and tell the others what had been seen.

The certainty of mathematical truths is not jeopardized when those truths are qualified, limited, and added to in science, technology, and daily affairs. Unlike works of art, which are sometimes greatly affected by the materials they use, mathematical creations maintain themselves no matter what the embedment because they occupy a distinct level of the rational at the same time that they are connected with what has been achieved on more superficial levels.

Set theory tries to free itself from the limitations which use, experience, or an actual (or even an imagined) world might impose on what it affirms. It envisages sets whose variables can take anything as a value—the self-contradictory, themselves, and, in all cases, what is represented by symbols and is never tied to particular items or to any particular level of the rational. The "creativity" of mathematics could, from that standpoint, be taken to be a mode of discovery and therefore to be able to reach only what is already there, awaiting precise, formal expression. Such formalizations, to be satisfactory, must be attuned to what mathematicians have in fact created.

Most set theorists seem to assume that whatever is intelligible, true, communicable, and demonstrable has an adequate, exhaustive mathematical nature and expression. Some of them go beyond Galileo to take all reality—not only what is scientifically knowable—to have a mathematical nature. Yet only the inability of mathematics to escape from its origins requires it to be pertinent to what happens to be available at any time, somewhat as the available instruments, paints, or canvases, conventional and accepted languages, and the like partly determine what can or cannot be created in the nonmathematical parts of other enterprises.

All mathematics has a possible application not because it always will or must find a use in science, technology, and daily affairs but because its creations are so many proper names of the intelligible constant that is behind and effective in all particulars. Although mathematics does not portray the cosmos, it does enable a careful reader of it to become aware of the omnipresent, malleable, controlling presence of the rational. Like every other kind of creation, mathematics provides a sign of what lies beneath all incidental and passing occurrences.

Even a set theory that takes account both of strictly mathematical truths and of what is expressible in terms apparently more comprehensive and general than those which mathematicians employ is unable to embrace everything. Art, politics, character, metaphysics, and theology are beyond its reach. Dismissing these fields as nonsense, because they cannot be expressed within the limits of set theory, makes explicit what this theory cannot do—enable one to comprehend what is outside its formalizations. Even the mathematics that set theory expresses contains only the residue of a mathematics already created. Because it must wait on novel mathematical creations to have a subject to speak about, it can do no better than offer the least distortive, clearest way to express and communicate what has been achieved. That is a good deal, but it is quite different from what creative mathematicians do and know.

Inference

To account for the separation and mutual involvement of mathematical units, we must turn either to a privacy or to the Dunamis. A privacy introduces limited additions to what is confronted. So far, it precludes knowing or using what stands apart from it. Only the Dunamis has the vitality and independence needed to make possible both a distinguishing and a holding on to different parts, no matter what these parts are.

The Dunamis plays a more conspicuous role in the arts and other creative enterprises than it does in mathematics; there it is confined, preventing it from reducing to transient moves the necessity that connects distinguished parts of the rational to one another. Formalism acknowledges no role for it, yet like every other enterprise it uses terms initially separate from one another and then effectively joins them. Those terms fix what is already marked out in the rational. An effort to deal with what is marked out in this condition, without using anything to distinguish subdivisions or to determine the outcome, would require an abstraction from all dunamic distancings. The overcoming of distancings demands acts, which in turn require the use of the Dunamis.

If one allows for the specialization and use of nothing other than the Dunamis, one will tend to suppose that mathematical creations are just momentary stopping places carved out in a pulsating medium. Presumably, the creations would vanish as soon as one stopped attending to them. Left unexplained would be the fact that others can subsequently reach the same outcome and can do so without being creative. Although conventions, decisions, and stable notations might enable a multitude to produce distinctions similar to those made by a creative mathematician, the distinctions would collapse into one another were there nothing to maintain and connect them. In the absence of the Dunamis they would merge or form an indifferent set of units.

There is paradoxical air about references to ultimates as lying beyond accepted particulars, for like references to anything else they inevitably employ and are caught up in words and their grammar, along with whatever referential acts these permit. This truth is no more intolerable than is the use of the unchanging word *becoming* to refer to what is not itself unchanging. The ultimates are reached from the standpoint of positions where they are interinvolved. They are not spatially, temporally, or causally distanced from those positions. Instead, they exist where actual occurrences are, but with depths of their own, intensively rich, self-contained. One arrives at them in intensive evidencing moves as less and less affected by what is used to begin a thrust into and use of them. Eventually one can go no farther. One's movements will have been overcome by the ultimates themselves as they become more firmly possessive and absorptive of what intrudes on them.

The rational is confronted as qualified both by ourselves and by the Dunamis. Bringing more of the Dunamis to bear on the rational emphasizes and affects the outcome of its joining with it. The informative character of mathematics is then enhanced, not jeopardized, for the Dunamis, though already operative there, enriches it by manifestations from deeper layers. As a result, the formally expressible components of mathematical truths are internally related with great effectiveness, matching the achievements of works of art. Those components thereupon achieve new meanings. "Larger than" in "Three is larger than two" has an import different from what it has in "This tree is larger than that tree." "Two" and "three" belong together; the trees, in contrast, are related in nature over distances. Nothing is gained if the Dunamis alone is accepted as real or effective, for that position would preclude significant intelligible articulations between fixed terms and relations.

Only human beings can infer, if inferences are what can be warranted by rules and can end with detached conclusions credited with independent features. These features are usually not known until the inferences have been carried out. No inferences make their conclusions be true; they can only enable one to arrive at such conclusions. A mathematician's creative passage from what has been achieved on one level of the rational to what is marked out on another can be assimilated to a kind of inference, provided one does not suppose that there is some antecedent confinement of the operation other than what provides a conceivable link between a distinguished level of the rational and that at which one might arrive.

Mechanically traversed steps present a necessity in a sequence; an inference freely moves to and separates an outcome from its connection with an already accepted premiss. Conceivably, some mechanism could bring the premiss alongside the conclusion to form a single, unified whole in which the premiss was enhanced by the conclusion it made possible. This outcome would not extinguish the difference between the two kinds of movements. Only inferences act teleologically to terminate at what is formally warranted. They have no predetermined path which they must traverse.

Rules justifying an inference neither report nor prescribe a course that has been or should be followed to reach a conclusion. If an inference straightway isolated a conclusion, it would still act differently from the way a machine does, for where the latter can do no more than start and stop, an inference begins and ends. It is a single act no matter how long it takes and no matter how many rests or pauses are introduced along the way.

The movements of a mechanical production fit an established joining of a start and a stop; an inference begins and ends. The limits of the inference can be joined in a justifying structure or rule that disregards the actual stages traveled from the beginning to the end. A mechanism moves in a fashion both antecedently determined and piecemeal whether or not its moves can be predicted; the moves of an inference are always new and single whether or not they are subdivided. Randomizing the moves of a mechanism will not free them from mechanistic control. There may be well laid out paths traversed when one infers, but those paths will be pulled into the course of the privately produced inferential move.

Most mathematicians carry out their inferences by passing from one item to another on the same level of the rational. Giuseppe Peano's so-called mathematical induction offers a good illustration. Having so defined zero and its successor that every other positive number is a successor, a particular number is reached from some accepted position by conforming to the so-called inductive rule. Another type of inference ends with what can be formally necessitated by assumed premisses. The different inferences, though occurring apart from rules and sometimes carried out without an awareness or consciousness of one, arrive dunamically at what has been or could be formally certified.

Beginning as it does with something held to be true and ending with another, formally certifiable truth, a sound inference proceeds in its own way to end at that truth as having a nature and status apart from that with which one began. While the inference may not have been carried out in accord with some specified rule, when completed its conclusion may be formally justified by such a rule—preferably one linking premiss and conclusion by necessity. The difference between a formal rule and an inference under it is captured in the contrast between "If x, then y" and

"Since x is true, y is true." The former has a hypothetical, the latter a categorical beginning. The former ends in what continues to be attached to the beginning; the latter ends with what is separately claimed.

There is no difference in principle between an inference from one number to another under the rule of mathematical induction and an inference from an experimentally relevant affirmation to what is claimed to be available for other observations. The two differ, of course; they begin at different places, conform to different conditions, and arrive at different kinds of conclusions. The number four, reached by mathematical induction, is distinct from its predecessors or successors but is not confronted as distinct except at the outcome of an actual inference to it. If it were created then and there, one would not be sure of having arrived at what had been arrived at before. An inference to it, whether or not conjoined with a rule purporting to express the nature of the rational, begins and ends at what has already been created.

An inductive or other rule may usefully help one to move directly and surely to conclusions, but one can also reach these conclusions by conforming to other rules. Sound inferences need not be straightforward or simple; it suffices if they arrive at a necessary consequence of what is assumed. No one has ever carried out the decimal expansion of the number four raised to the trillionth power. This does not mean that, though in principle reachable through mathematical induction, it is not already a distinct, genuine number or that there are not some truths we can now affirm of it. Otherwise, we would have to say that the existence of numbers and, of course, other mathematical units would have to be denied until they had been actually reached at least once and thereupon were somehow recorded and forever available. The Dunamis makes it possible for there to be an endless number of interconnected, distinct units on a particular level of the rational.

When introduced in the course of a creative act, the Dunamis enables distinctions already made to be interconnected. The distinguishable units, while they are interinvolved, will continue to exercise distinct functions. Just as the red in a painting is distinct from the yellow that is also there, all the while that the two affect one another's nature and role, so numbers, even those never acknowledged by anyone, are both distinct from and make a difference to one another. As distinct, they are the numbers we usually acknowledge; as making a difference to one another, they are those very numbers on a single, vibrant level of the rational.

There is no creativity unless a level of the rational is so reached that allowance is made for the presence throughout of distinctions produced on lower levels. That would be impossible were it not that the Dunamis is joined to the rational and that terminal units are demarcated there, fixed through the use of an established notation. The units would not be both distinctive and interconnected unless the Dunamis had interinvolved nuances and these nuances matched others in the rational.

If they did not, mathematics would be dependent on the persistent action of a privacy and, so far, be subject to numerous radical alterations.

Some inferences end not at another item coordinate with a premiss but at one of greater generality, to be justified through extensional or intensional rules. In the first type, "color," in the conclusion of the inference from "This is red" to "This is a color," is shorthand for "red or green or . . ."; in the second type, "color" retains its distinctive unitary meaning, one not adequately expressible in such a disjunction.

An intensional logic lacks an "or" operating between detached terms; for it, "or" is a component in a single expression, and "*x* or *y*" is a misleading way of presenting the conjoint disjunct "*x*-or-*y*." One could come to "*x* or *y*" from this by carrying out an intensional abstractive act. Extensional logic would, so far, have its warrant provided by an intensional logic.

The Dunamis can be privately joined to and used to add a vitalizing factor to a condition. This move is possible after one has arrived at it from what it has evidenced of itself. To get to it, one proceeds neither inferentially nor creatively—not the one because the procedure is carried out in a way that ends with something in need of no further justification, and not the other because other factors are not needed to produce it. It is there to be utilized at some depth.

Intensional inferences move from the thin to the thick, controlled by their conclusions. Although this fact has not usually been noted, it was not entirely unknown to Kant and Hegel. Kant, however, thought that one could infer intensively only if one started from something thick and moved toward nothingness, while Hegel supposed that one progressed over a series of distinct stages controlled by an omnivorous absolute. Neither did justice to the Dunamis, which has its own reality and richness, to be moved into in a distinctive way.

The red of a rose is different from a mere red. It is in fact an intensification of a mere red, produced and possessed by the rose. An inference from the mere red to the red as possessed by the rose necessarily ends with what is richer than the mere red. If an intensive inference begins with a mere red, it can tell us that a red belongs to something and is affected by it. It will also tell us less than "rose" does, for this refers to what is shaped, has a size, odor, stem, etc. Because a mere red tells us less than "red of a rose" does, we must engage in an intensive inference to move to the latter from the former.

All inferences occur outside formal frames; they can never be adequately expressed as they actually occur. It suffices for a knowledge of their logical use to know that if we engage in extensional moves, we arrive at something to be detached and maintained apart from a complex whose outcome is together with its beginning, and that if we infer intensionally, we arrive at what is denser than the premiss, often more powerful and able to take over. In appreciations, similarly, we begin with an acceptance of that with which we are to end, but it is not yet spelled out. We must then live through it, to end with the entire work functioning as a sign.

Formal frames indicate positions where one is to begin and conclude inferences, disregarding what is done along the way. One usually sets up such frames only after having engaged in justifiable inferences. Mathematical formulae do this. This recapturing is eminently desirable, for it enables one to recur, and in quite mechanical ways, to what may have once demanded incomparable creative ability.

Passages into a deeper level of the rational, and into recesses of the Dunamis and privacies, can all be treated as inferences justifiable by intensional rules. Equally well, they can be treated as direct and noninferential, beginning with thin instantiations of some ultimate and terminating in it at some depth.

Both the Platonic and the Hegelian dialectic are supposed to offer intensive ways of getting to better positions. There is no need to keep dialectic confined to Plato's and Hegel's uses. Conceivably, it could move through well-established positions. If these positions were due to the activity of the outcome, as Hegel thought, the outcome and perhaps its steps as well would already be laid out. But one can voluntarily engage in a dialectic (which is perhaps what Plato thought) or be irresistibly led from one stage to the next in an economic-political history (as Marx held). None of these thinkers allow for anything to be created, since they take every step to be assured by that at which one will finally arrive, to be what has already been established, or to be subject to an irresistible force.

Creativity depends on one's ability to reach ultimates as they are apart from oneself and from one another, to specialize them, and to bring these together. Rarely does one stop at in-between stages or try to contemplate or explore what is reached. That is a task for a philosopher. No use of a dialectic need be made to get to the ultimates. One can move quickly and directly to them from what is already present in limited forms in whatever there may be. It is also possible to stop along the way to note what is being done. One concerned with creatively using an ultimate on the next available level or layer must get to it as part of an effort to specialize and use it together with other factors. Since there are apparently an endless number of levels of conditions and layers of the Dunamis, a stop at any one of them will be quite arbitrary, though perhaps no more than one might then be able to manage.

Instead of trying to extract evidences of ultimates from particulars, as philosophers may, creators begin by reaching positions in themselves whence they can at once focus freely and directly on the ultimates, preparatory to making specialized use of them. Their concern is with producing what will best yield the sought excellence. If successful, they will end with what needs no other justification than that it is as good as anything a human could end with, given those particular opportunities. The acceptance of what an inference ends with is not so justified. If it does end with the eminently desirable, the inference will be satisfactory, but in order to justify it, its beginning and ending must be sanctioned by a premiss and a conclusion connected by an acceptable rule.

A formally presented plurality has its units alongside one another. None makes a difference to the nature or role of any other. To alter them so that they make such a difference, the Dunamis must be so brought into play that its involvement will allow what is distinguishable to be interinvolved.

We tend to speak as though there were nothing but a plurality of disconnected objects in the daily world, mainly because we assume that the space and time there are indifferent receptacles. Objects are not entirely indifferent to one another; they only seem to be so in our reports, for these abstract from what occurs and from the qualifying Dunamis. As a result, they present rigid articulations of what is transitory and singular.

The presence of the Dunamis in the rational—or anywhere else—does not threaten the intelligibility of what is distinguished in it. Both the Dunamis and the rational maintain their integrity and power as ultimates no matter what thrusts toward and into them. Both remain unbounded all the while that they qualify one another. There is no point in either where the other must come to a stop; it continues with less and less force until its presence is hardly discernible. The condition, as well as the Dunamis, maintains itself while the other makes itself effectively present in it in a progressively weaker fashion. Separately and together, both the Dunamis and the conditions extend beyond the borders of any group of items.

A formula is not very useful except for those who operate within the dominating confines of the rational in a way that precludes the Dunamis from doing more than faintly distinguish and join what is fixed there. The Dunamis, so far, is at the service of the rational. The reverse is also true. The rational impinges on the Dunamis to mark out what is not otherwise distinguishable in it.

Ultimate conditions affect and are affected by one another. Voluminosities, affiliations, stratifications, and coordinations, are intelligible; the rational, conversely, is subject to them and thereby extensionalized, stratified, with its units coordinated and affiliated. The separation and joining of distinguished parts of the rational are as direct as are the separations and joinings of subdivisions of the other ultimate conditions.

Neither the rational nor the Dunamis stands in the way of the other; each, on its own, qualifies what is distinguishable there. Once this qualification is made, the outcome can be fixed by using conventional notations. Because the Dunamis is fluid, vitalizing, at once spreading out and holding together what it terminates in, no analysis will ever do it full justice. The fact does not disturb mathematicians, for they are interested mainly in the rational. When attending to what they create there, they often ignore the Dunamis or accept it as though it were a part of their privacies or acts of creation.

One might take some as yet unproved theorem of great generality to be a primary creation and then go on to express it formally in such a way that other truths could be derived from it. Neither creative nor uncreative mathematicians do so. The former produce new truths and afterward join them to previous achievements, while the others are content to use the outcomes. Today, many are confident that privately produced mathematical creations have a status apart from their creators, though few are so confident regarding the status of musical compositions.

Many seem to believe that mathematics anticipates or promotes work in technology or science; fewer think that privately created musical compositions need to be justified by a performance. Scientists do not speak of remaining true to the intent of mathematicians in the way that performers speak of remaining true to the intent of a composer. This difference is due in part to the fact that science is taken to have its own method, topics, procedures, tests, and achievements, while performances are viewed (often by the performers themselves) as being no more than mediators or agencies by means of which a composer's work is made available. Were this view right, no performer would be a creator.

Some students of everyday language suppose that it alone is real or primary or that everything else should be understood to be a function of it. No provision is made for understanding its users, the total meaning of what is done supposedly being entirely contained in what is publicly expressed. If this view were tenable, it would have to be added that mathematics is confined to the use of accepted symbols and that its acknowledged creators are no more than suggestive innovators in the production and manipulation of these symbols. Their achievements would be somewhat like those of innovative deputies and legislators—a view that agrees with the belief that all detailed work is carried out within the confines of a paradigm introduced by some influential figure.

Conceivably, one might take such a paradigm to be a creation. It would then have to be understood in terms similar to those pertinent to the understanding of the work of some influential artist. A paradigm, though, is at best the outcome of what Peirce called an "abduction," the producing of a hypothesis to be tested and justified by experiments and discoveries that others might carry out.

In an abduction, one moves beyond the point where other hypotheses have been used in order to generate one having a greater scope. That does not suffice to make the outcome a creation. Creations do not simply present something to be used; they make something radically new by joining ultimates under the guiding control of a gradually realized excellence. Abductive outcomes are too abstract and bound to a prospective use to be equated with what mathematicians create.

Scientists are members of a community. Though they form a single group of thinkers, mathematicians, like artists, are engaged in carrying out radically individual work while depending on the materials they use to render their creations available to others. Each member of the scientific community, like the rest of us, has a private side. Instead of using what he can to produce an excellent work, he will, so far as he belongs to the community, go no further than to bring about what is pertinent to what is being done.

Scientists reach as far as they can while they hold on to what their community accepts. There is creativity in science, but it is not occupied with paradigms. Instead, as elsewhere, it produces new, particular excellences by privately joining conditions, the Dunamis, and an ideal prospect and having the result embedded in appropriate material.

Like other creators, mathematicians free themselves from the habits and interests in which they have been previously involved and thereupon deal with ultimates in personal ways. Like other creators, they are emotionally affected in the course of their creative activity, but their emotions usually lack the color and turbulence characteristic of those lived through by many of the others. The flatness of their emotions is due in good part to the fact that mathematicians rarely have a clear topic in focus—and it is topics about which strong emotions usually swirl.

That mathematicians are emotionally involved in their work is occasionally acknowledged in referring to the excitement aroused in them when they learn of a creative mathematician's entrance into a new level of the rational. That excitement is a more subjective form of the emotions undergone when one progressively participates in a rational condition or which erupt when note is taken of some scientific creation or discovery for which a mathematician provided the clue.

Whether or not they attend to what scientists or others might be able to use, creative mathematicians produce not just what is new but also what makes an advance on what they or other mathematicians had creatively achieved. Their creations are synthetic products, bringing together multiple factors. They support the view that no purely analytic truths are possible. Even "$x = x$" is synthetic, for at the very least it uses two distinct "x's" to refer to the same object.

Mathematical Truth

A synthesis, Hegelians claim, is needed in order to overcome what would otherwise be irreconcilable oppositions. The needed synthesis is, they say, performed by a necessitating absolute. Mathematical creations, if for no other reason than that they are created, cannot have been so necessitated. Previous achievements commit later creative mathematicians to producing something else. What is then created can be formally reinstated as though it had been deduced.

What mathematicians affirm is true; what they deny is false; what they cannot show to be either is indeterminate. The statement $2 + 2 = 4$ is true; $2 + 2 = 5$ is false; $x^n + y^n = z^n$, where n is greater than 2, is indeterminate, a theorem no one has shown to be either true or false. It is also the case that "This is a chair" may be true or false and that "This chair will collapse tomorrow" is indeterminate. "Truth", "falsehood," and "indeterminate" are used differently in these two places. "This is a chair" does not achieve its truth as a consequence of a creative act; "Zero is a number" once did. One does not create or devise a proof in order to end with "This is a chair." A contingently realized possible truth is different from the outcome of a fresh mathematical creation, for the latter ends with what is necessarily true. If it failed to do so, it would leave us with a still-indeterminate prospect.

A creator and a noncreator face indeterminate futures. The one is directed at a prospective excellence, not yet able to unify what is pertinent to it; the other is directed at an empty possibility which is not altered even when it is enabled to be present. Different actions are needed to give either of them a place in the present, the prospective excellence being used as a guide for what will enable it to become determinate, the possibility receiving a filling without thereby being affected. A prospective excellence takes over, affecting what made its realization possible; a possibility remains passive, both when realized and when not. Both are initially indeterminate, but whereas the one exercises control and can become more and more determinate, the other continues to be indeterminate even when it is enabled to be present.

A lasting peace is possible but may never be achieved; a created truth is not possible, yet it can be realized. The sting of this paradox is removed by treating possibilities as derivatives from ideals. In that case, whatever occurs must fit within the compass of a gradually realizable excellence. A cosmic teleology might then be operative, but we have no evidence that there is such a teleology, either latent or effective.

A creative mathematician, like other creators, is committed in multiple ways. What he himself has achieved, what he is beginning to discern, the prospective ideal, and what has been created by his predecessors—all these factors play a role in his creations. One of his commitments will be stressed more than others at a particular time. Were he primarily committed by what he had done in the past, he would still have to be distinguished from himself or others as having to make good the losses previously caused. One commits oneself but is obligated by what one has done. One may—or may not—commit oneself to meet obligations, but whatever is decided, it will not affect them.

One may or may not commit oneself to do what is required in order that an excellent work be produced. If there is no commitment, or if the commitment is not met, what is prospectively excellent will not be realized. Meeting commitments to do what is needed so that an excellence is realized is a creator's way of making what is indeterminate become determinate. If successful, he will have transformed his indeterminate prospect into an actualized, effective excellence.

Different actions are needed to realize different prospects. Since new creations in mathematics add new determinations to what was previously created, they make evident that what is determinate in one context may be indeterminate for another. Much as a man can be determinate as a present individual and yet may receive new determinations by becoming part of a society or a state, so a mathematical creation, while fully determinate in relation to some items, will receive new determinations from whatever gives it new roles. If this claim raises doubts, they may be dispelled by noting that what is determinate can always be further qualified when set in new situations. Even the finished past acquires new determinations from present events. A world war became the first world war when a second followed decades later.

This conclusion would be avoided if one held that nothing was fully determinate unless it were a part of every context, including that which the future might provide. One would then have to deny that any creation could ever be fully determinate. The law of excluded middle would not apply, since nothing would, on the hypotheses, be just this without also being that—or, more precisely, there would be no this and no that but only a "this and that," without distinct units or parts.

A created work has its items unified, not bounded off from one another; the items in it are conjoined not in a single "this and that," but in a "this with that." There, each item is both determinate and determinately together with others. The recognition of the kind of determinateness belonging to each component and unit makes it possible to distinguish them. *Six* obviously loses nothing by being included among all the numbers. It remains as it was but can obtain further determinations by being set alongside other numbers, whether natural or not.

Pragmatism leaves one with no way to decide whether or not a claim is rationally justifiable. The opposing realistic view has its own difficulties, claiming as it does that truths adhere to assertions that are themselves connected to things external to them. That doctrine implies that some truths are tied to occurrences in the remote past. Yet we can speak truthfully about the past only by giving it new determinations in the present and, so far, maintaining it there. To get to that past as it was, one would have to extract it from the present, thus depriving it of the determinations it has there acquired.

Referents of assertions have the terms of those assertions internally connected. When their common referent is ignored, those terms will so far be externally related, indifferent to one another. In "Six is a number," "six" is attached to "number" and with it refers to "six" as one among all numbers. "These are all the numbers" refers to a unified totality in which the numbers are distinguishable but not separated. At every stage of its development, mathematics provides a single truth within which more limited, similarly constituted truths are found, some of them initially created, others stemming from these.

Machines do not stop because they complete some venture; they are so structured, programmed, and energized that they cease to operate at the end of a particular period of functioning. Whatever unifications the outcome might have will be due to a program or to an interpreter of the data. It is difficult at times, though, to determine whether something is the outcome of the working of a machine or is what a human being may have unified. The fact that unifications and their loci are sometimes difficult to discern does not compromise the claim that a machine cannot produce a mathematical truth or carry out mathematical operations, not even of the most elementary kind. No machine can add or subtract; none can affirm that six is a number. The supposition that a machine could carry out any of these tasks rests on a confusion between numerals and numbers, between a notation and that to which one might refer what has been notated.

There is no denying the greatness of Plato, Aristotle, Kant, and Hegel. In different ways they exposed many basic, hidden, and previously misconstrued realities. It was their chosen task to do so. They did not themselves create anything, nor did they claim to have done so. What they said was original, making evident how inquiry into what is presupposed by every thing and act can be brought to a close. Had they done nothing more than say something arresting, they would, as some of their opponents claim, be indistinguishable from those who were clever, and nothing more.

What philosophers accomplish is distinctive and surely unlike what mathematical and other creators do. They know that if they are honored as creators, they will at the same time be denied to be what they seek to be and what they think they are— self-questioning and persistent, attempting to express a plurality of interrelated, root, permanent, and important truths about the universe, the cosmos, nature, the human realm, individuals, and their signal combinations and divisions.

Philosophers do not, as great mathematicians do, try to realize an ideal truth by making primal use of a rational condition and concluding with a created excellence. Although some philosophers have been overly influenced by mathematics, there is no warrant to the supposition that they would otherwise have nothing to do but criticize what had been done by others or that they were reduced to producing "likely stories." What a philosopher affirms is like a daily truth in its dependence on realities to which that truth is to be adumbratively joined. Those realities, like others, are constituted by a union of all the ultimates. Philosophers offer accounts of those ultimates which make them more evident and underscore their more interesting interconnections.

Unlike mathematicians, who join what they create with what has been previously achieved and thereby provide more and more determinate exhibitions of a single, inclusive excellence, philosophers have as their task the comprehension of what is essential to the being of any and everything. If they rest content with what others affirm, they have stopped philosophizing at that point. Other enterprises can do no more than provide them with suggestions and point up neglected aspects. Were philosophers to try to imitate mathematicians, they would have to use the rational as the locus of their productions; were mathematicians to imitate philosophers, they would not occupy themselves with creative work embedded in the rational.

Truths, I have already remarked, have a triple import. They are objective, referring to what exists apart from them; conformal, referring to what is at the other end of a single continuum; and embedded in that to which they refer. No enterprise is occupied solely with one of these aspects; an emphasis on it does not sunder it from the others. Although mathematical truths are usually taken to be purely objective, holding forever no matter what happens, they also conform and are integral to what is created. The conformal side is the most conspicuous, allowing a mathematician, without losing hold of what is created, to distance himself from the creation and so use it that what was previously achieved can be joined to it.

Mathematicians, whether creative or satisfied to explore consequences, seek to end with what holds apart from all contingencies. Still, their achievements, despite their universality and their separation from the world and its vicissitudes, are all dated. Mastery of this point faces two difficulties: (1) although what was once created in mathematics is always true, creations vanish if not fixated; (2) while beauty is gradually realized in what is creatively achieved by an artist and in a form whose presence depends on him, mathematical truths are either altogether present or absent and do not seem to depend on the mathematician for their existence. The issue has already been touched upon; it is time to face the difficulties directly.

1. Truths are normally taken to characterize expressions which reinstate, in a new form, what exists apart from them. Were beauty understood in this way, it would re-present what was intrinsically beautiful. Great works of art, however, do not re-express beauties encountered apart from those works. Their achievements are not variants on what might be seen or recorded about objective occurrences; they are new. At most, what is encountered serves artists only as an occasion, topic, or theme. Even realistic artists subject familiar scenes, people, and dwellings to transformative demands. The creations of mathematicians are like such creations—and also like some more humdrum productions—in requiring the use of privacies, the meeting of various commitments, and the utilizing of ultimate factors. They are also embedded in a commonly accepted notation, thereby enabling the created result not only to be preserved but to be communicated and used.

Whereas, in works of art materials qualify what is otherwise achieved, in mathematics the qualification is primarily produced in the opposite way, with a notation being given an import by what it is serving to preserve and convey. Since mathematical notations introduce separations and connections which creations lack, they require one who is concerned with understanding mathematical creations to avoid the qualifications that the notations introduce.

2. Unified items support and enhance one another. The excellences pervading them still allow them to continue to have their own bounded natures. The items may also pass away. Unless an achieved excellence could continue to be, it would have to pass away when these items do. This passing away does not occur. A mathematical truth and other excellences continue to be because the items in them continue to be in the form of interlocked units. While there is no way to hold on to the past as it was when present, it is still possible to unify what is in the past by utilizing it as factual, without depth or power, merely determinate, bounded and encompassed.

A mathematician's creation is organic, a single unified truth. What he produces is so far like a leader's creation of a glorified people. That result, too, has room for other creations, many of which were achieved earlier by others. In art no similar provisions are made for the presence of beauties previously created.

The benefits that creations may bestow on productions in other disciplines or occurrences at other times have no effect on its excellence. Otherwise, nothing would be excellent in and of itself. A painting, of course, may be affected by its placement in relation to other paintings and objects. Though it may then be difficult to get in a position where it can be properly read, it will still continue to be self-enclosed. Similarly, mathematical creations remain what they are, no matter how used in science and technology, at the same time that they can be related to what lies beyond them. The fact that they can be produced without explicit reference to previous scientific and technological established truths or to prospective uses breaks the back of those forms of language analysis and conventionalism that take a formal expression to be true only when attached to what exists. The kernel of truth those views contain is preserved in the observation that there are intermediaries which make it possible to connect the creations to those independent existents. Just as a message may mediate a sender and a recipient, so a mathematical formulation may mediate a creation and the data that concern others, whether scientists, technologists, or accountants. But also, just as a message may continue to exist no matter what sender and recipient may then do, so the language of mathematical truths may continue to exist no matter what is done by a creator—or by a user of his work.

If a mathematical creation were the strict counterpart of an artistic one, it would be produced outside the rational condition that it specializes and uses, or an artistic creation would be located inside a primal voluminosity. If the first, creations in science would not differ from those in mathematics despite the fact that mathematical creations persist while scientific ones may not and that scientific work is often successfully carried on without reference to mathematical creations. If the second, those occupied with the spatial arts would have to begin and end in ways radically different from the creators of temporal and causal arts do.

Although artists usually begin at a position neutral to both the voluminosity that interests them and the Dunamis they use, they often give a greater role to the Dunamis than mathematicians do. The fact is so obtrusive at times that it is sometimes supposed that artistic creations are produced as counterfoils to mathematical creations, making use of a primal voluminous condition only to add an incidental stability to a primal vitality. This view is encouraged by those who suppose that the Dunamis alone is real and that mathematics and science, and the philosophies that build on them, produce only abstract, distorted representations of it. The claim that the only reality is a primal process, momentarily stopped by distortions and falsifications, is up against the fact that mathematical creations have distinguishable components which frequently match separated items occurring apart from them.

In every creation, conditions and the Dunamis are privately specialized and used together and with the result sustained with the help of resistant material. A creator's private contribution, though, is less evident in mathematics than in other types of creation. The fact could be accommodated by holding that the different types of creation differ in the degree to which privacies contribute to the final unified outcome, but one would then also have to hold that the different types of creation result from different kinds of intrusions by privacies, with one type of creation becoming more vivid, personal, or available than others. Such a view seems to be behind the common inclination to take mathematicians to be discoverers rather than creators. Nothing can be discovered, however, unless it already exists, requiring the overcoming of barriers, space, time, irrelevancies, and perhaps also a change in direction or attention so as to make the discovered be more evident.

A discovery reaches what is already determinate, but hidden or bounded off from what is now known. It provides what it uncovers with new determinations, owing to the relations the uncovered has to the already known. It may have no predecessors and may be the outcome of great effort, ingenuity, and daring. It may both excite and delight. It does not depend on a gradually realized excellence. A creation not only makes use of such an excellence but with its help produces a new reality, self-enclosed.

Not carved out of a condition as a mathematical creation is, an object of art has no status apart from a privacy until the ideal excellence takes over and the result is embedded in obdurate material. In mathematics, a creator's work is persistently sustained by the rational condition he is creatively using. His achievement occupies this condition. Were there no fixing of the result in a notation, his creation would still have a place in the condition where it had been produced, though it would not yet be available to others.

Like other creators, a mathematician produces what is other than what he could have anticipated. Like other creative activities, his makes a difference to what is finally arrived at. His conjectures and probings are directed toward what refers back to and adds to what he has used. Thrusting this way and that in the effort to produce what fits in with and is both enhanced by and enhances what has been done, he makes the excellence to which he is committed become more and more determinate. The more determinate it becomes, the more surely will the different items he produces be turned into interinvolved functions. Whatever the level of the rational he successfully enters, he creates a single, undivided truth.

If a creator could understand his own motives, he would not thereby become a better creator. Nor can anyone help him learn what must be done to produce what is excellent. For him to create, he must freely bring ultimates together again and again. If he is a mathematician, to begin his new venture he will accept a level of the rational already mastered by other creative mathematicians. Were he the mathematician who made the first step into mathematics, he would have, for the first time, entered a low level of the rational from a position outside, making use of some actual object, perhaps a numeral or a measured square, to start him off. Today creative mathematicians begin where other creators left off, producing on quite a deeper level of the rational what will be unified there.

Despite the lamentations of some, particularly writers, that they are unable to accomplish anything for a time and have to sit forlornly before an emptiness they cannot understand or fill, many creators, and others as well, are able to work steadily. Those who are not creative may bring about what is desirable and important. As the proliferation of mathematics journal articles attests, noncreative mathematicians, like noncreators elsewhere, may not only be productive but may also make important contributions to the field.

Mathematicians who are occupied with the solution of problems, perhaps self-set, move from what they know or accept to outcomes not envisaged before, by them or by others. They neither create nor discover. Instead, they specialize, punctuate, explicate, bring about something new within the frame that a creator provided. Sometimes what they end with is startling and may open up avenues for a host of other endeavors. What they do is desirable, often useful, perhaps even able to stimulate a creator. They may solve particular problems; a creative mathematician, in contrast, solves an indefinite number in a single move.

Problem solving allows what has been achieved to determine what is next to be done; creativity, in addition, is subject to the demands of a sought excellence. When a creator faces the same problem that others do, he allows himself to be governed by the ideal he seeks to realize and sets himself to use the ultimates in forging his answer. He also uses his privacy with greater boldness. The result could be lodged in his privacy in the form of memories. Since these are not always reliable and change their strength and content quickly, he has to utilize common notations to give his work a steady, objective, available form. While immersed in his work, he is still partly separated from it and is therefore in a position to appreciate what he has done. Throughout, and at the end, he may even look at the result as though it were not created by him.

It is not usually remarked that a mathematician's work, like that of other creators, is suffused with feeling, reflecting the difference that the prospective excellence makes to what is being done, particularly since the feeling is faint and irregular at the beginning and quickly frozen at the end in his notations. Were the feeling absent, a mathematician could create while unconcerned with realizing an excellence in the form of truth—or truth, unlike other excellences would not be a singular making a difference to every part and its connections.

Because each mathematical creation brings alongside it what has been created before, the result, though lacking the depth and force of the feeling that an artistic work contains, is often more astonishing than what artists produce. Differences between these two kinds of ventures have led some to place them in a hierarchy of better and worse. That practice and its outcomes might be justified by referring to differences in degrees and to kinds of pleasures conferred and to the congeniality of the different conditions they use and finally signify. These justifications, though, refer to effects, not to the works. When one attends to the fact that truth is an excellence, no less able than beauty or other excellences to unify what enables it to be realized, there seems little point in claiming one or the other to be better, purer, or more worthy of admiration. Although truth is not beauty, nor beauty, truth, there is no need to put one above the other. While the arts may give greater pleasure to a greater number, mathematics has more uses in multiple fields, in one of which, science, another form of creativity can be carried out.

The Scientific Enterprise

Science is commonly thought of in one of two ways: as a plurality of created truths about the cosmos or as an accumulation of discoveries clarifying or adding to our knowledge. The one attends to bodies and their interplay; the other deals with these as qualified by man's interests. The two views belong together. Sometimes the creations provide new ways for relating the discoveries; sometimes the discoveries provide particular confirmations for the creations. Both may employ mathematics; both may have practical applications. One or the other, or neither, may take on a mathematical form or find a use. The scientists who focus on theories await confirmation from those who observe and experiment; those who observe and experiment look to creators for explanations and sometimes for linkages to other observations. The one makes use of a deep level of the rational; the other attends to what observation and experiment reveal. I will here attend mainly to theoretical physical science.

The scientific enterprise comprises both creations and discoveries. It carries out its task by following six distinctive procedures: (1) abduction; (2) induction; (3) observation; (4) experimentation; (5) prediction; and (6) the production of a distinctive set of claims. The first five are occupied primarily with what can be discovered, while the sixth offers a partial counterpart to creative mathematics. The six together are utilized in creative scientific work, though this or that scientist may concentrate on just one or a few of the first five.

1. "Abduction" is Charles S. Peirce's name for the method by which scientifically useful hypotheses are produced. These hypotheses free inquirers from the limitations to which their present observations and knowledge are subject, facilitating an appreciation of things pertinent to what has been accepted. It proceeds by freeing what is observed from its specific forms to obtain an abstract formulation applicable elsewhere. At its best, it is so expressed that allowance is made for variations on, additions to, and modifications of that with which one began.

Good abductions are not to be expected from those unfamiliar with a field; strangers cannot know what is relevant or irrelevant to what has already been accepted and therefore what is or is not to be utilized in reaching an abductive outcome. A good abduction does not simply remove details; it provides a formulation that is applicable both to that from which one began and to that which occurs elsewhere or at a different time. It can be used, too, to get one from and to ultimate conditions, the Dunamis, a background, a foreground, the past, and the future.

A good abduction allows one to anticipate an indefinite number of occurrences related to some that have already been acknowledged. That it is a primary agency for obtaining knowledge of any kind is a major tenet of John Dewey's Instrumentalism. Were it alone permitted, other good scientific methods would be ignored and no provision made for creative scientific works.

2. What we know is grounded in the present. Instead of then moving to an abductively formulated hypothesis pertinent to new situations, one may inductively take what held in the old situation also to hold in the new. Conceivably, one could take the move to be abductive, claiming that what has occurred is to be found again, but one would then overlook the fact that it is possible to pass directly from an accepted to a new situation that is expected to have the same characteristics as the old. Where abductive outcomes offer a kind of intelligible connection between what was known and what is to be newly characterized, inductions make do with habits of expectation, taking one into new situations as perhaps having the same pattern as the old.

Instead of directing one to make new observations, as abductions do, inductions serve to keep one functioning as before. The inductively reached outcomes are likely, plausible, and in consonance with established ways of acting. They need no grounding in the nature of things, for they do no more than promote a continuation in some particular mode of activity.

We protect ourselves from cataclysmic losses by carrying out a plurality of inductions in many places. In science and other disciplines we pass from place to place and time to time using many inductions. Only a reckless gambler stakes everything on one inductive move. Usually, though, only a few inductions are expressly noted. Even a gambler makes a plurality of inductions about the continuance of the game, the value of his chips, and the payment of debts, but he focuses on the induction that occurrences in which he is interested will, if independent, conform to a law of averages. They will so conform, but only in the long run; indeed, the run may be so long that it can never be credited with a definite end. The gambler's induction is careless; the inductions of scientists, in contrast, are carefully calibrated to what has proved successful before. Techniques and instruments successfully used in old situations, moreover, are inductively taken by scientists to operate successfully in the new and to sustain there the lessons of the old.

3. Both abductions and inductions start and end with what is observed. The observed item may be the object of a casual act of attention, or of a disciplined judgment distinguishing the important from the unimportant and the revealing from the obtrusive. Botanists, geologists, naturalists, and chemists remark on what others, not at home in the areas, usually fail to consider.

Good observation is inseparable from the determination of the roles that items play in complex situations. Not entirely separable from abductive and inductive moves, or they from it, an observation may require these moves to help one become alert to the presence of crucial occurrences, much as good observations are needed if good beginnings for abductive or inductive moves are to be made. In science, the observations often require a focusing on distinctions, relations, and aspects playing crucial roles. No one, as Peirce noted, other than those at home in a field, knows where to look and what to concentrate on. No theory obviates the use of a trained eye, shrewd surmise, a well-directed imagination, and knowledge of what is relevant.

4. Not all that is important is obtrusive. Nature must sometimes be tricked into revealing what otherwise would remain hidden, distorted, or irrelevantly modified. Experiments must be contrived to make evident what is relevant to one's suppositions. Background factors must be brought forward; those to the front must be pushed aside; the possibly adventitious must be forced to appear. These activities usually depend on the use of instruments to bring to the fore what otherwise would not be discerned.

Much in the history of science is calibrated with instruments employed at that time. Without these instruments, the results would not have been obtained; with them, the results have often been quite different from what otherwise would have been known. What we learn with the help of instruments is isolated, connected, or emphasized in ways it would not otherwise be. While they enable one to note what would be missed without them, they also hold it away from those neighbors with which it interplays.

Experiments prod nature and the cosmos to reveal what is not evident in the ordinary course of observation. They focus on pivotal occurrences, demarcated areas, sluicing, separating, or joining what seem to be items indifferent to one another's presence and operation. Their use inescapably turns a complex situation into one in which some items are separated from some others and then related in new ways. Sometimes the experiments will confirm what theory makes it plausible to expect; sometimes they will give some items new roles by placing them in contrived situations where they are forced to act and react in new ways.

Botany, geology, and other supposedly observational, descriptive, and classificatory ventures also experiment in their placement of observers and in their determination of the times and places where observations are to be made. Experiment puts special questions to nature, sometimes obtaining its answers just by providing boundaries and occasions, thereby enabling what is otherwise hidden to become conspicuous.

5. Abduction, deduction, observation, and experiment all have a predictive component. When experiments end with something startling or when observations reveal the unexpected, this result would often be passed over were there no expectation of that kind of outcome. It will already have been predicted loosely—guessed at as that which was being sought to fill out a gap not clearly noticed.

Literally, a pre-diction requires saying in advance what will be encountered, but this interpretation does less than justice to what is learned, for one never knows exactly what will be encountered. One must sense the relevance of what is freshly observed to what has already come to be known—and conversely. Just as a question or a propositional function has no mere blank into which some content is set, so a prediction prefigures the kind of outcome to be obtained. However, so long as one does not specify precisely what is to be encountered, a prediction will be hard to distinguish from a shrewd guess.

Predictions often follow a route laid out in some theory or express what experiments point toward. A doctrine of total necessity takes them to state what unavoidably follows on what has occurred. So far as that is possible, predictions would have to await only the passage of time in order to be fulfilled. If, as is usually true today, the rigid determinism of the past is abandoned, predictions will be taken to end not just in particulars at some later date but with what is general, awaiting instantiation.

Various scientists emphasize one or more of these activities rather than others. If they are active in a particular branch, they will differ in the ways they act within an accepted way of proceeding, with conspicuous achievements being credited to one or a few. A refusal to allow for what all do will contract the scientific community unduly or oversharpen the divisions between those who lead and those who follow. Those who follow are not to be relegated to the position of just agents or occasions, occupied with details. All may be equally devoted, disciplined, and active.

Many scientists are not creative. Like noncreative mathematicians, they depend on others to open up new areas. Still, carrying out their work within the compass of what great figures have made available, they do more than add punctuations or other incidentals to what has already been set out on a grand scale.

There is warrant for distinguishing a Newton, an Einstein, a Bohr from the mass of scientists. So far as the latter do not commit themselves to realizing an ideal prospect by joining ultimates again and again to end with a single unified outcome, they are rightly denied a position alongside the creators. Yet no less than those creators, they are obligated to be honest, careful, and precise, if only as a payment for making use of the scientific community's inheritance and support. Cutting away the illegal and immoral connotations of the term, the noncreators could be likened to forgers, for what they do is intended to fit neatly within the established creative enterprise.

The prospect that concerns scientists, like the prospect that concerns mathematicians, is an ideal whose realization involves the preservation of what has been previously achieved. Unlike preservations in mathematics, which allow the old to continue on its own level of the rational while being made part of and thereby altered on a new level, previous scientific achievements are often accepted only after being reinterpreted or altered. The beginning and outcome of combustion was known long ago, but the phlogiston theory that once served to explain it has now been abandoned. What was later learned affected the way in which an account of combustion could be fitted in with other types of occurrence.

If, as Peirce thought, scientists might all agree some day as a result of having finally come to the end of their inquiries, they would be part of a single community in which what they might separately know would mesh perfectly to constitute a seamless truth. There would then be nothing hidden, no reason to do anything more. The methods, accomplishments, and promise of science, as it has actually been carried out over its history in an ongoing, contingent world, make such an ideal community an implausible eventuality.

As members of a present community, scientists carry out similar methods of discovery and confirmation and respect the consensus of those working in other subdivisions of the enterprise. All are part of a distinct body of inquirers, carrying out similar abductive, inductive, experimental, observational, and predictive procedures. There is no need to suppose that they will ever reach the stage where all that is affirmed is given a mathematical form. Descriptions, reports, classifications, and orderings will always find a place in science since its orientation is not toward what can be precisely formulated but toward what can be expected, encountered, or warrantedly surmised.

A purely formal mathematical account must always be subjected to constraints to enable it to be a mathematics for the actual cosmos and not for a merely possible one. Whereas mathematical creations must meet no other demand than that they yield truths able to accommodate the old, those in science may require that the old be accepted as having a new import, explicable in new ways or expressible with more precision. Heavy bodies fall faster than light ones today, as surely as they did in Aristotle's time, but the fact is accounted for differently today from the way it was then. One would be able to treat science in a manner comparable to that appropriate to mathematics only if one allowed old explanations still to be pertinent even though one had accepted a later different explanation of the same occurrences.

Science continues successfully without any creators, occupied as it is only with learning what in fact occurs. What is subject to change is the import of its certified claims. Mathematics, in contrast, changes by expanding its scope. It need cling to no facts except so far as its creations are traced back to the initial numerals and diagrams from which the first mathematical acts began. Were one to put aside the new kinds of outcomes accepted over the course of scientific history, its formulations could be viewed like the numerals and diagrams initially acknowledged by mathematicians. One would still, though, be faced with the fact that new scientific theories often allow some of the old no role whatsoever.

Theoretical scientists generally find it desirable to make use of great mathematical achievements. Some, in the spirit of Galileo, identify a fixed segment of mathematics with the structure of reality. When they do, they introduce determinations, making a difference to the meaning of the mathematics they use. That fact has been insisted on, particularly by Dewey, in such a way that no sense could be made of the idea that pure mathematics contains many truths for which no application has been or may ever be found. Application, he thought, not only transforms what is applied but reveals it to have been "abstract," "empty," an instrument awaiting use. That view readily leads to the reduction of mathematics to a limited set of theorems, science to technology, and technology to an agency promoting the enrichment of human existence. This is a highly cherished objective, to be sure, one eminently worthy of devoted thinkers, but it is not what concerns mathematical and scientific creators. These seek to produce what is excellent. If they are scientists, the excellence will be exhibited in a cogent account in which all that can be learned can be coherently joined, with each part clarifying and being clarified by the others.

A mathematician may express new creations in established notations which stabilize truths previously affirmed. A theoretical scientist may utilize those same creations in his own way in his own theories. Detached from the rest of mathematics, the creations will be involved with what is encountered or acknowledged outside mathematics. The creations will then acquire roles they did not have before. All the while, they will continue to be fixed in the rational, undisturbed by what happens elsewhere.

Theoretical scientists may create as surely as do mathematicians. Whether or not they take account of mathematical creations, they, too, can use the ultimates to produce units promoting the realization of a unifying excellence. What they affirm will be offered as being pertinent to the actual cosmos. When this is conceived as a space-time, causal complex of interacting, knowable bodies, the mathematical truths used will have their ranges restricted and, as a consequence, will thereby acquire distinctive, limited natures and roles. As long as science is occupied with what occurs in an actual space-time, what is expressed as being in it will function in limited ways and, so far, will acquire new properties.

By carrying out mathematical operations as pertinent to what is done in established, restrictive ways, science alters them, qualifying the mathematics by the realities to which it is then referred. The mathematical truths will not be affected. At most, they will be added to what is scientifically expressed and thereupon provide a kind of general certification for limited truths referring to particular matters of fact.

Theoretical scientific formulations occupy a domain of their own. What in mathematics has the status of a truth has for this domain a different import, since it there belongs together with correlatives referring to presumed parts of the cosmos. The expression $x + y = y + x$ has one meaning when taken to be specified by any numbers and quite another when taken to be restricted to numbers attached to aspects of the cosmos. When the result is viewed formally, the restriction to cosmic occurrences will be abstracted from and thereupon treated as though it made no difference to the meaning, nature, or operation of what is expressed.

In speaking of all or some men, we evidently speak of the same kind of beings, restricting our reference in the latter case to a subdivision of those allowed by the former. That, at least, is the traditional, so-called Aristotelian view. Modern logicians, in contrast, usually take the "all" to attach to any intelligible nature and the "some" to attach to such a nature only so far as it is a part of one or more actual occurrences. One need not subscribe to that use of "some" in order to recognize that "all" and "some" have different ranges. Even when it speaks of "all" items of a certain kind, science operates in the area that formalists mark out with their references to "some." Also, the simple expression "four miles per hour" does not divide a distance in space by a period of time. That is surely impossible. It correlates the two. The four and the one are adjoined to the miles and the hour. They are what is to be added, multiplied, and so forth, just as they would were they attached to something else. Nothing done to them affects the correlated miles and the hours.

A purely mathematical science is impossible since science always joins mathematical terms to what has a reference to a cosmos, having an existence and course distinct from the mathematics used to articulate its claims. What science borrows from pure mathematics inescapably acquires a new meaning because it is then confined to what has a nature and career in a cosmos with a limited magnitude, a distinctive temporal pace, and processes to be discovered only by carrying out controlled scientific procedures.

When Pythagoras showed that different, mathematically definable positions on the strings of a harp precisely matched designatable tones, he did not show that the tones were mathematical units, combinations of them, or reducible to them. Instead, he made evident that the tones had a mathematically expressible nature. By plucking strings at measured positions, he produced certain tones, not others, but he did not thereby show that the tones were or were not creatively produced. If they were not, the outcome lacked a needed, undivided interinvolvement of note with note in a newly specified and utilized structure.

The Einsteinian formula $E = mc^2$ is intended to show the relation that energy, mass, and light have to one another. The c, as representing the speed of light, is said to be absolute, beyond any possible increase. The expression does not tell us about the nature of energy, mass, and light but only about the relations holding among their numerically characterized units. In effect, energy, mass, and velocity are treated as having units which are transformable into one another. As c^2 clearly shows, light, and consequently mass and energy, are not dealt with in the formula; instead, it shows how a number pertinent to a mass or energy can be made to yield a pertinent number for energy or a mass.

Einstein's creativity was partly expressed in his claim that mass, energy, space, and time are interinvolved in the cosmos and that quantities used in connection with them can be dealt with in established ways. When he related energy, mass, and light to one another, he tacitly supposed that they were different aggregations of the same kinds of units. His creativity was not expressed by his interrelating various numbers, but by his interrelating different cosmological occurrences, each understood to be constituted of the same kinds of entities. As so expressed, light, energy, and mass are transformable into one another by carrying out well-established ways of multiplying, dividing, and transposing different numerals. A formal relating of space, time, mass, light, and energy would not show them to be connected in fact.

Einstein's formula was the outcome of a creative venture in which a number of primary cosmic realities were understood to be joined in a radical, revelatory way. That his account has been accepted as paradigmatic for other physicists makes evident how helpful it is to see mass, energy, and light attached to comparable quantities. Because space-time, the curvature of space, the bending of light, the conversion of mass into energy, and the like—though it is with these that current scientific theories are concerned—are affected by the nature of that to which they are attached, scientists can refer to different types of occurrences while dealing with them as though they were expressible in comparable mathematical terms. Yet, when terms are dealt with as merely mathematical in nature and import, they are not identifiable with what is attached to referents of actual occurrences and regions.

The creativity of scientists is sometimes exhibited in the ways in which different dimensions of the cosmos are joined to mathematical expressions. Nothing is then done to the referents used for space, mass, waves, or any other pertinent item. When the mathematics attached to them is made available for mathematical operations, that to which they had been theoretically attached is not affected. Both scientists and mathematicians bring mathematical entities into new relations, the mathematicians doing so by moving into new levels of the rational, the scientists by accepting what the mathematicians create and then attaching it to the referents which interest the scientists. Despite great scientific advances, the notations and formulae previously used may continue to be used.

Those concerned with being "scientific" ignore not only what is not usable in science but also what is outside its scope—privacies, rights, religion, art, creativity, other types of inquiry, and transcendents—or try to restate these in terms pertinent to cosmic entities. Such attempts inevitably require one to stand outside all in order to see how they might be able to fit together. Even the justification of the use of mathematics in science requires one to do something like this, for it is necessary to establish a position above or between the two in order to be able to examine them objectively.

The assessment of the merits of science is not a scientific task carried out within the limits that science accepts; nor does it ground and justify a scientific understanding of the cosmos. The ethics that scientists accept, the community of which they are a part, the mathematical creations on which they depend, their abductions, inductions, predictions, observations, and experiments—these are not reducible to what is otherwise discerned or surmised about the cosmos. A purely "scientific" view precludes even an understanding of the creativity of scientists.

Once a creation has been completed in mathematics, it will be embedded in the rational. To make use of it in science, substitutes for it must be found and then attached to cosmic referents. To keep them attached over the history of the subject, they will have to be modified or, at the very least, be brought into new contexts and altered in meaning.

The history of mathematics is continuous, that of science episodic. Yet creative mathematicians seem separated, sometimes over long stretches of time, while creative scientists sometimes tread quickly on one another's heels. This is not an essential difference, and there seem to be periods when the positions are reversed.

The formulae that interest mathematicians often fix what has been created; those used by the sciences are often foci for achievements past and future, subject to ready, formal manipulation. Each mathematical creation is complete but can adopt what has been achieved; the creations of science are incremental, carried forward by the community with whatever changes are needed to unite what is known with what is subsequently learned. The ever-expanding, changing nature of the scientifically acceptable truths precludes the maintenance of an achieved excellence except as confined to a particular epoch. In the arts such a confinement would be the outcome of the acceptance of taste as a criterion of merit; in science it shows the retroactive effectiveness of new creations; in mathematics it reveals the superior status and accommodative powers of the newly created.

Scientific truths are truths in a history. Like all historical assertions, they are based on present evidence. So far, they provide a truth appropriate to the data and a reference to what will, over a period of time, be transformed.

A reference to the beginning of a temporal transformation contains terms whose interinvolvement awaits a reference to a past that provided a beginning and to a transformative agency enabling one to arrive, once again, at the initial item. Such references are never completely satisfactory, not because there is a necessary mixture of falsehood in what is claimed but because what is claimed never reaches what could fully sustain it. The only embedding that such assertions can have is in the present, where they express both objective and conformal truths about the past.

Most members of a scientific community concentrate on experiments or observations. A treatment of science as though it were a purely theoretical, formally expressed discipline accords these experimenters and observers only a subordinate, instrumental status. Few scientists are creators, no matter how ingenious their experiments and thorough their observations, but they also are not mere agents or subordinates, even when conducting experiments and observations within the compass and under the direction of some established outlook. Their experiments and observations offer splendid means of obtaining needed sustaining and graining material for theoretical affirmations.

Sooner or later, science uses the empirically known to punctuate and give added meaning to its theoretical truths. So far, it produces only limited, confined creations, inseparable from the cosmos. When well read, its claims will enable one to signify the rational as operative on and through bodies. These bodies, experientially reachable in principle, are theoretically expressible as part of a single account whose singular history precludes crediting the bodies with the kind of career possible to mathematical entities.

Appreciations of the work of science, like appreciations of the work of mathematics, are not possible to those who are not trained to understand what is affirmed. One needs guidance in order to read splendid work in areas where one lacks needed technical knowledge. One may, of course, respect what is done and may be able to make dexterous use of the formulations these works endorse, or even accept what they affirm as alone able to make clear whatever occurs. What is endorsed by mathematicians and by the scientific community may even be accepted by others with more confidence than what is endorsed in other fields, mainly because it can be backed by proofs and evidence, but there is no warrant for supposing that mathematics or science provides all that is needed to understand whatever there may be. In science especially, an acceptance should be accompanied by the awareness that what is endorsed today may be radically transformed later in order to fit new findings. Many philosophers, in particular, seem unable to master this lesson. As a consequence, the grand edifices they erect are cheated of their foundations with the passage of time and the progressive growth of scientific knowledge.

Attention in science is mainly directed at what is present, confronted, and manipulated, with traits defining other claims to be acceptable, irrelevant, anomalous, or prospective. One looks elsewhere to see if what has apparently found support will be confirmed, be defeated, or require alterations. Only a small part of science is created and thereupon able to serve as a frame to accommodate older creations and discoveries after these have been restated and thereby enabled to cohere with what would otherwise require its rejection.

Science conserves by altering, whereas mathematics both preserves and enhances. Paradigm theory, in holding that the great creative work of science occurs on a level of generality under which the rest of the scientific community operates, risks taking scientific thought to be more monolithic, more completely under the guidance of some great creator than it is in fact. There are and always have been scientists who spend their energies in dealing with possible alternatives to some more or less established view, while others occupy themselves with claims about what fits in with what all accept at that time.

Even when scientists seem to be restating what has been achieved in mathematics, they are occupied with carrying out nonmathematical procedures. They surely attend not to the rational, as providing both a condition and a locus for what they create, but to what holds as a matter of fact. Mathematical truths may be used to enable the scientists to express clearly what has been observed or surmised and sometimes to suggest new directions where investigations might be successfully carried out. As a result, the range of those mathematical truths will be limited at the same time that they will continue to express what has been created on some level of the rational. Scientists are more like poets than mathematicians, but also more like realists than romantics; the methods and achievements of science provide its practitioners not with matches of what occurs apart from them but with persuasive ways of explaining and reconstituting these events. They offer not well-grounded certainties but the best available answers to basic, cosmic questions.

Some physical scientists are genuine creators. They may or may not use mathematics, even to provide useful structures or suggestions. What they cherish are formulations having a power to unite special terms to express truths pertinent to the cosmos. Freely joining conditions and the Dunamis to refer to what is to be followed by empirically verifiable occurrences, they try to express their views with precision and to sustain them by observation and confirmed predictions. What is affirmed is maintained until shown to be in error, to be too broadly expressed, or to be irreconcilable with the currently accepted account.

Science progresses, not only by discarding what has proved untenable but by understanding daring abductive moves that make possible a better, more systematic, more comprehensive view, accounting for a host of confirmable truths. Just as there are beautiful poems containing beautiful stanzas, some splendid stanzas in poor poems, and some poor stanzas in excellent ones, so there are truths containing truths, other truths encompassed in larger false accounts, and falsehoods contained in truths. Beautiful stanzas and limited truths, because excellent, are self-contained. At the same time, if part of larger excellences, they will be intimately connected with other parts.

When scientific achievements are given mathematical form, some abstraction is made from the content, since this content is caught up in what happens to be. Few today would hold to the necessitarian view of the cosmos that once prevailed; if resurrected, its necessities would still not be identifiable with those of mathematics, since they are confined to this cosmos. Necessities that are not instanced do not interest it.

What a scientist affirms will not necessarily be read by him, either in the course of the production or afterwards, in the ways in which later scientists may. What he affirms will probably be dated, hemmed in with unnoted irrelevancies and mistaken assumptions that later developments may expose. If science paid more attention to what it had already achieved, it would be the most historically minded of all creative enterprises. Instead, it is content to use what it can. It does not now, and perhaps will never, exhibit a single, all-encompassing excellence. What it achieves is a plurality of unifications of the already known, guides to experiments, and contributions to or frames for new as well as old theories, some of which are used as occasions for new discoveries and creations.

Unable to know what the cosmos is except in its own terms, physical scientists cannot even know whether what they offer are fixed truths about it. They must be satisfied to hold on to what is not definitely known to be irrelevant, false, incoherent, or in conflict with what apparently has a sure grounding. What they affirm are truths different in kind from those acknowledged by mathematicians and historians and in daily life. Still, what the scientists affirm is readily accepted by the others. This is not because the truths are useful—much of science is not. Nor is it because they are more plausible, since what is affirmed often goes counter to what daily observation reveals and most believe. What it affirms are not truths in the sense in which mathematical creations are truths, but what is cogent, offering a better account than recognized alternatives.

When detached from all references to the cosmos, scientific creations are incomplete, so many hypotheses awaiting comprehensive articulations into which particular occurrences will fit. Though thinkers today know that Aristotle suffered from having tied himself down to a questionable astronomy, Descartes to a Galilean mathematical view of the cosmos, and Kant to Newton, too many today are ready to commit a similar error and accept the cogent claims of relativity theorists and quantum physicists as though they were final truths. Still, even a philosophy that wishes to deal with what lies beyond the cosmos ought to concern itself with what is always true of and in it. The results should, among other advantages, underpin not this or that particular epoch in scientific endeavor but the entire scientific venture and whatever truths it may attain.

We now face two difficult points: (1) works in science are created in ways differing radically from those in the arts and elsewhere; (2) feelings are present in what is created and therefore presumably even in apparently rigid scientific formulations.

1. Creations in different ventures are carried out differently in one sense, similarly in another. They differ in being directed at different prospective ideals, in the conditions of which they make primary use, in the kinds of parts they produce, and in the kind of unifications with which they end. They are alike, however, in their concern for excellence and in requiring commitments from their practitioners.

Science shares with mathematics a concern for attaining truth. Yet it is willing to settle for truths holding for limited parts of the cosmos and expressed in ways that are often tolerable for only limited times. Its truths are different in nature from those created by mathematicians. There is excellence in their creations only as they cogently represent truths germane to an objective reality. The excellence of a scientific creation can therefore be discerned only by those aware of what is at once subject to an ideal prospect and has a real referent.

Science is cogent because its creations, just so far as they find some dimension or part of an objective reality to sustain them, are true of it as it exists apart from them. One who attends only to the formulae in which the outcome of scientific creations are embedded will therefore miss what is being affirmed. When scientific creations are later found to be untenable, one may say they had been trued by an aspect of reality, but not in its full reach and depth.

While a mathematical creator enables one to grasp the nature of an effective primary condition, a scientific creator takes this condition to be operative primarily with others in a domain occupied by bodies. Since the truths of mathematics are preserved by being joined to new creations, and since new scientific truths may require the rejection of the old, what functions as a sign for mathematics will be quite different from what functions as a sign for science. The one ends by opening one up to the nature of the rational, making use of richer and richer agencies. The sign used by scientists opens one up instead to the same rational, but as operative on bodies.

Only those technically proficient in mathematics and science can read their affirmations so that the rational is finally made evident in the guise of a power affecting everything, and more particularly what is in the cosmos. Platonists and rationalists know this. The fact that everything is subject to the rational must not, though, be allowed to obscure the fact that other conditions are also operative and that their roles are made evident in other creative ventures. There the other conditions have a reach and power comparable to that which mathematics reveals the rational to have.

The current practice of extending the idea of creativity to cover the work of all those who exhibit some originality in some area is to be countered by sharpening the difference between creativity and spontaneity, inventiveness, ingenuity, and the like. The term should refer only to the production of splendors which, when well read, open one up to final conditions as pertinent to whatever there is. It will then be possible, as it is in science, to identify as creators those who work within restrictive limits, provided only that analogues of the scientific community can be found, assuring that good readings of the achievements will open one up to ultimate conditions effectively operating in limited ways.

2. The scientifically tempered ignore the arts—and ethics and history—or translate these endeavors into formalities in which limited units are joined together. Reciprocally, when confronted with the austere formulae of theoretical science, some doubt that it could be creative, particularly since there seem to be no feelings present in its results. A layman will rarely discern any excellence there, prospective or realized. Yet were feelings not present in these creations, we would be unable to understand how they differ from mere ingenious suggestions, possibilities, or expressions of these or from what is only technically well done.

Feelings are produced in works by the excellence that is there being realized. The ideals realized in the creative work of mathematicians and in the creative work of scientists yield distinctive feelings. Since the feeling in mathematical works is present only when the previous mathematical achievements are brought up to and joined with what is created on a higher level, only one who envisages mathematics as a single work can be aware of the feeling in it. A failure to discern that feeling is one with a failure to grasp a created truth in mathematics. Similarly, a failure to discern feeling in a scientific creation is one with a failure to recognize and live with it as a creation.

The feelings in both mathematical and scientific creations are like those in other kinds of created work in the sense that they reflect the insistent presence of an excellence in what is done. They have a different tonality and rhythm in the different ventures and vary in the degree that the ideal is effectively operative throughout. Awareness that a feeling is present keeps an appreciative reader of these creations from occupying himself with notations, formulae, deductions, or applications.

The statement $x + y$ is a single expression. To assure that it is treated as such we set it in brackets. The entire expression will be properly read as a single whole only if the brackets are used as occasions for attending to what they enclose. This approach should be taken since the full force of the syntheses that concern mathematics and the sciences depends on the operative presence of an ideal truth or cogency in the entire enterprise.

The present observation about the difference between mathematics and science, and the presence of feelings in the creative works of both, points up the desirability of checking what is said about creations in one area by what is said in others. The understanding of scientific creative work allows one to see some warrant for extending the term *artists* to apply to all those who are occupied with realizing ideals other than beauty, just as the understanding of the nature of art alerts one to the presence of feeling in all created works.

4

The Good Life

Individuals

From THE BEGINNING to the end of a human life, the body is sustained, possessed, and used. From the beginning to the end of the life, also, the body both structures and limits one's actions. The acknowledgment of that double fact leads to the familiar supposition that, in addition to a body, each human being has a mind or will, able to exist and function independently of the body.

Each human is both able to use and is limited by his body. Most can engage in guided, successful activity. The claim is warranted—if it is sheltered from unwarranted additions and some more basic truths are acknowledged.

Recognition that humans have bodies does not require one to hold that they are unable to be affected in nonbodily ways or that their bodies make no difference to what they privately do or undergo. Nor need the recognition that they make private decisions or that they privately suffer pain require that a privacy be unaffected by what the body does and undergoes. Thought and act, hurt and pain affect one another.

One way to account for the fact that individuals have separately functioning, interplaying privacies and bodies is to assume they have souls, somehow able both to dictate to the privacies and bodies and to cause them to affect one another. Whether or not one accepts the idea of a soul, and whether or not it is taken to exist forever, to reappear again and again, or to be divinely introduced into an organism and thereby convert this into the body of a human being, provision must be made for the fact that each human is an unduplicable reality possessing and using a privacy and a body.

The idea of a soul has no greater warrant than this, that not everything true of living beings can be explained by considering their bodies and that such a soul enables one to account for the human nature of the beings in which it presumably resides. The nature of individuality will still be left unexplained. How and in what sense are souls unique? How could each be other than all the others and other than everything else? How are the souls related to bodies? How are they able to affect bodies, and these the souls? Also, were animals other than human beings credited with souls, these souls would have natures and carry out activities different from those credited to humans; as a consequence, it would have to be said that part of what is common to both humans and nonhumans would have to be suppressed, or some active parts in humans would have to be latent in the nonhumans.

At present, it is mainly in religious circles that references are made to souls, usually accompanied by the denial that there could be individual human beings unless souls had migrated into humans from some previous residence or were divinely created and inserted into humanoid organisms at some time. What is needed is an account of human beings showing that there can be individuals with independently acting, interplaying privacies and bodies without needing to have recourse to the idea of a god of whose reality no one can be sure and whose actions originate where no human understanding can reach.

This is not the place to present a full account of the nature of humans, their individuality, and their essential constituents. It may prove helpful, though, to note some of the salient, persistent, radical differences distinguishing human from other living beings and both from what is not alive. We will not arrive at a good answer, however, unless we can also explain why only humans are able to perfect themselves. Could they do so in ways comparable to those by which excellences are produced in the arts, mathematics, science, society, and state? Unless such questions are answered, what we say about humans can at best be partial and more likely than not superficial and biased.

Existent actualities, both human and subhuman, living and nonliving, small and large, weak and strong, simple and complex, are constituted by a joining of nuances in conditions to nuances in the Dunamis. That claim carries forward the classical view that every actuality is constituted of a form and a matter, differing from this view principally in its recognition of the irreducible reality of a number of distinct, primal "forms" (conditions) and a "matter" (the Dunamis) that is at once potential, powerful, and dynamic. The convergence of the conditions and the Dunamis at a common point yields a primal ideal, able to be specialized as the ideals of beauty, truth, the good, glory, and justice. The first two have already been dealt with; the last two are the topics of the chapters following this. The present is concerned with the creative venture of realizing an ideal good.

In other studies, particularly *Beyond All Appearances, First Considerations,* and *Privacy,* I have tried to make evident how one comes to know the ultimates and how they interplay. For the present, it suffices to point up those aspects of the interplay that lead to the understanding of the nature of human beings and what they can do, and particularly of the nature of the characters they build up over the course of their lives, as well as the characters they creatively produce.

Both the conditions and the Dunamis are ultimates. Both have intensive depths. The conditions allow for a distinguishing of an endless number of levels; the Dunamis, of an endless number of layers. On each level and layer there are multiple nuances, distinguishable but not bounded off from one another. The conditions and the Dunamis insist on themselves, with the consequence that nuances in them occasionally meet to constitute actualities. It is therefore possible to find evidences of every one of the ultimates in every actuality. If such evidence could not be found, our examinations, procedures, and accounts must be incomplete, and perhaps in error.

As singulars, the conditions and the Dunamis join in two ways, with the conditions dominating over the Dunamis to constitute an unlimited field and the Dunamis dominating over the conditions to constitute an unlimited region. The joinings of the conditions and the Dunamis as undivided singulars make it possible for every actuality to be locatable in the field as a body and in the region as a privacy, without loss to the actuality's integrity as a distinct being. The primal ideal, resulting from a convergence of the conditions and the Dunamis at a common point, assures the persistence of the limited ideals that creators seek to realize.

Although there have been strong contrary views expressed in the East, and sometimes in the West, only conditions are usually acknowledged. Sometimes even a subordinate role for the Dunamis is precluded. Consequently, actualities have been conceived as no more than dense parts of the field in which conditions dominate over the Dunamis. Although the reverse emphasis on the subordination of the conditions in regions is less common, it approximates the connection that the psyches, selves, and privacies are respectively taken to have in panpsychistic, idealistic, and existential accounts.

It is not enough to acknowledge the presence of unlimited but specialized forms of ultimate conditions, for throughout their range they are qualified by the Dunamis, which has a subordinated but still effective role throughout the field. Because of it, the field vibrates and changes; because of conditions, the field also is voluminous, intelligible, coordinative, affiliative, and evaluative.

The universe is the outcome of the copresence of nuances in the ultimates. The cosmos is a specialization of the universe; there, bodies are bounded off from one another in a field. Living, and more specifically human, beings are all located in that field, without compromise to their natures and activities in a more specialized historically qualified nature. The cosmos contains aggregates of bounded units; nature contains colonies—the most familiar of which are those of bees and ants, and the most arresting the Portuguese man-of-war—and organic, living beings. Each of these entities is the product of a joining of limited portions of the conditions and the Dunamis.

Each organism also embraces subordinate actualities, acting in some independence of what contains them. The neglect of those subordinates prevented Aristotle from seeing that in ideal circumstances all bodies in a vacuum must fall at the same rate since the fall is determined not by them but by the similar units they contain. That, however, is no warrant for denying that organisms have their own ways of acting and that they sometimes determine when and at what rate their bodies will pass from place to place. When one walks, all the contained bodies are taken to a new place at a rate they affect but do not wholly determine. The pace and outcome of the moves are functions of the interplay of the complex organism, the parts, and whatever control it is possible to impose on the body's moves.

In a free fall the contained units are the primary determinants of the rate and the outcome; when an organism acts, the complex is the primary determinant. Only in a vacuum would units be unaffected by the complex that contains them; only in a world where unit bodies played no role would complex beings be unaffected by what they encompass. Only in special, limiting cases does a complex, and the parts it contains, contribute equally to the nature, pace, and outcome of what occurs.

Human beings acquire and exercise powers not possible to other beings. They may assume responsibility, speculate, and create excellent works. They may also create excellent characters in themselves and in that sense and to that extent are able to create themselves. To see this self-creation, it is necessary to point up the ways in which humans are like other types of actualities until we arrive at the point where their radical difference from all others can be signalized.

The meeting of a nuance in a condition with one in the Dunamis yields an *individuated* actuality. This actuality is distinguishable but not wholly separable from other individuated actualities produced by the joining of other nuances. There can be a plurality of such individuated beings because there are many nuances in both the conditions and the Dunamis. The beings are there distinguishable but not wholly separable one from another. Region and field are in balance there.

Some members of the cosmos are not only individuated but *individualized* as well, at those places where the field (constituted by the dominance of conditions over the Dunamis) is counterbalanced by the region (constituted by the dominance of the Dunamis over the conditions). Individuated beings are between their constituting conditions and the Dunamis; individualized beings are between a field and a region.

The cosmos is a field in which the Dunamis plays an essential though subordinate role. For some, the acknowledgment of fractals, quanta, chance, and chaos provide indications of the presence of the Dunamis and its role in the constitution of a cosmic field as well as in the individual actualities within it. No one can foretell whether or not the reverse emphasis—on the dominance of the Dunamis over conditions and thus of the presence of a region—will play a similar role in the future of controlled inquiry. If a region were also acknowledged, both as distinct from the field and as dominant over it, new types of investigation and experiment would be required, with the outcomes having to be reconciled with what is otherwise known of occurrences in the field. Today, controlled inquiry is mainly directed at the cosmos as a field of individualized bodily beings.

Humanists take account of a region as dominant over the field; the physically minded reverse the emphasis. Evolutionary theory, emphasizing the role of history as constitutive of nature, exhibits both strands. The naturalists' tendency to describe and classify and to keep to history, at the same time seeking to command the respect of traditional scientists, makes the presence of the region and field at once disturbing and illuminating.

Nature is always on the verge of being conceived in an overly humanistic or cosmologic form. To account for nature before the advent of human beings, and to contrast it with nature as humanized, a "cosmologized nature" should be distinguished from a "humanized cosmos." This distinction will allow for an epistemological treatment of a cosmologized nature as a subdivision of the humanized cosmos, as well as for an ontological account of the humanized cosmos as a subdivision of a cosmologized nature.

Living beings, before there were humans, were members of a cosmologized nature; since the arrival of humans they have remained there, while also being members of the humanized cosmos. In both, they are individuated and individualized. So far as they are the former, they continue into the field and region; so far as they are the latter, they continue into the conditions and the Dunamis.

Humans are *individuals* distinct from the field and region which meet at them just so far as they are constituted by the conditions and the Dunamis; they are distinct from the conditions and the Dunamis just so far as they are where region and field meet. They can be distinct from conditions, Dunamis, field, and region because, as between the conditions and the Dunamis, they stand away from the field and region, and, as between the field and region, they stand away from the conditions and the Dunamis. Equally, they are positions from which all four radiate, the first two more and more intensively toward ultimates that are apart from them, the other two into what stretches alongside them. We cannot suppose that individuals ever attain a position where they are exactly between the four, but they exist in contradistinction to the conditions and the Dunamis so far as they are also between region and field, and in contradistinction to field and region so far as they are between conditions and the Dunamis.

There are as many individuated beings as there are nuances in the conditions and the Dunamis that are in fact joined; there are as many individualized beings as there are places where field and region are in balance; and there are as many individuals as there are beings that balance what they are as individuated and as individualized. What is individuated is able to stand away from the conditions and the Dunamis because it continues into both the field and region. What is individualized is able to stand away from both field and regions because it continues into conditions and the Dunamis.

Each individual is an individuated and an individualized being. As the two together, it is self-centered, able to emphasize its individuation or individualization. Because an individual is both individuated and individualized, it is able to be apart from the conditions, the Dunamis, the field, and the region. All individuals can, therefore, be characterized as having the same kinds of constituents and yet be apart from these constituents and from one another. Constituted of the same ultimates that the nonliving are, each exists in the same field and region in which these can be located. Each allows as well for a distinguishing of its individuated and individualized aspects and can therefore be viewed as though it were simply a unit together with other individuated or individualized beings.

Human beings are individuals—and more. They are in a distinctive, humanized world. There they deal with other beings in terms requiring reference to distinctive human powers, interests, and acts. It is as members of that world that we first come to know them, with some abilities no other living beings possess. Only humans can commit themselves to realize and then use an ideal objective to guide and control their creative activities.

It is sometimes impossible to understand what human beings are and do except by supplementing what we know of them as in nature with what we know of them in the humanized world. Some of their creative work requires their subjecting what occurs in nature to new kinds of acts to enable them to function as material for and in what is created.

Each human being is both autonomous and conscious, the first because he possesses specialized versions of the ultimates out of which he is constituted and for which he provides a center, the second because he possessively adopts the region and field that stretch beyond him. Were he not autonomous, his existence would be jeopardized by the independent actions of the ultimates; were he not conscious, he could be located in the field and the region but could not provide them with a common meeting place. He possesses all four—the conditions, Dunamis, field, and region—but does not absorb them. If he did, nothing would be left to constitute anything else or to provide a place where other actualities could exist. Nothing that an individual can do destroys the independent status and roles of the ultimate factors, the region, or the field. ·

Some nonhuman beings apparently are also conscious. If so, they, too, provide midpoints for the field and region. None, though, is autonomous; all are properly dealt with as members of groups. The attempt to deal with humans as though they were like these beings, just delimited parts of a society, an economy, state, culture, and the like, can succeed only by neglecting the fact that humans are autonomous beings.

As humans mature, their autonomy becomes more steadily maintained at the same time that their consciousness becomes more qualified. The two together constitute a privacy. This privacy is specialized over the course of life in the form of a plurality of epitomizations, such as sensitivity, sensibility, desire, mind, and will. At one extreme, the privacy will be interinvolved with the body; at the other, it will carry out acts independently of what that body needs or does. At the same time, by virtue of the body, each individual will be locatable, law governed, associatable, coordinate with others, and possessed of a distinctive public value.

Humans can bring their privacies to bear on their bodies; they are also able to affect their privacies by their bodies. The privacies and bodies thereby acquire new roles and new meanings. Some of the bodily activities take place with no express control being exerted; some private activities, having nothing to do with bodily activities, may also be carried out.

Human beings are able to use their privacies and bodies separately and also jointly, with the one or the other in a dominant role. Concepts are formed with no necessary regard for bodily acts or needs; weight and strength characterize the body. Purposive action and pain make evident that a privacy and a body sometimes impinge on one another; the emotions exhibit the outcome of the mutual involvement of a dominant privacy or a dominant body.

Each human body has its own nature and ways of acting, occasionally behaving in uncontrollable ways. All the while, some things that it does may be privately assessed, redirected, slowed, insisted on, or kept to a course from which it would tend to stray. If a human being were entirely subject to his body, by itself or as having a place in the larger world, he would be able to do no more than react bodily. Were he then credited with the ability to focus on and eventually realize a prospective excellence, he would, paradoxically, have to be credited with a power not expressible in bodily terms. In effect, his body would be tacitly assumed to have a privacy enabling it to act in ways no other bodies do, while still being subject to a control, direction, and use and thereby enabled to bring about what a different privacy demanded.

Although all living beings have privacies, able to affect and be affected by their bodies, only humans make evident in their acts and achievements that they privately determine some of the things their bodies do and that, with their bodies' help, they often bring about outcomes of no particular pertinence to the bodies' needs or welfare. Such outcomes are reached when humans create in the arts, mathematics, society, and state. They also do so when they perfect their characters.

Character

Confronted by others, a being may remain where it has been, move toward or away from them, or, if living, ready itself to deal more effectively with them. The kind of reply it provides frequently enables it to overcome irritants and imbalances and thereby to be better able to continue, to be healthy, and perhaps to grow and mature. From some items it will withdraw; others it will use; to still others it will adjust. Such actions will not justify taking it to have an ideal prospect in view or to act to realize that prospect. Unless the body were a kind of privacy in a confused form, as Leibniz held, it could not be properly treated as though it had a mind and will of its own, even a blurred one.

If a living body could of itself seek its own health, it would need no objective to dictate how it should act. What can be warrantedly claimed is only that disturbances in certain parts may sometimes evoke compensatory answers elsewhere in the body, enabling it to function in a better way for a time. As nothing more than a living body, it is repelled by some things and attracted by others, but if it is not committed to realize an ideal prospect, it will not act to become perfected. If we assume that the body is well attuned to the world, requiring nothing except conformity to its ways, there would be little else to do but to live and prosper, provided that the privacy and the individual did not make demands of their own.

We might account for the actions of nonhuman living beings as being due to evolution and the effects of experience. Once, though, we come to humans, a new tactic is needed, for humans are able to forge private plans and can sometimes determine how their bodies are to act. Much of what is outside the body's reach is both powerful and indifferent to its welfare; if it were not possible to take private account of these externals, survival would too often be a matter of happenstance. Sometimes one should and can make the body withdraw when it is being lured to advance, to advance when being pressed to withdraw, to hold back when pulled, and to act against obstacles.

Lower organisms act as single beings, not as aggregates of distinct parts; they do not invite the blunders and disasters that beset humans, particularly when the latter try to create. Bees do not try to make something excellent; faced with a prospective excellence that they sought to realize, they would fall dismally short of building replicas of their well-ordered hives. Although they seem more successful than some birds and bears, which make obviously faulty nests and lairs again and again, their success does not mean that they never blunder, never open themselves up to grave dangers, or lack all spontaneity.

As all living bodies do, the human acquires habits. Some of those habits are residues of repeated past activities; other habits are acquired by the mind, will, and desire. All groove new acts along paths followed in the past, many of them successfully. A human also acquires habits relating himself as an individual to his consciousness. The habits by which an individual is related to his consciousness form his "second nature," his acquired character. He uses those habits when he acts privately. He also uses them when he commits himself to realize a prospective excellence. That commitment is usually undertaken without his paying particular attention to the body's needs and powers and sometimes even in opposition to its tendencies, its entrenched habits, and many of its activities.

One with a strong character will act through his privacy, where others are deflected by bodily demands. That privacy has many effective epitomizations. Some of these, such as sensitivity and desire, deal with what is pertinent to the body; others, such as speculation and commitment to an ideal, may be carried out in considerable independence of what the body needs. Occasionally they will make a difference to the way the body acts.

A man knows himself, is self-conscious, so far as he confronts his consciousness. We are accustomed to speak pejoratively of one who does so, so far as the self-consciousness denies to public acts an acceptable social form. Whether or not a man is self-conscious in this or in a more desirable way, just aware of what he is, he uses his character to determine how his singular privacy is to be epitomized in a plurality of distinctive kinds of acts. Were he to create, his character would be used to keep his privacy steadily directed at a prospective excellence.

Character is built up in good part because an individual so controls his body that he is able to concentrate on the use of his privacy. To strengthen that character, it will be necessary for him to act on the body so that the need to control it is reduced.

Bodily habits may be produced with no concern being shown for the privacy. For much of one's life, in fact, one acts mainly to satisfy bodily demands, thereby building up bodily habits. Those habits may help one concentrate on the use of the privacy and thereby more readily strengthen the character. The ways that the body habitually acts do not suffice to achieve this strengthening. Whether unguided or deliberately performed, bodily acts cannot do much more than determine the extent to which one may avoid a private attending to the body and thereby be in a position to make a steadier use of the privacy. Without that use, a persistent private commitment to an ideal, and efforts to realize it, would either be inexplicable or be the outcome of habituated uses of the body.

Different epitomizations of the privacy are brought into play when an individual acts through the medium of his character. He may occasionally ruminate or in other ways allow this or that epitomization of the privacy to act on its own. His acts will then seem to be vagrant, uncaused, when in fact they will exhibit the ease he has achieved by escaping from pressing bodily demands. Character, instead of being built just by habituating the body, is the outcome of individual determinations imposed on the body to make it easier to use epitomizations of the privacy.

A creator is sometimes aware that he has created something excellent before he embeds it in sustaining, graining material, since he used his consciousness to sustain it. He has too many private interests to be able to sustain it in this fashion for long; his creations deserve embedding in more obdurate material than his consciousness can provide.

Many can be trained to act with bodily ease and grace, to turn in one direction rather than another again and again, without apparent effect on their characters. Were this not so, all great athletes would have strong characters. Character is expressed in what each does bodily only if the acts are mediated by the effective use of the privacy as a singular plurality of different powers, ready to act and be directed by him as an individual. If his character is to promote heroic bodily acts, he must use it to make a private use of the body. One who just endangered his body without having used his character to determine privately what the body should do is not a hero; at best, he is one who is well disciplined, readied, with a body to be counted on.

Although their characters are strong enough to keep them steadily occupied with realizing an ideal excellence, some creators exhibit regrettable attitudes and behave deplorably. Wagner is one conspicuous example of a bigoted, crass, selfish man who produced great works. Some creators, like the young Mozart, seem to be attracted by an ideal rather than to be committed to realizing it; the ideal seems to flow into them and, so far, does not demand the building of a strong character. Their defective, undeveloped characters are often evident in the stresses they undergo, the selections they make, and what would otherwise be inexplicable lapses, interfering with the full benefits their incredible abilities could enable them to realize. Since they do not have habits for making the best use of their privacies, it would be better to say that they are unusually responsive to an ideal and thereupon able to do what others could not.

Character is not mere habit, and surely not bodily habit. It is matrix of controlled, stable ways in which an individual can make use of his privacy. His privacy may then act on the body, sometimes only incidentally or repressively, in the course of focusing on and providing a prospective excellence with determinations. He does so by specializing and using conditions and the Dunamis to produce units that help to realize the prospect. The result must be fixated by material if it is to have a status and being of its own when the creative act is over. What is created by composers and others who emphasize what they privately discern, as well as by performers who concentrate on the masterly use of materials, are private achievements given material grainings and sustainings.

Viewed as a singular, character is the controlled habit of favoring a private attitude, disposition, or inclination. Viewed distributively, it is such a habit operative in a particular expression of any one of them. One slips from the singular to the distributive use and back again without reflection. The former is favored when we speak of those who are judicious or reflective, the latter when we speak of them as excited and impulsive. When both dealt with as a singular and distributively, the favored way will allow for qualifications of the other and an occasional emphasis on what would otherwise be subordinated.

If no use were made of the privacy, there would be no knowing, preferring, deciding, or willing, no planning, anticipations, imaginings, or reconnoitering. These mental activities would either be ignored or would be reinterpreted and assigned to the body. Yet human beings sometimes force their bodies to go where they will be constrained or even endangered, despite the bodies' demands. If they do not attend to their bodies when they create, and at other times as well, their bodies will still play a role.

A creator's persistent occupation with realizing an ideal depends on his so using his character that it affects the privacy and thereby enables it to act as needed. Since the outcome would vanish on being achieved unless it were embedded in something independent and constant, one seeking to create must use material to enable his work to persist. If his privacy had a nature all its own which could be maintained in contradistinction to, yet still be made part of, its different epitomizations, it could be used to provide the material for what it is committed to realize. Instead, one must look elsewhere for this material. In the arts, one uses paints, stones, sounds, movements; in mathematics, numerals and diagrams; in society, the people to be glorified; and in the state, rulers and ruled in order to stabilize whatever justice is attained. If one seeks to perfect oneself, a similar use must be made of an acquired character. The very same character that makes it possible to attend to and act to realize a prospective excellence gives the result the lodgement it needs.

Every creator expresses himself through his character, which affects what he privately does regardless of whether he is occupied with perfecting himself or with producing some other excellence. If he is to satisfy his commitments, he must join a distinctive condition and the Dunamis again and again. His self-perfecting is so far like every other kind of perfecting. All make use of an acquired character to realize a prospective excellence through private acts joining specializations of the ultimates. In all, distinctive units are interrelated in distinctive ways and a unification produced.

At each step in the course of a creative venture in perfecting oneself, primary account is taken of a distinctive condition, the stratifier. This condition is joined to a layer of the Dunamis under the guidance of a distinctive ideal, the good. The stratifier, like all other conditions, adventitiously combines with the Dunamis again and again, thereby determining the lived value that beings have relative to one another. Present in every reality, just as surely as extensionality, the rational, the affiliator, and the coordinator are, the stratifier can be used like these conditions in a distinctive way in a distinctive kind of creative venture—the achievement of an excellent character. This achievement, like other excellent outcomes, depends on the use of an acquired character.

As already noted, each individual is a juncture of the nuances of all the ultimates and has a position in a field and region. Each individual is a concrescence (to use Whitehead's term) of a nuance in each of the ultimates. Instead of necessarily perishing as soon as it comes to be (as Whitehead supposed), each individual can exist and act for a time. It will, though, pass away sooner or later because other joinings of nuances in the ultimates get in the way of its continued existence.

Each individual has its own integrity and can interact with the outcomes of other junctures of the ultimates. Some of those outcomes may be individuated beings; others may be individualized as well. Some beings of both sorts are contained within the bodies of individuals. Those bodies are themselves junctures of ultimates and are sometimes controlled by the individuals, directly or through their privacies.

The cosmos contains only individuated beings, constituted solely by a meeting of consonant nuances in undivided ultimates. The independent nature and activities of the ultimates make it possible for any one or a number of individuated beings to arise and to pass away. As long as there are individuals, there will of course be individuated and individualized beings. None of the individuals will exist for more than a limited time, but as long as they exist they will also have the status of individualized and individuated beings.

The passing away of a living being does not jeopardize the existence of cosmic individuated or of natural individualized beings; it will not extinguish all that the living being encompassed or prevent its individuated units from being related to other units in the cosmos. Because an individual is also individuated and individualized and can act in ways which affect these, its distinctive acts may make a difference to the ways they function in the cosmos and in nature without entirely denying them the ability to be and to act outside qualification or control by humans.

The units and complexes within an individual may persist in the cosmos and in nature after that individual exists no longer. Since they will not then be subject to the individual's decisions and adventures, the units and complexes will not be quite as they were before. While the body has its own nature, limits, demands, and ways of acting, a living being occasionally makes it move where, when, and at a rate that being determines. Items within the body will then be at positions not accountable for on cosmic grounds alone.

The movement of a foot depends on the ways the muscles, tendons, and blood act. When a horse paws the ground, the time, place, effectiveness, and import of the occurrence will be altered. When a child stamps its foot, its character is used to express a will, an intent, or an emotion. The child makes evident that with the advent of human beings, what is in the cosmos and nature is no longer entirely explicable without reference to an acquired character's effect on human acts.

Beings that are alive affect the ways their bodies act at times; if conscious, they feel many of the injuries their bodies undergo. Only human beings, though, are able to use their privacies to carry out distinctive activities and bring the result to bear on their bodies. Only they can attend to an ideal, to be creatively realized by using their acquired characters to determine how to carry out private and public acts. They use their acquired characters, too, when they guide their privacies to help realize an ideal. One such ideal is the good, to be realized as an excellent character. This character provides a signal role for the stratifier.

Stratification

Apart from those who rest with the idea of human appraisal of whatever there is, or of a god who orders all items in a fixed hierarchy of dignities, there are few who acknowledge the pervasiveness of value. If the first group were right, nothing would have a value in itself or have a higher or lower standing in an objective hierarchy of values. A horse would be neither better nor worse than a horseradish except that thinking made it so. If the second group were right, the value of something would be due to a divine decree. On neither supposition would the excellence of a created work be accounted for; it would be present only insofar as it was so judged by humans or so decreed by God.

Plato is the great exception, for he acknowledged the existence of an effective conditioning power ordering whatever there was as better or worse. He also took it to be the only condition that was constitutive of the real and identified it with the ideal that all men should and some men do seek to understand and accommodate. If he were right about these additions, there would be no need to act and no way to create; one could do no more than overcome inattention or get rid of barriers to the enriching presence of that one primary, perfect reality. Plato would make one reduce creativity to a process of discovery, recovery, or imitation of what is forever.

What occurs, and also what is created, either has or lacks a value. If the former, the item will take a place in a hierarchy of better or worse. If human beings or God were the source of the value, they would have had to bestow a value on themselves or be totally without value. If either alone had a value, it would be indifferently connected with what else there was and would not be better than they were, but just different.

Every complex has a value as a singular at the same time that its parts have ordered values relative to one another. It may have better parts and have them better related than those possessed by a superior being; a healthy fish has better-ordered parts than does a seriously sick, defective man. Yet it has less value as a whole than he has. The values of each are one with their positions in a hierarchy in which they and others are ordered by the same stratifying condition.

A thing is on a low level of a hierarchy of values but may contribute to something having a high value, and conversely. The stratifier operates on human beings as singulars from a deeper level than when it is operative on others. It insists on itself, as every condition does, but from different levels, as limited by other conditions and by its interplay with the Dunamis. It is not something striven for. Since actualities are constituted without supervision or control, the stratifications they acquire relative to one another will not necessarily help them achieve an excellent outcome in themselves or anywhere else.

One strives to realize an ideal; one does not strive to specialize or use a condition. The ideal is indeterminate and must be provided with content. A condition, in contrast, is insistent, though it must be accepted if it is to be used.

The deeper the level of the conditioning stratifier that is expressed in a created work, the higher the status of what it helps constitute. An excellent work has great value not because of the values of its parts—they might be of a low grade—but because the realization of a prospective excellence requires that a deep level of the stratifier be expressed there. A piece of wood, a stone, paints, or sounds may contribute more to the constitution of an excellent work than something more precious, such as a human being, an animal, or a completed created work. They may supplement others more effectively than what is on a higher level of value.

If what is done is interconnected by a gradually realized good, a deep level of the stratifier will be utilized over the entire work, although that level may not necessarily have been operative in the production of the different parts. Even in those creations realizing an excellence other than the good, a deep level of the stratifier is utilized over the entire work. Contributing to every produced part, the stratifier will affect them to a degree it otherwise would not.

The different insistences exhibited by various conditions underscore the differences among them. Each helps one to realize a distinctive prospective excellence. That use may not end with the condition dominating in any part. At the end of the work, though, it will have a dominant position and be what the prospective excellence will act through as it unifies the parts. It will also be signified by the completed work as a condition affecting all there is. While it is the achieving of excellence that enables a finished work to function as a sign, it is the dominant presence of a condition that dictates what the sign is to signify.

A work of art is extended just as stones are; unlike a stone, its extension has a dominating role in the whole. All the while, the stratifying condition will play only a coordinate or subordinate part in the produced parts. Realization of the ideal good, though, will end with the stratifier dominating the other conditions in the finished work; that work will in turn signify the stratifier as an insistent unlimited power affecting everything.

The good as merely prospective is not itself very good. What is excellent is that good or some other ideal made concrete, transformed into a unification of parts, dominated by the condition of greatest pertinence in that venture. That condition will not usually play a major role in constituting the parts of a created work, but it always dominates the others when the work is completed.

The stratifier plays three roles in all creations: it relates each creation to other kinds of production as the greater to the lesser; it is a constituent of every part of a creation; and it is in the whole as a condition through which the sought excellence will be expressed as a unification of the produced parts. As a dominant condition in a completed work, it makes the work a sign of that condition as an objective power, affecting everything.

The more completely a prospective excellence is realized, the more definite will be the roles played by the parts. Some of these parts will be forced back and others brought forward in the course of the gradually achieved realization of the prospect. Each will also have a constituent owing to the stratifier and will have a stratified position in the final unification.

When used deliberately, the stratifier operates on what has already been partly constituted by itself and all the other ultimates. Consequently, the best work is in a world where the stratifier functions as one conditioning constituent among others. Nevertheless, each created work will be stratified as objectively superior to other items because it is made as a unified singular in which the stratifier operates on a deep level.

Some of those who seek to create, on finding themselves falling short of producing an excellent work, attribute their failure to an inability to keep irrelevancies from intruding. Some suppose that the inability reflects a weakness of will; others take it to be the unavoidable result of the finitude of man. They agree in holding that the obstacles could in principle be completely overcome. Yet all occurrences face insuperable obstacles and are unexpectedly affected by others in unexpected ways. If someone perfected himself, he would still be influenced by other beings, sometimes exactly in the way he was before.

Although nearly everyone would hesitate to place a great work of art or some mathematical creation above the most disreputable of human beings, many, perhaps most, would place a society or a state above all else. That would require that different types of excellence be arranged in a hierarchy of better and worse; it would also disregard the fact that neither a society nor a state is an individual and so could not use a level of the stratifier that humans can.

Much is gained by having human beings act in consonance, but if none of them benefits as an individual, the gain will accrue only to a group. To overcome that difficulty one would have to attribute the status of a stratifier to a society or state or suppose that some power bestows that status on them. The excellences a society or state might achieve could be on a footing with those that a single human might produce, but only if it were separately conditioned by the stratifier to the same degree.

Creations produce new unifications. All the while, the factors their creators utilized continue to act as though nothing had been created. In every creation, therefore, one finds unities as well as a unification, entities bounded off from one another, even while they are interinvolved. No creation breaks completely with the past or completely accommodates or is accommodated by the needed factors. Still, all creators use the ultimates on their own terms and thus do more than reestablish or relocate what is available to them.

During a creation, the ultimate factors used to produce the units continue to act as though nothing had been created. Consciousness continues to be consciousness, and the individual continues to have many other interests. Because creations never wholly absorb what they use or exhaust the powers of what produces them, they always leave much that is unutilized or unexpressed.

A creator follows one joining of parts by another under the aegis of a prospective excellence. If primarily committed to realizing the good, he will also have to commit himself both by his past actions and by what is foreshadowed. Those seeking to teach rightly place great emphasis on their pupils' commitments. It is the pupils alone, after all, who must satisfy them. Their commitments should also ready them to do this rather than that at a particular time and place. Committed to realizing the good, they must promote its realization; committed by past acts, they must produce a needed supplement; committed by what seems to be required, they must try to produce it.

Both those occupied with realizing the good in themselves and those who are not may favor certain habits, tendencies, and activities rather than others. The two will act in some accord with what others are, tend to do, and need, and may be able to benefit them. They will vary in the degree to which they commit themselves and to what. Sometimes one with a fine character may even fail to provide benefits to the degree that others do. These others, though, cannot be counted on as much, for only one with a fine character has a perduring base from which to carry out desirable acts, continuing on a particular course despite distractions and obstacles.

Those who have and those who have not been occupied with realizing the good in themselves pass judgments on their own tendencies and activities and on the excellence of their characters. Both can act in some accord with what others are, tend to do, and need. Both, too, can act to benefit others. If one of these fails to provide what he should and can, his habituated character, if strong, will assure his continuing to act in certain ways for the most part. Only one who has such a character can be counted on to act well to the degree that others cannot since only he has achieved a persistent base and strong tendencies to act in this manner. If he succeeds in realizing the good in himself, he will have converted his strong character into one that is perfected.

It has been already noted that one may create great works of art and still have a poor character. Artists, mathematicians, leaders, and politicians may be quite cowardly and selfish. One may be a great creator in one kind of venture and be singularly insensitive or incompetent in others. The so-called Renaissance man, at home in all fields of creation, is a myth, nourished by identifying novelties and inventions with creations, calculation with mathematics, and theory with leadership or statesmanship.

Each kind of creative work requires one to ignore what is needed in the others, though there is no preassignable degree of neglect, suppression, or modification that must be persistently maintained. Unless one type of creation be put above the rest, a commitment to any one will be as justifiable as a commitment to any other. If so, a self-perfecting will not necessarily be a venture superior to the perfecting of anything else.

There is nothing that prevents a Newton, a Pound, or a Churchill from acting despicably any more than there need be anything to prevent a saint from writing poor poems. Yet, unless these creators tightly seal off one side of themselves from others and thereby avoid expressing themselves as individuals who act through the use of their habituated characters, they must leave some mark of their weaknesses in their creations. Creations require individuals to begin their work at private positions behind their ordinary activities. Their character failures may not then be as palpable or their consequences as distressing as they are when expressed in interplays with others. What is then made evident in any case is that moral character may affect not only creative work but other acts as well.

The dominant role of a prospective excellence forces irrelevant private tendencies aside without depriving them of all influence. Those tendencies still make their presence felt in the choice of topics and in the time, place, and nature of the flaws that crop up in the creations. If this were not true, creators would not be individuals expressing their habituated characters in actions. At best they would be aggregates or would provide avenues through which some force surged and somehow ended in the production of great, quite impersonal works.

Epitomizations of a privacy are achieved sequentially. It takes time before an infant, with its sensitivity to pain and pleasure, acquires responsibility, will, and other advanced powers. Each of these powers has some independence from the others; it may even be exercised in opposition to them. Each also has a place in a stratified hierarchy of abilities in which those acquired later have a value greater than the earlier.

Mind and other epitomizations of the privacy presuppose and have a greater value than sensitivity or sensibility. That is one reason why creators must retreat far back into their privacies before commencing creative work. If they are prodigies, they have not had time enough to forge strong habituated characters. Their characters neither promote nor prevent a ready yielding to the ideal and an eliciting of needed acts, but if their characters do not contribute to their achievements, they could not properly be said to be creators. They would rightly be called "prodigies," from whom future creative work is to be expected.

When engaged in creative work other than a self-perfecting, creators do not make specialized use of the stratifier or make this an ingredient in a final outcome. Some other condition will instead be stressed, without precluding other roles for the stratifier. Someone seeking to perfect himself will not only make use of a deep level of the stratifier but will be valuationally joined to others. The feeling that the prospective good introduces will spread throughout the result. Even one who has achieved the noble man's self-mastery, the wise man's unruffled calm, or the hero's control exhibits the good as pervaded by a distinctive feeling tone.

The stratifier is utilized at every stage in a creating as one condition among others, joined with the Dunamis in part after part. Conceivably, it could be dominant in every part and not be so in the completed work. This would be the outcome if the parts did not jointly contribute to the realization of the excellent prospect. It is not great acts that make a great man, but acts so fitted together that the good is most fully realized in him.

Like every other condition, the stratifier is a constituent in whatever occurs. Like them, it still remains available for further use. As pertinent to a multitude of items, each with its own nature and a well-defined role, it may impose determinations having nothing to do with what is being sought or needed. Apart from the use of a sought excellence, the Dunamis, and the privacy, the stratifier's specialized presence in the privacy would end with just a scaling of epitomizations, while leaving them to act as they may.

As used together with other factors, the stratifier enables epitomizations of the privacy to function as well-demarcated, well-ordered powers. These powers, when guided and controlled by the good, will be related as dominant and dominated. If the interplay of privacy and body is to end with the individual acquiring a splendid character, all the distinctive parts of that character will have had to be unified by the realized good. The character's excellence will not preclude its independent status as coordinate with other creations, its affiliation in various ways with whatever else there may be, its intelligibility, its distancings as well as distensions, or its place in a hierarchy of better and worse entities, created or not.

Like every other condition, the stratifier is an essential constituent of the several parts of the realized ideal and of the work as a whole, both as the work is by itself and as it is together with others. The stratifier need not benefit that in which it is a factor; it cannot of itself assure that what it governs will so function that something desirable will be achieved. Nor will a joining of it with the privacy provide assurance that the whole will be benefited.

In all items, and therefore in all created works as well, the stratifier plays a role, together with all the other conditions, the Dunamis, the ideal, and the privacy. Left without the guidance of a sought excellence, there would be no determining the degree and manner in which the privacy will be utilized and joined to the body. That guidance is more and more effective the more one progresses in the realization of that excellence.

So far as it is unrealized, the good, like other ideal prospects, remains indeterminate. As virtuosos and prodigies make evident, it may quickly obtain a filling without being able to exhibit any feeling. If the prospective ideal could receive determinations only in this way, one would have to do nothing more than remove obstacles to its presence in a new setting. No feeling would be produced. But creations always require that work be done to realize an ideal and thereby enable a feeling to pervade a unified product.

Perfecting the Character

Neither the privacy nor the body of an individual is a substance, self-centered, going its own way in complete independence of the other. They are separated from and interinvolved with one another from birth to death. Initially, and also usually, the body plays a prominent role, but again and again the privacy dictates what the body is to do. The habitual ways in which a body and a privacy act separately and jointly builds an acquired character, the separate ways being primarily agencies for expressing what one will do. That character is used to realize a prospective excellence, and therefore a good character.

The fact that admonitions and supposedly justifying rules are so conspicuously used to turn the young toward the path of becoming excellent, combined with the belief that the desirable outcome is within anyone's grasp, seems to lie behind the common belief that a good character is had by filling in details in a native innocent and presumably fine human nature. The supposition is less common in the East than it is in the West, owing in part to the fact that so many in the East think that excellence is acquired by escaping from irrelevant constraints, bad habits, and self-imposed limitations, thus opening one to the eternal. Surely it is desirable to reach that stage, but that will require more than acts of constraint, removal, or negation. The advice offered could help pupils to get ready to be perfected. It will not enable them to be so. If they are to become wise, noble, or heroic, they must work at the task of acquiring a good character.

The perfection of a person, like any other kind of excellence, requires the joining of conditions and the Dunamis in act after act under the guiding control of the good. That outcome would not be possible if the individual did not use a well-habituated privacy and body. If successful, he will become excellent and so far stratified as equal to any other creation. He will not cease then to be the individual he was or lose the habits and hence the habituated character he has acquired.

Creations depend on a joining of conditions and the Dunamis again and again in such a way that an ideal prospect is realized as a unification of what has been produced. The creation of an excellent character is no exception. The fact that the outcome is realized in the habituated character that has been built up over the years means only that the creative activity will be able to be persistently carried out in a distinctive way.

To create an excellent character, one makes use of the habituated character that has been gradually acquired to govern the way the privacy is used. One must commit oneself to bring about the ideal good not only by means of but in the very character that has been achieved through the habitual performance of various acts. All the while, one will continue to be, able to act on and interplay with the body as it carries out its own activities.

Human beings, who alone can achieve excellent characters, must concentrate on realizing the ideal good in themselves. Only a few try to do so, and fewer still succeed. Most occupy themselves with needs and problems having a bodily import, with a few concentrating on the use of some such epitomization of their privacies as the mind or sensibility to bring about other results. All subject now the privacy and now the body to restraints.

High-spirited horses, persistent cats, faithful dogs, and similar living beings sometimes awaken admiration by continuing to act against strong resistances. Unable to create, they cannot properly be said to have excellent characters. Well habituated, they do nothing to realize an excellence in the habituated characters they have developed over the years. Instead, their characters function not as intermediaries between themselves and their privacies but as conduits between themselves as private and what they do publicly.

It takes a well-habituated character, operating through the privacy, to sustain efforts to create an excellent work and also, therefore, an excellent character. Yet the former is acquired mainly without effort, helped in part by training, teaching, and attempts to duplicate the acts of others. No training or repetitions make it excellent. At best they will enable one to find a prospective excellence that is attractive enough to elicit a commitment to realize it. Such a commitment requires a deliberate forsaking of a concentration on present, particular satisfactions in favor of a prospect to be realized for no other reason than that a splendid result may thereupon be achieved.

A prospective excellence is different from a possibility. Whereas the former acquires determinations through acts devoted to realizing it as an operative unification of a plurality of separately produced items, the latter can become only an aspect in something present. No one is committed by a possibility or committed to making it become present. If one wanted to acquire riches or to win a race, one would not have to commit oneself to bring it about. What had to be done would be no more than what enabled the possibility to become an aspect of something present. Some acts may have to be followed by others for this enabling to occur, but none of these acts will be subject to a controlling governance by that possibility.

A series of occurrences may be anticipated and produced, at the end of which a possibility might come about that might have been identified along the way, but that will not suffice to permit one to equate it with a prospective excellence. One is attached to such an excellence by a commitment and acts to make it more determinate and effective; a possibility is filled out by being given a position in the present as an aspect of what occurs there. A possibility awaits a filling; a prospective excellence, in contrast, affects the work that is done to realize it.

Both those who enable possibilities to be filled out and those who realize prospective excellences make use of their habituated characters, the one to keep the possibility in focus, the other to enable the prospect to become more and more determinate and enhancing. An actualized possibility, when hard to bring about, may not have been worth the effort.

A subhuman organism is not an aggregate of distinct parts and does not strive to be perfected. The neat mounds made by ants require no reference to any ideal; the ants are not concerned with realizing beauty, truth, the good, glory, or justice. Consequently, they never risk making the blunders or suffering the disasters besetting those who create. Ants take no great risks. Were they faced with a prospective excellence that they sought to realize, they would surely fall short of achieving replicas of what they now can do so well.

Sometimes human beings use their bodies to sustain what they privately achieve. To do so, they must reach a position in themselves where they can use their private powers. This effort might require them to neglect much that they need. All the while they will continue to have their own natures, course, powers, and habits. Inevitably, they will add tendencies, requirements, and insistencies of their own to what they set out to do. If they try to perfect themselves, they must so act that an ideal good is realized in the very habituated character that is carrying out the activity. If the result is biased toward the privacy and especially the mind, they may become wise; if the bias is toward the body, they may become heroic. If the first, they will be primarily reflective, judgmental; if the second, they will be primarily alert, responsive, active. To be noble, they would instead have to maintain themselves between these two poles, sometimes emphasizing acts along the lines of the wise, and sometimes along those pertinent to the heroic.

Privacies and bodies have distinctive natures and carry out distinctive acts. The effect they have on one another ensures that at least one of them will play a significant role in the result. Usually they give one another a new import by making use of the habituated character. In some accord with the pace and nature of the body's development, a privacy becomes ever more complex, acquiring such distinguishable epitomizations as sensibility, desire, mind, and will. These epitomizations are able to act in considerable independence of the body, to dictate to it, and to utilize it as support, agent, or supplement. All play a role in efforts to forge a good character.

Those looking to understand an ultimate and how it acts must not merely contemplate it. Instead, they must first attend to evidences of it in actualities and then so use what they isolate that they terminate at that ultimate. They may contemplate the ultimate, but only after they have privately moved toward it. That act requires that some of the body's insistencies be deflected or blocked. An interest in such self-control—or in the desirability of being guided by what is awesome and abiding—may hide the roles that the emotions actually play. These roles are not only unavoidable; they deserve to be emphasized both in creative ventures and in more routine activities. Freed from particularized interests, they charge one's activities, even those involved in one becoming a perfected being exercising a strong control over what is being done. At all times, these emotions, whatever the kind or the grade, are to be distinguished from a feeling, marking the effective presence of gradually realized excellences over the course of a creation.

It is sometimes easy to differentiate feeling and emotion when attending to creations in art. It is harder to do so in other creative ventures. Even so, the two should be distinguished. The emotions are lived through consciously; feeling pervades a created work. The production of an excellent character is inevitably charged with feeling, as the outcome of the insistence that a sought excellence, the good, manifests throughout. It will continue to be present as long as the excellence is.

Although almost everyone is aware of the presence of feeling in a work of art, its absence evoking such characterizations as "dead," "flat," "exhibitionistic," and, of course, "lacking in feeling," it is hard to discern it in creations in which notations and actions quickly take over. Because individuals are privately perfected by a realization of the good, it is even more difficult to separate out the feeling that is present, it being inextricably joined to the emotions that the individual undergoes when struggling to express himself through a use of both his privacy and body.

The noble, the heroic, and the wise are all loci of feeling, usually more readily discernible by others than by themselves. The dominant note is provided by the excellence as present throughout. Effectively unifying otherwise detached parts, it is exhibited with multiple stresses, thrusts, and thicknesses. Together, these qualities show that the work is a superlative singular, worth living with.

Some persons are too austere, too rigid, too unbending, too unforgiving of themselves or others. They are not noble. They are not even heroic or wise, despite a formal correctness in what they do and perhaps intend. The good does not enrich their characters or quicken what they do. Were the good effectively present, they would be able to engage in acts no study of the good or of character would allow one to anticipate.

Emotions exhibit the effective dominance of the privacy or the body in consciousness; they there fluctuate in nature and in tenacity. Rarely does any continue at that same pitch for long. At one time the privacy and at another time the bodily contributions will be dominant. There is therefore nothing to be gained by replacing the usual view of the emotions as essentially private and taking them instead to be essentially bodily. Emotions are constituted by a meeting at a common point of subdivisions of region and field—which is to say, when a privacy and a body are jointly possessed by an individual.

As the privacy and body vary in their influence on one another, they affect the nature, course, and tonality of the emotions they constitute. These emotions in turn qualify the course and outcome of what is being done. An angry man is an angered one, angrily striking an angering object, which may not even have been the occasion for his anger. It terminates in what angers: that is sufficient. An innocent child may be struck and yet be thought to deserve the blow because it innocently looked on.

Sometimes anger is desirable, as surely as is fear, jealousy, or joy. It is not they but their excesses and inappropriateness to particular situations or tasks that is to be condemned. Whatever the emotion and how it is expressed, it shows an overinsistence by the privacy or the body in consciousness. A sealed-off, separate privacy or body would preclude the existence of any emotion. Some stoics and sages aim at achieving that state, as though they could free themselves from their bodies. They, like the rest of us, interplay with other humans, interact with what they may happen to confront, and possess both their bodies and their privacies.

The simplest act of withdrawal into privacy requires a confrontation, a rejection, and a pushing aside of the body—and thus an involvement with what was to be ignored. Stoics, and sages as well, emotionally assess what they profess to reject. Opposed to them are those who try to immerse themselves in bodily activities. With others who are forced to labor to the point of exhaustion, they, too, are unable to avoid the exercise of private powers, if only to suffer and perhaps to resent the drudgery.

The good is one excellence alongside others. Ethical and religious concerns have tended to conceive it as that which all other excellences specialize. The Romantics stressed beauty instead. Philosophers are inclined to put truth first; communitarians give that role to glory; both democrats and communists claim to be concerned primarily with justice. Awareness of the merits of each help us avoid placing one of these desirable achievements above the others.

The noble, the wise, and the heroic occupy themselves primarily with realizing the good. If they realize other ideals as well, they might incidentally strengthen their characters. If they did not already have strong characters, they would not have been able to persist in the difficult task of making it excellent. A strong character is needed if one is to acquire a splendid character. The realization of the good in oneself is embedded in the very character which sustains the realization. A similar strength of character is needed to bring other creative ventures to a successful close.

Everyone builds a character of some kind during his life and uses it in a distinctive way when engaged in producing an excellent work. If we spoke of one occupied with realizing that good as already good, we would paradoxically suppose that one must be good in order to become good. One who seeks to be good, like other creators, makes use of whatever character he has acquired through his life. If that acquired character is strong, he will be able to keep steadily at the task of perfecting himself.

The steady, insistent use of an acquired character is not to be identified with the will, for the will is just one epitomization of the privacy alongside others, able to be exercised without reference to what else is present, to what ought to be done, or to the rights and powers of other actualities. It could be ruthless, heedless, used by one concerned with overcoming others, denying them their property, health, or continuance. In and of itself it is neither good nor bad. A so-called good will is a will used by an individual to insist on certain acts being carried out; it is not better than a will insisting on less desirable acts.

It is not exactly correct to say that a character is good if it so directs the will that a desirable outcome is realized. A character is good only if it is pervaded by a realized excellence. One would be more prepared to achieve this realization if one had made use of a strong character to get the will to back up a commitment to produce the excellent. The will would then be well directed before it was used.

Like every other creator, one concerned with becoming noble will be confronted countless times with the adventitious, accidental, aberrant, and obdurate. These occurrences will have to be mastered in order to bring them in consonance with what else is needed in order to realize the ideal good. One who would be noble must make a deliberate, willed effort to find a place for them.

It is tempting to suppose that the good is already determinate and needs only to make itself present or that humans might, through efforts to do what benefits others, enable it to take up residence in themselves. The supposition, so tempting to

Platonists as well as to the religious, is modified by those who believe the incursion of the good awaits the arrival of a few perfected beings whose presence will inspire the rest to imitate them. What is not made clear is why the good is supposed to be pertinent to any of them, why it should seek lodging in what could never be worthy of it, and how, if it is already determinate, anything could prevent it from being present.

An interest in what is readily produced or might be expressed turns one toward a possibility, with no need to engage in creative activity. To become noble, one must instead try to join ultimates again and again under the guiding control of a gradually realized ideal. Only then will one be able to end with a unification of various acquired tendencies and habits. The ideal is indeterminate, remote, faintly attractive. It is glimpsed again and again—a fact evidenced in the warranted appreciation that everyone has of the noble and sometimes of the wise or heroic.

Everyone on his own, so far as he is free from attending to some private or bodily demand, can glimpse the good and other excellences. In daily life one operates with a rough assessment of what others are and do, usually noticing indications of defects in the inadvertent, unguarded, hardly perceptible movements they make. Occasionally some signal act will alert one to the presence of a superior character and the good realized there. Few will do anything further. Many are overanxious to avoid failure; others find the effort to realize an excellence to be too difficult or to require too much time. Most people tacitly assume that one may acquire a desirable character without taking the same risks or making the same efforts a creator must. To keep occupied with realizing the good, it is at least necessary to restrain tendencies to focus on possibilities awaiting a filling and to give up the idea that one needs only to clear away whatever prevents an excellence from taking up lodging in oneself or elsewhere.

How can we know why some persist in their creative work while others do not? No account of external circumstances can fully account for the difference that a glimpsed excellence makes in their lives. Where a Rimbaud stops a brilliant career as a poet at nineteen, a Confucius tries throughout his entire life to become wise. Neither tells us why he acts as he does, in good part because, like other creators, he is preoccupied and has little interest in knowing just what was used or how.

Keeping the ideal good in focus, one who would be noble acts to realize it and thereby perfects himself. Those who seek to be wise or heroic emphasize the need to perfect the privacy or the body, the one using the body on behalf of an effort to give the privacy a greater role, the other reversing the emphasis. Nobility takes account of both. Not rigid, it slips sometimes toward the one or the other. There is some warrant, consequently, for saying that those who are wise or heroic are noble both because they specialize nobility and because, when this excellence has been achieved, it is sometimes expressed as the one or the other.

No positioning of oneself preparatory to engaging in an activity is ever entirely freed from the influence of habit or experience. If it were, it would be possible to make a ready use of any factor and any specialization of the ideal and thereupon engage in any one of a number of different creative ventures. Ideals, habits, memories, and expectations always play helpful but still only limiting roles.

Neither the privacy nor the acquired character has the power to create, though each has a nature of its own and does act in some independence of the body and the individual who makes use of it. The source of all enrichments is the human individual, acting on his privacy through the character he has acquired. What should be praised or blamed, therefore, is not the privacy or the acquired character but the individual who uses that character to realize an ideal.

Quite early in his career, each individual exercises his sensitivity in what seem to be random ways. Quite soon other epitomizations of the privacy will usually be developed and used independently of the body. It takes a while, though, before anyone uses an epitomization of the privacy either to produce something without bodily import or to dictate how the body is to function. Only when one arrives at the stage where use can be made of the privacy without regard for the body is one in a position to create anything, including a perfected character.

To be creative, it is necessary to begin to act privately at a point where activity is not limited by the body or by any of the privacy's epitomizations. Much of what is then done will neither be supervised nor directed. An individual can exercise the needed control, though, through the mediation of his established character. If he seeks to be noble, he will insist on and govern what is then done, expressing himself through his character and limiting his activities by his consciousness of the excellence that is then discerned. The privacy's most recessive epitomizations—mind, will, and responsibility among them—will be brought into play to function in consonance with the habituated body.

These observations go counter to the tenor of Aristotle's account of what humans ought to do. For him they are to become full-fledged members of, and participants in, a splendid state and must therefore acquire habits of acting which will enable them to be well-functioning units there. Although in other ways Aristotle took account of the distinctively private occupation of individuals with what was forever, he did not make room for their engaging in all their private acts or even in all those acts which are pertinent to what must be done in a state. Not the least of these occupations is a private readiness to promote the realization of justice for both ruler and ruled.

There being no need to treat a political or public life as a source or precondition for the attainment of a privacy, any more than the converse, a human should not be viewed as a detached, private being who may subsequently find a place among others. From the beginning to the end of his life, each is an individual with a privacy whose consciousness is in part a consequence of his possession of his body. If the excellence he is to achieve is to perfect his character, he will have to use his privacy primarily, and his body secondarily, to make it possible for him to focus on and gradually realize the good. This good, like other ideals, is indeterminate at the beginning of a distinctive, creative venture serving to realize it and becomes more and more determinate as the work progresses.

Each type of creation requires that its creator use his established character to commit him to realize a distinctive ideal. Whereas artists are prepared to take account of an ideal that is to be realized over an extended stretch, and mathematicians try to realize an ideal within a freshly reached level of the rational, those who would be noble try to enrich their habituated characters. Since the result will be primarily lived rather than attended to, its nature and operation will seldom be noticed. Nobility is gradually attained by making possible the increasing unifying control of the ideal good through the provision of combinations of ultimates in the form of stresses and leanings. The result might not have ultimate factors joined in better ways than they are elsewhere.

What is finally achieved by any creator is excellent because, and so far as, an ideal has been realized. All the while, the factors utilized over the course of the work will continue to be and to act as though nothing had been created. In every type of creation, there will be subordinate unities separated from one another which continue to be interinvolved with others. Those unities may provide avenues through which actions are carried out all the while that these unities are caught up in the unification that a realized excellence provides.

There is no one whom we surely know to have a fully perfected character. The best of humans is limited, subject to eruptions of emotions, different insistencies of the various epitomizations of the privacy, the particulars of daily life, and vagrant impulses. His perfecting requires that his privacy primarily, and the body secondarily, be enhanced. The expression of virtue requires that the two act in consonance.

The noble live distinctive lives. Beginning where knowing and desiring or other private activities could not yet have begun, they fulfill their commitment to realize the good in themselves. The heroic are primarily concerned with what they do; the wise provide a basis for sound judgments and controlled acts. Whereas the one is ready to act, the other wills to understand, and to understand so that he properly wills. The hero also realizes the good in himself, and the wise takes what he knows is good to deserve realization everywhere as well. These, though, are not their primary concerns.

Heroic humans retreat from involvements with their bodies, and from other humans as well, to be in a position where they can begin to act effectively. The wise retreat instead from involvements with their bodies and others to enable themselves to be one with an excellence deserving to be everywhere. The heroic are more attuned to what occurs; the wise have a cosmic reach. The heroic are selfless, though self-centered; the wise are impersonal, though their wisdom is individually insisted on. Either of them, neither, or both may be religious. Conversely, some deeply religious men may be wise or heroic, or neither, with their religious activities having little effect on their characters.

Although it is the heroic who are often religiously dedicated, it is the wise who usually speak of the eternal. The wise tend to use religion to justify their assessments, whereas the heroic use it to justify the characters they have acquired or the acts in which they engage. Both try to use the good privately in such a way that the body is led both to sustain it and to make it easier for others to engage in similar efforts. One who is noble, though, favors now the one and then the other way of expressing his achieved character, with the neglected emphasis continuing to play a role both in the constitution of the character and what is thereupon done.

Some heroes are quite naive, with little understanding of the values they preserve and enhance. In turn, some who are wise are not heroic; they may be quite indifferent to the need to face and overcome dangers to themselves and others, contenting themselves with contemplating what they take to have these and everything else as instances. Both may have made an effort to become noble, with the one emphasizing the need to act appropriately, the other the need to assess correctly. Both states can be achieved in peace, but only the heroic ready themselves to exhibit their qualities in war. Both interplay with others, but only the wise insist on remaining apart from the rest even while they interact with them.

Receptivity to the good is good because it depends on a prior ingression of the good, or it is good in quite another sense from that which the realization of a prospective excellence produces. Other kinds of excellence also affect occupations with them and thereby the process of realizing them. If we suppose that the ability to be committed to the good reveals one to be already good, it should then also be said that the occupation with beauty, truth, glory, or justice reveals that one is affected by these ideals before one does anything to realize them. The supposition is gratuitous.

Classical thought supposes that occupation with a rational condition is alone worthy of a human's greatest efforts. A condition is here confused with an ideal. Only conditions are insistent, specialized, and used to constitute actualities; prospects await actions before they are able to be realized. The difficulties are compounded if the Dunamis and the individual are neglected.

In referring to the emotions as essentially turbulent, disturbing, or confusing, attention is usually directed at those particular emotions that reflect the way the body strongly affects the privacy. When interested in the emotions as adding an irregular vibrancy to the privacy or the body, or when, instead, interest is directed at the arousal of fear or growth of confidence, attention is turned toward the ways the individual makes the privacy act. In daily life the emotions are elicited by what the body confronts; they may then explode in the consciousness, not be well controlled. An individual usually favors private contributions to the constitution of his emotions, particularly when he readies himself to carry out some private act. That is one reason why the emotions have been taken to be of paramount importance in creative work, despite the fact that some creators are coldly calm as they go about the difficult work of making something excellent. One seeking to create exercises control over what he does privately and bodily from beginning to end of his effort to turn a prospective excellence into an actual unifier. If this truth be recognized, enough perhaps has been conceded to make indifferent the question whether or not the connection was made by one who was acting emotionally.

The tonality of a creator's activity reflects the presence of changing meetings of the privacy and body in the individual's consciousness, whether he creates or merely goes about his daily affairs. At no time will his privacy lose all connection with his body, cease to be affected by it, or have no involvement with ultimates, himself as an individual, his character, or some prospect. If it could, the privacy would be blocked off from the body and would be possessed either by no one or by one who kept it apart from the body. Separated from the body, consciousness would be a purely private product, making a mystery of the fact that one is conscious of one's body and some of its activities.

Character and Virtue

Few, if any, provide for all their own needs or protection. All at birth depend on others for their food and care. Most benefit by being in a family or group; the few who do not so benefit have reached that position because they were once helped to survive. Everyone is born into a world where language, customs, and uncounted agencies are already available. The most abused and downtrodden, the humiliated and enslaved, as surely as the freest, strongest, and gayest, have all been helped.

If one sought nothing more than a good position relative to others, one would at best end by being well adjusted to them. Because sufficient effort would not have been devoted to self-perfection, the result would fall short of the excellence a human being could realize. Although we admire independence, self-sufficiency, and a splendid character, we know that there is still more to achieve.

Sometimes we admire those who pursue what they take to be required by a god. Occasionally we admire those who have achieved wisdom, those who are heroic, and even those who have noble characters, though they may not have done anything to benefit others. Those who, like a Buddha, refuse a final enlightenment in order to help mankind, or a Christ who sacrifices himself for man's sake, awaken both wonder and admiration. They are proof that there is a conceivable excellence involving concern and even sacrifice for others. Others, though less than these figures, also awaken admiration if, while imperfect, they act to benefit mankind. We commend those who remove obstacles in the way of another living a healthy, free, full life or who help someone improve himself. Neither sort of activity needs a perfected character, though a strong character is surely necessary for keeping one at the task.

A man could be selfish, callous, and thoughtless and yet praiseworthily help another. One explanation for this fact is fairly common: no one, it is said, is cut off from all the rest; each is able to exist only so far as he sustains and is sustained by others and will be at his best only if, like part of a healthy organism, he promotes their existence and functioning. A second explanation treats the benefiting of others as supererogatory, beyond any demand of duty, and the more praiseworthy for that. Neither answer is satisfactory, and for much the same reason: each looks for its justification in what is not human. If men are interrelated, they inevitably interplay; if they functioned as though they were parts of an organism, they would act, not on behalf of others but for the sake of making the supposed encompassing reality function well. Yet we know that it is good to help others for their sakes and not for the sake of some hypothetical superorganism. Nor is helping others entirely outside the scope of one's duty as a human being. It seems correct, therefore, to say that the good is able to be realized in only an unduly limited form in any individual, leaving it not yet fully realized, somewhat as the realization of beauty in one work leaves it still able to be realized in other works of art. Those who perfect themselves still face and still need to realize the good elsewhere.

Help extended to the unfortunate is eminently desirable—even mandatory. Indeed, everyone is somewhat unfortunate, needing help, though not in the way or to the degree as are those who suffer or are seriously disadvantaged. To act on behalf of the unfortunate is to act to realize the good in them in part and to make it possible for them to realize it further. One need not have become perfected in order to act in this manner.

One need not be good in order to benefit others, nor will one necessarily become good if one does benefit them. Villains are sometimes incredibly generous and kind; many a philanthropist wants to make sure that his generosity is widely known and appreciatively received. Since realization of the good in oneself can be carried out independently of the good made available to others, to say that one occupied with realizing the good in others—or even in oneself—is good must mean that that activity is superior to others because it produces a way for the good to be realized. The act need not be creative; it does not need to be occupied with realizing a prospective excellence but only with enhancing someone else without his having to do anything. It would be an act of virtue. Were such an act carried out by one who had a strong but defective character, it would exhibit the good in the way beauty is sometimes realized by one who, without making use of a prospective excellence, gives beauty the lodgement it needs. The act would not be creative, but it would still be commendable, desirable, what should be done. It could never be more than an episode, never certain to fit in with anything else, precisely because it is not guided and controlled by the good. It would, consequently, be close to the kind of achievement possible to a master of technique who here and there produces exactly what a creative act would require.

What is done for others provides an opportunity for them to enhance themselves. Those who successfully guide the young toward the stage where they can function well within a society or state may also demand respect for all the limitations then insisted on; if they do, they may thereby deny the young occasions for becoming perfected. To help others most, their distinctive needs must be satisfied in such a way that they are able to promote their own perfection. Their perfecting may require acts that a society or state may not be able to appreciate or use and may in fact denigrate or punish.

The good and the other ideal prospects are so barren, so remote, so powerless that there is nothing for a creator to do with reference to them except enable them to become more and more determinate by being realized as unifications of the factors used in a distinctive venture. If one is to realize such a prospect, he must commit himself to it and produce various things because it requires them.

Other creators can be as insistent on realizing their prospective excellences as is one committed to realizing the good. All could commit themselves to their distinctive prospects to the same extent and may meet their different, particular commitments with equal success. Still, the satisfaction of a commitment in one area or time may be easier or harder than it is in others.

The good does seem to commit one more insistently than do other ideal prospects. It is surely more pertinent to his character than other excellences are. More congenial, it is not for that reason more readily realizable or even of more concern. Were it an inescapable part of every other prospective excellence, one could explain the commitment of creators occupied with these excellences as being the result of its presence. Beauty, truth, glory, and justice would then be special cases of the good. If so, art, mathematics, leadership, and a creative political existence would have to be taken to offer special forms of the ways one acquires a splendid character. With as much warrant, it should then be possible to take the realization of any of the others to be superior both to the good and the rest. Excellences, though, are superior to other kinds of outcomes without themselves being scaled relative to one another.

Commitment to the good requires one to produce determinations for it. Other types of creation require that other kinds of determinations be provided for other prospects. All face similar problems and must solve them in related ways, for all make use of the same ultimates to realize equally indeterminate prospects.

Like other persons, those who are noble, wise, or heroic are obligated to make good whatever losses in value they bring about. Those obligations may not be important to the production of excellent characters. Yet were they pushed aside, the venture of realizing a splendid character would be compromised. To produce a splendid character and to make good the losses in value one brings about, demands a strong character, not necessarily one that has been perfected.

Each man should help others not solely as a consequence of having committed himself to realize the good but in part because he is obligated to do so. That obligation, however, enfolds a commitment to do what it requires. Apart from that obligation there is only the commitment to realize the prospective excellence somehow. One persistently failing to meet his obligations has a "bad character" not because he has not realized the good in himself but because he has not provided a recompense for whatever losses he has brought about. It would be more accurate to speak of him as failing to carry out good acts, where these acts are understood to be the outcome of desirable habits enabling him to enhance others.

The prospective good to which the noble commit themselves and which they realize in their characters deserves to be realized in other ways as well. Like everyone else, they reduce some beings and injure or neglect others whom they might have helped; like everyone else, they are therefore caught in the human predicament of being required to make good whatever values they have to sacrifice to make them be what they are.

A noble character is a private excellence. Its attainment does not free one from obligations to make good whatever losses one's presence, status, previous actions, and opportunities have entailed. If the obligations are not accepted by one with a splendid character, he will not have done everything that the good requires of him, since he will not have replaced the losses his existence and course entailed.

Like other prospects, the good is midway between limited possibilities and a primary, indefinite ideal, constituted by a meeting of conditions and the Dunamis at a common point. One passes through this point again and again, sometimes pulled toward the primary ideal, sometimes toward a possibility. It takes effort to stop at this midpoint; it takes a strong character to keep focused on it. More determinate than the primary ideal, the midpoint is still an ideal, less determinate than any of its realizations.

Although not more determinate than or superior to other objectives, the good is more congenial to one's character than other ideal prospects are. Yet all the while that one is committed to realize it, one may turn in other directions. It is tempting to turn aside when it seems possible to obtain quicker or richer satisfactions or to obtain them without much risk of failure. A commitment will keep one directed at an ideal only by and large, overall, awaiting actions which fill it out and thereby make it more and more determinate until it is finally realized. Renewal of the commitment, and repetition of acts serving to satisfy it, may make the effort to create take the form of a distinctive habit. Much as a painter may get into the habit of painting every morning, not as an exercise but as a means for producing an excellent work, so another may get in the habit of trying to realize the good at a set time and place.

To live is to become habituated and, so far, to be readied to function without reflection but with some assurance of success in familiar situations. Good habits, backed by health and intent, make it possible to act to fulfill a commitment to realize an ideal prospect, making it be more firmly involved in what one is and does. Those who act to their own detriment may have built habits as strong and effective as those used by others who act to realize the good. Habits of the former often hold them in a firmer grip; sometimes they only seem to do so.

Bad habits sometimes encourage the production of still others which are worse and which might control one to a degree that other countervailing habits do not. Vice, one is tempted to say, feeds on vice, while each virtue seems to require a distinctive effort. The idea, though, has no more warrant than the supposition that there is an insidious power at work, pulling everyone away from what ought to be realized. Vices are habits no more joined or separated from others than virtues are.

Satisfaction of obligations depends on the production of compensatory acts; it makes good a loss. Each person should compensate for what he has reduced in value. If he meets those obligations, he will not necessarily realize the good or promote its realization rather than some other excellence or some other outcome. Creative ventures are not ways for creators to meet their obligations. To attain to nobility one engages in a distinctive creative activity. Use should be made of the very ultimates specialized and joined in other creative ventures, while favoring a different condition and ideal prospect and satisfying different, particular commitments.

Each man stands apart from all others, but never to such an extent that he ceases to be a human among humans. No commitment or achievement could drag him from his place among them. There is a healthy obduracy in everyone, defying the efforts of tyrants, planners, teachers, legislators, and judges. It is maintained apart from all habituation, whether good or bad, testifying to the existence of a free individual behind all expressions, able to make use of his character to carry out private acts and to have his body act in ways counter to what others prescribe or demand.

By acting in a particular way again and again, one becomes more and more habituated, readied to carry out a course of action without thereby being denied the ability to change the direction or role that the activity and the prospective outcome play in determining what is achieved. Habits add starch to the acceptance of commitments and to what one tends to do. They may enable a privacy to be so directed and operative that the prospective good will be realized. If they did not support efforts to realize the good, a commitment to it would be indistinguishable from a longing, qualified by its terminus but having no necessary effect on what one does or should do.

Operating without being noted, habits—and therefore the character—ease the performance of certain acts. They make it unnecessary to attend closely to, and assure a rather constant occupation with the realization of a prospect. Creators act best when they function within the area that their characters can control. All the while, the good continues to be a prospect. Otherwise, not only would acts and their outcomes not necessarily supplement one another, but there would be no good to be realized.

We cannot provide or force anyone to have a good or bad character. A good character results from the creative individual use of a strong habituated character. If a bad character could be similarly produced, there would have to be a prospective "anti-excellence" focused on and creatively realized. One who decides that he will live a frivolous, dissolute, or despicable life must of course enable this possibility to become present in himself.

Malice, gluttony, and dissoluteness are not negatives. Conceivably, their possibility might become conspicuous, sustained in the present, and filled out with multiple particulars. One might then resolutely act in accord with that outcome. At best, one kind of act will here be joined to another and thereby enable a possible wickedness to be present. This would have no insistency; it could not unite what is done. That lack will not preclude the forging of habits that enable the possibility to find support in the present. One's acquired character can be overlaid by a regrettable possibility. This is not yet to replace it with a created, deplorable character.

The acts due to an excellence have the excellence in them; those due to a possibility give it nothing more than a lodgement. It is not weakness of will that characterizes the wicked, but a failure to unify their characters, with all the parts interinvolved and enhancing one another. Clusters of habits might be built up, making possible effective, well-grooved actions, but the units in the clusters will be poorly joined.

There are no perfect villains. Nor are there perfect noble, wise, or heroic men, for no creation is without flaw. A villain falls short of perfection not because he has been unable to realize the prospective good but because he has bad habits and a wrong objective. In place of an occupation with the realization of the good, he makes use of his will. His will, backed by a strong acquired character, is occupied mainly with the control of bodily acts. Where the noble use their acquired characters to commit them to realizing an ideal prospect, the villain keeps his will operating on and through his body. Thought and other private activities are made subservient to that will, not allowed independent roles.

A few can rightly claim an ability to teach others how to promote the achievement of nobility. Over the centuries, and in different lands, they have taught those ready to submit to training and thereby have their private attitudes and acts so transformed that a strong and then a good character was achieved. The Confucians and Aristotelians, among those teachers, have held that what was most needed was a change in the habituated ways in which their pupils acted. Religiously oriented thinkers instead ask those in their charge to focus on some transcendent reality and to behave as this reality prescribes. Both occupy themselves primarily with one task, giving others only subordinate roles and occasional attention. Unfortunately, what is needed is not just an avoidance of habitual ways, even those ostensibly having nothing to do with the realization of a prospective excellence, but the use of them to sustain what should be achieved. So far as the habits are expressed in bodily activities or in what issues in these activities, a privately achieved excellence will both qualify and be qualified by what is bodily done.

Established uses of the body must be so joined that they sustain and articulate whatever excellence or degree of this has been privately realized. Its ways must not be allowed a persistent domination. Otherwise, one would be forced to fit within situations which could obscure what has been achieved and sought and thereupon risk distorting or reducing whatever degree of excellence that has been or might be realized.

In a creative venture not devoted to achieving nobility, there is considerable diversity in the way the same prospective excellence is realized by different creators. In contrast, the good, though realized in unduplicable individuals who have built up distinctive characters by carrying out acts and building up habits others do not, is so effective in each that it overrides most of the differences in the different characters. One concerned only with having and expressing an excellent character needs only to keep focused on a prospective excellence and to realize it.

Those who have established splendid characters are alike in having made successful use of the same prospect. The difference between one noble being and another is due mainly to their individual uses of their excellent characters, and thereby their privacies and the prospective good. Others, not concerned with realizing an excellence, are alike in their use of some epitomization of the privacy, such as the will, and their enabling some possibility to become present. Despite occasional emotional outbursts and aberrations, they insist on having their way no matter what the circumstance; in contrast, the noble, despite their free, fresh use of ultimates and a prospective ideal, keep themselves functioning within the ambit of their commitments.

The noble and the base act as unique individuals; each uses a strong habituated character, but whereas the one puts his acquired character at the service of the ideal to be realized, the willful insist on expressing theirs. They thereby provide a new locus for a possibility and are in a position to use it to enable some other possibility to be infused in what is publicly done. A noble being is somewhat like a composer who plays his own work splendidly, the main difference between them being that the first is an individual enhanced by the excellence he realizes, whereas the second enhances a work distinct from himself.

Nobility is less the product of a making than is art, since it has less resistance to overcome. This does not mean that it is easy or that most of those occupied with achieving it or its variants reach their goal. The result in both is a reciprocal inter-involvement of a plurality of functioning units, with the one requiring a conquest of what is obdurate and the other an appropriate sustaining for the excellence. Since most of one's habits promote activities having other outcomes, if nobility is to be attained, distinctive habits must be acquired and others so altered that they keep one steadily involved in the same project. Something entirely new will be produced that is not reducible to or explicable by reference to any of the factors utilized. At the very least, the classical view that creation is a making must therefore be extended beyond its usual confines, namely the transformation of the resistant nature of actual objects, to the utilizing of private and bodily habits.

If one is to become noble, one must be free to realize the good in oneself. Backed by a strong resolution, the state that is achieved can be indefinitely maintained. The Epicureans and Stoics, otherwise opposed, agreed on this point, the former stressing the acquisition of an attitude of friendliness and considerateness, the latter detachment and self-control. These are desirable results, but they do less than justice to what one could and should do in private and in public. As Hegel observed, Stoics do and must attend to their bodies and the world in order to be able to suppress them. The Epicureans—neglected by Hegel in his *Phenomenology*—do not agree on when or how one might pursue other excellences.

In no creation is there ever a complete control of the various items to be unified. One is able to act "out of character," pursuing limited objectives expressing the dominance of this or that habit or interest, or to be so occupied with the good that the means to make it present is overlooked.

Practitioners of psychoanalysis help others overcome distorting or unwanted tendencies by tracing them back to privacies and then trying to stratify them in new ways. Whereas the Confucian and the Aristotelian try to change or improve habits, and the religious-minded take the object of their primary commitment to be all-powerful, the psychoanalysts are content to overcome blockages and distortions and thereupon allow an apparently innocent or perverse being to come to the surface. None promotes creativity. At best they persuade some of their patients to free themselves from undergoing undesirable or regrettable private experiences or from the compulsion to express what is not satisfying or desirable. That freeing may help clear the way; it will not contribute to the creation of a fine character, or anything else, unless it is possible to create just by expressing oneself well.

Creativity benefits from expressions of spontaneity, making use of new courses and openings, but it is never rightly identified with or subordinated to them. The man who creates is in control of what he uses, even while letting himself be carried along by his work. Whatever spontaneity he exhibits is used together with well-entrenched habits.

A fine character can be achieved before it is expressed in act. It is a product, not a potentiality. An occupation with developing desirable habits through training and admonition, and an occupation with the free exercise of private powers, will fall short of it. They will not get one to be fully noble or even to be wise or heroic. When such excellences are attained, one is able to become so positioned that he can manifest them in act and thereupon enable others to reach a similar stage. A splendid character may function as part of another excellence. It will do so when one becomes an individual-with-other-individuals, all expressing the characters they have acquired either over the course of daily life or through creative acts.

A mathematical creation is completed by bringing previous achievements to its level; a noble character is augmented when used to help others to perfect themselves. In both cases a creation will be completed in one sense, but not in another. In both a sought excellence will be realized in a limited area and be supplemented by acts operating in another. If the supplement is not provided, the realized excellence need not be jeopardized. When it is claimed that a work of art requires someone to appreciate it, it is also tacitly taken not to have been completed by the artist. The claim cannot be allowed even if it is supposed that the work was excellent before being appreciated.

Appreciation resembles the perfecting of another by a perfected man, since it enables a prospective excellence to receive an additional realization. This addition will not supplement the first perfection, but it will allow the first to be part of a complex in which the excellence was present in another part. Nobility is creatively realized only in an individual. If he enables it to obtain a foothold elsewhere, he does so without engaging in a new creative act.

Those seeking nobility will often take advantage of what their predecessors did or taught. All the while, they will eat, dress, speak, and move about as the rest do, more or less ignoring the stratification to which their privacies and bodies have been subject and whatever excellence they may have achieved.

That one has an excellent character must be made known by its owner. The people who believe that they are able to discern its presence by noting the look or appearance of its possessor are often mistaken. Nevertheless, one often does manifest in look and attitudes what one is privately. Were one to place emphasis on use of the mind and will, with a consequent skewing of the character toward the exercise of these epitomizations of the privacy, the fact might be made evident in the use made of language and assessments. Were one able to be heroic rather than wise, emphasis would instead be placed on attitudes and efforts tied to the mastery of difficult and dangerous situations.

There are wise men who speak of losing themselves in the eternal. To attain that goal, like reprobates who become saintly, they must not only free themselves from their pasts but give up trying to perfect themselves. Sometimes they are identified with those who have opened themselves to deeply grounded layers of the Dunamis. They may do something similar, but only as part of a creative activity that also involves the use of the stratifier, the sought good, and their characters.

Because of the conditioning stratification, different epitomizations are transformable into so many different agencies for virtues and other habits of acting. Aristotle's familiar set of moral virtues—courage, temperance, liberality, magnificence, self-respect, gentleness, truthfulness, wit, friendliness, modesty, and righteous indignation—were supposed to be achieved by finding a position between the extremes of excess and defect and had to do primarily with the proper use of emotion or the carrying out of actions. His list must be considerably modified, and surely added to, if account is to be taken of such epitomizations of the privacy as preference, choice, the assumption of accountability, and responsibility. These epitomizations he slighted or ignored. More important is the fact that he took it to be sufficient for one to acquire habits—which is what he took virtues to be—by practicing them on the way to possessing them. That surely is not always necessary. Generosity and kindness do not need preparations or preliminaries.

Saints are sometimes wise, often heroic, even noble, especially when occupied with realizing the good in a strong character and in expressing the outcome in desirable acts. They are, nevertheless, not properly treated as beings who have achieved excellent characters. They so habituate themselves that they are able to concentrate on becoming one with a supposed final reality. They try to make themselves receptive to it by cultivating humility or submissiveness. There is nothing they could do to benefit that reality. The noble, wise, and heroic, in contrast, have made themselves be excellent. They alone benefit a prospective good by realizing it as the excellence of a character.

Robert Neville, in his original and challenging *Soldier, Sage, Saints,* takes a sage, a purely wise man, to have both self-knowledge and a knowledge of the world. By providing a personal locus for truth he is thereupon enlightened. Taken to end with a knowledge of what is ultimate, he is quite different from a saint, with his ardently expressed singular desire. Knowledge, though, has too great an involvement with concepts, articulations, and truth-claims to be able to do justice to the concerns of a sage.

There are widespread religions that take saintliness not to be possible unless prepared for and then sustained by a god and, so far, not attainable by any individual on his own. Nobility, wisdom, and heroism, in contrast, can be achieved through the unaided use of a character built over the years.

It has long been recognized that works of art open up a good reader of them to discern a root voluminous power operative in every occurrence. Occasionally a Platonist has taken note of another power, the rational, available to those who know how to read mathematical creations. Other ultimate conditions have powers of their own; only when we successfully read created works do the great magnitude and power of a condition become evident. One oversimplifies by taking what is then discerned as "being" or "God" or "nature." Being is too undifferentiated, God too self-contained, and nature too limited to do justice to the multiple, independent, differently functioning conditions one comes to know after successfully reading created works. To become acquainted with a noble person is to confront one of these conditions, the stratifier, as intrusive on every occurrence, thus giving the occurrence a standing in relation to others that it would otherwise not have.

Everyone builds a character of some kind over the course of life. This character is given distinctive emphasis when a creative venture is carried out; it must be employed in a distinctive way if it is to be enriched by the good. Seeking to realize the good, one is like other creators, making use of whatever character he has acquired during his life, attending to an ideal prospect, committing oneself to realize it, supplementing each part by others in accord with their prospective and actual natures, until one is able to confront a primary power having an effect on everything. The mastery of the fact that someone is noble, wise, or heroic is one with the recognition that he has confronted a primal power ordering whatever there be as better or worse.

5

Leaders and Enthrallers

Defective Leadership

LEADERSHIP is rarely included in studies of creativity. Dealt with at length by historians, it is hardly noticed by philosophers. Robert C. Neville is an exception. He has examined some of the marks of great leaders under the heading of "spiritual soldiers." He is interested, though, not in their creativity but in going beyond the secular, familiar treatments that concentrate on leaders with limited, mundane interests and achievements, to focus on those who have had highly developed "wills." An adequate account of creative leadership must make provision for these persons, since some leaders, like Washington, Grant, Lee, de Gaulle, and Castro, were for a time soldiers with that kind of will. There are some, too—Hitler, Churchill, Mao—who are leaders of both the militia and the populace, though not themselves great soldiers. A great leader, like Mohammed, who elicits a new unity from a manifold of separate and often antagonistic groups could perhaps be accorded the status of a soldier. One who, like Moses, leads a frightened, homeless people for a considerable period of time, should not. Such leadership apparently does not require heroism. Like a Machiavellian prince, a leader might exercise firm control; he could also be a Franklin Delano Roosevelt, giving form and direction to the hardly articulate aspirations of a people.

Often enough, the successes of great leaders have been short-lived. Many leaders have had grave defects of character, while the leadership of others has proved to be a prelude to disaster. Even the greatest of leaders sooner or later reveal themselves to have only a limited vision and often to be unaware of trends and oppositions to be mastered through new creative efforts. Their achievements frequently breed a foolish confidence that they are infallible, that the people are completely submissive, or that past victories, often against great odds, assure continued success.

A great leader need not have a noble character. He may be neither wise nor heroic. He may be the source of grave injuries, exacting so high a price from those he benefits that the benefits are not worth having. What great leadership does de-

203

mand is that the leader help a people achieve a glory otherwise not realizable. The people here function for him mainly as material to be restructured, controlled, and made to serve an objective that it has not yet made its own. Unlike what is used in other creative work, the material used by a leader is human and living, each unit having distinctive rights and dignities and carrying out roles other than those the leader makes possible, desires, or endorses.

Although it is national and international figures who come to mind when one looks for an instance of a great leader, it surely would not be correct to suppose that leadership can be exercised only on a large scale. Leaders of small states, cities, tribes, villages, and, today corporations can be as creative as those who mold larger groups. A painting using a large canvas is not necessarily greater than one using a small. The leaders of large numbers, moreover, are able to produce large-scale, excellent outcomes only by making use of intermediaries. As a consequence, their work may require less creative labor than is needed when smaller groups are well led.

All mankind should be glorified. Great leaders of large groups may make it possible for that outcome to be achieved more readily than others can. Some leaders of small groups, though, unite their members at an incomparable depth and with an intensity that enables them to become beacons for the rest. Their achievements must be judged on their own merits before their value for mankind is considered. Creative leaders usually produce sealed-off outcomes, just as great sculptors do.

A leader's task is to overcome a people's lassitude or opposition, to stimulate its will to cooperate, to persuade it to become a locus for the realization of an ideal glory. Whatever the course, shape, and agencies he uses, he will be successful only so far as a people is unified through his actions and its responses.

The singular excellence with which a leader is concerned requires him to do more than exercise ingenuity or use force. The people must be prompted, aroused, directed, and guided. It may be resistant, will surely be unpredictable, and could be seriously fragmented. Although stone and words are effectively subjected to what sculptors and novelists create, they have some independence, enabling others to come to the creations from the outside; a leader, in contrast, is defied not so much by his people's being caught up in a larger world as by its nature and career. Although he may influence and alter it, he can never entirely control it.

To be glorified, a people must be both receptive to a leader's guidance and act to embody the excellence he wants it to embody. Since the leader is thereby confronted by material over which he lacks sufficient control, he must usually act for longer periods than do other creators. Yet what he achieves normally lasts for only a short period, requiring him to act again and again, with little real warrant for the expectation that when he is no longer, the people will continue to be and act as it had.

Other creators make use of conditions different from those a leader stresses. They also use different layers of the Dunamis, privately face different prospective excellences, and creatively join these excellences in distinctive ways, to end with an outcome that no others achieve. Each creator is inclined to set above all others the excellence that concerns him, but he has no warrant for this evaluation.

The head of all his people, a leader need not have reached his position legitimately. Leadership can also be exercised by one who, like Jeanne d'Arc, is not officially in command or by one acting through intermediaries having grand titles, distinguished rank, and considerable power. None of them need prevent other kinds of creative work. By allowing for other creations within or outside the scope of his own, a leader need not jeopardize what he himself has produced. Were any leader to take his creation to preclude other kinds of creative work, he would diminish the possible import and possible benefits obtainable from his own achievement.

Like every other creator, a leader must concentrate on a particular kind of task. Though he himself may be forced to neglect other work, there is usually no need for him to prevent its being carried out by others. From the standpoint of history, culture, civilization, and the nature and promise both of individuals and of mankind, those who deny a place for other creative works are less worthy of admiration than those who provide for these works. What a leader would have be realized is not compromised by some of his people acting to create in the arts, mathematics, or in themselves, either outside, within the compass, or under the influence of the glory he insists on. No creation, though, requires the promise or presence of any other kind.

Leadership at different places and times is faced with distinctive problems. As a consequence, it is exhibited in many different forms. As is true of other creative work, what is to be produced by a creative leader is an excellence unifying a plurality of units—here individual human beings. The result has some ability to act on its own. It continues to act in the absence of a leader, perhaps in the ways he had prescribed, but sooner or later without regard for his original conception. When he is no longer effective, what he achieved may be quickly followed by dispersal, mob rule, or revolution.

No leader ever succeeds in getting a people to continue to live completely as he would have it live, in good part because its members act independently of one another and ignore whatever the leader sought or realized. The existence of individuals, each with his own inalienable rights and privately initiated acts, inevitably stands in the way of a leader getting the people to act solely as he requires or desires. Each individual—particularly if young—lives and thinks outside the confines which regulate and define much that a leader would have him do.

For a leader, his people, like the material used in other types of creation, contributes to the nature of what is finally produced. Like other material, it is neither completely probed nor fully subjugated. The people, in addition, has a distinctive power no leader can ever fully tap, carrying out its own activities and interlocked roles no matter what he would have it do. A people, even when it is effectively restrained, molded, and led, may give evidence of defiance, factions, and a yearning to overthrow what may have earlier benefited it, and it may continue to do so for a considerable period. Since leadership is exercised on a people, which has not only a distinctive obstinacy but a course of its own, problems are faced by a creative leader other than and apparently greater than those set by the materials that are used in other creations.

Creative work enriches the very materials on which it depends for its continuance and stability. Whatever spoils that material endangers the whole of which it is a constituent. Because, as elsewhere, the material is not wholly pulled into the work, it is able to provide a stability and give a grain and role to what is created apart from it. A people differs from other materials mainly because the human beings of which it is composed are joined and yet remain separate from and independent of one another. They may envisage and pursue other prospects and make new assessments of what they once approved. What is presented to them is never merely absorbed; it is reacted to, accommodated, modified, and sometimes jeopardized.

A leader works directly on a people. Affecting it largely through inspiration and persuasion, he cannot become a successful creator unless he takes account of what the people can be made to do. To succeed he must, like other creators, retreat deep within his own privacy, for only then can he make best use of the factors to be joined again and again if an excellent work is to be produced. He must take account of the ways in which different men are able to associate so that the people will exhibit the glory he would have it possess. That prospect requires him to be aware not only of established customs and practices but of the fact that the interests and demands of individuals color and may radically alter what they together are, need, and do.

The glory a leader envisages can be promoted only if he takes account of the people's established customs and practices as sustained by independently expressed and therefore changeable individual attitudes and acts. That requirement turns him into a kind of primary organ, serving a distinctive organism whose nature and course depends in part on what other organs do. A leader acts on his people, as existing apart from him, in light of what he thinks it is, is about to do, and should be and what he thinks he can get it to do and become. Making use of it as existing and functioning independently of him, he commits himself to realize an ideal glory in it, with its aid. Often most effective when exhorting or instilling fear and thereby exacting the kinds of actions he desires, a leader would be no more than a preacher or provocateur if he did not do something else. Sooner or later he must unite himself with his people and, so far, act within the compass of a common, prospective, gradually attained ideal glory. It is this glory that he seeks to realize and will usually try to keep in operation.

A people clings to an acquired glory for an indefinite but limited time. That glory has to be creatively realized again and again if a people is to remain glorified. A leader must therefore yield enough to what he controls, directs, and enriches to allow for its active participation. Otherwise, the glory he makes possible for the people will not remain relevant to it for long. That outcome will be quickly manifested in a loss of a distinctive feeling-tone of the people, a sure mark of the end of the effective presence of a created excellence.

All creators must accommodate the material they use, since otherwise it would not be well utilized and at best would provide only an external, indifferent place where the work was given a public position. A creative leader must do more. He must yield enough to his people, while continuing to control, direct, and enrich it, to allow for its active participation. Great leadership, in part, and surely part of the time, gives way to what it molds.

A leader must be more attentive to what his material is doing and promising to do than other creators are. To carry through his special creative venture, he must join an affiliative and other conditions to a specialized, vitalizing power many times until a unification of his people results. Because he depends for his effectiveness on the accommodation and contributions of the people, he can guide and control it only within limits. What he finally accomplishes, with the people's help, will be primarily defined by him, but it will be realized and maintained by the people on terms it provides.

The outcome of successful creative leadership, like the outcome of other successful creative work, is a distinctive excellence. Although incomparable, it is coordinate with the excellences that are realized through other creative ventures. Like theirs, it specializes a more general ideal constituted by the convergence of the ultimate conditions and the Dunamis. That ideal enables the excellence appropriate to the distinctive creative venture of producing a glorified people to continue to be prospective even when it is realized.

When other types of creation are carried out within the provenance of the achievement that concerns a leader, they make use of conditions, layers of the Dunamis, prospects, and acts different from those that concern him. Since he may block or proscribe the use of what is done by other creators, he can prevent them from acting as they otherwise would. What he cannot do is stop them from withholding their private consent, from being lax where he would have them act enthusiastically, from being indifferent to the glory he would have them jointly promote and enjoy, or from letting it slip away from them.

Incomparable as an individual, each creator is also incomparable in his activity, though sharing with others the same concern that an excellence be realized through the production of needed, supplementary parts. Each creator acts on his own, makes a distinctive use of ultimates, and carries out a distinctive course of activity. Each achieves a unification, produced by bringing parts together under the aegis of a sought excellence. Different ventures use different conditions, produce different parts, and join these as no others join theirs. Poets bring words together differently from the way musicians unite sounds. Leaders differ from both, using exhortations and acts to produce a unified people.

What is created cannot be reduced to concepts. This is true even when the creation is expressed in language, symbols, or notes, all subject to rules. This truth does not imply that there is something mysterious, inexplicable, beyond all comprehension in any creation—or, for that matter, in anything—but only that each has its own being and career. Understanding by means of concepts dissects. Creations are singulars, embracing a plurality of emphases, thrusts, and functions.

A reading, though not creative, requires more than a removal of encrustations in a work or of blinders from a reader. Such removals would at best allow one to attend to the feeling present in a work and thereupon enable one to become aware of the operative presence of an excellence there. This end is surely desirable, but it is also far less than is needed for a work to be properly appreciated. At the very least, appreciation requires attention to the ways a realized prospective excellence enabled the various parts to supplement one another and finally made it possible to discern the condition that was used throughout—here the affiliator—as a primal power operative on and in every occurrence. A creation of any kind—not just the tragedies of which Aristotle took such acute note—opens one to a distinctive ultimate as operative behind and on every particular. Unfortunately, the knowledge of how to read a creatively led people is still in a primitive stage, with historians lagging somewhat behind bolder commentators and anthropologists.

What is created affects and is affected by the individuals using it and by the conditions it finally makes available to a good reader. Like every other entity, it is also affected by what has already occurred and may possibly occur and by the other factors that make it possible for it to be part of a world where other things are. A full account of a creatively led people, consequently, will require an examination not only of its production, the ways distinctive factors are united, the unification produced, and the outcome of an appreciative reading but also of the ways the work comports with other creations and with other kinds of objects, present, past, and future.

A full understanding of creative leadership, like the full understanding of any other kind of creation, requires a focus on the distinctive uses made of what operates everywhere to bring about what would not exist in the absence of that particular creative venture. It also makes evident what an appreciative reading should reveal, leaving to other studies the roles the creation plays in history, economics, religion, and commerce. What is most significant for creative leadership is no more and no less than a distinctive activity, ending in a realized excellence. Anyone concerned with knowing something about the contribution made by an individual leader will attend, therefore, to the specificities he introduces into the prospective glory he seeks to have realized.

The Nazis showed that the primary affiliative condition can be so expressed that a people can be pulled away from all others. The same condition, as opened up by Mohammed, exhibits it as able to act as though backed by a divine power. A good reading of what they did presupposes the creative production of a well-led people. Without this supposition, there would be no way to read the outcome except as an interplay of many separate units or as the product of undirected changes in acts and positions.

The problems that knowledge of creativity faces adds nothing in principle to those which the knowledge of anything else does, though creativity is, of course, involved with distinctive issues. Like all knowledge, it attends to something other than itself. We need not suppose the existence of some radical "other" which holds such others away from us. If it did exist, we would not know that it was there.

From the beginning to the end of our lives, we are involved with "others" within our bodies, in the world, as ultimates, as an ideal, as things, in what is created, and as known. We succeed in distinguishing ourselves from all of them preparatory to acting so that their independent natures and careers are better mastered in thought and deed. Beginning our inquiries, readings, and creations in a muddle, we escape by more and more withdrawing into ourselves preparatory to facing and making a controlled use of what we confront. Creators have no more advantage here than do the rest of us, but they are better able to move back from the muddle, to use what they then discern, to commit themselves, and to carry out controlled acts by which distinguished items become interlocked functions in a singular, unified, splendid work. The conceit of great leaders—and some other creators as well—is owing in good part to their forgetting the contributions made by the ultimate factors, the ideal, and the material they use.

There is no naturally glorified people comparable to the awesome Rockies or the Atlantic Ocean. If there were, an undeveloped mode of life could justifiably be equated with or deemed superior to a deliberately perfected one. Even those creators whose lives do not awaken admiration produce what is purer and more revelatory of the roots of things than many admirable but undisciplined men do. Free though the less disciplined may be from the corruption and follies of civilization, they are also less free from the unanalyzed daily world, where all knowledge begins. They may be adroit and effective in the course of their everyday existence, but they never entirely master it.

Creators never achieve their results just by themselves. Nothing is spun out of a naked psyche. Each uses the same ultimates and his own distinctive privacy but only one of a number of ideals and a distinctive material. Precisely how any one of them acts is not known. Fortunately, one can create and understand what creativity is and achieves without having that knowledge, though there is nothing amiss in a creator or anyone else having a good understanding of what he is doing and can and does accomplish.

Our main praise should be reserved not for individual creators but for the work they carry out. We need not then suppose that the creators are mere vehicles or instruments without power of their own. If, as is true of the noble, a leader is the locus of what is achieved, it is still necessary to distinguish him from what he creates. It is the creation that must be appreciated and read, the creator deserving admiration mainly for his dedication, abilities, and work.

A successful leader elicits efforts by individuals to contribute to the unified nature and actions of a people. Each member of that people should act together with the others in supportive ways and make possible the sustaining of the glory the leader would have them jointly embody. Each member has a privacy that is able not only to be expressed through his body but also to engage in distinctive acts in its own way. Without losing his irreducible separateness, each is able to be in a position to benefit from what all jointly are and do. Though each may benefit from the common excellence, the perfecting of all may fall short of a perfecting of any one.

A leader who dealt with a people as though its members lacked privacies would not lead them creatively. Instead, he would neglect or distort much that needed to be supported and encouraged. If he were to persuade individuals to behave as though essential aspects of themselves were undesirable or nonexistent or to suppose that those who were different from them in origin, religion, speech, or manners were to be injured, he would get in the way of their being together as mature individuals.

When others are denigrated, an undue emphasis is placed on the boundary separating one part of humanity from the rest. As a consequence, what is inside the boundary will be distorted. Boundaries are always two-sided, between the inward and the outward. Anyone who concentrates on what is excluded necessarily overlooks or misconstrues what is inside. Since what is excluded may be able to spoil what is included, a creative leader must so unite individuals, as having associated natures, that they can be unified by the glory he committed himself to realize. Since this glory can be realized in the people only with the people's aid, a leader must provide for the presence and action of what the people would otherwise neglect or abuse.

One who misconstrues the prospective glory, or what the people should do to become perfected, is no true leader. He may be just an enthraller. At times it may be impossible to tell them apart. An enthraller may sometimes even be hailed as a great leader by others, as well as by the people he is injuring. A genuine leader acts so that his people is glorified; he alone is a creator in the same sense that a great sculptor is.

Somewhat like a copyist, an enthraller can do no more than hold separate parts together. Keeping a people directed at bringing about what pleases, excites, and may even unite it, he is unable to glorify those he persuades. Instead, he hurts the very people he claims to lead. Some who have been signalized as being great leaders have been no more than such enthrallers. Acting on only a segment of mankind—as a leader also does—these enthrallers deal with it as existing in opposition to all others. Usually they will refer to some special nature, history, destiny, or divine act as separating their people from all the rest of mankind.

It is hard to find a leader who has really understood the nature of his people, and harder still to find one who has known what individuals are and what mankind should become. It is also hard to find one who has avoided all enthrallments of those whom he leads. It is therefore right to say that only when they together move toward the stage where they enrich one another's work are they maximally creative. Alternatively, we should identify as creative leaders only those who, despite flaws and failures, succeed in producing what is excellent on the whole in a world where other glories are realized. Creative leaders at their best so produce a unification of a people that the joining of all men in a final, single unification is promoted.

Although a crisis makes it easier to arouse a people, the actual work of leadership is best carried out under stable conditions. It is unnecessary for a leader to take a people into, carry it through, and finally win a war; his abilities can also be exercised, tested, and successfully expressed in peacetime. Indeed, it is more likely that he will enable the people to achieve an excellent, steady outcome if peace prevails.

None among a people may be noble; none among the noble may fit well with the rest of the people. The excellence that individuals can achieve separately is distinct from and may not be present when a glory is sought or realized.

Excitement and enthusiasm may bring a people together only for short times. A great leader, while taking advantage of such opportunities, is also occupied with what is richer, more stable, and valuable. All the while, he might insist that he is trying to do what will redound to all mankind. Enthrallers, too, claim to be trying to benefit everyone, but this claim has not kept them from instigating wars, encouraging slaughter and mutilation, or at the very least denigrating those who fervently believe and follow some other program, use some other set of works or words as guides and truths, or find other justifications for major prescriptions and proscriptions.

Inevitably, the occasions and access available to a leader, even his need to be effective, require an initial and perhaps an eventual concentration on but one part of mankind. Too often, this concentration will end by his rejecting what is outside his provenance. He may, and usually does, take the very existence of others to challenge the existence and claims of his people. References to its exclusiveness and singular nature may of course sometimes be necessary if he is to make headway in leading it, but if he is to avoid enthralling, he must use the denigrations of other peoples only as unavoidable and eventually harmless devices for eliciting a desirable common effort in his own.

Religious leaders are occupied mainly with providing fulfillments for what they take to be divine commands or divinely sanctioned standards. Consequently, they act at the service of a presumed excellent being who exists apart from themselves. They do not wish to treat this excellence as a mere indeterminate prospect whose mediation will perfect mankind. Instead, they want a people to function so that there will be a great good given to each one. Where creative leaders act to realize a prospective glory, these leaders claim to do little more than prepare for the arrival of another kind of excellence, presumably more enriching of each human being than it is possible for members of even the best-led people to become.

Some religious figures speak as if they believed a people could be so organized that a divinely sustained condition would characterize them all. Where creators actually realize ideal prospects, infusing what occurs with what they discern and bring to fruition, these religious guides state and clarify what they take to be divine commands, expressed primarily against a background of what is supposedly absolutely right or wrong. Individuals are told to obey those commands without question. If they do, they are assured, they will be enhanced to a degree otherwise not possible. If their religious guides are to avoid the charge that they are believers in magic, having the divine under their control, they should claim no more than that they promote a demanded occasion for their divine being to act, presumably to enrich everyone. None of these guides, according to their own accounts, can do more than ready a people to be receptive to gifts from a god who apparently refuses to provide them unless the people is so prepared that it will not pervert what it receives.

A religious guide claims to be an intermediary between God and man; a leader, occupied with enabling a people to realize a glory without supernatural assistance, requires that the people be receptive to what is being done by him. The promised glory is taken to be attainable by the people only if it acts in certain ways, sustained by the leader's vision and promises. He may speak of himself as a mere medium by which the glory will be achieved, but unlike a great religious figure, he will take himself, and is taken by others, to give that glory a unique form and appropriateness.

A religious figure tries to tailor his message so that it turns a people into a possible locus of a divinely produced enrichment or endorsement. He rightly denies that he is creative. Whatever creativity he engages in he interprets as a means for conveying a message or promoting an enrichment, not as a means for organizing a people. Instead of trying to make himself transparent or to be nothing more than an occasion for divinely produced goods to descend or be enjoyed, a secular leader contributes to the glory which his people is to possess.

Even when a religious figure prides himself on having been selected for his task and a leader modestly claims to be just an instrument of destiny or even of some god, they still differ from one another both in motivation and act. The one claims to be only an intermediary; the other acts as a contributor. There will be times when the one will shade into the other. One skeptical of the divine role a religious figure claims to have but aware of the transformations he brings about in a people will deny that there is any essential difference between the two. So will one who is skeptical about the ability of any human being, without divine aid, to help perfect a people. The first will take religious figures to be self-deluded or malevolent; the second will take secular leaders to be confused, self-centered, or even monstrous. So long as a religious guide thinks of himself as transmitting a divine message or command and a leader sees himself as occupied with enhancing a people, the two will remain different in intent, and usually in accomplishment.

Conceivably, there could be great religious figures who, like secular leaders, were concerned with having a people glorified. Moses and Mohammed provide good illustrations. Such figures could be properly viewed as secular leaders only if it is denied that they are agents for or transmitters of divine demands. Conceived as deceivers, they would be supposed to use references to a god as ways of making a sought leadership effective. They would, so far, differ from other leaders mainly in the roles accorded to supposed divine injunctions in bringing about a people's secular unification. It is one thing, however, to suppose that such religious figures try to deceive a people by professing to transmit divine demands, and quite another to suppose that they are themselves deceived while being actually concerned with trying to perfect a people.

So long as religious figures believe themselves to be acting on behalf of a god, they remain separate from creative leaders, for the latter use references to a deity primarily as means for persuading a people to act so that, apart from all else, it is glorified. Sometimes it will be hard to distinguish between the splendor that a conformity to the supposed demands of a divine being is said to bring and the glory that a creative leader promises. Still, the religious will be concerned with the people as receptive to a gift, while a secular leader will be concerned with having his people be transformed by what he makes available. Only the latter contributes to the production of a glorified people.

The ideal glory that concerns a leader beckons him, as that which is to be specialized and made determinate by the people, with him acting as an inspiration, guide, and intermediate. Were a religious figure also a leader, he would suppose himself to be so engaged in using what he believes his god to provide that the realization of a divinely sustained excellence would be promoted. Some great religious figures have retreated deep within themselves, beneath the encrustations of particular ways, and have acted in comparative freedom from personal biases. Selflessly occupied with reaching, obtaining, preserving, and promoting the good of a people, they are not creators. Nevertheless, they deserve to be set alongside great soldiers, sages, mathematicians, and artists for making superlative contributions to a perfectible humanity.

Like other creators, leaders begin close to the center of their privacies, cutting behind their established habits, resisting temptations to do something else, having little regard for personal gain or their own welfare, envisaging a great outcome, and acting in highly effective ways. Joining a level of a specialized, affiliating condition and a distinctive layer of the Dunamis again and again on behalf of a prospective glory, they try to elicit an accommodative response from the people. If successful, the people will become fraternized, supplementing one another's efforts.

At his best, a great leader exhibits some of the virtues, passions, dedication, and concentration of a hero. Like him, he may be wracked with fear and doubts he may hesitate and even backtrack. He may not see clearly what he must do, or why. All the time, he will give himself to performing a stupendous task without undue concern for his own safety or possibility of reward and often with little or no regard for the opinions of others. Like every other mortal, of course, he longs for esteem; he, too, needs to be buoyed up by some public expression or other sign. Still, despite great danger and in the face of considerable risk of failure or disaster, he will dare, be resolute, and both shrewdly and sensitively vary his emphases to vitalize, mold, and organize his people. His objective is the people, glorified, fraternized, undefeated by the aberrations of some of those constituting it. No other people, not even the forces of nature, he believes, will prevent his people from being glorified, if only it does what he prescribes.

The topics and themes that interest many creators indicate something of their motives and their defects. The defects rarely have as serious an effect on the lives and destinies of other human beings as the work of a leader does. Inevitably, the material he uses—the people—is used without regard for the individuals who both contribute to and exist apart from it.

As one looks back on a leader after he and his people have long since passed away, one cannot altogether free him from the persistent stench of vulgarity arising from his unwarranted intrusion into the lives of others. He fails to show an adequate respect for them in their severality. No achievement of a leader can justify his overlooking, suppressing, or trying to extinguish the fact that each human is an individual with irreplaceable rights deserving satisfaction.

A leader must exercise good practical judgment at the service of what he seeks to achieve. This prospect is not usually what he expressly affirms. Primarily occupied with unifying a people, he may not remark on this fact. His success depends in part on his people so responding to him that what he presents to it is enriched. Ideally, the glory he makes available will be adopted by his people in such a way that the individual members will be enhanced in consonance. That enhancement, however, is a matter outside the leader's control. Often it does not interest him, since he is occupied mainly with perfecting a people as a single entity. Yet it is individuals who, beginning at their privacies, so express themselves that they form a single people, having its own nature, course, rhythm, and power, where glory can be effectively embedded.

Inspiration

All of us can and on occasion do cut back behind our daily inclinations and habits to stress what is private and to make use of our habituated characters. Rarely if ever do we reach a point where our particular concerns or established habits play no role. As a result, we are readily convinced that anyone able to go beyond the point where we incline to stop is privileged or cast in another mold. A great leader, like some other creators, may then seem to be superhuman, engrossed in bringing about what no one else could.

Opening up a vista, a creative leader makes others aware of the importance and possibility of what might otherwise be no more than a beguiling illusion. Often he will be taken to have combined a singular innocence with great shrewdness, the first because he seems to be indifferent to personal interests and to be remarkably publicly spirited, the other because he seems to sense as no others do the singular, pivotal points at which basic decisions must be made. He is not content to recommend that an ideal glory be realized; usually he tries to address the people so that it will make a concerted effort to help him realize it. If successful, the people will show itself to be united, presumably in the way the leader endorses. Even when he lives in luxury, bedecking himself with marks of authority or with supposed signs of divine favor, he may be viewed as one who is above the vanities, selfishness, and self-centeredness of ordinary persons. Part of his success depends on making his people believe not only that he is concerned with the realization of their excellence in a way no others are but that he is so sensitive to the nature of what happens that he can make events serve the sought end. His trappings will often be taken by him and the people to proclaim his remarkable difference from all others. If he has distinctive marks, they will be viewed as certifications of his singular nature and his unusual ability to deal with crises, powerful forces, recalcitrant obstacles, and the grand objective in unduplicable, effective ways.

Nobility, wisdom, and heroism are only occasionally expressed, coming to the fore mainly on special occasions. As a rule, leadership is exhibited steadily, sometimes quietly, sometimes insistently, and sometimes by continuing a course previously established. Although the status of the leader may be established at a particular time through some signal act, it will be maintained partly through his determination of the way in which he, the people, and the sought glory will continue to be joined. The result, even when exhibited in a series of effective acts clearly produced by the people, will be treated by him, and often by others, as being mainly due to him. He will consequently be credited with a power whose acknowledgment suffices to evoke needed responses without any particular effort having to be made by him or by the people.

A hero has courage in the form of a steady character as well as an ability to exercise self-control. He will carry out daring moves on behalf of others, despite grave personal risk. If a leader were heroic, he would subordinate expressions of his own courage to efforts to glorify his people; he may then reveal weaknesses and vices not tolerable in another hero. Just as surely, a hero may have too narrow an objective to be able to function as a leader of a people. A hero may act without reflection, giving himself to the issue at hand, seeking success in a particular venture where he may have to risk life and limb. A creative leader instead occupies himself with the realization of a great objective, willingly sacrificing what is precious—even the lives that the hero would otherwise protect—for what presumably enriches all the rest.

A leader may express himself with humor, irony, and wit, may avoid risking injury in personal encounters, and may protect himself with guards and barriers. He may slight friends and intimates, sometimes even betraying and sacrificing them. He may express admiration for those he strongly opposes, may be devious, go back on his pledges and promises, discard those who have helped him, and embrace those who have opposed him, if these tactics appear to provide the best ways for advancing the outcome he seeks. If he succeeds, he will usually be forgiven for grave faults in character, and even in execution.

Like a painting that has long left the studio, the achievements of a leader are expected to continue even when he is no longer alive. To make that possible, he must retreat within himself to the point where he can move in any one of a number of directions to join specialized powerful factors in tight unions. No more than anyone else, of course, can he in his retreat reach his privacy as altogether unrelated to all else. Still, like other creators, he must begin deep within it. He will then not only be in a position to attend to ultimate factors but will be able to unite specializations of them again and again in the course of the production of a final glory.

All creators produce manifold parts subject to the guidance and control of a gradually realized prospect. The prospect that concerns each type of venture is distinctive in nature and role, though all are equally indeterminate at the beginning and become operative unifications at the end. Other creators usually benefit from their creations more than a leader does from his, for he is too caught up in his task and too involved with a large number of issues to have much time to savor what he is doing or has accomplished. While the other creators are also immersed in their work and often find themselves hindered, baffled, on the verge of failure again and again, they usually also have a better grip on their materials than a leader does. A people is rarely as steady as things are. When most compliant, it sometimes effectively resists being required to act in new ways.

There are usually no techniques which leaders master prior to their creative ventures. From the beginning, most work with virtually the same skills they had when they were part of the people. All learn by doing. When other creators learn in this way, it is usually only after they have gone through some training, in which they often botch what they try to achieve. A leader is denied that privilege. He may receive good advice, may have an opportunity to polish his rhetoric, and may learn from his mistakes, but he is given little opportunity to experiment on many, or for long. More conspicuously than other creators, he will usually end with what is quite different from what he intended or wants to endorse. He plays hunches, surmises, responds rather than thinks or controls, owing in good part to his beginning where he is most receptive to an affiliative condition, with the consequence that he is inclined toward the exercise of his will. He limits the exercise of his will responding to the demands of the ideal glory, to what has been done, and to what seems next to be required. He wills to keep himself committed in these ways or to act so that his commitments are met. These uses of "will" express partial forms of a distinct epitomization of the privacy used by an individual acting through his character to determine the insistence some epitomization of the privacy is to express relative to another epitomization or to some bodily act.

A leader is inspired by the prospective glory he seeks to realize, just as other creators are inspired by other excellences, though in other ways and with different effects. When we speak of artists as being inspired, though, we usually intend also to refer to the fact that they are being primarily influenced by the distinctive factors of which they make use. Inspiration is here taken to be a sudden quickening of their privacies by primal forces over which they have no control, whether issuing from themselves or from another, perhaps even a mysterious source. For a creative leader, inspiration is instead an effect wrought by an envisaged glory, arousing and directing him to use his will to keep him engaged in realizing that ideal to a degree not otherwise possible.

No less an excellence than any other, realized as others are, a unification in the role of glory is initially faint, indeterminate, not notably attractive. One needs to read much into it to make it worthy of full attention and to elicit a successful effort to make it determinate. The prospects facing other creators are equally thin; in addition, they are remote from what interests most men.

Glory, particularly if expressed in myth, attracts everyone, but not enough to make them act to realize it. What a leader discerns of it has to be brought to bear on the people in such a way that it pervades the whole. Could paints be aroused to hold onto a prospective beauty, they would imitate a well-led people. Could a people act the way paints do, they would passively await a leader's manipulation of them, enabling an excellence to be realized without any necessary benefit to them.

Whereas an enthraller is occupied primarily with transforming a people, using a glorious prospect as an excuse, a leader is primarily occupied with perfecting his people. Whereas an enthraller changes a multitude, a leader provides a means by which a people is able to change itself. The one is an insistent, persistent force, the other a power enabling a people to perfect itself. Both are accommodative, for nothing can be used or even destroyed without account being taken of what it is and can do. Judo stresses the fact more than other sports do; diplomacy carries out the same enterprise in a different way. A leader, unlike an athlete or diplomat and remote in intent and method from an enthraller, carries out his process of accommodation under the guidance of the excellence he has committed himself to realize. If a leader is not to turn into an enthraller, and thereupon cease to be a genuine leader, he must accommodate and not merely act on the people. Only in that way can he enable it to become glorified, enriched by the prospect that inspires him. The realization of his objective is no less important to him than the realization of a different objective is to a different creator.

The prospective glory prompts a leader to act on his people with new energy, to overcome its resistance, and to make better use of other factors. His use of a people as material enables it to contribute to the presence of the sought excellence. In addition to providing a sustaining grain for what he privately produces, the people both give his work a public role and enable him to fixate the import that the sought glory has for him. He alone is the creator, but one whose material must help him bring about the outcome he has envisaged. Just as he must accommodate the people to be better able to lead it, so, too, it must accommodate him to be better able to benefit from him.

A leader moves the people to focus on the ideal he envisages and to be prepared to realize it for an indefinite length of time. If successful, the people will contribute to the realization of its own glory, and its members will function as though they were actors so well directed that they independently performed in a way that would be approved by their director. If a people is successfully led, it will try to accommodate the ideal glory in itself again and again—or more precisely, when account is taken of its changing population, it will try to embody the ideal over a period in which its acts change with corresponding changes in membership and circumstance.

Where another creator focuses primarily on what must be done to realize an ideal, a leader keeps his objective in focus as that which awaits action by his people. His ideal is faced as having a depth, allowing for the realization of a dimension of it as an effective transformer of the people, while the people continues to confront it as what is to be realized then and later.

In discussing the creation of a great character, it becomes clear that an ideal prospect, despite its realization as a unifying force, continues to exist apart from all use. Emphasis on the ability of a realized excellence to be effective elsewhere, found to be conspicuously true of the good, brings out the fact that what is behind the different ideal prospects which concern different creative ventures may operate on and through what has already been perfected. The ideals pertinent to particular ventures specialize the same primal excellence in distinctive ways. Their equal indeterminacies and merits do not preclude their quite diverse realizations.

A leader seeks to transform his people so that a prospective ideal will be given a new location and role. Success, for him, instead of being just the outcome of a conversion of an indeterminate prospect into a determinate unification in or by him, requires the people to act on its own to have the ideal realized in it. It would therefore not be seriously amiss to speak of the people as though it were a cocreator, though one must then overlook the fact that the people does not often attend to a prospect or act to realize it. Usually it does little more then reorganize itself, changing its activities to provide a place for the ideal that the leader makes alluring.

No people is ever completely unified. Its individual members continue to express themselves independently of what they constitute together. Whatever glory it achieves soon fades, its members being at once too resistant and too independent to serve just as material. A people, because it is the outcome of the joining of individually grounded insistencies, quickly qualifies and may even soon separate itself from the excellence it had acquired.

Leadership depends on a people so acting that the unification the leader makes possible will in fact be operative. A leader, consequently, must not only promote a prospective glory but must get the people to act as he wants it to act. His achievement is jeopardized by those who express themselves without regard for the glory that he would have unify all. Despite the fact that a people must continue to act in distinctive ways if its glory is to continue, and despite the fact that it may do so when the leader is no longer present or even remembered, it would still not be correct to say that a people is creative. Whatever glory a people may possess in the absence of a leader not only depends for its existence on him but at best will be accommodated, not creatively realized by the people.

Despite both democrats and Marxists, it is impossible for a people to organize itself so that it focuses on and realizes an ideal glory on its own. It needs promptings and help from myths and celebrations, from evidences of past achievements, and from reminders of past and sometimes of present wrongs. Having no privacy, it is unable to commit itself to an ideal. It would be wrong to identify it with a community or to take it to be the precipitate of some group or context, depending as it does for its existence on the presence and acts of constitutive individuals, each with his own privacy, acting on his own.

Usually focused on glory in mythic form, a leader acts to give it an effective role in the constitution of his people. His primary concern is not for the people but for the excellence he would have it enjoy. If he occupied himself primarily with enhancing the people, he would not be its leader, but its reformer. Evidently, there is a reformer inside every leader, for no matter how much he influences the people, there is a part of it that escapes him and that he must get to act so that the realization of the sought outcome is promoted.

There have been charismatic figures able to arouse a people to work to its detriment, Hitler being the latest in a long line. Neither he nor any of the others was a creative leader. At most he was an unusually successful enthraller. Had he been a creative leader, he would have made a different use of the people, enabling it to achieve an enhancing unification. The evils he and his gang wrought were carried out persistently, with ingenuity and success. They inspired a multitude to act as though it could become glorified, all the while that it was being corrupted. The evils they produced were ingeniously conceived and were carried out inventively, but that was not enough to make their work creative.

If, with medieval thinkers, one refers to evils as being essentially negative, lacking the features which are in consonance with the nature of their perfect god, the absolutely positive, one would have to look to another power, the devil, to account for the fact that evils get in the way of the good. The evils the Nazis produced were as positive as the goods they destroyed, hindering, corrupting, and sometimes destroying, blocking, and overcoming what some believed to be divinely endorsed.

A glorified people neither distorts nor compromises what each member is or can do as an individual or what other people may be able to achieve. Because a leader cannot know in advance what his own or other people need or will do, or exactly what the result will be, none can know in advance that he will be successful or exactly what guise his success will assume. Each must act on his people as malleable but still obdurate material, to be accommodated even while it is being effectively led.

Like the pauses imagined by a composer or a poet, the distances prescribed by an architect, sculptor, director, or choreographer, the stops that punctuate a novel, the distinctions made in mathematical theorems, and breaks in the intentions of the noble, there are distancing separations in a people. They do not fragment it but rather join its members in a tensioned, internally constituted singular. Those members are all publicized individuals, effectively thrusting toward one another, affecting one another's public import, without destroying their ability to make distinctive, privately grounded contributions to the whole.

An enthraller who organizes a people to act to its own detriment can begin at a position apparently as far back in his privacy as any creator can. Instead of then focusing on the glory to be achieved, he will usually accept some alluring possibility or will frame the prospective glory in beguiling but dangerous myths; he will then impose it on the people preliminary to injuring the people as well as others. Even when he makes use of the same level of the affiliating condition and the same layer of the Dunamis and speaks of the same ideal prospect, he is radically different from a true leader because of the different roles he gives his prospect, the different kinds of actions which he carries out, and the different things he requires the people to do to itself and others. Where he uses his objective to stimulate the production of what is destructive, a creative leader uses his objective to unify and, so far, to enable his people to become fraternized without being set in opposition to other people.

To be a creative leader, one must be more than inspired. Nor will it be enough to be so guided by an ideal glory that one is able to prompt a people to act cooperatively. The people must be prompted to work together in a way that glory will characterize it. If this approach is not taken, a people might still be enabled to act in better ways than it had. Although not yet ready to have the ideal realized in it, the people might be guided by someone attentive to the same ideal that a creative leader is, but who, at the very least, will have detached the prospective excellence from the primal ideal it continues into, thereupon denying it the persistence and balance it needs and there obtains.

An effective guide could make a prospect attractive; he might persuade a people to act to realize it, but if he is not creative, he will not so act on what they do together that their excellence is promoted. A creative leader transforms his people in such a way that many of its members will act in mutually supportive, enhancing ways. Those members of it who are passive or indifferent may also contribute to the outcome, somewhat as rests contribute to a musical composition.

A leader's creativity is completed only when what he acts on, his people, has been turned into a means for realizing the sought glory in it, with allowance being made for the realization of the glory later and elsewhere. Because he sees himself as the main reason for the success his people might achieve, he is perplexed by his defeats, unable to account for them. His usual recourse is to blame either the people or forces beyond anyone's control.

No one is genuinely creative who does not withdraw from involvements in minor and routinized activities, if only for relatively short periods, nor is anyone creative who does not avoid introducing distortive stresses into what is to be done. A creative leader is free from such faults; he also enables a people to function together more effectively than it otherwise would or could and thereby to make its own contribution to the presence of the glory in it. His creativity is not jeopardized if the people misunderstands any of the factors used in realizing the ideal glory. It is jeopardized, and indeed cannot be realized, if the people do not want to accept that glory. Like all other materials, a people contributes to the nature of what is achieved, but unlike others, it will not only provide a place, a grain, and a sustaining for what is otherwise achieved but will vary in some accord with what its encompassed units need, desire, and demand.

The outcome of a leader's act is sometimes so conspicuously different from previous achievements that one is readily inclined to speak of a people as having been broken up into antagonistic factions before his arrival. Yet whatever fragmentation there might have been is overridden by the members' joint accomplishments. No leader turns completely alien beings or groups into a single unified people; instead, from beginning to end he deals with them as fitting together in a single totality. Since what he acts on already has individual members carrying out interrelated roles, the final outcome can never be his alone. He depends on the people's readiness to be enhanced by him as active, not as passive, beings. Because of their strong common bond, he must act as though he were one with them. The supposition that the times produce a needed leader for an aggregate of indifferent individuals builds on the neglect of this vital point. At the very least, a leader exposes and utilizes a bond that has been buried but that is still effective and is discernible by him if he really is a leader.

A people may be receptive and with favorable circumstances may push someone forward. It may sustain him as a leader for a while, provide him with opportunities and occasions, supports and supplements, and perhaps enable him to act more readily and effectively than he might otherwise. Even though his final success will have depended on the support and contributions of the people he leads, if he is creative, the excellence realized must be credited mainly to him.

Although one can distinguish and possibly isolate the conditions and the Dunamis in what is achieved—since they are present in whatever occurs—glory is not found as a distinct item in the created outcome it helps to constitute. As are the ideals in other types of creation, glory is exhausted in the unification it finally provides for the parts produced in the course of a creative activity. That result must be preceded by the leader's facing the glory as an indeterminate ideal, while the success of his efforts will depend on his getting the people to contribute to the process of getting the glory to be fully realized in it. A creative leader so realizes an ideal glory that the members of a people become role bearers, supplementing one another.

If the various factors in a well-led people were to come together apart from its leader, what would be achieved would be the outcome of a meeting of impersonal forces. Were the leader or anyone else to act solely as a single person, he might still be one who had somehow been caught up in a process larger than himself, a process that utilized him in the same indifferent way that it utilizes anything else. This is the way a leader is sometimes envisaged by those who think that what he does is but an expression of his place and time. What this view overlooks is the fact that he has a will of his own and that he acts on a people, itself acting independently.

Contextualistic theories rightly take a leader to exercise a power others do not and perhaps could not master. They hold that a people and its leader are part of larger groups, cultural, economic, historic, and linguistic. They should also allow for the fact that a leader subordinates what may have conditioned him to what his creative work requires. When he acts to realize an ideal glory in his people, he does not thereby extinguish his own or their separate reality any more than he avoids influences from the past, determinations by the ultimates, or actions by others. All the while he will continue to have a center and independence of his own. Like every other creator, he is always more than what he does.

Were one to look to heroes and others as the primary determinants of the course of the world, he would tend to overlook what they had to utilize. Nothing is gained by swinging to the other extreme to acknowledge only the work of history, society, economics, or some similar controlling power. All play a role—but so do individuals, who qualify and are qualified by one another, and surely by what is created, without thereby losing their independent existence and ways of functioning.

There is no people whose members are not individuals; we know of no individuals who are not part of larger groups. If we begin with the one, we terminate at the other, which then takes over. The fact that there are contexts which exert great influence on what they embrace does not stand in the way of individuals existing and acting independently of and sometimes in defiance of them.

A leader usually has a short career. Often he is soon overthrown or pushed aside. An occasional Napoleon may be able to return to exercise his leadership again, but his career, too, will have only a short span. Unlike other creators, a leader will not usually know how to become creative again, in part because he lives too much in terms of what he had accomplished and in part because he readily becomes enamored of a particular way he thinks glory is to be realized.

Most creators, after futilely trying to create again, either give up the effort or try to recapture the power they once had. It is difficult for them to give a true recounting of the decisions they made, the problems they faced, the challenges they met, or even exactly what they accomplished or how it was achieved. A leader, in contrast, sees himself as one who once made clear, crucial, well understood, practical decisions which were effectively blocked or carried out, the one because of him, the other in ways beyond anyone's control. Failure, he thinks, is not traceable to him; success, he thinks, is not to be credited to others. He believes his life is golden, though unfortunately not properly appreciated and never well judged. His memoirs are reports mainly of failures by others, for he believes that he was well empowered by the prospect he sought to realize but was betrayed by what, on his own reckoning, was feeble and unworthy. His memoirs tell what he would like us to believe; our documents and our memories make clear that he became one who, at the very least, was self-deceived.

Fraternity

A fraternizing people is the outcome of the realization of a distinctive condition, making individuals singularly pertinent to one another as both receptive and supportive. When they are joined in this way, a number are ready, with the help of the Dunamis, to be made into a unified, glorified whole. Were a people not led, and therefore not able to be glorified, it would at best constitute a nation. Such a nation takes account of a prospective glory, mainly in its celebrations. Without a leader, though, a people will not tailor its activities to become glorified, since it will not yet have a single, well-defined objective by which to guide its actions. Any glory which it may believe itself to be sharing will be an afterglow of a history it has accepted as its own. Much of that "history" will be fiction. The people will not be unified by this fiction, though it may speak as if it were.

The realization of glory requires a leader who both acts to realize a relevant excellence and uses the ultimates to promote that realization. Without a leader, a people could form a single fraternity but would not embody a realized glory, for though it would be intimately joined it would not have accommodated what would enable it to act as a single set of interlocked, intimately joined, functioning units. The realization of the glory depends on the presence of a fraternized people receptive to the glory that a leader makes effective.

Could a people unify itself, it would be creative, or else a unification could be brought about without help from any creator. A people, though, lacks a privacy and therefore cannot focus on a prospect. Nor is it able to specialize and use ultimates. Individual members of a people may feel that they are kin; they could even be fraternized by the affiliating condition and act as members of a single nation. That nation would be a kind of noble being magnified, but there is no private base from which it could be creative. For glory to be present, there must be a private focusing on it as a prospect and a private effort made to unite ultimates, carried on in some independence of what must be done to unite the result with material—here, the people. This end will not transpire if there is no one who attends to the ideal glory, trying to integrate it with the people.

A leader is no more unselfish than are other creators. Even those who seek to be noble act to enhance not themselves but their habituated characters. By themselves, these characters are distinct from the beings who constitute, have, and use them. Individuals utilize characters which, while never entirely sunderable from them, have separately produced natures and roles.

The members of a nation share a common history, tradition, practices, and destiny. Their daily lives make routine whatever splendors may have been obtained through a leader. Yet what the people achieve there, apart from a leader, may at times be able to enhance it and its members to a degree no leader had before succeeded in doing. Enemies may force a nation's members to be more interinvolved with one another than they otherwise would be. They will still not be unified, for unification is one with a realization of an appropriate excellence.

A leader is attuned to making a people have its members be interinvolved and receptive to the glorious prospect that is to be operative there. Usually he exhorts, cajoles, arouses a group in an effort to elicit appropriate responses from the rest. Because he sees himself as the reason for any success that the people may achieve in the venture of becoming perfect, he is perplexed by his defeats. Usually he is unable to account for them in any other way than as being due to what could not be controlled—particularly the people. It is evident to him that the people did not respond and behave properly, because of its irrational, native incapacities or willfulness or because forces operated in ways no one could master.

It is not difficult for a leader to give credit to himself for unusual abilities, character, and power and yet see himself as frustrated by weakness, indifference, or the obstinacy of what is supposedly endlessly malleable. How this paradox is possible he never makes clear, largely because he fails to recognize that his people is made up of individuals with private powers, intentions, desires, needs, and insistencies of their own. An understanding of his creativity requires one to recognize these factors and to see that he must be so placed that he is able to transform what is strong enough to act in opposition to him. The people's separate existence and activity need not, though, detract from his creativity any more than the settled meanings of words a creative playwright uses need detract from his.

Like every other creator, a leader privately specializes the condition with which he is occupied. He tries to unite it with specializations of other factors but gives the conditioning affiliator the primary role. Turning toward the affiliator, he delimits it preliminary to making it and the other ultimates an integral component of the people. His chief commitment is to the prospective glory, which he cannot realize without rendering the people maximally receptive to it.

Guided by the ideal glory, sensitive to the presence of the Dunamis as well as to the people's stable ways and tendencies, a leader progressively brings about its unification by enabling the people to become more and more accommodative of the prospect. Since individuals have their own natures, interests, and ways of acting, he depends on them to form a people apart from him. They will do so to the extent that they are receptive to the affiliating condition, apart from what the leader might do. As a consequence, he must adjust his use of the affiliator to theirs. This adjustment may not be easy, for he and the people here act independently.

It is an affiliated—that is, a fraternized people—that is to be led. To lead it, a leader must bring the affiliator to bear on it while trying to realize the prospective glory. Since the people has already been constituted by the affiliator—and other factors—and has then accommodated it, a leader not only must make independent use of the affiliator while realizing the ideal prospect but, in addition, must adjust his use of it to the people's. To be glorified, the members of the people in turn must modify their fraternization to accommodate what the leader takes the prospective glory to require.

We have here a conspicuous illustration of the fact that ultimate conditions are irreducible, inexhaustible powers. Whatever exists is constituted by nuances in each condition meeting nuances in the others and in the Dunamis. So far as the stratifier is dominant, the people will be fraternized. A creative leader's use of that very same stratifying condition introduces another fraternizing demand under the aegis of a realized glory. The stratifier, though, plays its greatest part in the achievement of a noble character. It also helps constitute the individual and is utilized in forming his character; it is also available for use in achieving nobility. An affiliative condition has a related role in the constitution of a glorified people. Other conditions operate in cognate ways in other types of creation, as the chart at the beginning of the book makes evident.

If a people does not sustain and enrich what is made available by a leader, it can still contribute to what is achieved. Its leader may do no more than exhort it and may have to await its response in order to have a proper locus for what he would have it embody. His creative activity will not be completed if the people is not used as responsive, sustaining, graining material, any more than any other creative activity could be completed without use being made of its own kind of sustainer. The material at both times makes the creation a rather stable part of a larger world.

Although able to affect a people deeply, a leader cannot control it entirely. It maintains itself against him no matter how compliant it is or how well attuned he is to it, in part because of the efficacy of the affiliative condition that is one of its constituents. He independently specializes that condition and uses it together with the Dunamis to make the people receptive to the prospective excellence he would have it embody. Other conditions will also play a role, though this role will usually be quite minor. The Dunamis will usually be quite evident, aiding the people to vitalize the affiliative condition.

A leader must transform his people, as existing and acting apart from him, until it so functions that the sought glory is both realized there and is able to stand before it as a lure. The transformation will be due mainly to the people in its reply to his exhortations, promises, and directings. If other creators did something similar, they would, no matter how successful, remain focused on their prospects. If a leader were like them, he would be content merely to unify the people and not be interested as well in having it continue to sustain the realized ideal.

Like other prospective excellences, glory is minimally determinate—just enough to distinguish it from other prospects as well as from the primal ideal which all the excellences specialize. A leader faces it as a distinctive but still largely indeterminate prospect. Where the noble produce a series of particular acts, all enabling their prospect to be more determinate in them, a leader deals with his prospect as that which he would like to be deeply entrenched in the people.

Apart from being joined with other factors in a creative act, an ultimate is joined with others without control or guidance. There is no deducing its presence or operation. It is known by attending to what is present and then, in a single move, evidencing it. After it has been reached, the process of evidencing can be theoretically dissected into a beginning, course, and end and be given a canonical form. The Dunamis, too, can be reached in a single act, both as evidenced and as an ultimate to be specialized and used. Like the conditions, it, too, can be formally characterized.

Characterizations do not affect the ultimates. They continue to act as undivided singulars both when they insist on themselves and when they are specialized and used in creative work. Fraternalization specializes all, but it emphasizes only the condition. It continues to be operative after a leader has ceased to act. After he stops his active leading, it will usually not continue to be effective for long in the form he gave it. Often it will be hard to discern. Unfortunately, there is no way to know in advance the exact moment when it will no longer be evident.

A creative leader privately attends to and uses the affiliator, specialized as an effective fraternalization. Joined with a layer of the Dunamis, the affiliator enables the prospective excellence to be progressively realized. Only so far as a leader enables the excellence to be realized in a people can he be its true leader. Until then, a supposed leader will at best be engaged in the act of becoming a leader. He may then be hailed or designated as one—even as a great leader—but he will not have that status until he has in fact enabled an ideal excellence to be determinate and present as a singular, unifying, felt glory. The affiliative condition that the fraternization specializes will still continue to be and be able to act. It will always have its own nature and power. A leader gives it a special effective role at a particular place and time.

A creative leader is both helped by his distinctive habits and limited by the manner in which these habits restrict and qualify his use of the ultimates. He differs from those who are content to cajole and guide a people in his insistence on having glory realized and in his success in getting the people to act to become perfected by it. While using the same factors and guided by the same ideal that his people is ready to accept, he continues to differ from the people in the way he attends to and relates the affiliator to the other factors and, consequently, in the way he effectively promotes the people's fraternization. The people may fraternize apart from him, but his concern with realizing the prospective glory adds to his and the people's effective use of the affiliator. Were he to act as other leaders do, he would still differ from them in his interest in a particular people whose members have their own unduplicable privacies, activities, and careers. Usually, over the course of his creative activity he will join similar specializations of the same conditioning affiliator to different specializations of the other ultimates. The fact is not usually as conspicuous as is the leader's changing involvement with his people at different times, in different circumstances, in the light of its changing interests and efforts, and in a changing environment.

No used condition is ever entirely free from qualifications by the others. An available condition, before it is used, is affected by the others in distinctive, limited ways. Before there is any attempt to utilize it, it is also vitalized by the Dunamis and qualified by a prospect. In creations, these qualifications are enriched through a new, distinctive use of all the factors. Ultimates can be and are brought together again and again, in fresh ways, to produce what is different from all of them. Recognition that the various factors in a creation are already qualified by one another makes it necessary to understand an excellent work as the outcome of a meeting of what is never exhausted in any act. When they are deliberately brought together, each of the factors will already have been affected by the others. No thinking about the way they are brought together in mutually supportive ways could do full justice to all that occurs. Even if one had a clear understanding of each ultimate and of the ways all were again and again joined, he would be unable to grasp just how they are combined. Fortunately, the failure is not here important, for what is to be learned from a study of creativity is not the way parts are produced by joining specializations of ultimates but how they impinge on one another under the influence of a gradually realized excellence.

Before a leader transforms a people, he must transform his specialized versions of conditions and the Dunamis, making them both more accommodative of one another and more in accord with what the people are and need to become. If he is to transform and enrich those he leads, what he joins to the people must be modified by his awareness of its nature and functions.

Like every other creator, a leader needs to work in two different ways: he must privately combine various factors and must embed the result in recalcitrant material. He may, as dancers, actors, and orchestras and some sculptors, architects, and painters do, pass almost imperceptibly from the first stage to the second. That he does so is evident from the fact that he is not usually surprised that the material he uses alters the outcome.

No understanding of a people completely encompasses it. This does not mean that the people or its transformation is unintelligible or that the outcome cannot be anticipated, but only that its effect cannot be fully known in advance of its occurrence. Brought into the compass of the creative activity, a people plays a role in the final work as surely as do other contributors and can be subsequently isolated there without being denied its independence.

Like a privacy, conditions, the Dunamis, and the ideal, materials always have some status of their own. Whether they are sounds, words, movements, metals, numerals, things, people, or governed beings, they, too, are the outcome of joinings of ultimates. That is why they can be compatible with what results when the ultimates are creatively used.

A leader yields to his people as others must to their material to have the sought excellence embedded there. This embedment requires that the nature and needs of the people be respected. Since the best envisagement of a people tries to understand the difference the people will make to whatever is offered to it, its leader must take account of it as having an independent being and course. If successful, he will deal with it as a reality apart from him. Before he comes to that point, though, he has to take account of the ultimates to which he and the people have already been subjected and which have in fact already constituted them.

A people led is a people so changed by its leader that it turns what he makes available into a part of itself. If the leader fails to change the people, it will not be able to be perfected. He will then, at best, have provided an irritant or a grace note for what functions as though he had never lived. Approached initially as that which is to provide a locus for its leader's private achievements, a people helps turn the leader's outcome into an aspect of itself. The utilized thereupon becomes a utilizer, the transformed a transformer, the locus a possessor.

A leader would not be a creator to the same degree as artists are if he did not begin deep within his privacy and make maximum use of ultimate factors. Since he is in part a historic product, one who has been a member of a people, perhaps of the very people he leads, he can never free himself from his material to the degree most other creators can, even when those others are historically toned and influenced by previous events. Also, what he uses is qualified by what he has undergone as well as by what he both expects from it and aspires to.

Like an artist, a leader works on material distinct from himself. Like a creative mathematician, what has been created is utilized by him in new efforts and achievements. Like one with a noble character, he provides the excellence he achieves with an opportunity to be realized elsewhere. Like the participants of an ongoing, excellent state, he needs the help of those with whom he interplays. Unlike them, he gets what is distinct from himself to act so that it not only sustains the excellence but itself becomes perfected. His work is enriched by what he has learned, just as surely as it is guided by what he seeks to achieve. Both helped and limited by his past and that of his people, he will be inclined to use the former and defy the latter, except when it supports his aims. In his absence, some individuals might still forge distinct bonds, take up different but interlocked positions, engage in supplementary tasks, and as a consequence form habits of speech and action which not only keep them in accord but help them to be more securely and better united. They will not, though, be the locus of a sought glory. To achieve that end, they need a leader.

It is often difficult, if not impossible, to distinguish between the outcome of a people's acting in consonance on its own from the outcome of a leader's creative use of it. A led people will sometimes surprise by suddenly demonstrating that all along it has been acting with considerable independence of its leader. Because a leader usually wishes his work to last indefinitely, he may try to have a stable government follow him, one that will effectively codify what he has achieved. He may try to train others to continue along his lines. Whatever he seeks and whatever he does, his leadership will sooner or later give way to a routine version of his intentions and work, making necessary another venture, so quickening the people that it functions in a new and possibly desirable way.

The affiliating condition a leader uses is expressed as an effective power, turning a people into a fraternized whole. Joined to other factors, the condition will bind the people more or less tightly. The degree and manner in which it incorporates the leader's union of factors—with him inspiring and the people supportive, with him exhortative and guiding and the people accommodative and active—will differ from time to time.

Because of what the people do to accommodate the affiliating condition, its fraternizing will differ from what it is as merely mediated by a leader. Because of him, the people will be organized in a way it would not be otherwise; because of the people, the organization will become integral to and affected in a way and to a degree that the leader cannot control or even anticipate, not because it is mysterious but because the people has its own nature and ways of functioning. No one can know in advance just what the outcome will be, for it is worked out then and there. Inevitably, the people will contribute to it no matter how dominant, how determined a leader may be. The result, consequently, may be quite different from what he might have envisaged or endorsed.

A leader cannot avoid depending on the people for his final success. He needs it to turn what he makes available into a part of itself. Whether or not it does so, the people will itself interplay with the ultimate factors, accommodating them just as surely as they are accommodated by the people, whether or not the people accepts them in the guise the leader provides. Inevitably, the people will qualify the ultimates, maximally by altering its course, minimally by adding details.

The envisaging of the specialization and use of needed factors by a leader is initially carried out by him alone, but their final role will be dictated more by the people than by him. Although it is he who keeps focused on the desired objective, the outcome still has to be independently sustained and qualified by the people. Even when he provides the people with what it needs and wants, his objective will be modified in ways he does not fully determine and which may not be in full accord with what he would have the people be or do.

The members of a creatively led people are not merely together, acknowledging the same leader or even acting so that his intent is manifested in what they do together. Subject to the affiliating condition that he would have it embody, a people provides for its own continuation on its own terms. If collaborative, many of its members will attend to a common danger or difficulty and thereupon act to meet it effectively.

One of a people's members, or a number in succession, may lead in meeting a common challenge, but none will function as a true leader. Remaining among the others, though for a time having a pivotal role, the one who is to the fore may be uninterested in having a common glory realized. A creative leader acts differently. Even if he reaches his position because he has successfully worked together with a people, he sets himself apart from it. Instead of playing a pivotal role in a collaboration, he acts to make it possible for the people to become further fraternized and thereupon more receptive to becoming glorified.

Fraternity specializes an insistent affiliating condition to which a leader subjects an already fraternized people to allow for the presence of the glory he seeks to have realized for and in it. He may not concern himself with working through a government with laws or with using other restrictive agencies to make the people more malleable and receptive. Instead, he will try to get its members to become better attached to one another in a single unification throughout which the glory operates. He is most effective if the people is receptive to his urging, for then the people will more readily alter its course to progress toward the stage he would have it achieve.

A fraternized people is an outcome, constituted in part by a specialized conditioning affiliator constraining it at the same time that the condition both acts on and is accommodated by it. The affiliating condition thereby becomes a component in activities serving to make the sought glory become fully operative for and in the people. Since humans have their own independent status and often can dictate how they will act, what they have once achieved they might conceivably destroy, bring to a sudden end, or continue in some other guise. They therefore face a leader with the problem of mastering what has a more obdurate nature and course than other materials usually have.

The factors a leader joins and insists on, primarily through his exhortations and portrayal of the glory to be achieved, are joined to the people mainly on terms the people provides. Other creators, too, are limited by their materials. In some of them, the material may also be independently acting humans. These persons though, will not usually be well affiliated, awaiting further affiliations promoted by a leader and enabling a sought glory to be present as a unifying power.

When religious figures appeal to individuals to love one another or to do what will push them to the limits of their abilities, they want them to act so that the desired outcome will be realized with the help of or by an eternal being. They could therefore be said to offer just a different grounding for the ideal objective a people is to realize. If so, they would still differ from secular leaders in the claims they made for themselves, the kinds of exhortations and formulations they provide, and the warrants they offer for what they say and do.

Whereas secular leaders take themselves to be distinctive instances of humankind, the religious take themselves to be divinely chosen or somehow privileged. The first see themselves as principals; the others see themselves as mediators of some eternal demand or command. The secular leaders may find it most desirable to speak as if they were sanctified or to suppose that they have been divinely plucked out of a multitude. The work they do will still be secular work and for a secular end. Conceivably, they might so unite a people that it would be responsive to religiously toned expressions. They might use religious terminology and speak of themselves as being chosen or even as having been asked to carry a burden they would rather not assume. But if they were to act simply as agents, not as principals creatively realizing a final glory on the way to having it fully realized in the people, they would not be true leaders. To be leaders, they must appeal not to conscience or faith but to the people as able to be glorified. For a leader, a religion is never more than one of a number of means used to make the people more pliable, receptive, kept together, for his concern is not with a religion or its object but with the people to be glorified, perhaps with religion's help.

Fraternity is the specialized form of the affiliating condition that a leader would have a people embody. If he were concerned only with it, he would have to deny it the support and enhancement it obtains from the Dunamis and would have to await the people's accommodation of it. Although there is no avoiding the independent contributions that the people, the conditions, and the Dunamis make to the final outcome, the realization of the glory depends mainly on the leader's successful completion of his part of the venture. He alone is the creator, with the people contributing a sustaining component, for he alone brings the various factors together so that the prospective excellence becomes more and more determinate, awaiting only a transformed and transforming material to give the creation a steady locus. Although it is the leader who uses and specializes the needed factors, and although he combines them in his own way, the people still has its own inextinguishable nature and mode of operation. His is a new product, both carried and altered by the people the sought glory is to enhance.

Democracies often err in supposing that great leaders will be great rulers. Successful generals are readily elected to high office, where many of them make painfully evident that there is a striking difference between great leadership and great ruling. It is usually later seen that the electorate, and sometimes the generals, have confused an ability to arouse and solidify a number with the ability to provide a people with needed governance. When a general, or someone else who has been able to inspire others to carry out difficult and dangerous work, turns to politics, it is not surprising to find that he does not know how to make justice prevail and is forced to leave the task of ruling to others. If not well controlled, these others, his supposed agents, will begin to rule instead, but rarely with the independence and power required if a people is to be well governed.

Somewhat like a comic who finds that some unplanned gesture awakens a welcome response, a leader is inclined to accept all desirable outcomes as due to him. Since he treats many of his failures as a result of forces beyond anyone's ability to control, it is not difficult for him to think of himself as infallible, even divine, needing no special training, as other creators do, and therefore to be treated as a special, unusual human being. Although he is successful only so far as his people sustain him and carry out his vision in its own way, he credits it with doing no more than offering an occasion for his singular nature and acts to be exhibited. Paradoxically, he may give himself less credit than he deserves, for it is he who gets his people to the stage where it is able to make a significant contribution to the realization of its own perfection. His creative leadership enables his people to act so that what he envisages, and whose realization he promises, finally operates as a unifying glory. It is not necessary that he know this or know exactly what occurs.

A people is more readily ruled if it has been well led. Not well led, it may have to be subdued, kept in line. So far, though well ordered, it will not be on the way to making possible the continued presence of a suffusing excellence. Only when this excellence is achieved will leaders and people be one; only then can a leader be confident that his will has been successfully exercised and a people unified in act as well as in spirit; only then can a leader's inspiration and acts end with a quickening of the people through its realization of what he willed. Although the creative work is the leader's, the final outcome will be due to both him and the people.

A leader's success is more likely the more surely he builds on what the people will likely do. Without supplementations by it, he would be just a dreamer. As subject to him, it is open to alteration by expressions of his will. All the while, it has the power to reduce him and his achievements to nought. This reduction may sometimes occur in a single moment of disillusionment or through a sudden common occupation with other matters. A leader sculpts in momentarily frozen water over whose continuance he has no firm control.

Sometimes a leader supposes that it is good for a people to act as a mob, frenzied, with its members so excited, so interinvolved, that it acts with exceptional energy. However, if the people is not kept within bounds, if its tendency to act as a mob is not restrained, it will prevent the attainment of the objective to be realized and often destroy the leader in the process.

References to a prospective glory pertinent to a people, and realizable so far as it takes itself to be specially privileged to realize it, promotes a tightening of the way in which its members fit together. The people is thereby enabled to act as though it has a future no others have and which it will sooner or later realize, especially if guided by a leader who has made this realization his concern. At the same time, the people must be held in check. If it is held by accepting a leader's decisions as its own, the glory he focuses on will become the glory it is to embody. For this to happen, its members need to be joined to one another with an intimacy they do not share with others. The result may have to be preceded by exhortations, the threat of disaster, an invocation of a common heritage and destiny, or an insistence that the people is special and its present status undesirable. What is said and done by the leader will thereupon serve as a means for getting the people not only to be inspired and directed but to act so that its members will be intimately interlocked in function and in spirit. The distinct individuals who compose it will then share in the excellence that unifies all, as though they were mutually functioning parts of a single body.

On its own, a people cannot be joined with the same success that a creative leader enables it to achieve; it needs him to arouse its acceptance of the affiliative condition together with other factors in the course of a creative realization of a prospective glory. Were the members of a people not fraternally attached to one another, the people would lack a needed connectivity. The affiliator, when used by a leader to provide a distinctive structure, contributes to the people's achievement of its needed fraternalizaton. Because of the effective presence of the sought excellence, the people will be suffused with feeling. Like the feelings present in other creative work, this feeling will be faintly evident to an appreciator at the beginning and become more and more evident as his reading proceeds. Although noble characters and a well-led people are affected by what is experienced privately, they could not themselves experience the feeling others discern them to sustain unless they could assume the position of self-appreciators. That would require them to know themselves in the way others could. It is enough for them, though, to become perfected; they have no need to appreciate the result. The fact does not interfere with their becoming aware of the growing effective presence of their perfecting ideal and, therefore, of an excellence being realized. They would, so far, differentiate themselves as appreciators from themselves as objects of appreciation. The noble are able to do so readily. It is harder for a people to carry it out; conceivably, the people could be glorified and not experience any glory and, so far, act as a virtuoso does when he plays a great composition. That this failure to experience glory does sometimes occur becomes evident when one takes note of the complacency that often sets in soon after a people has attained what it accepts as such a state of glory.

If a people took itself to be glorified but was not in fact well unified, it would express a common attitude, but this attitude would not necessarily make a difference to the way its members were effectively joined. The operative presence of that glory, though, could be noted by others if they were alert to a feeling pervading the whole. They would then be in a position to use the unified people as a sign of a primal power effectively affiliative everywhere.

One can slough off the splendid part of any culture and take the contributors to it to constitute a glorified people, with the rest serving as external supports, though deriving little benefit from the result. Concentrating on the selected segment, freeing it from its political side, one might then take the residue to be a separate, glorified people. Its distinctive achievements could thereupon be treated as so many interplaying components. Such a process of isolating a splendid part of a definite whole has been carried out in many places and times. It is sometimes the way Renaissance Italy and the antebellum South are treated. The procedure, though, yields only a simulacrum of a genuine glorified people since it requires a selection of some individuals and items and a meshing of them in ways involving an abstraction from what in fact occurs.

The classical Greeks are sometimes referred to as a glorious people. The judgment is made on the basis of the incomparable works some of them produced in art, philosophy, and politics. Overlooked is the fact that these were the achievements of a small number and had little effect on the rest. It was a people untroubled by the practice of slavery; it denigrated women and ignored the plight of those who labored.

A good reading of a created work allows for the signifying of a condition as effectively operative in a way nothing else can be. If we use what we initially discern of such a condition to guide our reading of it, we will also be able to grasp it in a way we otherwise could not. Many have learned how to read creations in the arts in this way and have thereupon become aware of the controlling power of conditioning voluminosities. A few have learned how to read mathematical creations so that the power of an irreducible, rational condition becomes evident. It is much harder to read a glorified people so that it finally functions as a sign of an equally basic and effective affiliator. Since the feeling tone that glory introduces into the whole is not easy to discern, it is not uncommon to miss the fact that an affiliative power is operative throughout.

The Vitalization of the People

A population is an aggregate of individuals. Strictly speaking, it is an abstraction, for individuals are always so interconnected that they are prevented from being just separate units, each bounded off from the rest, having no bearing on one another. However, they can be dealt with as a populace which, though just a collection, is more than an aggregate of units. A people, in contrast with both a populace and a population, encompasses interinvolved individuals, each with his own privacy and rights, acting in consonance. The result has a distinctive nature, past, future, and ideal objective, with members more or less affiliated in different ways at different times. With the help of a creative leader, the members will be joined with a greater degree of intimacy than they otherwise could.

Unlike a composer, whose major work may be done before it is given a stabilizing notation, a leader—in addition to his private production of a juncture of a specialized level of a condition and a distinctive layer of the Dunamis joined to an ideal prospect—works directly on the people. A director of a play or dance, a conductor, and a drill sergeant do something similar, differing from a leader in being willingly restricted by rules and in requiring a greater submission by those in their charge.

A leader is occupied with the conversion of a loosely joined people into one intimately interinvolved, structured, vitalized, and glorified. His major problem is to get the people to act as he thinks it should to attain that status. Giving little weight to the criticism of others and wanting to have the people act in a particular way so that the sought excellence is realized in it, he tries to elicit its support. Just as radically individual in his attitude and activities as any other creator is, giving little weight to criticisms, he, unlike them, tries to get his material to act on its own so that a needed sustaining grain is obtained.

With the help of mass media, it is possible today for a leader to make a direct appeal to a large number. In earlier times he may have had to rely on agents, acting on hunches based on rumors and reports; today he can reach millions. Whether he affects them directly or works through intermediaries, he is never reducible to the status of a unit among them. To have an ideal glory be realized in them, he uses his privacy in a distinctive way. Most of the abilities he has, some of which he may exercise in carrying out other tasks, play such a minor role in what he does here that they could be safely assumed to be absent. Often he may forget that they are operative.

A leader tends to suppose that after his departure what he says and decides will have somewhat the same import that it had when he was present. Yet if he is no longer active, he can at best only suggest. Usually he will nostalgically urge the people to function as it did when he was actually leading it, forgetting that the times have changed, that many members of the people have been replaced, and that what he had achieved has effects making necessary new acts perhaps quite different from any that were pertinent at the time when he was effective. It is sad to see those who were once great leaders speaking and acting as though all that the people need is their suggestions or admonitions. A people must be creatively led if it is to be glorified. This end no advice can produce.

Something may have been learned by a leader over the course of his venture. Shrewd guesses, based on what has been learned in rather similar circumstances, might later be made about the ways in which events will develop. His advice might still lead to disaster if it is not accepted with a grasp of the changed nature of the people and the prevailing circumstances as making a difference to the import of what is suggested. If someone tailored the knowledge he had acquired to make it pertinent to a present situation, he would not yet produce what an actual leader does. To be effective, he must also transform his people to make it be both more receptive and contributive.

A well-led people shares in a common attitude. This attitude may be elicited by the leader but depends mainly on what the people are, want, and do. If someone just arouses a people, he will, more likely than not, produce one not well knit, not knowing where to turn or what to do. More likely than not, the realization of the prospect that the people may have vociferously and passionately endorsed will be precluded. A people not well knit responds to many irrelevant promptings and readily overturns what should have been preserved. Rarely does it obtain what would enhance it.

A people must be enabled to make its own contribution to the realization of its distinctive excellence, not as a creator but as transforming material. Even great figures sometimes fail to grasp the fact that their effectiveness depends on the acts of a people whose demands, needs, and course must be accommodated or satisfied. Those who try to do no more than subjugate inevitably spend time and energy in reducing the contributions the people could and must make to the realization of the outcome a true leader promotes.

Were a leader the only source of what is done, there would be no one led; a people would be no more than a collection of passive, perhaps endlessly pliable puppets. He would have no material that would contribute to the realization of the sought glory. If instead the people alone were to act, there might be someone who would exhort but might not lead. A leader must allow his people to make a needed contribution.

Like other creators, leaders would like to have what they produce be preserved without undergoing serious modifications. This preservation is best achieved by prompting individuals to accommodate the affiliating condition and thereupon be so joined that the sought excellence is realized in a fraternized, well-organized whole. No one really leads unless the people also act to promote the realization of the objective the leader accepts and would have the people embody. A dictator is not a true leader, requiring as he does that a multitude function as an obedient mass rather than as contributors jointly enriching what he provides. He is inescapably resisted, for the people has a reality and way of acting all its own, never entirely accommodating what he does or produces. Its actions are primarily determined by the joint responses of its members, directed at dealing with what is needed by, limits, or challenges it.

A people is the outcome of a meeting of conditions and Dunamis, but it is still able to be affected by and to accommodate junctures of themselves. It also has internally determined limits. Unlike its members, it is unable to make use of ulti-mates to promote the realization of a prospect. Lacking a separately functioning privacy, it is without sensitivity, will, or mind; all it can do is act as a single, frater-nized complex. Having no separately functioning body, it cannot occupy a position in the world where bodies resist, insist, and interact. Although different peoples oppose and may attack one another with the force and blindness characteristic of physical things, they evidently cannot do so by making use either of privacies or bodies of their own.

Not an aggregate, not an organism, without appetites or desires, a people still has a distinctive nature and mode of action that may be enriched by the achieve-ments of its leader. Understanding it requires a reference to the ways it stands apart from the factors constituting it and its receptivity to those very factors as they are joined by the leader. Not a man writ large, the people cannot be creative any more than it is able to eat or sleep. Though without intent or aim, it can yet become the locus of an ideal glory which will enhance it if it is sustained by its individual members, whether or not they attend to that objective.

A painter sometimes works directly on his canvas without having first made a sketch. A leader almost always works without a plan. He may set out a program and state what he will or would like to accomplish, but he may not follow the stated course or carry it out in a way that promotes the realization of the objective it was intended to enhance. His use of the people reduces the risk that the outcome of his work will be no more than an imagined splendor; still, the more he allows for contributions by the people, the more will he need to modify his ways to take advantage of its tendencies.

Individuals are irreducibly obstinate, necessarily giving a leader's decrees new loci and weights. Were a leader to become a dictator, he might turn the people into an instrument for the satisfaction of his demands, but it will still continue to remain outside his full control. When he injures and deforms individuals or stands in the way of their full development as persons, he depends on their contributions to the presence, nature, and actions of a single complex, having its own nature.

A dictator who sets himself in opposition to the people whose members are not only well joined but self-controlled makes himself less effective than he could be. The more surely a dictator lowers the status of the members of a people, the more surely will he be occupied with what is not worth controlling. His failure to take account of that fact offers little solace to those subject to his terrible decrees. Those who suffer under him are not recompensed by the fact or by the realization that his life is beset by rivalries and dangers. He does irremediable harm. He may enrich himself and enjoy privileges and the exercise of his will and his whims; he may be confident, self-centered; he may indulge himself as he sees fit, resting on what he has weakened. He may produce some benefits, all the while that his use of propaganda, lies, threats, censorship, and prison testify to his awareness of his people's independence. Cowed, a people can be made to work, but it will not do much to enhance what the dictator provides. He is at best an enthraller who may benefit a few for a while.

Even if all a dictator seeks is to be dominant, able to determine what a people should do, he must make use of what he is controlling. This material is not passive but ready to express a nature and power of its own, initiated by individuals as not yet manifested as so many public units. Sometimes he treats his horses and cars with more insight and success.

A people wholly receptive would not be led. What occurs may be desirable, but it would still leave the people impoverished. Something similar, but not as serious, occurs when glamour, fad, and momentary appeal play roles in other activities. Only creative acts end in the production of incomparable excellences. If these had no present appeal, little could be done but await those who could make an enriching excellence present and effective.

We can make provision for the training and reception of creators in many fields, but little can be done to assure the presence of a great leader. There is no assurance that he will arise at a particular time, any more than there can be an assurance that other types of creators will appear when needed. History is a series of blunders and stumbles, misdirection following on misdirection, arrested and redirected at unexpected moments, interspersed with sudden gains, some which may last for a considerable time.

Sometimes a leader appears when a people seems most unready; at other times he appears when it is expecting him. The memory of some past great leaders may not be entirely lost, leaving a people readier to carry on work that a new leader makes possible. That may be desirable; it is not necessary. Though many men are lax, despairing, discommoded, or self-destructive, a people is so alterable that its leader may sometimes be successful, provided only that he probes deep into the Dunamis and introduces a vitality geared to the use of an affiliating condition and a prospective glory.

Every actuality, human or subhuman, living or not, has its own center, nature, rhythm, insistence, and resistance. No matter how hard it may be to distinguish one from another, and no matter how well they fit together, each will have his own privacy and body by means of which he will mediate and possess specializations of the ultimate factors.

At once like and unlike, individuals are turned toward one another through the agency of the affiliating condition and the effective presence of the Dunamis. Affiliated and vitalized, and thus fraternally and dynamically interinvolved, they form a people whose individual members express themselves in consonance. Even while they are radically apart from one another, they are not only interrelated but able to become interinvolved in more intensive ways.

Like anyone else who has carried out a difficult task, a successful leader has made needed use of his own powers and what he has been able to lay hold of. Having managed to free himself from the usual restraints of habit and tendency, he is able to occupy a position where he can reach into ultimates to a degree otherwise not possible, while remaining tempted to act in ways he had before. He will probably not escape from that danger without being faced with another, unless he knows how to keep to a course that will end in the production of a glorified people. The particular condition and the level of it that he emphasizes, the layer of the Dunamis of which he also makes specialized use, and the ideal he is committed to realize— these may sometimes keep him occupied with trying to act as a leader long after he has ceased to be creative.

A condition is static, structural, cognizable. It can be kept in focus in a way the leader's own privacy, the Dunamis, and an ideal cannot. Whether or not that is done, none of the needed factors will be of much value to him if he does not try to specialize and join them, with the affiliative condition given importance that other conditions are not. A mythological portrayal of a realized glory might help him and the people to remain directed at this. The Dunamis in particular, with its fluid, vitalizing depths, while always available and active, will escape his full mastery. If he is a creator, he will lay hold of it and use it, give it a greater role than it usually has. If he does not, he will, more likely than not, end with a lifeless people whose members are not able to affect one another effectively and intimately.

To promote the responsiveness of a people, a leader makes skilled use of rhetoric. Rhetoric was once an important agent; today its study is neglected almost everywhere, except in theological schools where incipient preachers are taught how to exhort and persuade. Modern leaders are usually untaught masters of it. Not until rhetoric is once again made prominent in a fresh but critical spirit is it likely that there will be many who will be well prepared to be leaders, able to persuade a people to become vitally interinvolved without requiring a denial of its independence.

The Dunamis adds a needed vibrancy to whatever it affects. When joined to a conditioning affiliator, it binds and empowers what otherwise would at best be related as mutually relevant units. It would then be qualified by other factors as surely as they are by it. When not fully used, or not used well, it will overwhelm, getting in the way of a people's need to be effectively affiliated. Present everywhere, always operative, having a plurality of undifferentiated layers, it adds a vibrancy to whatever it joins.

Without neglecting the different things which must be done by different segments of the population, a creative leader must arouse, cajole, persuade, and guide. His success depends on his ability to balance a needed affiliation with a needed vitalization and thereby make it possible for his people to be enhanced by the excellence he realizes for and in it. The people on whom he works will already be differentiated by gender, age, status, and wealth. It will also be subdivided into clusters, of which families are the most familiar and most obdurate.

A creative leader will prescribe the kinds and vitality of the relations which are to connect the members and subordinate groups of a people. At the same time he will try to suppress or absorb what does not enable the people to be unified by the prospective glory he would have it embody. Were no account taken of the different abilities, inclinations, and needs that different individuals have, the outcome would be human beings unable to do much more than be excited together.

Like Hitler, an enthraller may state well in advance what he intends to do. Although on reflection his goal may be seen as horrendous, destructive, what cannot be obtained without tearing a particular people away from the rest of mankind and itself eventually becoming debilitated, an enthraller may be accepted with enthusiasm. Regardless of what he says, plans, or aspires to, he is not a creative leader, for such a leader enables his people to become glorified. He might cherish a prospective glory and may use rhetoric most effectively. Though he may for a while enable his people to be remarkably well fraternized, he will not enable it to contribute to its own perfecting. The glory that he promises is a counterfeit, brought to bear in such a way that the people is reduced in dignity.

Hitler did not take a loose aggregate of individuals and suddenly bring them together. He took account of their convictions, interests, longings, and fears, and was thereupon able to have them act together, apparently for the realization of their glory. Stalin put greater emphasis on a supposed inevitable course of history, all the while that he, too, acted as an enthraller. Each in his own way tacitly allowed for the separate functioning of the people while getting in the way of its actually becoming glorified.

Sometimes a revolution begins without a leader, only to have its gains solidified by one. Inevitably, that leader will be faced with the existence of dissident subgroups. Political opponents, workers, farmers, intellectuals, corporations, and bankers will form factions, some with guiding figures at the head, able to alter the course followed and perhaps causing their groups to counter what the leader supports. Usually they will make room for subordinates, mediators, and agents, who take it to be their task to increase the range and strengthen the influence of those they serve. At their best, though, they will instead produce fraternized, vitalized small groups to be further enhanced by the all-encompassing prospect the leader is occupied with realizing.

A fraternized people has individuals acting and working together, carrying out distinctive roles. If a leader could be content with the people doing no more than forming such a fraternity, a number might work well together. They would, though, still not exhibit the passion, the malleability, and the energy they should. A leader, even when arousing a people, must keep it within bounds, alert to the fact that it could readily turn into a mob, without steady loyalties. Even if a mob responded to the same myths and did so with more enthusiasm than a fraternizing people does, neither those in front nor those who follow in the mob will promote a common, prospective excellence. A mob is too disorganized, too variable in its moods and acts, to be able to provide the place a prospective excellence needs if it is to be fully realized.

The Dunamis is a single, pulsating, ongoing, irreducible, primal factor. In it there are passing undulations and mergings. Again and again it erupts in the form of partly distinguishable but not well distinguished occurrences, limited and qualified by expressions of a nuanced condition. The outcome may be individuals intimately together but not fraternally joined, not yet supplementing one another, insensitive to one another's nature and interests and therefore not yet a people ready to be perfected.

Although it is the leader who is creative, his work will be incomplete until his people is able to accommodate the result. Although it is not a cocreator, its supplementary action is nevertheless indispensable; it alone provides determinations for the sought objective and enables what the leader has produced to be fixated. It could not be a cocreator unless it could on its own so join conditions and the Dunamis that it enabled the ideal glory to be fully determinate in the form of an actual unifying power. Its individual members would then be intimately together, supplementary and responsive to one another's interests and, so far, able to become the fixated locus of a realized excellence.

A leader is usually aware of the need to invoke the Dunamis at a depth close to that which a mob exhibits, but able to be controlled by the affiliating condition. His task is to give full play to all the factors involved, the condition serving primarily to structure, the Dunamis to vitalize, the objective to guide, his privacy to act, and the people to accept and contribute to what he makes available. Individuals, without losing their radical irreducibilities, will then be parts of a people acting as if it were a single organism to which most of its members, perhaps all, will contribute in ways they may not understand but which they may sometimes suppose they themselves desire.

The Dunamis has an indefinite depth and an indefinite stretch. A layer of it vitalizes a limited number by joining them in a way no condition, private willing, or ideal could. All of us, in moments of terror or passion, suffer its presence and sometimes are aware of it and what it does. By itself, it arouses. It may overwhelm and send us off in a direction neither expected nor desirable. We are carried and occasionally whirled about by it, caught up in ways not within our control. Had we not been subject to steady conditioning, we would not be able to limit its effectiveness.

What the Dunamis does is often effectively hidden when a people occupies itself with removing obstacles, aims at available targets, or provides needed agencies for bringing about what a leader insists on. He, too, makes use of the Dunamis, turning it into a dynamic component in a people responsive to his urgings. If in the absence of a leader a people looked to laws, force, or a strong interest in an attractive objective to keep it active or restrained, it would so far be uninspired.

Were someone to bring a multitude to a sudden halt or send it off in a new direction, he would not yet be a creative leader. A creative leader commits himself to realize an excellence that will be well received by the people. Ideally, each member will share in and be enriched by the common excellence. None will possess it as his own; it is realized only by the people as vitally together.

A people could be well united if it allowed itself to live within the ambit of a common glory. Since there would so far be no sustaining by its members, the glory achieved would readily vary in force and quickly vanish as circumstances changed. A perfected people enables the excellence it embodies to counter what would otherwise change or preclude that excellence. Providing the people with a plurality of sustainers, its members enable it to become a single locus of the glory a leader would have the people embody. Because the individual members are distinct from the people they together constitute, each can not only share in the glory but enjoy in his own way.

Viewed from the standpoint of its members, a people is their common public presence; viewed from the position of a leader, it is material to be worked on. Taken by itself, the people has a nature and career carried on in independence of, but not in opposition to, the individual members. Attempts to reduce a people to an aggregate of individuals overlook its characteristic activity and nature and the glory it might embody.

Individuals together constitute a people, apart from any leader. Sometimes they separately move to the position where they are all subject to a common tradition and future and are jointly vitalized through their acceptance of some land as their own. When they do so, they pass from the stage of being together in a union to that of being members of a society. There will often be someone in front of all the rest. Usually, like the first bird of a wheeling flock, he will not inspire the rest to be better interrelated. Although he may be followed, even for a considerable period, he will not lead.

A leader is not one who is just to the fore; he enables a people to accept more readily the glory he privately joins to a condition and the Dunamis, usually by making it vivid and appealing. While continuing to be distinct, acting in ways the people do not, privileged, visionary, insistent, focusing on the excellence that is to be achieved, he remains in accord with the people without becoming a part of it. A necessity, he becomes unnecessary the more successful he is at helping the people to maintain a hold on what perfects it.

Other creators concentrate on conditions different from the one that most concerns a leader. Moving back into his privacy, behind the position from which he tends to act, he uses a conditioning affiliation in a way other creators do not. To enable the prospective glory to be realized, he also provides a public expression for what he privately envisages and does. He may not do this well. It suffices if he is able to find means for getting the people to be receptive to what he utilizes.

What the people on its own occasionally exhibits in its celebrations, festivals, and crises its leader utilizes for his own purposes. Usually he tries to bring a deep layer of the Dunamis to bear, both by making the people receptive to it, and by having it so subject the people that it is enabled to act in a new way. There is no complete possessing of the conditions or the Dunamis by him—or by the people.

Already present and effective, though not on the level or layer a leader reaches and tries to have the people accommodate, the ultimates independently enable the people to act as a single, vitalized unity, receptive to the unifications a leader promotes.

A leader is not able to control the Dunamis any more than he can control the other factors. Regardless of what he seeks and does, they remain irreducible and insistent. All that he or anyone else can do is make a limited, specialized use of the Dunamis and join the result to other specialized factors. Since these factors continue to be apart from him and any combinations of their specializations that he can produce, what he creates, like every other creation, will be able to be affected by them again and again.

In the Orient, where the Dumamis has been a focal topic for centuries, it is almost a commonplace that it is reached most readily and adequately by those who free themselves from daily involvements and thereupon attain a position of ease in the center of themselves, or perhaps at the center of all that is. If nothing more than this centering occurred, what would likely be achieved would be an avoidance by individuals of some of the tugs and blockages to which they are daily subject. Each might then be able to live more selflessly than before and free himself from the grip of daily habits. Slipping into the Dunamis unreflectingly, he would unknowingly form intimate bonds with others. Not alien to them, he would still not be necessarily well adjusted to them and, so far, would do little more than provide rudimentary complementary acts.

One hoping to perfect himself will employ the Dunamis to enable him to bring about an effective harmony of multiple private powers. If he is concerned with becoming a vital part of a society, he will keep in accord with its nature and course and thereupon act more effectively than he might otherwise. In the absence of a creative leader, though, he will not be able to keep the Dunamis operating at a needed depth and thereupon will not be prepared to be together with others in a single creative venture.

Creators usually use their privacies as sustainers for what is achieved through the use of needed factors, with publicly available objects providing fixities and grainings. A people carries out these roles more evidently and adventurously than other materials could carry out theirs, in part because it is made up of independently existing and acting individuals and in part because of what the leader does to it. When musicians, actors, and dancers perform, they do something similar, but because they do not act to perfect themselves, they do not deal with the available conditions and the Dunamis as do leaders or a people well led.

A composer's notations and a mathematician's symbols are materials with comparatively minor roles, the Dunamis being utilized by those creators mainly to qualify what was obtained by penetrating into a condition to an unusual degree.

The Dunamis, as brought forward by a leader, instead enables a people to be inter-involved apart from all other factors and to function in a distinctive way. Without its help, the people would be inadequately joined and insufficiently activated; as a consequence, they would not fully embody the prospect the leader focuses on.

Some grand event, an eclipse, a cataclysm, a sudden bounty, may arouse a people to a high pitch. Individuals, more or less indifferently together before, may then begin to move in a single direction, share in a common, intensive action, and exhibit a new confidence, determination, and sense of righteousness. At times they may even use the Dunamis on a layer and in a manner other than that appropriate to realizing the objective that concerns their leader. They will then succeed in producing only momentary outcomes, easily giving way to others, and will consequently readily move in new directions. An adventitious outcome has no native power or endurance. It continues only as long as circumstances permit.

A leader must stand apart and inspire a people to follow him and thereby move toward the stage where it is perfected. Jeanne d'Arc did this, uniting a distinctive objective with an effective way of relating and bringing an army vitally together and thereby making possible its functioning in ways no others could at the time. When she fell back or to one side, she still continued to lead, for leadership is not a matter of position but of disposition, not a status assumed but a role carried out. Like some other leaders, she acted steadily with a concentration and effectiveness others exhibit only for short periods, in unimportant places, realizing comparatively lesser objectives.

No responsiveness by the people, no acceptance of the Dunamis in the guise necessary for individuals to be interinvolved if a prospective glory is to be realized, eliminates the need for a leader to unite the Dunamis primarily with a specialized affiliating condition, each qualifying the other. The people, by being opened to the Dunamis as an independent power, is made into an effective carrier of what he joins. It can then function somewhat as performers do, as able to be subject to the Dunamis and to make independent use of it. It differs from such performers in being led, the leader's exhortations serving to get the people to allow more of the Dunamis to operate on, in, and through it.

Because his stress is on the Dunamis as operative in and through a people, it is a rare leader who is aware of it as an ultimate or even of the use he makes of it. Facing the ideal in his own way, he keeps himself focused on it even when the people seem not to heed him or when it fails to be subject to the Dunamis to the degree and manner required if it is to be perfected. Somewhat like an improvisational performer of a musical piece who unduly concentrates on the use of his instrument, a leader may rely on an agent who distorts what is intended.

Nothing maintains a fixed position steadily and forever. The Dunamis that a leader uses has its own insistence and intrudes in different degrees at different times, both on what he does and on what else he brings about. Although most successful if he makes good use of agents, he is often blocked by subordinates, even when they have something like the spirit he would have pervade them. What they say and do may so filter and qualify what he intends that he could be reduced to a monument, respected but unheeded. There need be no malice or indifference then expressed. Everyone readily falls into routines that blur what was bright before. Enthrallers, too, become set in their ways, confident that their successful past decisions assure future successes. At the beginning of World War II, Hitler acted against the advice of his generals, and events proved him right. The generals were right, however, toward the end of the war, but he was so confident that he was right once more that they were forced to carry on a hopeless endeavor.

Like every other creator, a creative leader must begin afresh, again and again. Unlike other creators, since he is not necessarily well disciplined, he will in the end be unable to make much progress. Most likely he will lose his grip on a conditioning fraternity, fail to reach the Dunamis at the needed depth, and not arouse his people to make the needed efforts. If death cuts him off in the middle of his venture, mediocrities will usually take over, trying to produce slowly what he most likely would have done quickly and forcefully. This or that individual leader may be needed at particular times, but just as surely there will be times when certain others should not replace him.

A leader may be more aware of the presence and depth of the Dunamis than are other creators, although he does not control it any more than others do. He provides for its effective expression from a depth below that where it usually operates, but so far as he is not able to control it, he is at best its agent.

A leader's position may have been long assured. Agencies of persuasion may have been in steady use. References to a common blood, history, destiny, mission, solidarity, chosenness, and the like are common and often effective means by which he will persuade a multitude. The people may be on the lookout for him, tensed, expectant, not knowing just what it is that is being awaited. Suddenly, without anyone knowing just how or why, a large number may suddenly be swept up in a common fervor, share a spirit sharply differentiating it from all others. The people may then turn suddenly toward one who had been relatively inconspicuous. It might choose him and assert that it will follow him. That assertion, however, will not suffice to make him their leader. At the very least, he must concern himself with having a prospective glory realized, quickened by the Dunamis operating on a people at a depth greater than it usually does.

Glorified Mankind

The idea of glory is referred to repeatedly in stories, myths, celebrations, and official histories. Instead of making its nature clear, these narratives effectively hide it. At best they make a people feel that it is special, rightly proud of what it supposes marks it off from all others. Yet like every other prospect, it is at first quite indeterminate. A creative leader, committing himself to realize it, provides it with determinations through his effective use of ultimates and by getting the people to embody it. All the while, both as an objective and as what is in fact operative, it will be treated by the leader as an excellence his people deserves to possess; indeed, he thinks that his people already possess it latently and that it will, with his help, unify the people as a mutually enhancing, interlocked set of functioning units.

Some historians take the glory that a people views as properly its own to be the inevitable outcome of its self-defined need to continue despite obstacles and failures. Cynics treat it as a self-delusion, or perhaps as the outcome of deliberate deceptions by malevolent enthrallers. An occasional philosopher such as Plato takes it to be an eminently desirable "lie" needed in order to get a people to become fine political beings. Others understand it to be the product of historic forces, propaganda, language, or a deception produced by dominant figures enabling them to subjugate the rest. For more positivist-minded thinkers, it is a confused outcome of individual efforts to act together or to interchange sentences. None of these explanations accounts for the fact that a prospective glory is given determinations by a leader and can be realized as a unification. Paradoxically, the successful realization of glory provides the greatest possible warrant for supposing it to be ungraspable or meaningless, since it vanishes as a distinguishable item—as do all excellences—on being made determinate.

Glory, we have already seen, is not the only ideal that can be realized. There are at least four others, each specializing a more general ideal. This is the limiting point of a convergence of all the conditions and the Dunamis, a meeting that occurs without supervision. The outcome is specialized differently in different creative ventures. There would be more or fewer specializations were there more or fewer primary conditions. One test of any account of creativity can therefore be provided by seeing if there are types of creations requiring use of still other ultimates or if the number of types of creative venture could be reduced.

If a man does not attend to the ideal glory, he cannot be a creative leader. Nor can he be one if he does not persuade the people to act as material and yet so exert itself that it is able to make the glory part of itself. Although there is a kind of knowledge involved in all conscious activities, and thus in the proper use of anything to bring about acceptable outcomes, and although there is a kind of knowledge involved when using the Dunamis or the privacy in a creative act, a leader will not be primarily concerned with knowing these agencies, any more than he is with knowing the nature of the prospective glory. He does not differ in this regard from other creators. None is particularly interested in understanding what must be done, or even the outcome, either before, while, or after it is realized. The accepted task for each is to create, not to contemplate.

Creativity is an honorific term. Those who use the same factors as creative men do but end with what corrupts and may destroy—no matter how ingenious, innovative, or inventive they may be—are not creative, unless creativity could be properly credited to those who do not produce what is excellent. It is therefore not properly applied to a god who supposedly made our defective universe or who, as some suppose, is occupied with maintaining it. Only humans beings create, for only they can produce particular excellences—or more precisely, the realization of prospective excellences beyond any preassignable degree.

No one who fails to produce a unification of parts, no matter what his intent or accomplishment, is truly creative. He might be admired and applauded. If he awakened admiration in a multitude and succeeded in getting it to imitate him or to follow his recommendations, he would not yet be its leader. To be a leader, he would have to so inspire a people that it was receptive to what could unify and benefit it. Since the creation will be completed only if the people is in fact perfected, he must not only get the people to act in certain ways but needs to have the people actually unified. Since this unification is not possible unless the people makes it own contribution to the result, a creative leader will be concerned with getting it to do this. What is achieved might last for only a short time; that, though, may be time enough for him to be its leader.

When one thinks of the destruction that enthrallers bring about, one may wish to refer to them in more pejorative terms. *Enthrallers*, though, does describe what they are, and *enthralling* the activity they carry out. The destructions and losses they promote may sometimes be explicitly insisted on as correlatives or preconditions for realizing a sought glory. When a people is so enthralled by one who corrupts it that it takes him to be a great leader, destruction will for a while be equated with a step in construction, debasement with a precondition for enrichment, and delusion or self-glorification with evidence of leadership.

Some men do not suppose that a leader or the people must do anything for a people to become glorified, supposing that the glory is already real but remote, perhaps making a people inescapably but unknowingly move in a direction of which it is unaware. These teleologists minimize the roles of both leader and people, taking them to do no more than provide opportunities for the independent arrival of the excellence. They match those who think the good awaits a propitious time to become an ingredient in a character, perhaps after the way is prepared for what presumably needs no help or prompting.

Leaders of large numbers may be better known than those who lead fewer. Also, their use of intermediaries may make their work easier than that required for smaller numbers. Because great leaders so unify their people that they may seem to (and may in fact) challenge the right of other people to pursue another course, it will eventually be necessary to look for a leader of all humanity, and then perhaps to a state in which everyone lives a well-regulated life, with ruler and ruled supporting one another.

A leader need not have a title. Leadership could be well exercised by one not officially in command, as well as by one who believes himself destined to have the excellence he envisages be realized. A leader ordinarily assumes that the achievement of glory is inescapable if only his people will accept his guidance. He may think of the people as being forced to act at times in ways that deflect it from realizing the accepted objective. He will then see himself or the people as having been unfortunately compelled to act at a time or place requiring an occupation with various preliminaries, to need props, or often to overcome great dangers and obstacles. The same objective will continue to be acknowledged, but its promotion will be postponed until some new path becomes available. For a time he will be forced to act as though he were only at a preparatory stage in the production of an excellent outcome, while continuing to be dedicated to the task of realizing it. He will then be like a poet who has not yet forged the precise phrase for what he discerns, while continuing to be confident that he will succeed.

A creative leader acts on the assumption that the excellence he cherishes will be realized, although he and the people may for a while be forced to attend to other matters. He may insist even more emphatically that the people continue to act in ways he endorses. No matter what the people does or how hard he must struggle with adverse circumstances, he will continue to be concerned with the realization of what he takes to be the people's proper and perhaps destined end. If the obstacles are too great for him to overcome, he will usually blame the people, perhaps for having become unworthy of the excellence he wants it to enjoy. In his eyes, the realizability of the ideal will not have been affected in the slightest; it will still be for him what would be inescapably realized by a people worthy of it.

A people has an independent status and way of acting; sooner or later its leader recognizes that it also has an unavoidable, unconquerable side. As long as he is successful, he will have little occasion to notice that fact. When failure seems unavoidable or has already arrived, he will usually take the people not really to be his, for if it were it would surely act so that the objective was achieved. More often than not, he will decide that he made no errors, unless it was in thinking that the people was worthy of being glorified. As is true in other ventures, it will then be hard to determine whether he created an excellence with many flaws or so botched his work that it is not excellent at all. In any case, he will take failure to reveal perversities and wickedness elsewhere, forcing him to concentrate on tactics and, so far, be unable to exhibit his mastery of a grand strategy for bringing about what is sought. Failure for him is always the fault of something untoward; his only fault, if fault it be, he thinks, is having too great a trust, being too much occupied with a prospect that deserves but does not receive a needed backing.

Someone insisting on a future that a people is predestined to serve, or doing nothing to remove obstacles to appropriate action, would be indistinguishable from a dreamer or a madman. If he is called a leader by those who live generations later, it will be what he pointed toward, not his actual leadership, that will be taken to provide a warrant for the designation.

The excellence a leader seeks to have realized is present for him and for the people in different ways. For him it is a quickening power; for the people it is to be possessed. He wants the people to embody the excellence, with himself playing the unduplicable role of a necessary determinant. Occasionally, he will think of himself as eventually enshrined in the supposedly imperishable annals of history. Whether he does so or not, he must occupy himself with producing a glorified people. It would, therefore, not be amiss to take him, despite his conceit, to be more selflessly immersed in a work of creation, for longer periods and for the benefit of more, than are any other creators. Sometimes he will allow, sometimes encourage, sometimes forbid or prevent other creative ventures. Rarely does he offer good reasons why he does so, unless it is a good reason to say that other creative ventures get in his way, whether or not they actually do. It is surely wrong to suppose that other ventures cannot be pursued as well and on their own terms. The glory of a people will in fact never be properly realized unless it has room for other types of creative achievement, since these achievements not only enrich the people but enable one who reads them properly to get a better grip on conditions coordinate with the affiliative, which so effectively joins what otherwise would be more or less indifferent units. A good understanding of a creatively led people finally makes evident the affiliative condition's effective omnipresence, just as a great poem opens one who appreciates it to an all-encompassing, insistent time.

A leader concerned with benefiting his people maximally will provide for and encourage other types of creation as well. The notion that these creations will endanger his project rests on the mistaken supposition that a people can and should spend all its energies in achieving a single glorious status and that other creations are to be produced only if they help the people work toward, obtain, or sustain that status. A leader may sometimes allow for or encourage creative activities directed toward the realization of other excellences, but he rarely offers a better-grounded justification for his allowance or endorsement than he does for his denials. There is no reason to suppose that he or any other creator has a knowledge of the nature of other types of creativity, the excellence they achieve, or the benefits that might ensue. Neither here nor in other places does a creator have a special knowledge of what other excellences are, in prospect or in fact, nor does he know how to realize or to benefit from them.

Leadership is assumed and submitted to. Rarely is it appreciated in such a way that its factors are thoroughly understood. One who would appreciate what Franklin Delano Roosevelt achieved will not begin or end with a knowledge of him, the people, his creative activity, or even the glory that the people for a time enjoyed. Instead, one will attend to a distinctive, objective union of ultimates in which the affiliator dominates over other conditions and, with them, is joined to the Dunamis. If the outcome is well read, he will confront the affiliator as a power operative on and in everything. A differently led people will provide a different sign of the same ultimate. Nothing less than all led peoples joined in a single sign could take one into the depths of the affiliator.

The price one must pay for using any creative work as a sign of what operates on and in all occurrences is that no acquaintance is then made with any other operative conditions. That knowledge could be achieved only by getting all types of creation together to act as a single sign. A theoretical understanding of all the conditions would not suffice, since appreciations are always caught up within limited areas. The best possible reading of a creation can do no more than disclose one operative condition or another.

A connoisseur or a historian might try to get in between the place where one makes creative use of a single condition and the place where one understands all the conditions as separate or joined irreducibles. Were he an appreciative, good reader of all types of creative work, he would be able to discern all the conditions as operative everywhere. Since he would view each from a separate angle, he could not attend to them as jointly operative, irreducible ultimates of equal efficacy. They operate this way in constituting the common ground of all that exists. Separately and together they are more powerful and persistent than anything man can produce, providing a common base for the cosmos, nature, and the human realm in which all creations fit.

A leader may appreciate what other leaders have achieved. If tempted to copy their most effective deeds, he will, more likely than not, become an imitator, vainly trying to reinstate what fitted elsewhere into new situations needing new answers. This is the risk run by anyone who tries to learn what leadership is by studying the deeds of great figures in the past. It is good to learn what they did; it is better to learn what leadership is, requires, and produces. The nature of leadership may be learned best if one ignores what great leaders did, and surely what they said or thought. It is unlikely that the best leaders were the best students in institutions set up by the armed forces or business or that they will be excellent members of some bureaucracy. What is learned in neatly defined situations does not prepare one well for the rough-hewn world of practice, with its dangers and obstacles. The best one can do to prepare for leadership is to supplement limited, but open-ended, live experiments in leading with a respect for what a people is, does, and needs, backed by a knowledge of the best ways it can be persuaded to act to achieve its own perfection.

The leaders most closely studied in schools are often leaders who had not studied other leaders with care. What is true here is true in other fields. While no knowledge is ever to be disdained, and though masters can teach one how to avoid serious blunders and help one acquire needed techniques, they must not be allowed to impede fresh creative work. Just as no study of Beethoven will make one a great composer, so no study of Alexander will make one a great leader. But equally, just as a poor knowledge of the elements of musical composition will confront one with obstacles that a more knowledgeable composer would have avoided, so an ignorance of what leaders do will allow for otherwise avoidable blunders and omissions which rule out the production of a people becoming glorified. The risk of becoming crippled by what should have helped is always present. Like any other creator, a great leader may, of course, produce a work of such magnitude that defects caused by ignorance or poor techniques will be of comparatively little moment.

A creative leader produces a people set in contradistinction to others. Though not necessarily in opposition to his, these others may and usually will be viewed by him and his people as being both dangerous and defective—indeed, dangerous precisely because defective—standing in the way of the glory he and his people take to be theirs alone to achieve and enjoy. Though he might want to do so, he cannot seal his people off from all the others, and surely not from the past it has shared with them, their competing efforts to make use of available resources, or their attempts to prosper, if need be at the expense of others.

Like religions, each of them occupied with obeying a god presumed to be receptive to the willing acceptance of him by anyone—though perhaps completely satisfied only by those who have managed to subscribe to certain beliefs and engage in particular rituals—different people, each led by someone creatively occupied with specializing, using, and uniting ultimates and concerned with having his people be perfected, take themselves to be special, and inescapably opposed to what is defective. Often leaders see their people as alone destined to be glorified and alone, therefore, to have the right to be, to continue, and to prosper, with all others needing to be limited or converted. A leader will usually arouse, underscore, and promote that attitude to make it more likely that his people will function as he thinks it should.

A leader who succeeded in making a people work on behalf of mankind would still remain a leader only for that people. Conceivably there could be a leader who would enable all human beings to form a single nation, bounded off only from and by nature. Yet because segments of mankind are already effectively united in diverse ways, he, too, would be forced to tailor his expressions and activities to answer to their distinctive needs.

An appeal to what is common to everyone will never be entirely effective since individuals and the limited groups they form have different requirements. Were there a universal cataclysm, a common enemy, or some other commonly perceived threat, it is conceivable that some leader might be able to help all so that they formed a single unified people.

It is part of the appeal of an actual leader that he addresses a particular people as though it will eventually, by transforming others, produce a perfected mankind. Faced as he is with quite diverse, long established, almost ineradicable customs, he cannot realistically expect to attain that goal. It is perhaps also unreasonable to think that any leader is able to abrogate the opposition his people assumes toward others. Someone trying to be a world leader, and also taking account of the fact that human beings tend to form exclusive, closely knit groups, has to depend on help from other groups while occupying himself with his own. If he could produce a single unification of all individuals, as well as of all groups, all humans would be closely affiliated, with subordinate groups supplementing one another.

Human beings have a hierarchy of distinguishable private and bodily powers. To elicit activity from them at a depth not previously tapped is to get them to bring hidden powers to bear and thereupon to be in a position to introduce a new tonality into what is being produced. Each leader does this. A world leader would have to do it as well, while promoting the awareness and realization of what enables each individual to benefit the rest. Such world leadership appears to be at the back of the minds of many leaders. Typically, a leader envisages the world as an extension of the limited group he is in fact leading and the locus of the splendor his people is destined to enjoy. He might view mankind as though it were identifiable with his people as spread over the globe. A true creative world leader would instead seek to unify all peoples, concentrating now on this pocket and then on that, but always concerned with having a single, distinctive excellence be realized for and in all humans together. His concentration here or there would be quite distinct from the occupation of a leader of some limited group, for the latter work requires the leader to stop there. Even when he concentrated for a while at one place or another, a world leader would be occupied with unifying mankind.

There have been no genuine world leaders. An Alexander, in ignorance of the existence of other peoples, might suppose that he was one, but ignorance does not suffice to place him in that exalted position. An occasional religious figure, when he ignores national boundaries, approximates the required state. His emphasis, though, is on the glorious objective to be achieved, perhaps on its source, and more often than not on the objective as endorsed by what exists forever. Instead of vainly occupying himself with trying to transform this world, he concentrates on making a supposed destiny more vivid, it being usually supposed that a great good awaits everyone if regrettable limitations are overcome.

For mankind to be unified through the realization of an ideal glory, a very deep layer of the Dunamis must be tapped. This tapping might not be necessary if some group succeeded in eliminating or transforming all the others. It is surely required if there are limited groups, maintaining their integrity even while being joined to others. Utopians are inclined to slide over the fact, supposing that the way to achieve a desirable involvement is for everyone to give up all loyalties but one. Yet the most to be reasonably expected is that ordinary differences will not be allowed to turn into antagonisms and that destructive differences will be overcome.

A single, harmonious mankind is not inconceivable; it might perhaps be brought about by harmonizing all activities and interests. Yet the larger the group, the less likely it is that there could be a strong bond uniting all members. There is no determinate number of people who could work together to become glorified, but it seems unlikely that anything much will be done if limited numbers do not pull away from the rest, acting to make themselves glorified by accommodating what a creative leader makes available only to them.

It seems improbable that all mankind will ever be glorified, for, paradoxically, it would lack any human beings to exclude. Groups will apparently always be opposed to one another for reasons economic, social, traditional, and historic, some of them trivial, some profound. Different forms of glory are realized in different peoples, each giving a different import to what was indistinguishable only as long as it was indeterminate, not fully operative. Since it is a particular people that is led, the most that can be expected is that it will exist in harmony with others and perhaps contribute to the existence of a single, peaceful mankind, enriched by diverse customs, stresses, interests, and practices. A leader, whether his group be small or large, will never have more than a limited effect on this. Yet it is possible to envisage a position outside the provenance of all particular enterprises from which everyone can be seen to make use of the same data, but with emphases on different aspects. Indeed, it is only if one assumes some such position that it is possible to understand the different kinds of creation that are possible. A resolute inquiry into all the factors constituting every item, small or large, individual or complex, reaches what a utopian treats as conceivably joined in his imagined community. That community is inevitably overspecialized, with the ultimate factors joined in only one of many possible, limited ways.

Works of art can be completed, with external boundaries giving them new, ines-

capable roles. Mathematical creations produce areas in which previous achievements are fitted and external boundaries constituted at new positions and in new
ways. Noble spirits are primarily self-limiting in a world where boundaries are
imposed without regard for what is achieved. A well-led people, similarly, is
bounded off from others at the same time that it is together with others in a larger
mankind. With these, it has a place in the history of civilization. There, too, are
the states men sometimes create.

6

Created States

Political Justice

PEOPLE TOGETHER need and want a leader. If that leader is a creator, the people will become glorified. If he is unchecked, he will often act foolishly, trying to turn incredible dreams into realities, sacrificing what exists in the present, and getting in the way of what in fact should be done—in short, stop being truly creative. The remedy, worked out over the centuries, is to replace such leaders with cooperative rulers and ruled in a stable, law-governed state. There can be no assurance that such a state will do more than keep ruler and ruled together or that it will treat their needs properly. For that to happen they must be dealt with from the position of a common, perfecting, political justice. This is but one type of justice, applicable only to what occurs in a state.

Beauty is sometimes equated with the source or outcome of pleasurable experiences, truth with what may be useful, cogency with what has technical applications, the good with what satisfies, and glory with a distinctive mark or sense of superiority possessed by one's people. Warrant has already been provided for treating these ideals instead as different, equally basic excellences, produced by carrying out creative acts. In contrast to these often misconstrued ideals, the nature of justice is apparently well understood by everyone, particularly in relation to matters of primary interest. Justice demands that account be taken of whatever is relevant to adjudications and particularly of what bears on the life and prosperity of human beings. Too often it is specified and applied in a biased form.

When some individuals are dealt with in ways that others are not because they have a different color, gender, inheritance, or status, justice still requires that all who are subject to the same classifications be treated in the same ways. When some classification is characterized as unjust, an appeal is made to a more comprehensive classification, warranting a blaming of the first for introducing irrelevancies or distortions. Justice equates all beings so far as they have the same natures, abilities, roles, or histories—indeed, any feature relevant to a considered situation. It should not be credited with the power to make its demands effective. It is better to accept the popular picture of justice as blindfolded, indifferent to anything but the relative weights of contending claims, doing nothing on its own except to hold the scales in which different claims will be weighed, and presumably requiring that one tray have something added or subtracted until the two balance.

Everyone takes account of the demands of justice in some form, but few are interested in it as an ideal or as limited to the functioning of a state. Most are content to appeal to it solely to counteract what they take to be improper distributions of opportunities, goods, rewards, or punishments, both in and outside the compass of a state. They usually take it to warrant the provision of counterweights to the biased, unfair, or irrelevant. Everyone seems aware of being the equal of others in some respects, in some situations, or in relation to some things and therefore to deserve to be subject, with them, to the same determinants of what they are, must do, and deserve to receive.

The justice that is used to determine the way goods should be distributed is not an ideal or even a more limited prospect to be progressively realized through the performance of a plurality of acts. It is a measure. An ideal, though, does not measure; a measure is not made more and more determinate. The one increases in effectiveness and control as a creative work progresses; the other remains apart, unchanged by what it serves. The justice that is to be creatively realized requires no more of an appeal to a measure than a painting requires an appeal to some standard of beauty. If the image of a blindfolded justice holding scales is not to be reduced to a portrait of a measure but is to offer instead an image of a prospect to be realized, she must be accompanied by other figures enabling her to become actively involved in balancing the scales. Those others are needed, at the very least, to put something on the scales. If she is to help in getting the scales to balance, she must await the ways that the other figures will involve her in that task.

Justice requires rulers and ruled to act so that it can operate throughout. They may do so in three ways: they may act together as individuals, as subdivided into ruler and ruled, and as law governed. Each realizes a distinctive kind of justice— *ideal, political,* or *legal*. Only the first, like the ideals realized in other ventures, is realized through creative activity. Unlike other ideals, it presupposes the achievement of a more limited form—a political justice in an actual state. There rulers and ruled have to act as cocreators, independent of one another, but in consonance. This consonance is not likely unless what they do is elicited by a statesman, enabling them to have their acts, though carried out independently, be in consonance. Conceivably, they could accomplish this task by freely and adventurously acting independently, but they would then risk getting in one another's way. A statesman could help them avoid this difficulty.

The achievement of political justice requires ruler and ruled to act legally. So far as they do, they promote the realization of a justice that is exhibited in the constant ways they act together under *enacted laws*. In addition, account will eventually have to be taken of a *living law* as an integral part of the acts carried out in the state. Whether ideal, political, or legal, justice awaits the actions of the members of a state—the first as members in an already politically just state, the second as cocreators of such a state, and the third as occupied with enactments.

Political justice is ideal justice made pertinent to a number of individuals acting together. Unlike glory, it requires for its realization a people able to contribute to its own enrichment as well as to the enrichment of those who rule them. Conversely, it demands that those who rule, whether as individuals, legislators, or a judiciary, be so positioned that they both benefit those whom they rule and enable themselves to be enhanced as they otherwise could not be.

The realization of political justice requires successful creative activity. Yet, though the ruled—and sometimes rulers, too—repeatedly demand that it be realized, few deem it a prospect or act to realize it. If it does not take on the role of a more and more effective guide, sooner or later rulers and ruled will be in conflict or will at best impinge on one another only occasionally and then in minor ways. Usually the rulers, but occasionally the ruled, will have a dominant role. The former will be inclined to act through enacted laws, since these laws will usually be in accord with their interests, while the latter will be inclined to defy or evade some of them to satisfy their needs more completely.

A leader might yield to the demands of ideal justice. His leadership would, so far, be restricted to getting both ruler and ruled to function well together. The cherished glory he would have be realized will have been allowed to slip into the background, to be invoked only when either or both ruler and ruled slacken or fail to act concordantly. The political justice that could directly determine the relative positions of ruler and ruled would here, too, be the primary objective, with a prospective glory emphasized in order to evoke extra effort.

Elections are often won by those appealing to the glory a people will supposedly attain by becoming well ruled, but states are successfully run only when rulers and ruled carry out separate, supplementary tasks. That supplementation is promoted if they form distinctive complexes and act in stable, mutually supportive ways. Political justice presupposes that such a stage has been achieved and enables it to be perfected.

A prospect pertinent to both ruler and ruled, political justice is to be realized by their carrying out independent, supplementary roles. If they did not do so, they might still act consonantly and even help one another, but would not be occupied with realizing the unification of both of them in a state. They would be two bodies moving in different orbits, possibly without colliding, but doing nothing to reduce the likelihood of collision. Neither would be restrained by what was pertinent to and could enhance them together. There could, so far, be no assurance that they would become components of a just state. As a consequence, they might, even when acting in consonant ways, not act as well as they could and should.

With no power of its own, political justice, like other prospects, is radically indeterminate. It requires creative work by rulers and ruled acting in supplementary ways, even when they are occupied with carrying out their separate tasks. This justice, dictating how rulers and ruled are to function, depends for its realization on rulers and ruled acting independently, but in consonance. Conceivably, there could be someone with power enough to have his will prevail and thereby determine what others might do. Conceivably, he might insist that political justice be realized. That outcome, because demanded but not promoted by him, would not end with the realization of the sought excellence. Instead, it would turn the ruled into his agents, producing outcomes from which they might benefit but which they did not create. They would be somewhat like actors who, though enabled to have their roles well joined, did not carry out creative work. Only when rulers and ruled act both separately and jointly to realize an ideal political justice can they be creators of a just state. This requirement does not preclude some of them from also having the role of pivots, intermediaries, or focal points.

Rulers and ruled, like any other actualities and complexes, are constituted by the meeting of nuances in irreducible conditions and the Dunamis. Like other human beings, they attend to and make special use of all the ultimates. No matter how those ultimates are specialized and used by them or by anyone else, they will continue to remain apart from what they constitute and will therefore still be available for use on other occasions. What they constitute will have its own nature and way of resisting. If the constituted entity is human, it will not only be and act apart from the ultimates but will also be able to make use of them. Both when men form groups and when they are divided into rulers and ruled, they are constituted by the same ultimates, differently utilized.

Like other human beings, rulers and ruled have individual privacies and can assume accountability for what is credited to them. Both, too, are public beings from which and to which actions are directed. As components of a state, they are subject to political justice. To the degree that such justice is being realized, rulers and ruled will be acting as they should. For that to happen, a coordinative condition has to play a dominant role, and a prospective justice has to determine what is to be done.

A just political state is impossible if rulers and ruled do not provide loci for a primal, coordinating condition. They must specialize this condition by acting concordantly. Their groupings may have been produced without regard for any form of justice, but if there is to be a just state, they both must so act that it prevails. They will also be affected by the Dunamis in different ways, to make the resulting state not only well structured but vivified. In it, political justice will act as a singular unifier for two concurrent, vibrant groups.

Political justice would have but a limited, precarious existence and no well-defined course were its realization not achieved by both ruler and ruled so acting that their respective natures and promise were sustained and promoted through the use of laws benefiting both. The two are equal neither in numbers nor in power—nor should they be. While it is sometimes said that in a democracy the people rule, what is true is that they sometimes have an opportunity to determine who will act as their rulers for a while and, presumably, who will enact laws taking account of what both they and the rulers need separately and together.

From the standpoint of the ruled, rulers are primarily agents with limited tasks. From the standpoint of the rulers, the ruled are so many public beings to whom accountability is to be attributed in accord with the law. Although it is a subdivision of the ruling group that enacts and enforces laws, some of these laws must also apply to the rulers if the state is to be law governed.

The good character that some men develop may be used with benefit in any enterprise. That use will not make their venture superior or inferior to others any more than its greater market value or the cost of its production will make one work of art be superior to others. A state can benefit from the presence of men of good character—as well as from achievements in the arts, mathematics, science, and society—without thereby turning them into agents or instruments for it. Those creations, in turn, can benefit from their practitioners' encompassment in an excellent state without the state necessarily becoming an agent serving to promote or preserve them.

Even if the existence of an excellent state were essential to the existence of other kinds of created work, or conversely, the different kinds of creations would remain irreducible excellences. The excellence of none need be jeopardized by its acquiring an instrumental role. Their excellence will, in fact, usually be presupposed as providing a warrant for making instrumental use of them. As just caught up in a situation where it serves some other objective, its actual or presumed merit may make a desirable difference, contributing to the good of the other. All the while, all will remain what they were, internally constituted. As playing a role in some other context, they are so many bounded units. What they are as internally constituted may have prompted that bounding, but this will not affect their singular excellence.

It is good to have heroic men in a state. Without them, it might perish sooner than it otherwise would. Still, an excellent state could be built and might prosper in their absence. It is good, too, to have an excellent state; without it, heroes, sages, and other creations would be poorly protected. Even so, in its absence men can produce great works. Each type of creation may benefit from others. Whether it does so or not, the excellence of each creation will still be its own, untarnished and unqualified.

Political justice determines the ways both rulers and ruled are to act. Neither may know its nature or recognize themselves to be subject to it. They could and do live under well-written, enforced laws without being occupied with what would perfect the state or themselves. Unless they also act so that political justice is realized, they might continue indefinitely as privileged or disadvantaged. The state might then be stable and well run, but it would still have a defective, unbalanced nature, reflecting an improper but permitted favoring of ruler or ruled, the few or the many, the established or the new.

Democracies assume the ruled to be able to benefit most if they can dictate who their rulers are to be and the conditions under which they are to operate. Communist states take the rulers to be able to function best if the people do what is prescribed for them by "managers," the rulers here being understood to be acting solely in the people's interests. Democratic rulers also claim to be concerned with serving the people; in addition, they place great emphasis on the fact that they are elected and are subject to recall through regulated, fair, and open procedures. In both democratic and communist states, the rulers must ensure that laws are well written and are obeyed. In neither type of state is adequate account taken of what people are, do, and need. Today the difference between the two is largely a matter of organizational structure and political methods, particular laws, attitudes toward dissidents, and control of the economy, and not what they believe the realization of political justice to require.

As essential components of a just state, rulers and ruled differ not as positive and negative, good and bad, but in emphasis, tasks, procedures, and immediate goals. Each sees itself as currently having to concentrate on removing obstacles supposedly in the way of enabling political justice to be realized and a just state thereby produced. Both indefinitely postpone the date when their realizing of political justice will be finished.

The completion of the Marxist formula "from each according to his abilities and to each according to his needs" provides a good guide for understanding what political justice requires and therefore what rulers should express in laws and action. The completion has at least four prongs.

1. "From each according to his abilities" considers human beings from the outside, as so many possible contributors to a common product. Since each is at the very least the public origin of what is done, what each does should be referred to him as one who carries out needed public roles. A common outcome will thereupon be taken to be the result of proportionate efforts made by differently endowed or enabled individuals. Nothing so far is said about their need or right to increase their abilities.

Although collectives and institutions are unable to initiate anything and must look to individuals to make use of them as agencies, those institutions also have powers of their own, to be so exercised that adequate protection and benefits are provided for what they encompass. To take account of such institutions, this part of the formula should be altered to read "from all, separately and together, according to their abilities." Account must still be taken of the different kinds of abilities expressible by various types of individuals, with the strong differentiated from the weak, the mature from the immature, the enabled from the disadvantaged, and then as pertinent to particular economic, social, and political tasks. If all abilities are to be taken into account, consideration should also be given to such private powers as understanding, willing, and preferring. No reference will as yet be made to the abilities needed to create works of art, mathematics, noble characters, or a glorified people.

If "from all, separately and together, according to their abilities" were understood to demand the exercise of those abilities needed to realize political justice in an ongoing state, with other abilities being expressed on behalf of its perfecting, this part of the formula would finally have to be amended to read: "from all, separately and together, according to their abilities to function as cocreators of a politically just state."

2. Individuals differ in maturity, skills, and flexibility. They are more or less dexterous, more or less teachable. The abilities they happen to have are not the only ones they could or should have. If a state asked only for each to do what he was able to do, it would have to rest with what each happened to be. It would make no demand for the improvement of the people, even when that improvement was to the advantage of the state.

Both ruler and ruled should be helped to be and to act so that they could coproduce an excellent state. They would not be able to do so unless they had the ability to respond appropriately to whatever was provided. This part of the formula, therefore, must be amended to read: "to all, separately and together, according to their inabilities, so as to enable them to become cocreators."

Conceivably, a prospective justice could directly elicit needed activities from both ruler and ruled. If so, they would have to specialize the justice in different ways, or it would have to make different but supplementary demands on them. The first possibility requires each to understand the position of both together in order to determine its own share; the latter, instead, requires a prospective justice to split itself in two. The former is not likely, while the latter is impossible, since a prospect is initially both impotent and indeterminate. One must look instead to both the rulers and the ruled to act well in consonance.

3. "To each according to his needs" was understood by its formulators to be concerned primarily with food, shelter, instruments of production, and other eco-

nomically toned demands. The needs of men are greater than these, both in number and kind. Everyone needs companionship, guidance, training, education, advice. All are more than bodies and have more than bodily needs. Everyone must be helped to get what he privately needs and can privately make his own.

So far as individuals stand apart from one another, there is no control over what they do. An economy, like any other common context, stops at the borders of each. When it refers to consumers, it refers only to those who have removed common goods from a common store. It has no interest in knowing whether or not the items removed are consumed, thrown away, spoiled, or disposed of in some other fashion.

Unless it is supposed that the satisfaction of needs requires only their quieting or overcoming, to meet anyone's needs it is necessary to allow also for the producing or eliciting of still others. The satisfaction of these needs may require acts different from those provided before. Both ruler and ruled are to be enhanced by the achievement of political justice, with the satisfaction of needs for food, shelter, housing, and opportunity being satisfied in different ways apart from, and both before and after, that achievement. When that requirement is taken to be primary, with others still needing accommodation, each man will be seen to require others to be satisfied mainly in order to promote his own need to be perfected. Other needs, some of them quite insistent, will then be neglected or only incidentally satisfied,

Occasionally, enlightened patrons or men with power may ease the way for someone to carry on creative work. Not much more can be done by them than to provide opportunities and encouragement. These supporters fall quite short of giving creators, and therefore cocreating rulers and ruled, what they should have. What is needed is what enables them to create together, with other satisfactions taken to be either preconditions or consequences.

4. The very nature of a prospect defines what it depends on for its realization. "From each according to its needs" could have application here, just so far as "each" had a need to be perfected and, therefore, a need to realize an ideal. No prospect, of course, is benefited by being realized. It would be paradoxical to suppose that what is radically indeterminate has a need to become determinate, particularly since its realization involves its gradual disappearance as a distinct entity.

Justice, like every other prospect, has no needs, unless something could have a need to vanish on being transformed. A caterpillar could be said to have the need to become a butterfly, but unlike an ideal, a caterpillar is already an actuality. An ideal is prescriptive, making demands only on one who has committed himself to realize it. Creative work needs a prospect; a prospect needs nothing.

"To each according to his needs" and "from each according to his abilities" are intended to focus on individuals, the first clause referring to what would benefit them, the other to what they are able to contribute. If no specific assignments, restraints, and admonitions are expressed, it will be tacitly assumed that the task of rulers is to promote the interests of the ruled and that the ruled are to try to do what the rulers prescribe. The reality of the state will so far be ignored, or the state will be identified with a people gloriously united under a leader.

Because roads are now built, forests preserved, crops planted, army, navy, and air force prepared, debts accumulated, and restraints set in place ready to be enforced, those coming later have some of their opportunities expanded and others limited. When their time arrives, they will express their own interests and powers, altering, adding, subtracting, submitting, and rebelling in ways no one can fully anticipate. Yet, despite the fact that our posterity will use and do what we never envisaged or needed, the same prospective political justice that is available to us will be available to them.

Not necessarily antagonistic, rebellious, or law abiding, neither at peace nor at war with one another, rulers and ruled, in the absence of all guidance, would have to adjust themselves constantly in order to be able to continue without serious conflict. Their acceptance of the guidance of enacted laws would not necessarily promote the realization of a just state. Laws structure and articulate. In a perfected state they will be fair, well expressed, and well administered, with both rulers and ruled acting in mutually beneficial ways.

Creative ventures open one to risks of failure that could have been avoided had one's aims been more modest. These ventures withdraw one from familiar landmarks and well-established patterns, some of which may have proven most reliable. The pertinent ideal of one venture promotes the ignoring and sometimes the use or defying of what is required if other excellences are to be realized. Each creator makes others risk producing works inferior to what otherwise would have been more successfully carried out on behalf of their own objectives.

Rulers should both promote the interests of the ruled and have themselves supported and satisfied on the way to making justice prevail. This dual aim could be achieved without regard for ideal justice or any other such prospect. It might provide little or no room for creative ventures in art, mathematics, science, the formation of character, leadership, or for the realization of justice.

Because individuals differ in degrees of maturity, experience, good sense, strength, and health and in the possession and exercise of various private and bodily powers, an achieved political justice may satisfy them in different degrees and at different times. It does not require the individuals to become alike or interchangeable. To give each his due, it is necessary to act differently toward everyone. So far as such a policy promises to increase the distance already enjoyed by those who are advantaged over those who are disadvantaged, political justice will require that countermoves be made until everyone is able to act effectively for mutual benefit.

That prospect requires ruled as well as rulers to function in ways they otherwise would not. Although both rulers and ruled would benefit from realizing political justice, neither on its own can act so that this end will be brought about. Unable either to focus on or to realize the justice that is pertinent to both, they must be helped to act jointly and consonantly. For the most part, each will react to prevailing injustices, to what seems to be seriously amiss, or to what is to its advantage. The piecemeal remedies that are usually provided may obstruct the realization of the political justice that should prevail.

Political justice is made more and more determinate not by separate individuals but by a number, and then as divided into cocreating rulers and ruled. Something like this multiple determination happens when a game is played. Just as the members of the teams must accord with the rules of the game, individual rulers and ruled must act in accord with what the state requires. Appeals to patriotism, fairness, loyalty, and the like may help to keep both rulers and ruled functioning concordantly. It is their activities, and then as primarily directed toward the achievement of their own objectives in mutually supportive ways, that provide for the realization of a political justice pertaining to both.

Failures to have justice prevail may characterize long periods, in good part because there is no well-defined position from which a reversal might successfully begin. Sometimes the failures will throw one further back, although unduly limited outcomes sometimes provide good irritants spurring everyone on. When not themselves part of the process of producing excellence, unduly limited outcomes may still prompt a successful realization of what is sought.

The achievement of political justice conforms most closely to a common view that creations result solely from a masterly use of techniques. The techniques never suffice. To suppose that they could is to overlook the fact that each prospect has a distinctive nature to be realized over a series of acts in which a condition and the Dunamis are joined under limitations set by commitments to what has been done, to what is to be done, and to the ideal to be realized. By just carrying out a technique, no matter now splendidly, it is possible to achieve not excellence but something well done, in good part because one has concentrated on the use of material and, so far, neglected what else must be produced.

The concern of artists, mathematicians, individuals, and leaders with their respective excellences has its counterpart in those rulers and ruled who jointly provide for the incursion and consequent determination of the ideal that is to unify them. As with all other excellences, its realization will unify a plurality of items which, in its absence, would be only externally related to one another. The realization ends with rulers and ruled interinvolved, without canceling their independence, dignities, and rights, or their ability to act on their own.

The achievement of political justice requires cocreative rulers and ruled, each acting primarily as a separate group. If they are not in consonance, they will not benefit from the gradually enriching, effective transformation of justice into a unifying excellence. They still might act well, but only incidentally, not as interinvolved units and complexes.

Aristotle, in one of his accounts, took justice to be a mean between injuries done to another and to oneself, and thus to provide a kind of balance between two forms of injustice. That view requires one to know what injustice is, to deal with it in its particularity, and to take justice to be primarily rectificatory, remedial. Referred to as the prescription that one balance injuries suffered by oneself with those that others suffer, justice could be taken to instance the demand that there be laws determining the distribution or sharing of resources. So far, it would not await or depend on the occurrence of injustices. Sufficient account would still not be taken of other areas to which legal justice pertains, or of the rights of individuals to mature and to have their abilities and needs assessed from a common, neutral position. Since Aristotle took his state to be already perfect, the only political justice that he had to consider was one applicable to those who were taken to constitute it, all other individuals being held to be unable to share in the state or to assure its continuation.

Legal justice prescribes that everyone in a state is to be dealt with impartially, under laws, without prejudgment, acknowledging only what in fact occurs and perhaps what would then injure or enhance. Political justice, in contrast, demands that rulers and ruled act in mutually supportive and enhancing ways and that individuals, whether they have the roles of ruler or ruled, promote the state's nature and functioning. Although it stops with public beings, the perfecting of individuals as not yet public may still be promoted, even though they will be outside its provenance, privately carrying out other activities and engaging in other creative ventures.

It is law-governed rulers and ruled who are able to realize legal justice. The laws should themselves be just. The circle lurking here is dispelled with the recognition that laws, as they operate on ruler and ruled before the state becomes excellent, can enable both to act steadily and in consonance.

Political justice is not realized merely by overcoming inequities. If it were, there would still be no assurance that they might not crop up again. It is realized only when rulers and ruled so act in a state that they support and enhance each other. Like all other realized excellences, the justice will give new roles and meaning to what it unifies. Various individuals may devote themselves to seeing that it is realized. Acting freely, standing apart from others, they could occupy themselves with making it more evident and available. They could give it a musculature and scope that it otherwise might not have, but unless limited by what enables rulers and ruled to act separately and cocreatively, they will not provide political justice with the determinations it needs in order to be realized.

The Statesman

The recognition that political justice is an excellence cannot be sundered from the nature, source, and exercise of power by ruler and ruled to realize it. If either ruler or ruled were to act alone, the other would have to support or be an agent for it. Monarchists and totalitarians suppose that the ruled should indeed act in this way. Democrats and Marxists take the opposite position. Each pair precludes the enrichment that the other could provide.

A politically just state is the outcome of the interplay of separately acting rulers and ruled promoting the same objective. They could succeed only by happenstance if they were not able to complement one another. Only if, when pursuing their separate courses, they do in fact complement one another will they persistently act in consonance. Only then could an excellent state be produced and ruler and ruled be maximally enhanced, separately and together.

A just state needs mutually supportive actions by ruler and ruled, with some of the achievements of each providing needed and supportive activity for the other, somewhat as an opera, concert, performed play, or ballet depends on a number of supplementary contributors. Unlike these ventures, in which different actions supplement one another mainly in sequence, rulers and ruled have to act as cocreators, habitually and effectively together realizing a prospective political outcome. Neither of them alone can assure that a just state will be realized. If they acted in consonance at one time, there is no reason to believe that they would do so later, unless, at the very least, their activities were controlled by a common objective all the while that they occupied themselves with only this or that side of it.

There are at least four ways in which rulers and ruled might act independently and yet supplement one another so that a single excellence was realized.

1. Rulers and ruled could share in a common tradition, constituted by individuals with similar pasts and perhaps similar standards. They could be prepared to fit well together, realizing a single prospect through the production of compatible parts. However, since they would not aim at achieving this prospect, whatever consonance they achieved would at best be the unsought outcome of their established ways of functioning.

How could there be any assurance that they would continue to act in consonance? How could a state come to be if ruler and ruled had not acted apart from one another, each providing what the state required of them whether or not they considered or supplemented one another's needs? A common inheritance could be divided in opposing ways, but that will not assure that needed supplementary acts will thereupon be produced. A shared tradition helps keep ruler and ruled in consonance, but though it makes the consonance more likely to continue, it does not guarantee it. What has once been well joined may not be well joined thereafter.

2. Rulers and ruled might act in consonance if they have well-entrenched, pertinent, and successfully used complementary habits. Each could then presumably act in ways making ample provision for what the other does, each focusing on what is to be expected to confront both sides—but they could do so only if rulers and ruled were already in accord or, if not, were prepared to act so that such consonance would be achieved and maintained. There is, unfortunately, no way to guarantee that, left to themselves, they would not hinder one another, whether or not they found what they did to be a good way to act.

3. Ruler and ruled could conceivably act consonantly while functioning in considerable independence of one another. They might do so even when occupied with carrying out their distinctive tasks. Making use of their established attitudes and ways of acting, they could attend to what enables them to focus, not on what might be justified by the past or might be attended to when they act well together, but on a prospective justice. This independent activity need not preclude a reference to a shared tradition or to a present in which they functioned in considerable accord.

Neither ruler nor ruled can assure that the two of them will act independently yet harmoniously, even to bring about what benefits both. Each has its own singular needs and pursues its own objectives. No state may be able to harmonize them. Whatever direction it goes as a singular depends in part on how its constituents enable it to function, thereupon affecting what they themselves do. If a prospective political justice is to be promoted as the excellence of a state, an intermediary is needed between that justice and separately acting and sometimes antagonistic rulers and ruled. Rulers and ruled must, while separately acting for their own benefit, be enabled to act concurrently in mutually supportive ways.

4. It is the task of a statesman to provide separate objectives for ruler and ruled which, when realized, yield a single, politically just state. To achieve this goal, he must reexpress political justice in the form of distinct, supplementary objectives which the rulers and ruled are to realize by carrying out independent activities. Unlike either of these, a statesman will allow himself to be guided by the prospect of a just state, while leaving it to ruler and ruled to act as distinct powers, each engaged in realizing its own objective, for in the absence of accepted subdivisions of a single prospective justice, they readily get in one another's way.

A statesman is not a creator. He does not make anything and surely does not progressively realize a state by carrying out a series of acts promoting the realization of the excellence it should exhibit. Instead, he attends to a prospective political justice and thereupon subdivides the needed work into what ruler and ruled, while occupied with attaining their own distinctive objectives, are to realize together. He marks out the kinds of separate tasks they are to perform, not in detail, but in outline, with broad strokes, in the light of what he discerns of the nature of a prospective political justice. Political justice can be realized only if what he prescribes for each can in fact promote it.

It is the task of a statesman to prescribe, not to control. Attentive to the nature of political justice and aware of the ideal justice that it specializes, he must try to make evident what rulers and ruled are to do so that political justice will be realized in a just state embracing both. If content to persuade, particularly if he did so on behalf not of justice but of glory, he would act as a leader. Perhaps no sharp line can be drawn, marking off where he might act as the one, articulating, recommending, pointing the way, or as the other, persuading, guiding, occupied with having glory realized. Statesmen sometimes act as guides and try to convince, to inspire, and even to arouse, but so far as they are statesmen their efforts will be directed only at presenting rulers and ruled with distinct tasks, enabling them to become separately acting but still harmonious parts of a single, excellent state.

A leader who assigns various complementary tasks to different segments of his people differs from a statesman in not being occupied with having justice realized in independently acting rulers and ruled. He and a statesman have different objectives, make different uses of the ultimates, and produce different combinations of them. Most important, they are concerned with different outcomes. Where the one is occupied with glorifying a people, the other is content to show how independently acting rulers and ruled can so act that they realize a common, just state.

Occasionally a statesman may inspire, envisage a splendid future, and have what he cherishes be realized by others. Alone or with them, he may be able to produce an outline or a constitution in which the essentials of good ruling and obedience are made evident. No state would be produced in that way. Nor would anything be created, since the statesman would not have done more than enable rulers and ruled to act independently.

The statesman's task is to enable ruler and ruled to know what they must do if they are to create a just state. He does not simply inform them; instead, he presents himself as an effective guide who will show each how to act well and yet in accord with the other, without having to attend to the other or the prospective justice. The schema he provides makes evident what independent powers must do if a common, desirable outcome is to be achieved. Despite its importance, this outcome will not be identifiable as a prospect by either. Neither ruler nor ruled may attend to it. Instead, each will be inclined to focus primarily on what is germane to its own needs and promise. Consequently, if what the statesman recommends is not accepted in such a manner that ruler and ruled change their ways and act consonantly, they will drift apart and prevent the achieving of a single, unified, politically just state. Someone dictating to ruler and ruled alike would be a ruler to whom they were subjects; he would not be a statesman, but an absolute monarch at best and a tyrant at worst.

The excellence to be realized in a state is no less indeterminate than are the excellences pertinent to other creative ventures. A statesman does nothing to realize this excellence, his task being only to make evident the nature of the single, desirable outcome that rulers and ruled could achieve by separately carrying out the acts he recommends. It is they who must create by acting in distinctive but concordant ways. All he can do is provide them with the opportunity to be distinct, independent contributors to a common desirable outcome, able to benefit both. It they respond to his recommendations properly, they will function as cocreators, each producing what is essential to the achievement of political justice in a state where they will be dealt with as they deserve.

When a statesman discerns a prospective justice, he responds to it in a distinctive way. Using it as a guide, he prescribes what ruler and ruled are to do, thereby enabling them to face different, perhaps difficult, and surely quite general demands. Ruler and ruled are to carry out these demands in ways appropriate to different circumstances and thereby satisfy their own different requirements. A statesman is no sage; if he were, he would, more likely than not, make the same kind of recommendations to both, treating them as so many individuals and emphasizing ways they could achieve good characters.

An actual state, though falling short of what it could be, may still have many desirable features. It may expedite commerce, offer protection against common dangers, and have effective laws taking good account of what human beings are, do, could be, and should do. It might function well for a long time, even in the absence of any statesman. When he appears, he will make only general proposals, expecting them to be filled out by rulers and ruled so that they will continue to act concordantly, for mutual benefit. He makes different recommendations to each as different powers, contributing to the realization of the same prospect by carrying out separate roles. The outline he offers must therefore be used by them in different ways. It is of course desirable for each to be aware of what the other should and might do. Still, they could act properly and in harmony by doing nothing more than carrying out the segments of the task of realizing justice that a statesman has assigned to them.

A statesman may not be freer of faults than anyone else is. More likely than not, he will not be humble. He may even be overly confident, taking himself to have an insight denied to others. These defects need not compromise his judgment concerning the essential components of the political justice which ruler and ruled are to produce through concordant acts.

Only if the initial, undivided political justice that concerns a statesman is brought to bear on ruler and ruled in different ways will they be positioned to produce concurrent, mutually supportive acts. Rulers and ruled are cocreators just so far as they bring their privacies into effective interplay with that part of the ideal that a statesman allocates to them. Only then are they able to realize a single prospective excellence, of which neither might be aware and which is rarely of interest to either.

Neither rulers nor ruled, on their own, attend to the ideal that their state should realize. If they did, they would skew it toward themselves. Moreover, when either tries to take account of the other's needs and ways, it does so in ways colored by its own nature and predilections. A statesman is needed for each to see how it could so act that what it does for itself supports and is supported by, and enriches and is enriched by, what the other achieves.

A statesman can do no more than express in general terms what rulers and ruled are to do on their own. They must fill out what he presents, actually produce what he endorses, and thereby realize a politically just state, where the rights of all as public beings will be respected and publicly available satisfactions distributed accordingly. Had he power enough to compel them to carry out the tasks he assigns, he would have the two as his subjects. Instead, he awaits their acceptance of his designation of their separate, supplementary tasks. Those who had previously ruled would then probably be reduced to legislators, with the ruled made subject to their enactments.

It is possible, in the absence of a statesman, to know what rulers and ruled should do. Political scientists could have that knowledge. They do not, though, have a position between a prospective justice and those who could realize it. It is from that position that a statesman tries to present ruler and ruled with their different tasks, designed to promote the realization of a common political justice in the state embracing both. He clarifies and alerts, pointing the rulers and ruled in a common direction by subdividing a common prospect into distinct, appropriate, and acceptable objectives. Unlike a ruler, he does not threaten to use force to make his version of the ideal be realized, although it is rare indeed for him to be able to call on such force to support him. Like a ruler, he is primarily occupied with making good, practical judgments about the nature and consequences of what ruler and ruled are to do, but where a ruler focuses on the determination of how best to direct and order those who are ruled, a statesman occupies himself with making the parts of an ideal state so attractive and reasonable that rulers and ruled will accept their assigned portions of the perfecting prospect. If they do, they will be readied to function so that they will realize the single objective together, while doing no more than acting to realize their own limited objectives.

It is not a statesman's task to assure that rulers will forcefully carry out laws, even just ones, or to see to it that the ruled obey them, whether or not they then benefit themselves, the rulers, or both together. Still, since those who rule tend to impose their wills on those who are ruled, and since the ruled are not inclined to promote or sustain a common justice, a statesman will try to alert each to the nature, rights, needs, and power of the other. When most successful, he will elicit their joint efforts, often by making evident the benefits each will receive by carrying out indicated, specialized, supplementary acts. Since his is the practical wisdom of knowing what is pertinent to the realization of justice in a state constituted by both, he will display a flexible understanding of the probable course of events that will enable both to bring about and maintain a common, just state.

A statesman is eminently reasonable. Reasonableness, or *praxis* as some today are inclined to term it, has many forms. In all, it expresses a readiness to act effectively with reference to what is available, for the sake of bringing about what is desirable. In a state its use promotes the good of both ruler and ruled, an outcome not to be expected if they do not act on behalf of the realization of a political, and possibly an ideal, justice. Whatever state is achieved could be quite stable because of the continuation of inherited customs and practices, qualified by the efforts needed to take account of changing circumstances.

There have been unreasonable rulers whose effectiveness was due mainly to the force they were able to use to make the ruled do what might increase the advantage the rulers already enjoyed. One who would be reasonable when under the control of such a ruler has to act in some consonance with the ruler's effective judgments and willful acts, even when he tries to find ways to promote a better state. This course is not easy to follow, requiring a kind of silent, hardly noticeable satisfaction of many demands that do not evidently modify or violate what is decreed.

Unlike a political scientist, a statesman does not just present or justify what he would have be done. Unlike a propagandist, he does not try to make men change their ways. Guiding himself by a prospective ideal justice, he specializes it as a political justice and assigns to ruler and ruled the complementary tasks which could realize it. Indispensable to the achievement of a just state, he could still be said to be no part of it since he does no more than mediate a singular prospect and the subdivisions of it that are to be carried out by ruler and ruled. It is no less true that he is essential to it, for without him ruler and ruled would not continue long to act both independently and in harmony. His actual life may be quite short, but he could be said to continue in the form of a constitution, a tradition, and a common memory, thus enabling ruler and ruled to keep acting independently but still in consonance.

Even when flexible and innovative, able to change their courses, to compromise, backtrack, and initiate, rulers and ruled cannot be counted on to use ultimates so that an excellent state is produced. Nor can the most imaginative of statesmen, even one who is attuned to the course of events and has a good understanding of how rulers and ruled can and should act, do more than present them with recommendations of ways to function. Only in the best of circumstances will both ruler and ruled act to bring about what he would have them do, for their attention tends to be focused on what has to be done here and now, and then mainly to enhance or shore up their distinct privileges and promote their own opportunities.

Rulers are often brought up in cloistered areas and are educated to speak, dress, and behave in distinctive ways. When under scrutiny, they may occupy themselves with issues of signal importance, mainly in inherited ways. If strong, they may invade and take over another state, break into new territory, produce unanticipatable results, transform whatever they use, and then end with outcomes they credit primarily to themselves. They tend to be conservative, to want to preserve what has been tested by time, to continue to maintain their positions, and to be satisfied with the production of a controlling structure within whose compass the ruled will live peaceably, though perhaps unfulfilled and diminished. Once they are in firm control, they usually allow a larger scope to their fancies and follies. They would be stronger and sometimes more successful if they were more flexible, better attuned to what the ruled could do.

While often identified with a single being, particularly when given a special title indicating a status greater than that of any others, an individual ruler rarely acts alone. Usually he must make use of a complex government of which he is the ostensible, and perhaps may occasionally the effective, head. Sometimes he will need the backing of armed forces as well as of agents. Chiefly occupied with laws, structures, and fixities, he is inclined to minimize the power of the Dunamis, both in the ruled and as it is available to himself. Immersed in the present, interested mainly in what can be discerned in the immediate future, he also tends to overstress the need for immediate action, to slight what seems to be a far-off objective or to require the cooperation of many. These limitations cannot be overcome by his multiplying the number of governmental officials. Such intermediaries inevitably modify, delay, and deflect what they are supposed to transmit.

Creative leaders are not always available. It is possible to live without artists, creators in mathematics and science, or even noble men. Many, too, can live quite well in the absence of good government, particularly if they are members of a society in which shared prospects and tradition, cooperation and fraternity, stability and flexibility promote their continuation and prosperity. A state adds to these achievements. At the very least, its constituents, ruler and ruled, can be so positioned that they make maximum use of one another's abilities and achievements to realize an objective that neither alone could get into proper focus.

In the absence of a statesman, ruler and ruled may act in some consonance for a time, but they would not know how to act independently and yet promote the realization of a single political justice benefiting each separately and both together. More like the conductor of an orchestra than a composer, needing others to act on their own if the sought outcome is to be achieved, a statesman directs rather than controls, convinces rather than persuades. Unlike rulers, ruled, leaders, or performers, he is primarily a mediator, making evident and desirable what is to be done by others. Unlike a planner or theorist, he tries to be influential; unlike a leader, he does not contribute to the production of an excellence; unlike rulers or ruled, he attends to the undivided prospect that is to characterize the state as a singular. Taking account of the nature and needs of ruler and ruled as distinct, he emphasizes the desirability of their acting in harmony. He alone enables an objective to bear on ruler and ruled, as both distinct from himself and able to realize compatible, needed parts of a single just state.

Persons who together produce a constitution could be termed statesmen and taken to represent a single statesman or to produce one in the form of an effective document. In the first way, individuals would be treated as so many fragmentary forms of a single statesman; in the second way, one would have to attribute to the document some of the attributes characteristic only of human beings. Many of the difficulties then raised could be disposed of by changes in nomenclature. Of greatest importance is the recognition that a statesman is a needed intermediary between a single prospective political justice and needed parts of a functioning state.

Rarely do statesmen articulate their recommendations in a form relevant to the best interests of rulers and ruled. Rarely are their recommendations the outcome of reflections on the nature and role a political justice is to have in a state. Rarely do rulers and ruled carry out supplementary parts of a single task and thereby realize political justice. Still, any and all of these desirable outcomes could be approximated beyond any antecedently determined degree.

A statesman has completed his task if ruler and ruled on their own continue to act independently of one another in such a way that they make possible the better and more successful functioning of the other, thus realizing a common political justice. Could he get rulers and ruled to act persistently so that they both concentrated on their separate tasks and yet realized the common justice, there would be no further need of him. Since they will surely acquire their own habits, stress their own interests, and oppose one another many times, they must have persistent recourse to a statesman or to what represents him to assure their continued consonant activity.

Since a statesman is occupied primarily with focusing on and communicating what ruler and ruled are to realize by carrying out supplementary tasks, he will use his privacy in a way neither of them does. To make the prospect of political justice guide his determinations of their roles, he must persuade them to act as cocreators. Not a utopian, he will enable ruler and ruled to bring about an actual state in which they are able to benefit themselves and one another—but like a utopian, he will be aware of the nature of ideal justice and, though not in a position to realize it, will nevertheless make its realization more likely.

Only when rulers and ruled are occupied with realizing different, supplementary parts of the same objective will they act as a statesman recommends. They will then be joint creators of a politically just state. Since a mutually sustained and enriching political justice is best assured by having well-formulated, enforceable laws, a statesman will, in articulating the nature of political justice, also indicate the kind of laws that are to be enacted, carried out, and obeyed. If he does so, legal justice will be realized within the compass of a politically just state produced by rulers and ruled acting as cocreators.

Usually less emotional than artists are, a statesman is also less concerned to bring about a result that may never play an effective role in the world than a mathematician is. Less self-involved than a leader, he also may not be noble, wise, or heroic. Like all creators, though, he will privately specialize and use what he is able to discern of the ultimates. Since he is not a creator, he will do nothing to realize a just state; instead, he will present ruler and ruled with limited prospects germane to their distinctive natures, abilities, needs, and promise, thus enabling a singular excellent state, embracing both, to be achieved. If the rulers or ruled fail to heed him, or if they do not act as he recommends, there is not much that he can do to get them to change their ways.

The autobiographies of artists often highlight what are supposedly crucial incidents in their lives; creative mathematicians offer few indications of how they create; the noble rest content with achieving and exhibiting a self-mastery and then, when the occasion arises, making evident what they are; leaders favor what they think will persuade and may, in the calm of retirement, reveal the aspirations they had and the frustrations they suffered. Since a statesman stops short with making evident the nature of a perfect, attainable state, the most accurate, complete, and relevant account of what he thought, planned, and did could help one understand only the way he had made political justice pertinent to others.

Beauty is initially a bare, indeterminate prospect. It does not interest artists, though they do freely terminate at it, commit themselves to it, and over the course of their creative activity give it a greater and greater role. Truth is too general an idea for a mathematician even when he is interested in producing what has the greatest generality and an unlimited applicability. The good does interest those who would be noble, but it is too impersonal to attract those who cherish the enjoyment of readily attained goods. Glory is always somewhere in the offing, but it does little more than prompt a leader's elicitations of what a people is to do. Justice contrasts with all of these ideals in needing separately acting subdivisions to produce not what is excellent but essential parts of it.

Dust, gravity, light—all corrode works of art; traditions sometimes block the path over which creative mathematicians are to move; the noble must tailor their acts according to circumstance; leaders act on a people only partially closed off from the rest of the world. None of these creators has to deal with as many problems as rulers and ruled must. Inescapably affected by what has no regard for what a state is, does, and needs, neither knows what it requires or does all that must be done. A statesman, as well as rulers and ruled acting as he prescribes, are needed if a state is to be perfected.

A state has a nature and can be said to act and react, but what is in fact done is the work of individuals and groups carrying out roles. Their acts are privately grounded and usually directed at what is wanted and feared. In a well-led society, the members of each group will be interinvolved with the rest; in a state, what each privately initiates will have no other status than that of being the unacknowledged origin of what is publicly done.

Because political justice requires someone to focus on and specialize it in a two-fold, unbiased way, it needs the help of a statesman to alert ruler and ruled to the desirability of their carrying out supplementary acts. If they are to do so persistently, they must cooperate within the compass of the state they jointly constitute. Yet neither ruler nor ruled is able to envisage a state as able to satisfy both.

Rulers always have to exercise some force both because there are aberrant individuals and because the force provides an effective means for closing the gap between command and obedience. If the gap is closed only from their side, the state will not be able to yield more than a supposed common unification skewed toward the rulers and their interests. If they use force to get the ruled to act properly, they will make evident that they or the ruled, and possibly both, are not acting as they should. The ruled, in any case, always resists, both because no rule is perfect and because the distance between obedience and command has to be bridged from its side as well. That requirement reflects the independent status of the ruled and the fact that it takes account of the sought objective in its own way. Apart from an adherence to what a statesman recommends, rulers will at best provide only for a continued governance that does not arouse great disturbances, while the ruled will yield to demands which do not counter what it takes to be precious.

Rulers and ruled should join ultimate factors many times in ways which supplement each other's productions. At one moment, the rulers' needs, demands, or achievements are to be to the fore; at another, those of the ruled. If they are cocreators, their overemphases on themselves as apart from one another will characterize stages in the achievement of a just state in which they are mutually supportive. Only if rulers and ruled supplement one another's acts while doing what they can to have a common justice realized does each do what a statesman would have it do.

If one who ignored the complex nature of human beings, with their diverse impulses, established traditions, habits, and needs, and the bitter truths that fear makes many craven and that power increases the appetite for what it satisfies, he could do no more than assume the position of an imaginary statesman who was occupied with beings unlike any of those who now exist.

Leaders must be effective; statesmen need only to be plausible. A leader concentrates on exhorting and condemning; a statesman presents to rulers and ruled what they can identify as promoting their interests and the realization of a just state. Leaders can continue to be leaders even when the people contribute to the realization of justice; statesmen can continue to be statesmen even for an inspired, well-led people. These leaders and statesmen still differ from one another in aim, procedure, and accomplishment. Even when each carries out some of the roles essential to the other, they act in distinctive ways.

Rulers and ruled might mesh well together. They cannot be expected to do so for long if not effectively guided by what enables their independent activities and goals to be supplementary. If in the absence of a statesman or of a legacy effectively substituting for him, they promote a common, just state, it is not to be expected that their supplementary acts will continue for more than a short, adventitious span.

A statesman does not merely state what rulers and ruled are to do. He brings the common, prospective, political justice to bear on them in different ways. Since he is an active mediator, it is not surprising to find that those who duplicate the constitutions and structures of others who were progressing toward the achievement of a just state may not promote the realization of a just state for themselves. For the realization of justice to be promoted, the effective intermediation of a statesman of their own, relating the common prospect and the separately acting consonant powers, is needed. He may or may not cajole. It makes little difference, in fact, what devices he employs as long as he succeeds in enabling ruled and ruler to act in consonance while they go about their distinctive work.

A statesman need not codify what he would have rulers and ruled do. It suffices if he has been able to get them to be subject to the guiding control of a common objective, though neither may attend to it. What he endorses for those in his state may not be appropriate to those in another. Indeed, it would make little sense to present the program that was effective in his state to rulers and ruled in some other, with its different past, present, and likely future. When democracies or other types of states are exported, they undergo radical changes and as a consequence may produce not rulers and ruled independently producing the state both need, but what may, in fact, preclude their acting in needed ways. The cocreators of a particular state have to act toward one another in ways which differ from those required of cocreators in some other state, if for no other reason than that they have different traditions, habits, needs, problems, and opportunities. One who presented a blueprint or a constitution without effectively conditioning what rulers and ruled should do would not be a statesman, but at best one who marked out what a statesman should effectively express.

Rulers and ruled are most effective when they go their independent ways. Although a statesman cannot compel and may not succeed in getting them to act as they should, he is needed to enable them to act so that justice will characterize their joint, independently produced achievements. Although he neither acts nor leads, he effectively changes the ways a common excellence operates on both without their attention being necessarily directed at it.

A constitution represents a statesman. The fact is made evident when, in the so-called preamble of the Unites States Constitution, the purpose of the Constitution is stated by marking out its major objectives. These objectives can be achieved only by rulers and ruled carrying out tasks promoting and sustaining what the constitution "ordains and establishes." A statesman, unlike the "preamble," actually connects a single prospective justice to the diverse provisions that rulers and ruled are to satisfy as separate bodies.

The "preamble" to the Constitution does not express the Constitution's full purpose. Not only does that document put major stress on the nature and tasks of the rulers; it fails to attend to all the requirements of a just state and does not attempt to assign to rulers and ruled distinctive kinds of acts clearly designed to realize such a state. To be an adequate representative of a statesman, a constitution would have to mediate between a prospective justice and the rulers and ruled in a way that enabled stated parts of a single objective to become objectives for distinct, independently acting rulers and ruled. Some of the objectives and needed acts, or outlines of them, could be stated in the body of a constitution. The fact has been signalized in the United States Constitution in those amendments that guarantee equal rights for all, regardless of race or gender.

A statesman who tries to be creative is to be viewed with apprehension, for he cannot control or use those who alone will act. He would most likely emphasize what rulers are to do, seeing them as perhaps more likely than the ruled to be receptive to what is present and surely as better organized and prepared to do what will be to their advantage and therefore what will conceivably be carried out to promote the realization of a just state. More important is the fact that it is to the rulers that one must look to have particular laws stated and enforced.

In these days, when the idea of a final cause is dismissed as the confusing inheritance of an Aristotelian way of dealing with nature, the role of the statesman will be readily misconstrued. More likely than not he will be taken to be a ruler, veiling privileges in a language calculated to lull the ruled. One has then to resort to the courts to provide ad hoc determinations of what ruler and ruled are to do. Those courts will thereupon substitute a purpose of their own making or ascribe the work of a statesman now to the ruler and now to the ruled.

Courts which do not act to sustain or to impose a common purpose might act as one of a number of competing ruling powers. Were they set above the other branches of a government—in the United States, the executive and legislature— they would become the ruling division of the state. Although they cannot entirely escape from taking that position on occasion, they function best when they sustain a statesman's purposive determination of what rulers and ruled are to do.

Actual states may result from transformations of a people into the subjects of enacted laws. Those laws are rarely the outcome of efforts to make a statesman's formulations effective. Only now and then is a statesman available; even more rarely is he listened to. Only now and then do rulers and ruled work well together to bring about what he envisaged; only rarely do they do so deliberately. To limit and make up for these deficiencies, a constitution, checks and balances, voting, referenda, ready channels for communication, and interplay have to serve. These supplements may help ruler and ruled recognize and perhaps carry out their distinctive tasks. Were nothing more than this work done, the state would more likely than not be unsteady, not prosperous, not just, and would not exhibit what a statesman outlined.

A painting is produced on a particular canvas. A sonnet has a preset number of lines. A building at a particular site is subject to zoning laws, the impingement of sun and shadows, and the effects of the environment with its contrasting buildings and spaces. These and other works of art are created within accepted limits; when they are completed, they will be bounded off from all else. These boundaries and their producers are not integral parts of the creations, though like other extraneous objects they may intrude on and spoil what has been done. Unlike the prescribed length of a sonnet or the size and location of a building, what a statesman provides enables the contributors to a final, excellent work to act as supplements, realizing their own limited objectives under the aegis of a prospective common justice.

If poets were asked to collaborate in the writing of a sonnet in heroic couplets, with words appropriate to some special occasion, their work would be like the work carried out by well-guided rulers and ruled, though still quite different in conception, course, and outcome. Not only would they seek to realize beauty rather than justice, but they would have begun to work only after they had accepted prescriptions antecedently set. Rulers and ruled, in contrast, always remain free to modify recommendations made to them without ceasing to be cocreators. Whereas the limitations accepted by the imagined poets keep them at separated tasks having no necessary bearing on one another, rulers and ruled can, because of a statesman, contribute to the production of a single work in which what they severally do is so joined that each is enhanced.

A statesman presents cocreators with what they are to subdivide to produce a single excellence not otherwise possible. Like other creators, the cocreators have to make an indeterminate, ideal prospect be realized. Unlike the others, they need to have that prospect mediated by the assignment of distinctive correlative work which, if well carried out, will produce a just state. Since cocreators depend on one another to fill independent, necessary, supplementary roles, a just state is less likely to be realized than are other kinds of excellences.

A number of individuals in a constitutional convention could function in effect as a single statesman. His mediating role might be expressed in the constitution's statement of purpose. This statement will put in general terms what rulers and ruled have to specialize separately, and separately produce. The two will still continue to be distinct from one another, act independently, and require different demands to be satisfied. Inevitably, they will interact with one another. Rarely will each so act that the other's interests are fully sustained and promoted and its own well satisfied.

Justice demands that whatever there be have its nature respected and its promise promoted. Pertinent to individual privacies, bodies, groups, rulers, and/or the ruled, distinct states, and numbers of them, justice operates in different ways in the different places, depending on what it has to unify. Made relevant to a particular state, it prescribes that each act there be dealt with on terms relevant to the way the actor and others are affected. At different places and times it will require that stresses, expectations, and procedures be altered so that it can become more and more effective.

Unlike the units of interest to artists and mathematicians, those dealt with from the perspective of justice (like those dealt with from the position of the good or nobility) are privately grounded in humans possessing distinctive rights. Some of those rights are native; others are bestowed. Justice takes account of what is and should be made available if those rights are to be respected. It is one of the few prospects that needs an intermediary to enable creators to engage in different but supplementary activities. Performances that require guidance by a conductor, choreographer, or director offer analogues. Those intermediaries have a power and control possessed by no statesman.

The justice a statesman would have realized by cocreating rulers and ruled is political, at the fore of an ideal justice pertinent to every state. When political justice is realized, a state is positioned to realize that ideal justice. This justice enables the prospective political justice to have a status apart from the statesman, who thereby enables it to be an effective prospect. When cocreators carry out their supplementary tasks, the just state they realize brings forward the ideal justice to make its realization possible. All the while, both rulers and ruled will be subject to laws as so many special conditions they must meet when carrying out their separate activities. If they are to promote the work of cocreating rulers and ruled in a state, the laws must both instantiate a single Law and promote the realization of a legal justice.

Laws

We have seen that all actualities and derivatives from them, whether important or not, good or bad, passive or active, are constituted through the joining of different ultimates. So is every part of a creative work and that work as a singular, internally constituted excellence. In some parts of each work one or another ultimate may be dominant. Those parts may nevertheless be so joined in the final outcome that some other ultimate dominates over all.

In a created work, a realized excellence makes use of a dominant condition as the primary vehicle through which it unifies all the parts. The lines of a poem may exhibit the dominance of an affiliative condition, but a complete, excellent poem will be primarily a temporal excellence. In a state, the final, dominant condition is a coordinator. (I have sometimes referred to this condition as *being* since whatever there may be is a reality to the same degree as anything else, no matter how strong or weak it be. Since *being* has long been treated as referring to what is in or behind everything whatsoever, I now think it is better to use another term to designate what is only one of a number of ultimate conditions.)

The coordinator sets distinguishable items alongside one another. As pertinent to every state it has the specialized form of Law, which mediates the coordinator and a particular state, with the latter encompassing a plurality of public beings both as distinct and as together in groups. When Law is abstracted from its role as constitutive of the structure of particular states, it is sometimes called the "law of nations." Some theologians and some moralists go further and refer to it as "natural moral law," supposedly incorporating a supernaturally grounded justice and setting limits to the kinds of acts that are permissible. The theologians ground it in the decrees or being of their god. No such grounding is needed to warrant the acknowledgment of Law as a specialization of the coordinator. A great difference between one state and another lies in the different controls that Law imposes on what they do and in what is required of their rulers and those who are ruled.

If taken to express the nature of justice, Law—an instance of a condition—will be confounded with a prospective ideal. Unutilized, it is indeterminate but still different in nature from the prospects that are pertinent to creative ventures to be realized in distinctive ways, even within a state. Law requires that accountability be attributed and taken to entail rewards and punishments on the basis of public acts, whether or not private factors play a significant role, somewhat as accountability and its consequences are ascribed to commanders of ships for what their subordinates do or fail to do. All that matters is what can be ascertained about public roles, tasks, failures, and achievements.

Justice in its different forms—ideal, political, and legal—is matched by different kinds of law. Ideal justice is realizable if a state operates in accord with Law, an effective expression of the coordinating condition. It is realized as political justice in a particular state by cocreating rulers and ruled. If these act in accord with enacted laws, legal justice will also be realized.

Legal justice provides a determination of the viable rights particular beings have, dealt with as so many role bearers. Necessarily neglecting what individuals are and privately do, a state will act in accord with legal justice so far as it distributes its rewards and punishments on the basis of impersonal determinations of the outcome of law-determined discriminations. To do so, it must take account of the importance of the roles that individuals assume and carry out and of the ways rewards and punishments best contribute to the state's continuance and prosperity. Enacted laws, which allow for no reference to private intentions or determinations, cannot meet the demand that the distribution, no matter what the form, be in accord with what individuals have privately decided to do.

Enacted laws apply to members of a state both as singular and as together. Those members are to be treated as so many public referents for the state's attribution of accountability for what occurs. The ones that are taken to be accountable may not have brought about what was proscribed or may not have neglected what was prescribed. Nevertheless, they may be held accountable by the state, even one operating impersonally under good enacted laws. It is right for the state to hold individuals accountable so far as it is right to have accountability determined solely on the basis of enactments making attributions in the same ways and with the same consequences for everyone. What would not then come within the provenance of the state would, for it, be taken to be "private"—not as that which was lived through by an individual apart from all others but simply as a public occurrence that the state's representatives have defined to be outside its concern.

The "privacy" of which lawyers speak is a public area into which the state does not choose to enter. A home is public for the state if it is a suspected source of what is forbidden, and it will be held to be private just so far as no accountability is legally ascribed for what occurs there. Not only is that privacy quite different from the privacy actually possessed and used by individuals, but the accountability ascribed may diverge considerably from the accountability that is privately assumed.

A privacy is epitomized in desires, thoughts, will, responsibility, and other ways. These epitomizations are outside a state's reach and therefore outside its interest. When enacted laws refer to "intent," they refer not to what occurs in an individuals's privacy but to what the laws define as a relevant source of an ascertainable public act. All the while, men will continue to carry out private activities. Many will claim to know what they themselves, and frequently others, intend in their otherwise unreachable privacies and will make judgments that may diverge radically from those which the courts pronounce.

The "intention" that concerns a state is an accountable act assumed to originate in or at a publicly identifiable being. Since a state does not concern itself with the question whether or not an individual privately assumes accountability, it cannot promote the realization of itself as being able to do justice to what anyone is or does as an individual. Its representatives may demand expressions of contrition, public confessions of guilt, or evidences of regret, but they cannot get behind these signs to the beings who initiated the acts.

The realization of legal as well as other forms of justice depends on the existence of individuals who privately commit themselves to the task. Those commitments are made and carried through outside a state's capacities and concerns. It knows nothing and can know nothing, and it cannot interest itself in the question whether or not the accountability it ascribes is privately accepted.

Enacted laws are obeyed in states which are not created as surely as they are in those that are created. Unless the rulers as well as the ruled follow the recommendations of a statesman and thereupon act so that they are able to be compatible parts of a single, just state, the enactments will not be carried out in ways that promote the state's perfecting and consequently its becoming both legally and politically just.

Enacted laws, even where distinct and authoritative, do not necessarily provide adequate expressions of the Law. Produced by rulers, they are to be instantiated by the ruled—and should be by the rulers as well—as so many accountable, public beings. Their main purpose is to measure the extent to which what is publicly done is acceptable.

At its best, a plurality of enacted, enforceable laws, appropriate to what is done publicly, will express Law as pertinent to that state. These laws regulate public acts carried out there. Neither ruler nor ruled might consider or know the nature of Law, despite its being specialized in every enactment. Even those who formulate and enforce the enactments as part of an effort to realize justice may have no better understanding of Law than anyone else.

Legal justice is a prospect holding for rulers and ruled separately as well as together. It demands that all issues be dealt with on their merits, "given their due" for what they are and for what they entail in a state—a matter to be determined on the basis of publicly available evidence. No occupation with the formulation or application of laws, even under the limits of a constitution, will assure that it is ever realized. Nor will its realization be assured by a people considering one another's needs or desires or by their adding special provisions for those disadvantaged because of their past, gender, color, disabilities, or poverty. All that is required is that rulers and ruled act steadily together under enacted laws, forged in consonance with the demands of legal justice.

No one is merely a public person. If he were, he could not assume accountability for what he does or for what might be credited to him. His rewards and punishments would then have to be determined solely by an impersonal application of enacted laws with no regard being taken of him as one who privately and independently acts, sometimes without regard for what is publicly required and done. Were laws not subject to the demands of legal justice, the ruled could be well regulated but would not act so that the state is perfected. Legal justice requires that account be taken of the public rights that individuals and complexes possess. Prescribing that those rights be respected, it neglects what individuals privately are and do.

A state acts in accord with the requirements of legal justice only so far as it distributes its rewards and punishments on the basis of impersonal, law-determined decisions. To do so, it must take account of the importance of the roles to be assumed and carried out and of the ways the distribution of rewards and punishments can best contribute to the state's continuance and prosperity. Laws cannot satisfy the demand that the distribution, no matter what its form, be in accord with what individuals privately decide to do.

A government restricted to rewarding or punishing those held accountable for desirable or undesirable public acts emphasizes procedure. At best it exhibits the legal justice of due process, a procedure in which attributions are impersonally made. That procedure still allows some to be held accountable for what they did not do. Since it requires only that attributions be impersonally made in accord with established practice, due process may conflict with other, more personally relevant ways of determining what is to be done.

A good judicial system follows the publicly available evidence wherever it may lead. That does not assure that its decrees will always cohere with what individuals have responsibly produced. Some men have been found guilty in fair trials without even having had the means for carrying out the punishable acts. Some innocent persons have been convicted and guilty ones not charged because procedures, while eminently fair, objective, and careful, failed to get beyond what the individuals were taken to be and do as so many public units.

Enacted laws are distinct, authoritative, specialized expressions of Law. Needed to regulate the public acts of humans so that they do not get in one another's way, as units or in combinations, the laws express the legal structure of a state in a plurality of applicable forms pertinent to some of the things that are publicly carried out. Produced by rulers, laws define what it is to be an accountable public being. The efficacy of those laws depends on their bearing on the public actions of both ruler and ruled. They are properly applied to them because they are both subject to the state's determination of the nature and degree of their accountability.

Political justice provides a guide for a statesman, enabling him to determine what rulers and ruled are to produce together. He takes account of the roles these are to carry out separately, though in consonance, within the ambit of a state. Legal justice demands that rulers and ruled carry out mutually supportive roles. It presupposes, but says nothing about, their private acceptance of what is ascribed to them. Yet in the absence of such acceptance, men would be only public places where laws had application. In a state men are to function as law-abiding role bearers. If interested in having legal justice prevail, they will privately accept as right the state's impersonal distributions of rewards and punishments, openings and closings. If they do so, they will be not only role bearers but public, legally determined persons.

One who lives in accord with what enactments prescribe would be no more than a good public unit unless he privately accepted the accountability that the state credited to him as being right and therefore what the realization of legal justice demands. If only the ruled accepted accountability, the rulers in their exercise of power might act as the laws prescribed but would not consider themselves subject to them. If they are to make themselves be members of a legal, just state, both they and the ruled not only should accommodate the demands of political justice in the forms that a statesman assigns to them but must privately take themselves to be accountable for what the state credits to them. Accepting what is credited to them by the state as that for which they are privately accountable, they are then committed to carrying out still other acts. These acts, by fitting in with what enacted laws prescribe, promote the realization of legal justice. When rulers and ruled not only carry out compatible, needed public roles but accept what has been ascribed to them as that for which they are properly held to be legally accountable, the state's limits will be stretched. Only then, though, will the state accommodate them as independently acting individuals who accept as right what is publicly done for and to them. If this accommodation were not made, the ruled might promote the functioning of a state in which individual roles were carried out, but they would not back those roles with private acceptances.

The realization of a legally just state requires that the accountability determined by the application of laws be accepted by those to whom they are ascribed. Only those private persons who freely sustain what they are publicly taken to be and do, and indeed whatever they may be held accountable for, can be properly said to participate in the functioning of a well-governed, legally just state. That state provides for an interlocked set of warranted rewards, punishments, acceptances, and rejections, accommodating both those who do and those who do not privately accept what the state presumes their actions to deserve. It embraces them as publicly together, but still as having privacies, lived through apart from all others. Only if they hold themselves accountable for what the state ascribes to them, though, will they be privately in accord with what they are as public members of the state.

The laws formulated by rulers should be framed within the compass of Law if both their needs and those of the ruled are to be assured of satisfaction. Some of the laws will be good, some bad. The poor ones will differ from the others in one or more of three basic ways: they will not be well formulated; they will not refer to what is essential to identified acts or their consequences; or they will not promote the realization of legal justice. They remain poor laws even if remedies are provided to make up for their deficiencies. It would, therefore, make for precision to speak of well and poorly formulated laws, of well or poorly applied laws, and of wise or unwise laws.

Poorly formulated laws so carried out that legal justice was promoted are better than well-formulated laws that hobble or skew the functioning of the members of the state. Of primary importance is the operation of particular laws in such a way that legal justice, the impersonal determination and distribution of accountability for what comes about in the state, be realized. If law-abiding activity by both rulers and ruled, promoting the realization of legal justice, is to occur, the right of rulers to formulate and enforce particular enactments and to set limits for determining the accountability of the ruled as public beings must be limited. They should provide only for those determinations of accountability that promote a legally just state.

In the absence of an interest in the production of an excellent state, laws could be well formulated and provide eminently desirable structures determining the basis on which conflicting claims could be well adjudicated. If the laws were applied on the basis of what they might do to enable individuals and groups to act well together, legal justice might prevail. Since role-bearing rulers and ruled, even when acting in consonance, may not promote the realization of the state that a statesman would have them bring about, a legally just state may not become one that is also politically just.

Laws are formulated and also applied by some who lack interest in legal justice. So far, they can be no more than agencies for determining whether this or that act is to be permitted or forbidden and what its consequences are. Yet despite the fact that those who legislate may be in control for long periods and that many do not attend to the task of realizing justice over the course of a creative venture, whatever is formulated and applied will still instantiate Law.

No one in a state is a detached unit who first acts apart from it and later becomes subject to laws that bring him into or keep him in it. Rulers and ruled, no matter what they do, perform acts in which a coordinating condition is instantiated and may be in control. So far as the instantiation and control occur, the acts of rulers and ruled are Law governed, though not yet subject to any actual laws.

The members of a state are accountable role bearers whose acts incorporate a conditioning primal coordinator in a form it may not have in what is enacted. Because the enactments are imposed on what already has been structured by the coordinator, they can be more or less in accord. A similar situation arises when judgment is passed on the precision of something said. No one first produces a meaningless jumble of words and then sees how well it happens to conform to grammatical rules. Instead, all speak more or less grammatically. The respectability of the results may then be tested by seeing how the grammar exhibited conforms to one used as a norm. A legislator or ruler is like a grammarian who has the power to punish those who do not exhibit what is acceptable in what they say.

The members of a state produce more or less law-abiding acts, often without knowing the pertinent laws. Those laws are intended to serve as means for relating required acts or prohibitions to promised rewards, punishments, restraints, and opportunities. The acts the members constitute, with the help of specializations of the coordinating condition joined to specializations of other ultimates, rarely match the demands expressly formulated by legislators.

A tyrant increases the scope, threat, or use of force to make his will become effectively expressed. Inescapably limited by what he cannot control, he inevitably rules, in the face of what he and others believe, only with the help of the ruled. What he presents is inevitably qualified by them. When what he demands is not forthcoming, he has to threaten or use the power available to him. He cannot content himself with formulating broad principles and policy, for these, too, must be backed by force unless the ruled could be counted on to do what he insists on. If they could be counted on at some particular time, he would still have no assurance that they would continue to do so.

A state has rulers and ruled acting only more or less in consonance. Laws enable them to act in accord as accommodated, public beings. Were a ruler, whether one or a number and acting as a government or a controlling power, to stop with the formulation of laws, he would not yet have enabled justice to be realized. For that to happen, the laws must become part of the occurrences in which specializations of the coordinator are already constituents. The laws that rulers back may or may not benefit the ruled, but if the ruled are to do what the rulers prescribe, they must turn those laws into transforming components of their own acts. Since specializations of the same coordinator are already operative there, the ruled will both qualify and be qualified by what the rulers insist on.

Treated in abstraction from the complexes in which they act as structures or as imposed on those complexes, laws are exhibited in what both rulers and ruled do.

Conceivably, the structuring condition may keep them acting coordinately, but it will not assure their joint contribution to the achievement of a just state. In such a state, effective laws enable ruler and ruled to continue to be mutually supportive. Only so far as they are mutually supportive will they be able to promote the realization first of legal justice and thereby of political justice.

Like the rest of men, those who conceive their task to be the formulation of laws usually carry out their prescribed tasks without reflecting on the basic and general factors they specialize and use. Rarely are they aware of the prospective justice they should realize. Even the best of their enactments are formulated without attention being paid to the Law that these are to express in limited situations.

When in the United States and in some other modern states ruling is the work of legislators, the executive, and the judiciary, limiting and supplementing one another, preconditions are set for the guidance and enrichment of enactments by a well-presented, relevant, legal justice. Those enactments, no matter how thoughtfully and carefully formulated, will still be no more than intermediaries between Law and the ruler and ruled. They may have a prescriptive form and be backed by force. Both rulers and ruled may attend to them. Some may be useful, some harmful, some willful; some may be poorly, others carefully forged and imposed. In and of themselves they have only an arbitrary nature and scope. Only if they act as intermediaries for Law and, through it, for a primary coordinating condition will they make it possible for justice to prevail.

If the specializations of the coordinator by rulers and ruled are discrepant, the one in laws, the other in public acts, those who rule may resort to force to get those who are ruled to change their ways. Force would not be necessary if the determinations of the nature and location of accountability for what is done by the ruled were in accord both with what each privately does and what each is expected to do in public.

To make them effective all enactments have to be backed by a possible use of force. In its absence there is no assurance that the enactments will be carried out, for one cannot count on goodwill, established habit, or custom to guarantee that what should be done will be done. No private power is sufficiently strong or steady, well enough known or expressed, to guarantee that what is decreed will be produced, particularly if it has to be tailored to limited situations at special times. Force may be needed to back even those laws that promote the welfare of the rulers or ruled, and eventually the state itself. When laws are used to make men act to their detriment, one should expect that sooner or later ways will be found for undercutting and finally overcoming what is seen to be arbitrary or tyrannical, denying to individuals the status of private and public persons with natures and powers of their own or precluding those groupings of them that tradition and decent living require.

Neither rulers nor ruled will ever be exactly as statesmen or justice would have them be. If they could, there would be little more to do than wait for the rulers and ruled to express their natures, promise, and needs and for each individual to have his rights, appetites, and desires satisfied. Joining the others in ways dictated mainly by interest, circumstance, and opportunity, each can at best make a desirable contribution to the state of which he is a part. Good habits will keep him performing in well-established and perhaps proper ways. What he does will be given a distinctive spin and will be energized in a distinctive form. While the difference he makes to the outcome may be slight, playing no evident, appreciable part, it may not only make a great difference to him but may make a considerable contribution to the manner and degree to which legal justice is realized.

No set of laws can be laid down in advance as always holding for all. An attempt to do so would tacitly suppose that the ruled should not, could not, or would not do more than give the laws opportunities to be carried out. At the very least, the interplay of the laws and those who are subject to them must be guided by the prospect of a realizable, legal justice. Its realization will have ruler and ruled at once interinvolved and enhanced. If force is used, it should be to promote that result.

The abuses committed by rulers over the course of history have led to an exaggeration of the roles the rulers play. Two remedies have been offered: one, that their power should be reduced; the other, that it should be increased. If one concentrated on the state as a primary reality, one could instead take account of the fact that legal justice is pertinent to both rulers and ruled and that both should act in conformity to enacted laws. It would be an error to suppose that ruler, ruled, or the state itself has overriding rights justifying the use of men in whatever ways needed to promote the continuation and prosperity of any of the three. The objective to be realized is a just, internally constituted, steadily maintained, enhancing, singular, excellent complex.

Laws alone can never make legal justice prevail. Account must also be taken of the need to have law-abiding men carry out acts enabling all to prosper. In different limited situations, that need has different specific forms. Without the guidance and growing control of ideal justice, however, nothing more could be expected than that what is done to and for individuals will respect their equality as so many public units in a legal or a statesman-mediated state. Remedies would then have to be provided to overcome what might preclude the treatment of them as origins of public acts in a possible perfect state where ideal justice is realized.

What each individual is to do in a law-governed state ought to be determined by what he is as a unit role bearer acting in accord with good laws. These laws build on the understanding of what both rulers and ruled can be reasonably expected to do. Some persons, to carry out their tasks, would then have to do what is different from what others should. A concern with readjusting the relations of individuals to compensate for failures to enable them to exercise an equal right to be, continue, and prosper would then have to be so expressed that their equality was respected and the state enabled to prosper.

Operating in states which are not created as surely as they do in those which are, laws serve mainly to guide and coordinate the ruled. Each law ideally offers a distinct authoritative expression of Law. If rulers and ruled follow the recommendations of a statesman, not only will they act in ways which are in accord with what that Law prescribes and enactments express, but they will also enable a political as well as legally just state to be realized. There, rulers and ruled act in supplementary ways.

If there were a state where good laws were well carried out, those laws would still have to be accommodated in different ways and degrees in some accord with men's needs and desires. The parts of a machine, in contrast, react to the pressures and the kind of natures they have as so many bodies. Neither they nor animals can yield to privately expressed desires or wills to act in law-abiding ways. Human beings might be like such machines or animals if they could not, from within, maintain themselves as individuals in contradistinction to all else, if they had no inalienable rights or if they could not assume accountability.

Laws, even when backed by force, may elicit desirable actions, but there will never be enough laws to assure the realization of legal justice. It is necessary for rulers and ruled to initiate acts on their own and to insist on carrying out activities with an effort and energy whose effectiveness no laws can assure. Although invoking force or threatening it by either side will usually provoke efforts and acts not otherwise forthcoming, those acts may not be what is needed and, if they are, may cease with the removal of the force. The threat or even the use of force intimidates only a limited number for a limited time. It does not guarantee that what is done will promote the realization of an excellent state. It is also natively indifferent to the question of whether or not what is decreed or what results is good or bad.

It is never enough to get ruler and ruled to act in harmony or even to have the two act as mutually supportive individuals or groups. They must also be steadily governed by laws. Without that governance, their expressions would not be objectively stated determinations of accountability. Conceivably, they could adjust themselves to one another again and again, but if adjusting were all they did, they could achieve legal justice here or there, but would not, so far, promote political justice. It takes a legally just state to make a political justice be an effective prospect for ruler and ruled.

What a statesman recommends to ruler and ruled will enable them to realize a politically just state if they act as he would have them act. They will not do so for long, however, if they are not regulated by good laws. It is only because and so far as rulers and ruled act in accord with such laws that they can be counted on to act persistently as a statesman recommends and thereupon be able to realize a politically just state.

Laws might be quite narrowly formulated and rigidly enforced by official bodies. The range of application of the laws, while making possible their use in a plurality of diverse situations, might be irrelevant even to those who are willing to assume whatever accountability is credited to them. Part of the gap could be bridged in the course of the application of the laws if account were taken of the nature, tendencies, or acts of those to whom they were applied.

The best laws link public acts with what the state needs to have done. By enabling the state to function smoothly and be better able to have rulers and ruled act well together, the laws can promote the realization of a politically just state.

People rarely demand that they all be treated as equals. At most they think themselves to be improperly dealt with on this or that occasion. Those who sympathize with them demand that their specific interests be considered and sometimes even that these interests be given a preferential treatment to make up for losses previously suffered. The people may rebel in reaction to flagrant and widespread injustices or to what appear to be so. Laws dealing with them evenhandedly may be rejected as being inattentive to past wrongs or to denials of opportunity, as entrenching unjustified differences, as overlooking special rights and privileges, or as failing to make recompense for past legally or socially established biases. Not often, if ever, will those who are ruled, any more than those who rule, insist on laws that are fair both to themselves and others.

The formulation and application of laws do not often fully instantiate the equality expressed in Law as modified by the political justice the statesman discerns and as in accord with private, warranted assumptions of accountability. The laws may still enable a number to be so organized that a plurality of interlocking, mutually supporting roles is effectively carried out by rulers and ruled, both as individuals and as cocreators.

Good rulers, for whom a legislature is a part or an agent, try to get the ruled to provide supplements and supports for the laws which supposedly will make possible the realization of both legal and political justice. In the absence of such rulers and supplements, there will be a tendency to allow some leader to take over, with his nature and activities hidden behind grand titles. If the rulers have force at their command, they may forestall that move and get a people to act in prescribed ways. The rulers may overcome the people's resistance, though not necessarily its resentment and preparations to rebel.

At times of crisis, when crucial decisions must be made, those who have been ruling in somewhat routine ways may have good opportunities to join with the ruled in needed law-governed ventures. If legal justice is to be realized, both will have to act under the governance of effective laws. Success is not possible if that ideal is not kept in focus and made more and more determinate until it finally unifies the law-abiding rulers and ruled; it may take serious crises, though, to prompt both to act more coherently and effectively. Sometimes a leader may work on behalf of rulers, but if that was all he did, he would be occupied with achieving not justice but a glory to be enjoyed by those rulers.

Ideals are indeterminate, luring but not compelling, guiding but not constraining, more and more in control the more determinate they become. To be oblivious of them is to have nothing at which to aim, nothing to realize. When realized, they encompass a multiplicity of functioning units affecting one another. Those who take their task to be the realizing of a legally just state will do so only if Law is specialized in ways compatible with the specializations produced by ruler and ruled and if both take adequate account of the unpredictable, the unexpected, and the aberrant. Since these deviations are usually too many for the rulers and ruled to deal with properly, the prospect of legal justice must be so used that both are not only guided but controlled by it.

If rulers are to act so that a legally just state is to exist, they must interplay with those who are ruled and, together with these, engage in concordant activities. Circumstances may preclude the presence of some of the needed acts. Those who could rule well might be in exile or in prison; those now operative might lack good agents or be countered by a people not yet ready to act well in accord with the formulated laws, no matter how good these laws might be.

If rulers and ruled had their public beings taken over by a state and were treated as causes and effects for acts not privately initiated, what men take themselves to be accountable for would not always have a bearing on what the state does. Both rulers and ruled would then be in a state, but not as persons who privately initiate public acts or who acknowledge these to be acts for which and for whose consequences they are rightly held accountable. The status of a ruler or ruled would be a burden imposed by a state, limiting what they might do or requiring them to produce what might concern neither. They would be indistinguishable from pure souls joined to irrelevant bodies caught up in an alien world.

One could completely detach oneself from an involvement in a public world only by ceasing to exist. It is, of course, possible to think, will, know, and accept accountability while privately ignoring or defying the body's demands. This does not mean that one's privacy is ever completely cut off from one's body. A Cartesian "I think" is at one extreme of a single activity, at the other end of which is a body that grows tired. Life in a state is dependent on individuals separately giving their bodies effective roles there. Just as surely, life apart from the state depends on an individual continuing to be and act in some accord with others.

The question why some persons rather than others effectively rule seems in principle to be no more difficult to answer than similar questions about dominant powers in other areas; nevertheless, ruling faces obstacles the others do not. Not only does it have to deal with not altogether manageable individuals, but these individuals—even when compliant and able to work together and be cocreators—go their own ways. Rulers must deal with much that they cannot fully master. So must the ruled. No other type of creation depends so much on what is outside their creators' control.

States are forged within a largely unknown world. Cocreating rulers and ruled hold this world at bay for a while as they try to act on and in accord with one another in the course of their effort to produce a politically just state. In it the laws limit, provide articulations, promote order, and smooth the way for needed action, neither transforming those to whom they apply nor reaching them as private beings.

So far as rulers are not subject to any laws, they are rulers only for the ruled, not constituents of a just state who, with the ruled, act there in law-abiding ways. Laws imposed on the ruled need to be supplemented by others to which the rulers are subject; otherwise, the rulers will not be part of the same, legally just state. When they are most law abiding, enabling legal justice to prevail, both rulers and ruled will still continue to carry out a plurality of separate roles.

All the laws belong together in a single body of laws, some of them formulated long ago. A newly constituted state, while using newly forged laws, soon finds these laws modified by laws that once prevailed. If it had new rulers and new laws, it would still operate under limitations inherited from past enactments, the ways in which both ruler and ruled had lived under them, and the difference they made to one another. Precedent and custom affect both in ways in which even the training of artists in a particular school or tradition does not affect them, in good part because laws both specialize Law and mediate it and, consequently, are able to be joined to laws that had been operative before. The common-law tradition puts great emphasis on this fact, sometimes even minimizing the roles played by ruler and ruled as well as the justice they should jointly strive to realize. Where that tradition is not prominent, emphasis is usually placed on the legitimacy of a rule to certify that new laws fit in with the old.

At times of revolution, when new rulers are instituted and new laws insisted on, the need for rulers to be creative involves not so much an opposition to old laws as it does a demand that new ones appropriate to new situations be produced. At their best, the rulers will understand formulated and promulgated laws not as they then are but as they are to operate on and be received by those who are to live in accord with them. The new may make a great difference to the ruled, with its strong ties to the past, partly expressed in its habit of obeying. The rulers will consequently be most effective if they adjust their course and productions again and again so that the outcome is one to which the ruled also contribute. If the rulers neglect, minimize, or oppose the contributions of the ruled, they can do little more than offer recommendations, threaten enforcement, or use force.

Rulers depend for their success in part on the acceptance and accommodation by the ruled of what the rulers present. Prescriptive, and able to be forcefully insisted on, their laws will have well-defined structures in part determined by the established language. So long as no actions are carried out in accord with them, the laws will remain static, effete; if the rulers are not themselves subject to the laws, the state will be defective, for at the very least there would then be no limitation put on what the rulers might warrantedly do.

Political justice is applicable to both rulers and ruled. It is promoted if rulers and ruled produce a legal justice by living in accord with good laws that impersonally determine the nature and extent of their public accountability for what is done. Failures to act in law-abiding ways have to be rectified by compensatory acts by the rulers, the ruled, or both together.

If the ruled did not have their own integrities within which the Dunamis is a more or less dominant factor, they would not be able to respond flexibly to the rulers or be able to accept a governance by laws. Instead, they could do no more than provide units to be manipulated by the rulers and offer places where the laws could be instantiated. The Dunamis makes an independent contribution to both rulers and ruled, but only in a limited and qualifying form. Once a particular role for it has been established, rulers are in a position to mark off, more sharply than before, their use of it in an actual governance. The layer of the Dunamis they utilize will be affected and backed by others, more deeply grounded.

Rulers are able to impose a union of Law and the Dunamis on what is already qualified by these factors. Could they avoid all involvement with the Dunamis, they would not be able to act. A creative leader is alert to the ways the people are together and how they might be more intimately joined to become a locus of a realized glory; by contrast, a ruler has to be alert to the need to have the ruled function as a cocreator. Only if he does so will it be possible for the just state endorsed by a stateman to be realized by rulers and ruled together acting in law-abiding ways.

The Vitalized State

Men act in considerable accord well before there is a state. Tradition and experience make them aware of their different capacities as well as the need for them to work together to meet common dangers and to take advantage of common opportunities. Supplemented by the way they are interinvolved with one another through the agency of the Dunamis, they act collaboratively, often successfully and for long periods, as constitutive members of a common society. When they become members of a state, they do not lose their ability to act as they had in the society and, as a consequence, can be appealed to by a leader to overthrow their ruler.

For a ruler to be successful, provision has to be made for the continued functioning of the society with its characteristic mutual involvements. Apart from the state, it may still be possible for a number to collaborate quite well for considerable periods, with each member carrying out traditional tasks in different ways and degrees, depending on his ability, interests, and training. Such collaborations require not only guidance and control, dictating how mutually beneficial tasks are best performed, but also a use of the Dunamis to quicken both the separate activities and what is jointly done.

Were there no state, a people would act best if it allowed most of its acts to follow traditional routes. It would be fortunate if it could be guided by a great leader. If the people could then go on to become members of a well-organized, just state, it would be able to contribute to and benefit from the realization of a legal justice expressed through laws and thereby promote the realization of political justice.

A state is not needed in order to point a people toward an ideal to be realized; that is the task of a leader. Nor is it needed to enable a people to carry out its tasks effectively and successfully; custom and experience could suffice. A state is needed because it alone enables a legal and a political justice to be pertinent to both rulers and ruled, independently carrying out distinctive roles and acting in supplementary ways under well-enacted and effective laws.

A ruler's attempt to be a cocreator requires him to find a private position in himself where he is able to utilize the Dunamis, a conditioning coordinating Law, and a prospective justice. Although the Dunamis already plays a role in his every act and is utilized in all his efforts, he has to make further use of it on a deeper layer if he is to succeed in doing more than act in routine ways, affect the ruled only minimally, or merely focus on the prospect to be realized. He should use the Dunamis in three ways: to quicken his decisions and activities; to vitalize his occupation with the ruled; and to help him promote realization of justice. Since he is only a cocreator, what he does must be matched by similar utilizations of the Dunamis by the ruled. They, too, must quicken their decisions and activities, act on their counterpart, and strive to have justice realized. Although in his promulgations and acts a ruler alone seems to be active, and thus alone to quicken his decisions and moves by using the Dunamis, he needs the ruled as his cocreator, for no ruler can take adequate account of the ruled's needs and desires or of the individual, privately assumed accountability of its members for what is publicly done.

The ruled is more than an aggregate of single individuals. It comprises many groups having their own natures and needs. Ruling is directed primarily at these groups. When individuals are considered, ruling requires that they be dealt with as role bearers, not as private beings. A ruler might sympathize and, like anyone else, be able to grasp something of their separate privacies, but his activities as a ruler are concerned only with what occurs in public and with an accountability to be attributed on the basis of impersonal determinations of legally defined, public sources of acts or omissions.

The history of politics is primarily a history of the effectiveness of rulers and of the devices used to change the direction of the exercise of their power. Confucians are more concerned with what is privately initiated and particularly with the role that the Dunamis plays there. They focus on the problem of producing a proper attitude in individuals toward themselves and others. When they turn their attention to political issues, they look to a ruler as a kind of father who deserves to be obeyed. If the ruler fails to act to promote justice or some other desirable outcome, they try to get him to become a wise, ethical being whose reasonable actions will suffice to make "his children" rightfully obedient and consequently content and prosperous.

If there is wisdom backing what a ruler demands, obedience may be the correct response. Neither ruler nor ruled, however, provides the dynamism needed if there is to be an excellent rule. For a just rule to be realized, both ruler and ruled must open themselves up to a deep layer of the Dunamis and then confine its operation by having it joined to the coordinating condition. All the while, as cocreators in an ongoing, law-governed state they should be progressing toward the realization of both legal and political justice.

A cocreative ruler does not simply separate off a layer of the Dunamis in the course of his acts. He reaches beyond the layer ordinarily used, both to quicken what he himself is seeking to do and to affect the ruled. Unlike a leader, who is directly occupied with using a deep layer of the Dunamis to transform a people, a ruler uses one in the course of efforts to have the ruled meet the demands of enacted laws. Whereas a leader would like to have his people serve as the locus for a grand objective, a ruler needs the ruled to act independently of him as an equal cocreator. If he does not accept the guidance of a statesman, his laws will rarely be more than prescriptions or demands made on those who act independently of him. Because the Dunamis is an independent ultimate, one can never do more than provide limits for the layers he specializes and uses, leaving the outcome to be enriched by other, independent uses of it. Since the Dunamis could overwhelm what it intrudes on, one must limit its use. Consequently, a ruler involved in the creation of a state will use the Dunamis mainly to quicken his laws and bring it to bear on those whom he rules so that they will be able to act in new ways. At his best, he will look to the Dunamis to help him elicit the acts he would have the ruled perform.

If an obedient people does no more than fill out the roles assigned to it, quickened by the layer of the Dunamis that a ruler elicits, it will not thereby be denied an ability to act independently of him. If a ruler sets himself against the continuation or success of the response of the ruled, he will prevent its maximal contribution to the realizing of a legal and political justice. Both must make new uses of the Dunamis.

Stable states are possible because the Dunamis is there confined to actual practices. There, it is effective, insistent, acting on its own terms, but limited by other ultimates. A supposed common will would place no restraint on it. It may have a dominating or dominated role in whatever is done or envisaged, but that will not affect its existence and power. All ultimates continue to be and to insist on themselves no matter how they are specialized and used in creations or elsewhere.

If they are not to be doctrinaire, arbitrary, and perhaps inconstant and willful, rulers must conform to some laws. As has also been stated, they will in addition depend on supplementary outcomes produced by the ruled. A created state depends on the work of both, divided along the lines a statesman portrays, with rulers and ruled creatively carrying out their assigned roles.

Viewed from without, a state is well bounded, existing over time and space, with multiple relations to other states. Viewed from within, it is a pulsating whole, constituted by the interplay of rulers and ruled under effective laws. Its rhythm varies at different times. Occurrences within it will sometimes be credited primarily to the rulers and sometimes to the ruled, though they will usually involve some contribution from both. Both provide vehicles and avenues for the Dunamis, exhibiting and expressing it in partly opposing and partly consonant ways. If creative, they will join it to governing laws and thereby provide them with a needed vibrancy. All the while, the Dunamis will continue to insist on itself. The existence of a state through time and its ability to interact with other states and to affect the actions of rulers and ruled are in part consequences of the fact that the Dunamis operates in and through them.

Ruler and ruled, while affected by the Dunamis, enable it on a layer below that which they tap, to interplay more effectively with the laws and thereupon vitalize the state. Though the state depends on the concurrent actions of both rulers and ruled, it, too, will be independently quickened. Legal justice would not be present there were it not that the rulers and ruled, in their different utilizations of the Dunamis, made it possible for it to be joined in new ways to them as well as to the laws.

As a cocreator, a ruler deals directly with the Dunamis, uniting it with Law in order to produce a single, ongoing system of enacted, prescribing, effective laws. So far as those who are ruled are not also contributive, not enough will be done for a just state to be realized. Since the Dunamis is never possessed even in specialized forms, all that either rulers or ruled can do is to enable a layer of the Dunamis to be joined to a level of a condition so as to have justice realized. When so dealt with, the Dunamis will add vitality to a law-constituted juncture of ruler and ruled. Enacted laws will then merge into living law.

Living law, like Law, is more comprehensive than any formulation permits. Living law is also more vitally charged than is Law. Not specialized by any enactment, living law is so qualified by tradition and custom that it is undergone rather than known. Both ruler and ruled instance Law, are subject to enacted laws, and are quickened by living law, all at the same time.

Law makes evident that acts have ethical import; enacted laws structure a state; living law reveals human beings to be intimately joined under Law. Specializations and use of the living law may be confined to the rulers in their privacies, be set between them and the ruled, or be made part of the ruled. Neither side can do more than accept living law as charged by the Dunamis.

Good rulers are singularly vital. They act in consonance with the ruled, themselves independently vitalized. Were they to attend solely to the different kinds of activities that the ruled carry out, they would be caught up in what may no longer be usable and might stop their creativity before they had adequately involved themselves with the ruled. If they brought together an ideal justice and Law and perhaps took account of the contributions the ruled jointly make to their common endeavor, they or the ruled might still not invigorate the result. Rulers rule best when, in addition to enacting and imposing laws, they and the ruled are affected by living law.

The Dunamis is all-pervasive. It operates in the privacies of rulers, in their formulations and insistence on laws, and in their occupation with ideal justice no less than in the activities of those who are ruled. It is to be used to invigorate privacies, laws, and the manner in which the ideal is brought into play both in what rulers do apart from and what they do for and with the ruled. Account of it should be taken of it in all those places.

A creative leader quickens a people to act so that it becomes more intimately involved on the way to being unified to the degree and in the manner that a sought glory requires; by contrast, rulers depend on the ruled to carry out various needed tasks. To realize justice, they must adjust themselves to the activities of the ruled and allow for their activities as cocreators. All the while they must remain alert to what legal justice requires and how other factors are to be specialized and used. Inevitably, they make use of a coordinating condition as well as of the Dunamis. If creative, they will take account of the condition as Law, incorporate it as living law, specialize it in formulated, particular laws, and attend to the ways all of these are carried out. At all times they will use the Dunamis, varying in their use of it, while it continues to act on its own.

Even when rulers do not act, the ruled do. They might then avoid conflict with the rulers for a while but would not act to promote an excellent state. Under the threat of the use of force, they might act as the rulers require, but more likely than not they will then fail to provide the vigor, course, flexibility, or persistence needed if the sought outcome is to be realized. The most that the rulers could do would be to direct, qualify, and limit what was being done by the ruled so that the results were in line with what the rulers wanted to have achieved. Although it is the ruled as so many individuals who begin most acts and who may have to be subject to threat and force, rulers will not usually concern themselves with them unless the ruled are engaged in what is pivotal or conspicuous or have caught the attention of the rulers or their deputies.

Nothing will be changed in principle if just one person acts as a ruler or if the task is instead subdivided and carried out by a number, either in groups or as individuals. From the position of those who rule, the ruled are public units who act together in accord with what is prescribed. But the ruled will not, even when responsive to a statesman, always act as the ruler requires. Rulers have to insist that laws be carried out. They must not only seem to be reasonable but also make it appear likely that they will make their decrees prevail.

Rulers can formulate and apply laws for the sake of realizing a common justice. They make use of the Dunamis to quicken them. Rulers should do what they can to have good laws formulated and carried out well and to indicate what must presumably be done to have the ruled act so that they, too, move toward the position where they contribute to the production of a vital, legal, political, and just state.

Created and Noncreated States

There are few if any excellent states. Those that we might be willing to acknowledge—some idealized state in classical times, or perhaps the United States at its inception—are modified continuations of what was envisaged by statesmen. At best they exist in their idealized form only for a short time. Rulers and ruled change in composition, while laws are interpreted differently in different periods by different legislators, judges, and people. Changed circumstances, too, demand new interpretations. New practices, new territory, new challenges, and new techniques for dealing with these circumstances may turn a created state into a precursor of one not at all excellent.

If we are to respect the great difference that will forever set a created state, no matter how flawed, apart from one not created, no matter how well made, we should keep focused on the difference between a unification and a unity. The first combines functions, each affecting the others; the second embraces a plurality of distinct units, each with a separate nature and position. The functions result from the gradual realization of an ideal over the course of a creative act.

Many political theories suppose that a state is primarily a controlling power, mediated by laws, rules, customs, established practice, or language. The presence of individual public expressions, the Dunamis with its intensive vitalizing power, and the ideal in terms of which needed actions are there produced are misconstrued or neglected all the while that they are presupposed. There are no states if there are no human beings, with their own individualities and privacies, able to decide, assess, direct, control, and contribute to the existence of what they use and what might limit or control them.

A seriously flawed created state is radically different from one merely well crafted because, like every other kind of creation, it is produced in a distinctive way by individuals separately or in groups making a unique use of the same ultimates that other creators specialize and combine in their own ways. A prospective justice provides an opportunity for rulers, the ruled, and the two together to make a created state present and effective. Its achievement also depends on privacies, bodies, laws, the Dunamis, conditions, and fulfilled commitments supplementing one another and thereby promoting the realization of justice. Both the process and outcome will be influenced by tradition, by relations to other states, and by the outside world. With other states, a created state will fit within a single, larger context embracing all of them. There, each will exhibit in a distinctive degree and way an irreducible, ultimate condition, the coordinator, spreading between, controlling, supporting, and transforming both rulers and ruled.

Laws are general. None refers to individuals as so many singular, irreplaceable, privately acting beings. They refer only to public units, possessing only accredited rights; what is privately intended, suffered, or enjoyed is ignored. Even when someone is credited with less dignity than others and is taken to deserve less consideration, a law-governed, just state deals with him as a public unit who is in principle interchangeable with any other, particularly when basic rights are at issue. Laws relate only to publicly evidenced activities, to what can be publicly and impersonally reached, taking no account of what is privately done. What is not publicly expressed is always outside their reach. It is also outside the interest of rulers and the state. From the standpoint of both the rulers and the state, as well as the laws which express them, each human is no more than a public unit, an irreducible source and recipient of public acts. Punishments of heads of state, the killing of embryos or the aged, and other destructions of beings with privacies, have been sanctioned by states because distinctive publicly expressed or viable capacities were taken to be inferior to the capacities attributed to others or because it was held that their public existence or acts were not tolerable. The victims were, so far, viewed as just public units even when said to have natures, powers, and characters not discoverable through externally applied means.

Laws are properly applied only if they refer to interchangeable units or groups.

Conceivably, some group might contain only one member, but the law will then, like a good logician, distinguish that member from the group to which he belongs, taking him, in principle, to be replaceable by others. All the while, each will remain an unduplicable, noninterchangeable, self-maintained individual, with a privacy that no public nature, presence, or acts could adequately express. Each provides a public unit that the state makes subject to laws; in the state, each is but a role bearer whose acts are wholly public.

In a union and in a society, no less than in a state, the members qualify one another as so many public units. Whatever the assessment and use they separately make of what they publicly are, must do, and are held accountable for, each will still act as a private individual, entering a common arena in his own way but dealt with there as a public being. Restricted in the conduct of his personal affairs, denied rights, crushed, enslaved, he will still retain a being and a power that no one can reach or extinguish, though any number may get in the way of his expressions and reduce his effectiveness.

Rulers may sympathize with, love, or hate those whom they rule, but they can do no more, through their decrees and acts, than provide or deny them the right and perhaps the opportunity to act in public in various ways. As a consequence, the rulers are faced with a threefold obduracy, expressed in roles publicly carried out by the ruled as accountable beings, as legally recognized persons, and as individuals who express themselves from private positions. Reciprocally, the rulers themselves have their own threefold status as role bearers, as legal, public persons, and as possessors of privacies no one can completely penetrate.

An absolute rule, even one shrewd, flexible, and benign, promoting peace and prosperity, gets in its own way. At best its rulers act like a sculptor who has failed to work with his material, indifferent to what would enable it to contribute maximally to the final outcome. Because a ruler must work not just on others but with them, and because they frequently need help in order to be able to be satisfactory cocreators, he has to help them function well on their own. At any moment it may be desirable for either of them to be ascendant, but what is to be produced is greater than what could have been achieved if either always dominated the other. Greater weight, consequently, may need to be given for a time to the contribution of one to compensate for previous neglect or misconstrual. The balanced outcome that the creation of a legally or politically just state requires is brought about by tacking first in one direction and then in another.

A ruler who is unconcerned with creating differs from one who is so concerned mainly because he does not try to provide the ruled with whatever is most desirable to have in order for it to be a cocreator. As individuals, both continue to exist and act apart from the roles they carry out in the state. Even when there is no discernible difference in the way a ruler acts when a cocreator and the way he does when he is not, he will still have different tasks. A cocreator must try to make up for the failures of its supplement. It is this kind of response that the defenders of democracy apparently have in mind when they suppose that in their states a people will express itself so that sooner or later it will determine the import of the laws that the rulers insist on. The critics of democracy reply that the ruled cannot be counted on to act in ways which will benefit the ruled or even the ruler or the state because each is primarily occupied with furthering what it takes to be its own interests. Since those interests are best promoted if rulers and ruled act as cocreators, the two views could be made to cohere.

Although both rulers and ruled will always express diverse and often conflicting impulses, this divergence would be less likely were rulers and ruled to live under good laws justly administered. So far as the ruled alter the locus and course of the laws that rulers provide, they exhibit the kind of independence that other creators do when they adjust to circumstance. So far as the ruled affect the nature of what the rulers insist on, they add new meaning to the rulers' work. Inevitably, acting as cocreators, rulers and ruled together produce an outcome different from what either alone could achieve or from what the two could bring about by each following its own bent.

Whereas orchestras, actors, and dancers might provide new vehicles and may alter the nature of a production, rulers and ruled produce it together. If a playwright or a director were to interplay with actors in an attempt to realize a common objective, he would approximate a ruler seeking to produce an excellent state on his own, with the ruled acting as his material.

From the standpoint of a ruler, the contributions of the ruled are to be more or less good ways for enabling what he provides to be carried out as he decides. So far, a ruler will do no more than enable the ruled to act in steady, well-structured ways. But if a politically just state is to result and an ideally just one is to be promoted, both rulers and ruled will have to act concordantly under common laws, with each on its own providing needed parts for a final, single, excellent outcome.

Whereas in art, mathematics, and society creators are satisfied to carry out the difficult task of producing what may promote the enjoyment, understanding, or insight of others, those who seek to realize nobility or justice try to enhance the persons who are involved in the realization of these prospects. It is only a realized political justice, though, that benefits co-creators as units and in groups, for it alone embraces them as role-sustainers. Only if the rulers and ruled create together do they enable a final justice to be realized.

Creative work is difficult. It is pursued and successfully concluded by only a few, and then only at certain times. The splendid outcomes with which some end does not warrant the claim that creative efforts are always to be preferred. Other work may not only be more readily and successfully carried out but may prove to

be more useful than the created is. Still, excellence needs no excuse. It characterizes what needs no addition. It is self-contained and can exist without being well
understood or properly appreciated. What it achieves is best read when the several
parts, even when they promote a ready appreciation, are not fastened on, and attention is paid instead to the ways in which distinguishable functions enhance and
sustain one another within a superlative, singular achievement.

Each state has boundaries marking it off from other states, whether or not it or
the others are created. The boundaries are two-faced, terminating determinations
set by what is beyond them and imposing restraints on what is done within them.
These boundaries may be breached from either side, thereby turning the boundaries
into mediators. A created state is internally determined, with its limits defined by
its boundaries. In it, rulers and ruled are distinguishable, active stresses in a single
unification all the while that they continue to be apart as individuals. If the inward
side of a state's boundary does not coincide with its self-constituted limits, that
state is not perfect.

As an entity simply together with other states, created or noncreated, a state is
a single, bounded unit. Much as paintings fit more or less together with one another, so will states. Although the limits of a created state are inviolate, being constituted from within, it is subject to overlays and modifications by others which
interact with it. Such a state is in constant danger of being denied the status of a
self-maintained creation, somewhat as a fine painting might be seriously distorted
or destroyed if parts of it were modified. The Rothkos owned by Harvard have
changed from a desirable red to an alarming blue. Like a state in a world of states,
they have been affected by what has occurred independently of and external to
them.

A state that is not created has no limits, being distinguished from others only by
what marks it off from them in a common world. When a state is bounded this way,
its ruler and ruled cannot be well joined. If they act well together under laws in
such a state, they do so without being constrained by a common justice; even when
not acting at cross-purposes, they would not then take adequate account of what
they have to do.

A state, created or not, has a nature, career, limits, and boundaries other than
those characteristic of any of its components. It has its own history and its own
future; it competes with the others for natural resources; and it looks for help from
others to protect it from real or imaginary dangers. Only states make treaties or can
keep a peace agreed on in a convention of states. Only they occupy territories.
Although the rulers and ruled of a state together determine its course, it remains
distinct and powerful enough to affect both. Their acts also affect its relation to the
other states, each with its distinctive nature and career. Whatever excellence it has
may be spoiled by the ways the actions of the others impinge on its units.

If beauty is credited with making a demand on men, it still is acknowledged by only a few. Most persons cherish truth, but the truths of mathematics are of little interest to them. A noble spirit awakens admiration but does not necessarily elicit efforts to produce nobility elsewhere. Glory attracts, but it needs a leader to persuade a people to work toward its realization. In contrast, rulers and ruled, once they have set on the road where they act cocreatively, find that justice demands continued realization. In the absence of an ideal justice, they might adjust to one another with great success under good laws, but they would so far be no more than law-abiding co-workers. If it is just, a state embraces rulers and ruled acting to bring about what is to benefit both of them and the state as well.

Were all states together credited with a single nature, separate states would be distinguishable only so far as they were able to maintain themselves apart from that nature. Were some one state taken to be the only true state, the others would be at best no more than partial states lacking some essential factor—perhaps a ruler, laws, a law-abiding people, or a good interplay of ruler and ruled. A created state embraces all of them within its own limits. Justice stretches from one of those limits to the other, unifying complexes of rulers and ruled. Though it exists together with other states, it follows its own course. Other creations are in similar situations. Each fits into a distinctive setting, and this setting into a larger, without necessarily affecting the creations themselves.

Although the arts, mathematics, nobility, and leadership may be located within particular states and what may contain all of them, each creation has its own internally constituted limits. None is without a flaw. The flaws of actual states, though, are so grave that it is hard to entertain the idea that any of them could have been created. Yet were that impossible, statesmen could never be more than utopians, and rulers and ruled would never be more than compatible interactors.

No matter how peaceful its intent or how it concentrates on its own internal affairs, each state must make provision for its defense and place restrictions on goods, visitors, foreigners, and other actual or imagined sources of dangers. Each is forced to adapt its policies, budget, and laws in the light of what other states do and how they might be expected to affect it. Although the war of each man against all others, made famous by Hobbes, applies only to imaginary savages, it expresses quite well the relation that actual states have to one another. Hobbes thought that antagonistic savages, for their own good, had to accept a sovereign to rule over them, giving up every supposed right except the right to life. Because such a sovereign is so set in contradistinction to those who are ruled that he cannot benefit from their independent activities, his state is more defective than a state need be. That defect must be avoided if there is ever to be a single state embracing all others.

A ruler of a world of states, especially if they were not yet perfected, would need power to keep them in accord, or he would rule only on sufferance. Yet if he had the power, he would be both dangerous and limited, the one because he might not act as a cocreator and the other because he would depend on the several states to have his decrees carried out. Actual states can do no better than form alliances until the time comes when, identifying a common enemy, they see the need to work together, and perhaps even the need to produce a single, all-encompassing, excellent state. This state would not rule primarily over subordinate states but over all the people as a single, interlocked set of role bearers, interplaying with the ruler under laws. Groups within it would act as focal points to be granted some autonomy, but only to enable them to perform well.

It is not easy for those within a state to read it properly; nor is it easy for those outside it to do so. Still, if a state is created, we know that there will be a feeling pervading it, and that at the end of a good reading we will be able to confront the conditioning coordinator at a depth from which it expresses a power we otherwise might not detect.

Sometimes, faced with a serious crisis, ruler and ruled so interplay that the state seems to be pervaded by a feeling due to the presence of a unifying justice. That apparently was what took place in the United States when the New Deal began to take hold of rulers and ruled in the form of acts that made the nature of justice felt as a force, and many became aware of a primal condition equating all members, despite differences in status, nature, attitudes, and activities. Unfortunately, reports of that occasion are of little help to those who today want to experience the feeling of a pervasive justice and to be opened up to a primal coordinating condition.

If the claims of this chapter cannot be maintained, one will be left with the alternatives: no states are created; created states, unlike other creations, are not suffused with feeling; created states do not enable anyone to directly confront a primal condition as an unlimited power with an apparently unfathomable depth; or excellence, in the form of justice, is not a realizable prospect for a state. The only relevant issues then would be the nature and functioning of power, economics, custom, history, and the ways antagonistic groups try either to gain ascendancy or to find some basis for existing in comparative peace.

If a perfected state were impossible in principle, there would be something amiss here, perhaps in the supposition that a coordinator was a primary condition, that it could be used in creative work, or that it could open one up to a distinctive, omnipresent power. We would then have to dismiss the idea of a created state as an idle fiction. The struggles of modern men to provide for multiple devices to enable justice to pervade a state would then deserve to be condemned as wasted effort. We would have to proceed by trial and error, content to make improvements where possible. Although we cannot avoid proceeding in this way now and then, not only in politics but elsewhere as well, it is not the only way we can act.

There have been occasions when statesmen set some rulers and ruled on the path of enabling justice to be realized. Still, the brute fact remains: states today are many, primarily separated from one another as distinct, uncreated, complex organizations where rulers and ruled both interplay and get in one another's way.

It is rarely that all the ultimates play an equal role as constituents of what happens or is done. When they do, it is rarely for long. The cosmos, nature, the humanized world, and men are all overrun with contingencies because the ultimates meet in ways that nothing prescribes. Creations are no exception. There, whatever ultimate is stressed in the production of parts may have a different status in the final outcome. Whether it does so or not, it will, as we have seen in the study of the different creative ventures, make it possible to signify a distinct ultimate condition. A created state makes it possible for a good reader to discern the coordinator as a primal power affecting whatever there may be. Law and laws give new, specific meanings to that condition, making that on which they operate able to act in ways they otherwise would not.

If what is here claimed is warranted, we are now in a position to understand the ultimate conditions as able to be joined in all created works. If we are to confront each of the conditions in depth, it will be necessary to go through the difficult but exhilarating labor of trying to read all the different kinds of created work with appreciative care.

Although a creator may have little interest in carrying out the reading that appreciators engage in, what he does know is that from the beginning to the end of his work a power, beyond what he is, does, knows, or uses, comes more and more in focus as he nears the end of his work. Since rulers and ruled act as cocreators, neither of them can succeed in signifying a condition to the degree that a single creator can. Still, what they achieve is waiting to be well read. A statesman could undertake such a reading if only he would tear himself away from his memoirs and be willing to attend to what those he programmed actually created. Others must remain content to try to adopt his position if they are to see if what he would have had done by rulers and ruled was in fact done. If it was, justice will be found to pervade their state and the coordinator will be signified as an omnipresent and powerful force affecting everything. Until then, there can be no assurance that a state has been created. If it were impossible for rulers and ruled to function as cocreators, a state and the justice to be realized in it would not deserve a place alongside other creations and realizable ideals.

Although other creative ventures have been brilliantly carried out in the past, they all, together with the venture occupied with producing a legally, politically, and ideally just state, face a future where no success can be assured. New creations are neither guaranteed nor excluded because a particular type of venture has been successfully carried out, never has been carried out, or has even failed in every case. The fact that some ventures have had great achievements to their credit does not show that other great works in those areas will continue to be produced. What we now know is that what is needed for creations of all types is available, awaiting creators who can and will satisfy commitments to produce them.

If someone had the ability to read every type of creation, he would be able to grasp all the ultimate conditions as irreducibles, affecting everything from depths not discerned at all or at least not discerned so directly and with such a sense of their joint power. In the absence of such a polymathic appreciator, there is nothing to do in order to know what all creations could reveal other than to learn what the ultimate conditions are and the best ways they could come together. It is with a knowledge of those ultimates that this work began. The examination of the nature of their best joinings has been the major concern throughout. The warrant for the whole depends on its enabling one to understand the different creative ventures, each carried out in a distinctive way with distinctive results. If what is maintained here is correct, a good reading of all kinds of creation will make evident the nature of all the conditions that operate everywhere, and which the cosmos, nature, the humanized world, and men specialize in diverse ways.

Appendix

Index

Appendix

The Dunamis

WHATEVER WE KNOW is framed in concepts, categories, and theories. These provide structures wholly or partly conveyed in a grammatically correct language. Most thinkers take this claim to close off further inquiry, contenting themselves, and urging others, to do no more than rest here. All, they think, should occupy themselves with understanding and using a primary set of formulations and making evident how these are, could be, and must be displayed.[1]

These rationalists are opposed by two groups. One is composed of those who take a stand with a Heraclitean becoming, a Nought,[2] a Jungian unconscious, and the like. Another rejects the views of these—and of the rationalists as well. With Dewey, they take their stand between the other two. They are neo-Hegelians who accept experience, practice, history, language, or a common set of convictions as primitive. The other two views are thereupon treated as offering abstractions from a primal, inchoate whole and wrongly held to be realities or supposed to have references of their own. Whatever we can know or use is supposedly obtained from an aboriginal maw and is to be used as an agency for articulating, controlling, and organizing this, their original and common locus.

These two oppositions to the dominant, rationalistic view are faced with a common, serious difficulty: to express, communicate, and defend themselves, use

---

1. Heidegger takes this approach to be a tradition brought into focus by Plato and dominating Western thought until his time. This view not only ignores a long-established Asiatic view which insists on a primal nonbeing and inescapable "Way" but slights the role played by Plato's Receptacle, Schopenhauer's Will, and Kant's manifold.

2. Heidegger's "Nought" differs from others in somehow being positive and strong enough to be able to negate itself.

must be made of the agencies provided by the rationalistic view. In the attempt to avoid that embarrassment, recourse is sometimes had to negation.[3] The supposed irrational, as well any supposed source of it and the rational, are thereupon characterized as "unintelligible," "irrational," "nonbeing." The negative note is still present but not made evident when what is basic is instead said to be "brute," "matter," "the given," and the like. Such ways of referring make use of terms which are just as categoreal and affirmative as those they are intended to replace.

It would not be improper for the rationalists to reply that their categories are attended to when and as they are distinguished, both from what refers to them and from that to which they refer. Even the purest, noblest, the most through and through intelligible idea has a brute side to it. Every referent is distinct from that to which it refers, even when all it does is to reinstate it in a new form. If there were nothing resistant in a category, concept, etc., it would be something then and there created and sustained and so far would not only presuppose some noncategorized activity but would be without anything to which it might refer. In addition to having an obdurate component, and thereby making it available for a referring, it can have application only so far as it is faced with what is distinct from it. There are always three obduracies involved in any reference: one within, a second in that which refers to it, and a third in that to which it refers.

Intelligibility, unintelligibility, and experience are highly general ideas. All are faced with what is distinct from themselves. If they are said to be negatives, they still are positive enough to be able to negate what negates them. On being used, a reference is transformed into its referent without ceasing to be distinct from it. In the course of the transformation, any idea that refers to what is distinct from it will also conform to, be embedded in, and be integral to that to which it had referred.[4]

The three distinguished views have multiple variants. These variants may hide but do not eliminate the intrinsic defects of the views on which they depend. What is wrong with rationalism is not its use and endorsement of concepts, formalisms, theories, etc., but its supposition that they are or could be completely detached from what refers to them, from that to which they refer, and from their own obdurate beings. The irrationalists and the neo-Hegelians are surely no less mistaken in treating all articulations as necessarily distortive, falsifying, or irrelevant, since

3. For Thomas Aquinas, as for neo-Platonists, negation marks a falling away, a becoming less real. The view leads him to suppose that evil is radically empty and impotent. How such an enfeebled product is able to defy the all-positive God thereupon becomes an unsolvable mystery.

4. For a discussion of the three types of truth see *Toward a Perfected State*, SUNY Series in Systematic Philosophy (Albany: State University of New York Press, 1986), 81ff. It is there shown that it is not possible to detach them completely from one another. The upshot of the present study depends on and confirms that judgment.

that denies any intelligible way for them to express themselves and their rejections.[5]

It has been possible to deal here with all three views only because it has been possible to attend to all of them at the same time and thereupon see how they agree and disagree. Something similar is done when we distinguish references to the present, past, and future, to a book here and another there, or to an unexpressed belief or fear. The current, accepted use of a language, trial and error, and customary practices all leave open the question of why references proceed in different directions and how it is possible for one to note, compare, and contrast a number of them.

As the neo-Hegelians have maintained, we must begin with a rich, partly inchoate content in which we can discern a number of diverse factors. There is no reason, though, to remain with these thinkers when they go on to claim that those factors, when separated, are nothing more than empty abstractions and that they acquire meaning and value only so far as they help reorganize the initial content. Not only do they then necessarily treat their initial content as inchoate and unknowable, but they have no way of accommodating mathematics, ethics, law, other prescriptions, and communicable controls.

We do abstract from what we initially encounter. This, though, has no beginning or ending, real distinctions, or separated items acting in opposition and in consonance, where neither subjects nor objects are to be found. What is primary for us, where all our inquiries initially begin and to which they eventually return, is the familiar world of daily life. What we obtain from what is encountered there are not thin, impotent, partial versions of daily objects but truncated forms of insistent realities which have come together and constituted those objects. We begin with, and eventually return to, the outcome of the meeting of more ultimate realities which we come to know by using the attenuated forms they exhibit in what they together constitute.

Rationalists differ from the nonrationalists, and the two of them from the neo-Hegelians, in their use of different evidences. The three begin initially with what is encountered daily and never lose all hold of it. The isolation of imposed forms or conditions of individual contributions, and of a primary ground turns these possible moves into three different sources, each more insistent and basic than that with which one began.

Sometimes evidences of one type of ultimate reality are in ascendancy, some-

5. All references stand apart from, are attached to, and are transformed into their referents. When it is claimed that all facts are theory-laden, one still leaves the facts untouched. If the theories are appropriate, they will evidently conform to the facts. When the facts become theory-laden, the theories themselves have merged with them and are in effect embedded in them.

times another. None is ever cut off from the other two. An examination of each reality begins where they are together. That beginning is forced into the background when one attends to the evidences and then engages in the act of trying to reach what they evidence—the ultimate realities as they exist apart from one another and all else.

I have previously examined, in some detail, the nature and use of evidence of ultimate conditions.[6] Recently I have attended to the nature and use of evidences of individual privacies.[7] At that time and later, I have found it necessary to distinguish a third type of ultimate, the Dunamis.

> The Greek for "power" is *dunamis*. *Dunamis* is also Greek for "potentiality" and for "dynamic." The primal continuum is all these at once; 'dunamis' therefore is an ideal technical name for it. The *dunamis* has the vitality of Plato's receptacle, but it needs no demiurgos to divide it. One can identify it with Aristotle's prime matter, but only if, contrary to him, this is recognized to be insistent. Unlike Whitehead's Creativity, it does not make anything its creature. It is not more real but only more subterranean than individuals. The irreducible units which condense it are in turn to be understood in both Democritean and Leibnizian terms, the one emphasizing the bodily side of them, the other the private. (*Privacy*, 21).

> People are together with whatever there is, by being related in a common space and time, and in other ways. Eventually they disappear into that ground. That ground has been referred to over the centuries and in different cultures in many different ways—"Tao," "The Receptacle," "The Collective Unconscious," "The Will," the "élan vital", and "Creativity." All are somewhat overlapped by what I call the *dunamis,* to accentuate the fact that what is the ground of all is at once potential, powerful, and dynamic. However, it be designated, it is acknowledged by everyone to be internally indeterminate. Some take it to be radically unintelligible. But if it were this, it would be so below the level, where anything could be grasped, as to be undetectable. Always available, it is a flux where distinctions are being constantly made and unmade, without ever achieving the status of separations. (*Toward a Perfected State,* 22)

> A comparatively easy means for making a penetrating contact with the *dunamis,* and to realize that this has been done is to attain the state of being peaceably alone at the end of a fine musical performance, or by becoming involved in that or some other absorbing work of art. Sitting quietly in a great cathedral or in some other place of worship, on a lonely beach, in an open field, in a desert, a person has other opportunities for becoming aware of a

6. See particularly *Modes of Being* (1958; rpt. Carbondale: Southern Illinois University Press 1968); and *First Considerations* (Carbondale: Southern Illinois University Press, 1977).

7. See *Privacy* (Carbondale: Southern Illinois University Press, 1983), particularly part 1. There are anticipations of the view in *Nature and Man* (New York: Henry Holt, 1947).

vast reality whose boundaries are not discernible, and which seems to vanish when one tries to conceptualize it. In fact one always merges with it. (Ibid., 389–90)

Again and again I have been asked to expand on these observations. Many have found references to similar ideas in the East and West not to be very helpful, obscured as they are by formulations in negative terms, the use of contradictions, metaphors, and paradoxes, and the apparent need to accept alien cultural commitments. The challenge is as hard to avoid as it is to satisfy. The attempt must be made if one is not to end with affirmations without adequate backing, descriptions without possible application, and opinions masquerading as primary truths.

The Dunamis can be distinguished, encountered, and probed; it can be spoken of without shock to one's logic, good sense, and need to communicate. It has a number of distinctive, indispensable roles in the constitution of various types of entities and in the ways these function. Without it there would be no occurrences, no transitions, no contemporaries, and no causation. These are large claims, needing clarification and defense.

The Dunamis is encountered in at least nine different places:

1. It is immediately present in every emotion. Emotions exhibit the merger of privacy and body, each qualifying the other. In the absence of the Dunamis, the two might have a common boundary, but neither would effectively intrude on the other, at once qualifying and limiting it. The vibrant, turbulent, transitory nature of an emotion is due not to the body or the privacy which the emotion thereupon overwhelms or disturbs but to what is distinct from both and enables them to modify one another.

The privacy of a person possesses a body, making the body its vehicle. That body is not entirely passive; it qualifies what is privately expressed in and through it, giving it a new import. Reciprocally, the body affects the privacy, occasioning pains and pleasures, making aesthetic experience possible, and enabling one to act accountably in a world where others also are.

The so-called mind-body problem will remain without a solution as long as the emotions are attributed exclusively to one side or the other or are credited with two forms, one mental and the other physiological. We privately live through our emotions, but what is lived through is usually forced on us by the body. Whether we like it or not, we are compelled to take account of the body's presence, insistence, resistance, and functioning, its rhythms, location, and needs. Whether we like it or not, our bodies are privately possessed and are partly within our control. The double obdurate fact is exhibited by the emotions, themselves limited versions of the Dunamis, individually lived through.

2. Men collaborate in order to overcome challenges too great for any one to

master. Could they do no more than collaborate, they would be separated beings who might occasionally carry out mutually supportive roles but who otherwise would have nothing to do with one another. Each would be sunk within his individual privacy and would make contact with others only to counter what is beyond the capacity of anyone alone. Each individual would be a calculator, a metaphysical utilitarian, an economic being, making contact with others only to maximize gains and minimize losses. Yet whether they cooperate or not, without thought or intent they also more or less fit together as associated beings, living in and belonging to the same society as well as to smaller and larger groups.[8]

Cohesive groups require men to be both collaborative and associated, the one enabling them to work well together, the other enabling them to share a common spirit. The one depends on their dealing with common dangers and opportunities in mutually supportive ways; the other depends on their bonding, their acceptance of one another. Neither may be carried out consciously. A good deal of collaboration is carried on by habit; associations are sustained by tradition and exhibited in common customs.

The bondings of men in society, or in such smaller groups as families and clans and such larger ones as a nation or a folk, hold them together. Without these bondings, groups could be effective but not cohesive and could be expected to dissolve when some common enterprise has come to an end. The cohesiveness exhibits the Dunamis in a confined area. Each member of a group encounters and shares in it as an insistent, not controllable presence joining him to others, some of whom are quite distant and neither encountered nor known. The Dunamis provides a common tie, participated in directly but never entirely cut off from the rest of itself, the Dunamis as less accessible.

References to "forms of life," a common language, history, and conventions depend on an encounter with the Dunamis in some limited situation. Obtrusively present in some places more than it is in others, it is never entirely bounded off from any. If it were, there would be no awareness and no submission to a common tradition and an ongoing way of being together.

The Dunamis is directly encountered in the form of associations among limited numbers of actualities. These actualities share in it, participate in it, are caught up in it, without even thinking of it or knowing the way it functions. Always involved with others and therefore always involved with the Dunamis, different living beings form various segregated groups. It is not the promotion of the species or a struggle to survive that keeps the lemmings together while moving toward their

8. The first part of *Toward a Perfected State* deals with the origin and nature of collaborations and associations and the communes, communities, unions, and societies that their meshing produces.

doom. The Dunamis keeps them together, too, even when they compete, sometimes so violently that they injure both themselves and the others. Always involved with the Dunamis, each human, too, is involved by himself and also with it when and as he functions as a member of a commune, community, or any other group of interlocked individuals.

3. It is one of the oddities of the Whiteheadian view that it allows for no knowledge of contemporaries, nor indeed for any joining of them. All conversation on his view is zigzag. What one person said at one moment would be known by another only at a later moment, everyone being completely cut off from any others who might be copresent. Each, so far as he knows, could be absolutely alone. It is sometimes said that the difficulty is not serious since the interval between what is begun and what is received is so small. The defense is not strong. There is no way in which one could measure such an interval, for any measure would be applied in a present time; no measure ever stretches over an interval separating past and present.

Not only do we confront contemporaries; all of us enter into the next moment together, though some of us are sluggish and others are quick, some are running and others are asleep. In the absence of the Dunamis able to carry us all along, how could a number of independent beings keep abreast? Were we just together in space or in one of a plurality of space-time frames, no signal would be fast enough to enable us to be contemporaries or to keep us abreast.

To the degree that we make contact with the Dunamis, to that degree we are able to be together with all else. To the degree that we are subject to the Dunamis, to that degree are we able to be together with others—no matter how far distant they are—and pass with them into the next moment.

Were one to tailor his understanding of the nature of things to conform to the latest acceptances of physics, he would be unable to provide an account of all coexistents—or even of those entities which exist within a single time frame. Acknowledgment has to be made of the Dunamis if one is to understand how there could be contemporaries, how they could be known, and how they could both be independent and pass into the next moment together.[9]

9. Cf. "The Contemporary World," *Review of Metaphysics* 4 (June 1953): 525–38. Eight reasons are there offered why one must acknowledge contemporaries, no matter how long it takes for light signals to traverse the distance between them. It may suffice for the present purposes to refer only to the eighth, which observes that any bodies, no matter where they are in space, are related to others as larger or smaller. "Were some body freshly created and stuck somewhere in the firmament, it would not have to wait for weeks and weeks before it could have a relation of 'bigger than' to something here on earth. The theory that all relations owe their being to time-consuming actions, overlooks the static, constitutive relations of comparison which hold between all things." ("Static" should be replaced by "steady," the connection being constantly maintained by the Dunamis.) One might escape this conclusion by supposing that anything outside our time

4. The merely intelligible, the purely formal, is forever selfsame. Were it alone to be, there would of course be no process of discovering it, knowing it, or utilizing it. Were one to hold that individuals also existed and carried out a course of inquiry and discovery, they would have to be understood as continuing over a period of time, over the course of which they replaced a state of ignorance by its opposite.

A converse exaggeration on passage leads to the acceptance of a Heraclitean flux, with no one persistent enough to know or acknowledge it. Sometimes it is maintained that while everything is in flux, some things change more sluggishly than do others and therefore could be said to be relatively at rest. The claim is itself, though, offered as an inviolable truth, unchanged and presumably unchangeable throughout eternity.

There is not only change, ongoing, becoming, but conditions, able to provide stable structures and intelligible relations. The acknowledgment of a supposed flux existing in contradistinction to the fixed takes account of one way in which the Dunamis can be encountered. To know it is to stand apart from it and therefore to preclude the supposition that it alone is real.

To whatever degree and manner one acknowledges becoming, to that degree and manner one acknowledges the Dunamis. Only if it were possible to encounter sheer transition, mere fluidity, just an ongoing, would it be possible to encounter the Dunamis by itself. It would then be found that change has a thickness to it, that it is pulsational, vibrant, with an uneven pace. We can know this quality of change because we never stop at the surface of the Dunamis but always pass indefinitely beyond the surface into thicker and thicker layers. The more we penetrate it, the more evident it becomes that its various layers are continuous with one another.

Since change is everywhere, in privacies, bodies, societies, states, and the cosmos, and since it can be directly encountered in all, the Dunamis is always available. It is not necessary to turn one's back on what is known everyday, on nature or the world as understood by scientists, or even on what is certified by philosophers of science or language, in order to become aware of the Dunamis. Nor would it be desirable to deny that day gives way to night, that bodies move, that men speak, or that it is possible to carry out such logical operations as inference and substitution.

5. "Passage" normally refers to a transition from one item to another of the same type. Colors, weights, positions, and theories pass into other colors, weights, positions, and theories. "Coming to be" in contrast, refers to a transition from what

---

frame has an indeterminate magnitude, awaiting some connection with our frame before it can become determinate. One would then have to add that the objects in our time frame would, from the position of others, also have to be indeterminate. How they passed from one state to the other, and why, would be questions left unanswered. There is something defective in any position that requires some determinate objects to be taken to be indeterminate.

is not to what is, where "what is not" refers not to a Nothing but to something that may be other in type from that which replaces it.

I have attempted elsewhere to show that actualities are the products of fulgurations of the Dunamis fixated with the help of conditions and thereupon held away from these constituent powers.[10] The view makes it possible to avoid the supposition that each actuality is a special creation—readily admitted by all when account is taken only of subhumans, but not extended to man by some, thereby denying him a genuine place in nature. But even if it is supposed that man is outside the rest of nature only so far as he is being supernaturally sustained, it is not necessary to suppose that each individual man or "soul" is a distinct creation. Pigs can procreate pigs without divine assistance; can't humans procreate humans without its assistance?

Human privacies can and should be understood to originate in the same way that lesser privacies do. The argument becomes clear once it is granted that the most elementary fulgurations of the Dunamis are fixated with the help of ultimate conditions in the form of atomic monads, elementary bodies with sustaining privacies. More complex beings can then be understood to be the outcome of new fulgurations of the Dunamis, pertinent to a plurality of the atomic monads or other units, each having a private and a public side. The coming to be of nonliving, subhuman, and presumably human beings can all be understood to be the result of nuances in the Dunamis being fixated by ultimate conditions and then maintained by irreducible privacies.

6. Passing away reverses the direction exhibited in coming to be. Both have relative and absolute forms, the former taking account of beginnings or endings in other actualities, the latter starting from or ending in the Dunamis. A relative passing away leaves behind residua, aggregates, pluralities in place of unities; an absolute involves the loss of privacy and its control over a body. The latter is the result of a return of a being into the Dunamis, where it can never be more than a moment in a single undivided though endlessly differentiated ongoing.

To know that a human being is coming into existence is to know an actuality in its transition from the status of an unseparated part of the Dunamis to it as standing apart from it. To know that a human being is dying is to know him in the course of his merging into the Dunamis. At both times the Dunamis is encountered but not attended to. We must, though, understand it if we are to understand what it means for an irreplaceable, privately maintained individual to stand apart from all else for a while. Only because and so far as one continues to share in part of the Dunamis does one hold the rest at bay.

7. It was remarked under (1) that the Dunamis is an ingredient in every human

10. See *Privacy*, 16–29.

emotion, a vital, inchoate link between a possessive privacy and a resistant and somewhat independent body. The Dunamis is also an ingredient in every condition. Though every condition has an integrity of its own, insistent, able to be specialized in multiple ways without loss to its status as an ultimate, each acts on the other ultimates and there provides evidence of itself in the guise of a structure, or 'essence'. Each impinges on the Dunamis and is impinged on by it. To be acquainted with a condition is therefore to be acquainted with the Dunamis, since the latter insistently impresses itself on the condition and thereby makes it internally differentiated. The Dunamis does not entirely penetrate the condition; it does not and could not deprive the condition of its independence and independent activity.

Were it not for the intrusion of the Dunamis into the various ultimate conditions, there would be no tensional connection among their distinguishable units. Even space and time would be unextended, mere conceptualized wholes, or at best Leibnizian, confused versions of these wholes. The Dunamis enables these and other conditions to have distinguishable but not distinct, separated components and as a consequence makes possible "synthetic," informative judgments, not only in arithmetic and geometry but about justice, attraction and repulsion, structures, and excellence.[11]

Mathematics and other formal disciplines have terms distinguished in them. Those terms are interinvolved; they make a difference to one another. They belong together. No condition is self-distinguishing. None waits on actualities before it is able to be internally differentiated. None awaits the coming of men before it is able to be pertinent to whatever actualities there happen to be. The distinguishing is the outcome of the intrusion of the Dunamis on the conditions, independently of the existence or interests of men. That is why the conditions can have a bearing on what occurs in the absence of humans.

The Dunamis distinguishes and joins subdivisions in unchanging conditions. If so, there is no need to suppose, with Kant, that we construct whatever mathematical truths we know. Mathematicians occupy themselves with using the primary and persistent distinctions that the Dunamis introduces into a primary rationale whether or not they have application. Theoretical physicists, ethicists, and axiologists are also alert to differentiations already present in the conditions that concern them and engage in creative acts which make use of what they there discern.[12]

11. These judgments reflect the nature and function of Being, Substance, Rationality, and Value. These conditions, and their availability and functioning, are dealt with particularly in *Modes of Being, First Considerations,* and various volumes of *Philosophy in Process.*

12. The nature and content of synthetic, a priori knowledge evidently deserves to be reopened, freed from the space, time, and judgmental limitations to which Kant subjected them in his brilliant, pioneer investigations.

8. Creative activity, and, to a lesser extent, innovations and inventions make use of the Dunamis, for it is because of it that what is produced is distended, vibrant, nuanced, and unified. Taoists and Zen Buddhists have long insisted that we must allow the Dunamis full play both if we are to create and if we are to live as we ought. Some stress its separateness and independence, while others focus on the role it should play in human life. Both remark on its unduplicability, its resistance to all attempts to characterize it adequately, and the indispensable role it plays in art and virtue. But as they are inclined to overlook, conditions and individuals in turn intrude on the Dunamis, thereby making it both intelligible and accessible for use in limited endeavors. The use does not require a reaching to, or control of, the Dunamis as an ultimate reality existing apart from the others, any more than one must reach or use conditions or privacies as they are in themselves, maintained against all else.

An exaggeration of the faults of formalists has led too many defenders of the Dunamis to take the opposite tack and speak of it as though it were beyond all comprehension. Since they are able to distinguish it from the conditions that interest the formalists and from the actualities which are to make use of it, they evidently know enough about it to make it possible to state what it is. The statement does not exhaust its reality—but that is true, too, of statements about conditions, privacies, and the outcomes of the interplay of these with the Dunamis. What is clear and distinct may well be true, but only if it is about that which is so far clearly distinct from it.

Creators are engaged in making, not in knowing. They do not dwell on the nature of the different factors they use but straightaway bring them to bear on one another. That activity does not require the blocking out of all cognition. Although a concentration on the understanding of something requires a different focus and activity than does an effort to bring it to bear on other items to produce something, there is no necessary opposition between them. Production does not preclude cognition, though it does subordinate it, allowing it only minimal play. That, though, is enough to enable one, on encountering and making use of the Dunamis, to attend to conspicuous features of it and the way they contrast and fit in with what else is known.

9. Very few create. Most do no more than invent, innovate, produce novelties, or introduce variations in what has already been achieved. Almost anyone, though, seems to enjoy the sight of a sunset, a mountaintop, the startled moves of a deer, the tingling flow of a brook. An increasing number have come to appreciate works of art. In different ways and degrees, they allow the Dunamis to set the pace, determine the relations, and provide the emphases. These determinations are at once passed through toward a vast, unbounded, uncognized, irreducible, enriching, and

sustaining dunamic ground. Matching a creator's use and comparative neglect of it as an ultimate to be understood, those who appreciate allow the Dunamis, as caught up in a created work, to dictate their pace and stresses.

Although appreciation is quite different from understanding, emphasizing a yielding rather than a dissecting, a submission rather than a questioning, an acceptance of the global in place of the dissected, it does not preclude all knowledge. While our thoughts are pushed back, allowed to be overwhelmed when we are immersed in making, they are not thereby extinguished or undetectable. For short periods it is possible to be absorbed in an appreciated object and to encounter the Dunamis primarily in rhythms, pulsations, and pulls into an horizonless immensity—but often enough, and often too soon, one loses the object and becomes involved in the Dunamis itself.

There are surely more ways than these by which we can encounter and characterize the Dunamis. At moments of great intimacy we approximate a fine combination of association, emotionality, contemporaneity, and appreciation. In celebrations, passage tends to replace appreciation. Great scientific investigations focus on conditions, with the Dunamis allowed to take one from position to position without reflection or control. Instead of holding that the Dunamis is remote and inaccessible, it would be more correct therefore to say that it is omnipresent and for that reason not attended to, not made an object of knowledge except at special times. It is more like the environment in which we carry out our daily affairs, more like the circumambient air we daily breathe than it is like a stick or a stone, a plan or a clock.

The Dunamis can be characterized in other than negative terms, terms which are parasitical on other kinds of beings. Six stand out.

1. Confronted initially within the limits of particulars, or as involved with privacies or conditions, the Dunamis is evident in the distinctive grounding it provides each. Each in turn confines it without limiting it; no matter how it functions there, it continues to be and act apart from any particularities it might vitalize or join together. To know what is confined, and to be aware of it as not thereby limited, is to know the Dunamis as an associating power. Unlike a relation, which stops at its terms, the Dunamis continues beyond what confines it, pulling at its confined form, not allowing this form to interfere with it as unbounded, unlimited, without beginning or end.

To know that Tom loves Mary is to know a love in a specialized, limited form. To know that it is love that joins them is to pass beyond their particular involvement to a more pervasive, deeper ground, able to pull on every exhibition of itself, to express itself through this exhibition, and to be able to exhibit itself in other confined areas. The love is a conspicuous illustration of a universal fact: every connection between entities has a dynamic side, able to be discerned once one distinguishes what is bounded by particular entities from what is being active there. What is bounded is relational, an instance of a condition; a confined activity is the Dunamis on a particular, comparatively superficial level, unable to stop its thrust, as a single boundless ultimate.

2. The Dunamis is fluid; nothing in it is separated from anything else. Endlessly nuanced, it allows for no distinct units. The law of contradiction does not hold within it; it is vague.[13] That vagueness still allows for a sharp differentiation of it from conditions and individuals. Apparently, it is its vagueness that has prompted so many to speak of the Dunamis as though it were incomprehensible. Yet it allows for the use of other laws.

Whatever is said about the Dunamis will be said in repeatable terms and from the position of a condition or of an individual. The characterization is transformed the more intimately the characterization is involved with it, since terms set alongside one another are thereupon made to converge, both enhancing one another and terminating in a single, absorptive ongoing. When we sympathize with another's grief, we pass beyond a mere relationship to him in a public world. We then share in a more subterranean bond, to rest finally with us merged with one another, with those who grieve with us, and with others as well.

There is never a precise point to stop in one's sympathy, either in another or elsewhere. Sympathy has no parts, no well-defined base, no particular beginning or ending, for it is the Dunamis as partly and momentarily caught up in a particular, personalized situation. Still, though one's sympathy is directed at another, it is only part of a deeper connection which is sometimes faintly discerned when one attends to him.

3. The Dunamis is oceanic, limitless both in depth and extent, self-maintained, pulsating, making and unmaking distinctions within it. It would be all-absorptive, drowning every effort, denying every relationship, were it not for the double fact that it has degrees and never sets any one item apart from others. We can know it somewhat in the way we know a mountain or an iceberg, as the thrust-up part of what is mainly submerged, or the way we know a river as only partly exhibited within visible banks. Unlike these actualities, though, which we have come to

13. "The *vague* might be defined as that to which the principle of contradiction does not apply. For it is false neither that an animal (in a vague sense) is male, nor that an animal is female"; Charles Sanders Peirce, *Collected Papers,* ed. Charles Hartshorne and Paul Weiss (Cambridge: Harvard University Press, 1934), 5:505). Since there are no separate units in it, the law of identity also fails to hold there. Ultimate conditions instead exhibit a failure of the law of excluded middle: "The *general* might be defined as that to which the principle of excluded middle does not apply. A triangle in general is not isosceles nor equilateral" (ibid.). It should also be added that no inferences are carried out within them. In contrast with the other two, privacies, since they are not duplicable or formalizable, allow for neither substitution nor implication.

know because we have deliberately attended to what is below the surface, the Dunamis insistently manifests itself, exhibiting itself as that which is being maintained from beneath. It intrudes on us and pulls us toward it, a river in which we already are subject to an undertow.

4. The Dunamis insists on itself. It will not be gainsaid no matter what one does or how one thinks. The condemnation of thought by those who are concerned with the Dunamis does it a disservice, as though it could be extinguished, weakened, or deflected by any thinking. Other ultimates interplay with it and thereby constitute the familiar world of everyday, as well as the more esoteric objects of science and the products of creative activity. Each enables a superficial portion of the Dunamis to be operative without affecting its nature or activity as a single, irreducible, boundless ultimate. The other ultimates also insist on themselves, but in different ways and with different effects. When all the ultimates meet, they qualify and supplement one another without loss to their independence or their ability to continue to act in distinctive, independent, inextinguishable ways.

5. The Dunamis is internally self-fractionating, perpetually distinguishing and merging nuances. Allowing for no separations, it must be yielded to if it is to be apprehended as apart from the other ultimates. Did we not have our own self-maintained privacies, we would, on encountering it, be swept up into it, unable to distinguish ourselves; were there no independent conditions which could interplay with it, there would be no laws of nature, no generals specifiable in multiple ways in interplay with some layers of the Dunamis.

Whatever we know is caught up and possessed by what is known. Knowledge and the known are connected adumbratively. The role of adumbration was initially remarked in *Reality*. It was there said to be a component in all articulations of the nature of actualities, bringing subjects and predicates together more and more, to end with them as united by, and in, actualities.[14] Adumbration has an even more extended use, being inseparable from our use of proper names.[15]

14. *Reality* (1938; rpt. Carbondale: Southern Illinois University Press, 1967). For a critical examination of adumbration, see Robert Woods, "Weiss on Adumbration," *Philosophy Today* (Winter 1984).

15. The nature of names, particularly as referring to conditions and individuals, is examined in *First Considerations*, 68–79. In addition to the *adherent* names appropriate to actualities, e.g., "Tom Jones," and the *exalted* names of final conditions, e.g., "Being," there discussed, we must provide for the *alluring* names of the Dunamis, e.g., "Nirvana," "Tao." Both adherent and the exalted names were seen to have transposed forms when directed at one another. An *arresting* name is an adherent one used of conditions, e.g., "The Enlightened One." An *honorific* name, e.g., "Lord," is an exalted name used to refer to an individual. With the introduction of alluring names for the Dunamis, account will also have to be taken of transposed forms of them applicable to actualities, e.g., "Mystic," and of transposed forms of them applying to conditions, e.g., "Demiurgos." There will also be transposed forms of the adherent names of actualities, e.g., "Des-

6. Each ultimate mediates the other two. Conditions mediate privacies and the Dunamis; privacies mediate conditions and the Dunamis; the Dunamis mediates conditions and privacies. All three mediations occur in the actualities which they together constitute. In the absence of the Dunamis, conditions and individuals might conceivably come together, but the result would be nothing more than a fixed set of units set in a permanent frame. Were there no joining of conditions and individuals, there would be just a perpetual flux. Were there no individual actualities, there would be vitalized laws of nature, but no units to which they applied.

Just as controlled bodily acts evidence the insistent presence of privacies, structures, and relations, so ongoings provide evidence of the Dunamis. The different types of evidence are so many attenuated forms of what is evidenced; all are present in what the ultimates together constitute. The move from the evidenced to the evidence is intensive,[16] taking one into what is more insistent, more self-maintained, and absorptive of that which evidences it. But while the evidenced conditions are more wide-ranging than that which evidences them, and while privacies have a singularity and inwardness no expression ever fully captures, the Dunamis is absorptive, turning what reaches into it into a nuance of itself.

Truths about all the ultimates are at once objective, conformal, and embedded.[17] Still, those that refer to conditions are primarily objective, and those that refer to privacies are primarily conformal. References to the Dunamis, in contrast, are primarily embedded. If one were to speak of objective truths as having degrees of involvement with their referents, it would also be appropriate to say that embedded truths are more or less absorbed in the Dunamis to which they refer. The need to refer to the Dunamis in ways which are distinct from those needed to refer to the other ultimates, apparently, is what repels those who deny its presence and attracts those who affirm it. But the Dunamis, I have tried to show, is no less and no more difficult to refer to, encounter, and understand than are any other ultimates.

---

tined" applied to the Dunamis, as well as transposed forms of the exalted names of Conditions, e.g., "The Will" and "The Collective Unconscious."

16. The idea was anticipated in Kant's Anticipations of Perception. See, for example, *The Critique of Pure Reason*, A.166: "The *real* which corresponds to it [sensation] in the object (*realitas phaenomenon*) has an *intensive magnitude*, that is, a degree" (Norman Kemp Smith's translation).

17. "See *Toward a Perfected State*, 81ff.

Index

Names

Albers, J., 20
Alexander the Great, 253, 254
Alighieri, Dante. *See* Dante
d'Arc, J., 205, 246
Aristotle, 40, 52, 54, 67, 112, 127, 144, 154, 161, 167, 189, 198, 199, 201, 208, 267, 279
Augustine, St., 64

Bach, J. S., 43
Balzac, H., 43
Beethoven, L. van, 85, 86, 87, 253
Bergson, H., 72, 74, 83
Bizet, G., 59
Bohr, N., 153
Bolyai, J., 105
Bonaparte, N. *See* Napoleon
Brodsky, J., 29
Brouwer, L. E., 106
Buddha, 192

Cantor, G., 106, 131
Castro, F., 203
Christ, 192
Churchill, W., 203

Confucius, 188, 198, 199, 297
Cornet, A. Gaudi. *See* Gaudi

Dante, 43
Da Vinci, Leonardo. *See* Leonardo da Vinci
Dedekind, J., 116
de Gaulle, C., 203
Descartes, R., 15, 161
Dewey, J., 42, 150, 154

Einstein, A., 153, 156, 157

Fermat, P., 114, 119, 131
Fischer, B., 125

Galileo, 132, 154
Galois, E., 105, 124
Gaudi, 15, 59
Gauss, K., 105
Gödel, K., 104
Gogh, V. Van, 35, 63
Goldbach, 114

Subjects

Paul Weiss, Sterling Professor of Philosophy, emeritus, Yale University, is the founder and former editor of the *Review of Metaphysics*, founder of the Metaphysical Society of America, and founder of the Philosophy Education Society, Inc. He was a president of the American Philosophical Association, and he has received five honorary degrees. He was a visiting professor at the Hebrew University, the University of Southern California, the University of Denver, and the Catholic University of America. Weiss has published some thirty books, among them *Modes of Being, Nine Basic Arts, Sport: A Philosophic Inquiry*, and twelve volumes of his ongoing *Philosophy in Process*. Some of his books have been translated into Hebrew, Portuguese, and Japanese.